MW01713941

Series: *Studies in Drama & Theater*

1. D. Pietropaolo ed. *The Performance Text*

Cover: "Infographie" by Pierre Bertrand

# The Performance Text

edited by

Domenico Pietropaolo

LEGAS

New York Ottawa Toronto

**Canadian Cataloguing in Publication Data**

Main entry under title:

*The Performance Text*

(Studies in Drama & Theater; 1)
Papers originally presented at a conference held April 11-12, 1997
at the Graduate Centre for Study of Drama
University of Toronto
Includes bibliographical references.
ISBN 0-921252-90-0

1. Theatre—Philosophy—Congresses. 2. Theatre—Semiotics—Congresses. 3. Drama—History and Criticism—Congresses. I. Pietropaolo, Domenico, 1949- II. Series.

PN2018.P46 1999 792'.01 C99-900402-6

For further information and for orders:

**LEGAS**

P. O. Box 040328
Brooklyn, New York
USA 11204

68 Kamloops Ave.
Ottawa, Ontario
K1V 7C9

2908 Dufferin Street
Toronto, Ontario
M6B 3S8

Printed and bound in Canada

# Contents

# Acknowledgements

The papers in this collection were originally presented at a conference which took place at the Graduate Centre for Study of Drama, University of Toronto, on April 11 and 12, 1997.

As a conference topic, the idea of performance text seemed to us narrow enough for a fruitful discussion and yet sufficiently inclusive to allow for our different fields of specialisation.

As convenor of the conference, I would like to thank the authors of the papers, the technical staff of the Drama Centre, and all the participants who helped make the meeting a great success. I would also like to thank Professor Leonard G. Sbrocchi for his support and for his technical assistance.

# IN THE BEGINNING WAS THE WORD: TEXT VERSUS PERFORMANCE

Christopher Innes

Perhaps the central issue in studying drama today is how we evaluate physical aspects of performance: theatre as bodily expression, as opposed to the presentation of written words. Encoded in the process versus product dichotomy, the leading edge of the profession is taken to be improvisational work —sometimes formalized under the term "devising" — which by definition rejects text as a basis for acting and de-emphasizes, or even discards spoken language. Since this comes out of the exploration of non-verbal expression by Performance Groups in the 1960s, it seems appropriate to use some of their work as an example. Analysis of their experiments also highlights the cultural balance between various modes of communication, which is a pre-requisite for examining the nature of physical theatre. So it is the possible range of non-verbal languages, and their relative weighting against the standard verbal transmission of meanings, that I want to focus on.

It is hardly a coincidence that the Book of Genesis opens with such a categorical statement on the significance of language: "In the beginning was the word... and the word was God". The Bible truly is the Urtext of Western, European civilization, shaping and informing its values; and even if Jehova is reported as having SAID "Let there be light", what the Bible asserts —in its very status as "holy SCRIPTURE"— is the primacy of WRITTEN words. Our whole civilization is based on texts and their transmission. Indeed the fact that when Gutenberg invented printing, the first text to come off the press was the Bible, serves as a cultural archetype. So it is entirely logical that even the performative art of theatre should develop as a delivery system for written scripts.

Although the first —legendary— figure in theatre may have been an actor, and Aristotle points to the dithyramb (a pre-dramatic performance of music and dance) as one of the sources for tragedy, the origins of Western theatre that can be documented are all text-based. It might be argued that the most effective elements of Greek theatre were visual: the masks, or the dancing choruses after whom Aristophanes named several of his plays (*The Clouds, The Birds*). Yet the "granting of a chorus", the official term for approving a theatrical performance, was competitive and decided solely by written scripts.[1] Similarly the size and centrality of the *Orchestra* seems designed to emphasize patterns of movement, yet the most striking aspect of stages constructed in ancient Greece is their acoustic clarity. The amphitheatre at Epidaurus, for instance, is in fact an architectural arrangement for promoting the spoken word. Thus even as close to the origins of our theatre as Aeschylus, performance is primarily a tool for disseminating a written text to large numbers of people who, even if able to read, would have had little access to anything longer than a broadsheet when the only form of duplication was handwritten copying.

This dominance of text remained standard for all Western theatre up to the present century. Hamlet's instructions to the actors are entirely concerned with fidelity to a written script. Polonius may marvel at the Player's physical expression of emotion, in empathizing with the Hecuba he is describing — but those tears in the actor's eyes, however real, are illustrative: a way of communicating the written content of a speech that is itself derived from literature, explicitly "Aeneas' tale to Dido" in Vergil's epic poem. When 18th and 19th century spectators comment on Garrick or Kean, it is their accuracy in transmitting Shakespeare's texts that is praised. So it is hardly surprising if drama was traditionally seen as a branch of literature, and evaluated by literary criteria. Certainly the language of plays is always performative, rather than discursive.[2] But in all conventional drama the meaning is carried by the words; and the primacy of verbal discourse on the stage is indicated by the classical training in rhetoric for actors. Movement, grouping, posture, gesture were all illustrative, rather than independent signifiers; and plays, even in performance, presented "narratives" that were defined by words.

However, this practice changed radically in the twentieth century under the impact of modernism: first with Gordon Craig, who argued for abstract performances of pure movement (excluding even the actor), then through Antonin Artaud in the 1920s. Neither Craig nor Artaud had an immediate impact, though Craig's writings provided a catalyst for the alternative, experimental "little theatre" movement. But the ideal of "physical" theatre resurfaced with Performance Groups in the 1960s, and continues to be explored by contemporary experimental the-

---

[1] For a discussion of the use and development of the Chorus in Ancient Greek drama, see J. Michael Walton & Peter Arnott, *Menander and the Making of Comedy*, Westport CT 1996, 47f.

[2] For a discussion of t he performative basis of theatrical scripts, see Michael Sidnell, "Performing Writing: Inscribing Theatre" in *Modern Drama*, Winter 1996, 547f.

atre (the Wooster Group, Spaulding Gray). And with the change in practice, new critical approaches began to emerge. It is no accident that both happened at the point when theatre departments were set up in universities. Indeed, I would suggest that it was largely the need to distinguish their subject from the literature studied in departments of English —out of which many theatre departments emerged— that led to a focus on non-literary aspects of theatre. This, of course, has now developed into Performance Studies. The irony that the locus for exploring physical modes of communication should be academia, where above all the book rules, is often overlooked. At the same time, it can be seen as an early symptom, perhaps even the catalyst for the rejection of "the canon" that has so preoccupied the MLA over the last few years.

The inspiration for the 1960s Performance Groups came specifically from Artaud, whose seminal essays in *The Theatre and Its Double* first appeared in an English translation in 1958. One of his essays from the early 1930s famously declared NO MORE MASTERPIECES, opening the attack on canon-formation in a way that still reverberates in today's academic arguments. Artaud demolished the whole tradition of Western drama as "one of the aspects of bourgeois conformism" — and in addition to dismissing written texts as a basis for theatrical performance, Artaud argues

> that an expression does not have the same value twice, does not live two lives; that all words, once spoken, are dead and function only at the moment they are uttered, that a form, once it has served, cannot be used again and... that the theatre is the only place in the world where a gesture, once made, can never be made the same way twice.[3]

Though overtly aimed at "the idolatry of fixed masterpieces" (Sophocles, Shakespeare), this emphasis on the uniqueness of each theatre-event also provides the basis for valuing process at the expense of product in any performance.

Artaud proposed the ideal of a performance that would act on the spectator like Chinese acupuncture, directly affecting the central nervous system through the body (as opposed to communicating intellectually/verbally through the mind), thus returning "theater to... the physical knowledge of images and the means of inducing trances". These means were to be a "dynamism of action... in which violent physical images crush and hypnotize the sensibility of the spectator seized

---

3 Antonin Artaud, *The Theater and its Double* (trans. Mary Richards), New York 1958, 76, 75. All quotations are taken from this source because of its specific relevance to avant-garde performance groups.

by the theater as by a whirlwind of higher forces". And the effect would be analogous to the psychoanalytic treatment of making a patient "assume the apparent and exterior attitudes of the desired condition", which Artaud declared went back to an "elementary magical idea". This non-verbal "religious idea of the theater" was also literally pre-textual in seeking to return to the "poetry-through-theater which underlies the myths told by the great tragedians" — and it was grounded in Artaud's belief

> that the theater, utilized in the highest and most difficult sense possible, has the power to influence the aspect and formation of things: and the encounter upon the stage of two passionate manifestations, two living centers, two nervous magnetisms is something as entire, true, even decisive, as, in life, the encounter of one epidermis with another in a timeless debauchery. [4]

This emphatic emphasis on bodily expression and intimate physical connections is highly idealised, even fetishistic. However, it chimed with the politics of the counter-culture movement in the U.S. —where opposition to the Vietnam war, combining with the drug culture, led to rejection of all official hierarchies, including verbal logic— and offered an alternative, "authentic" mode of theatrical communication.

The question is: given the word-dominated culture of Western society, to what extent such an ideal is realizable in actual performance. If one imagines communication as a line stretching from discursive language at one end to silent gestures at the other, then the "narrative" of theatre generally occupies a middle space: both show and tell, allowing a degree of individual interpretation for each spectator within a set frame of common meanings. And the stronger the verbal element, the more focussed and specific (and intellectualized) the messages transmitted to an audience. The equation of course varies, with Alan Bennet's monologues or a minimalist piece like Beckett's *Not I* being at the purely verbal extreme. By contrast, in its ideal form physical theatre presents a completely non-linguistic narrative. But what kinds of meanings do physical images communicate? Is it possible to develop a vocabulary that is separate from and independent of speech? Can meanings be transmitted that are not automatically translated back into words in the minds of the receivers? Words are specifically defined referrants, while physical expression is a far more variable signifier — so how can one ensure that gestures have even approximately the same effect on different spectators? The work of performance groups offers a case study for such issues.

---

4 *Ibid*, 80, 82-3, 79.

Artaud's writings served as a manifesto for Peter Brook and the Becks' Living Theatre, as well as Joe Chaikin's Open Theatre and Richard Schechner's eponymously named "The Performance Group". And the development of the Living Theatre, who became the model for many of the American groups, exposes the problematic nature of Artaud's ideals. Their early experiments were still text based: productions of *The Connection* (an intensely realistic portrayal of drug addicts by Jack Gelber) and *The Brig* (Kenneth Brown's brutal depiction of life in marine prison). However the documentary quality of these scripts encouraged an extreme degree of actuality in performance, and led to extensive verbal improvisation, with the core meaning carried by the *mise en scène,* which expanded to envelop the whole theatrical event. The actors in *The Brig* were required to live by the prison rules for extended periods as part of the rehearsal process, while mimicking the yelled army orders transformed the words into non-verbal sound-language. In *The Connection* actors stayed in character as addicts during the intermission, panhandling members of the audience. And this blurring of pretence and reality, together with the self-expression allowed by improvising, meant that "the actors began *to play themselves*" which Judith Malina described as "a very important advance".[5]

Following up on this line, the Living Theatre defined their aim as turning performances into "an absolute communion" with the audience. The aim was therapeutic —both for the actors, who would be enabled to transcend physical limits of performance by breaking through their own psychological inhibitions, and by extension for society as a whole through liberating the spectators from socially imposed repressions— thus effecting "the transformation of the demonic forces into the celestial".[6] The fullest expression of this came in *Paradise Now,* first performed in 1968 and elaborated over the next two years on tour in Europe and across the United States.

This production included sequences of action first evolved for such earlier Living Theatre performance pieces as *Mysteries* (1964) or *Frankenstein* (1965); and indeed such an element of repetition is characteristic of most performance groups who reject verbal texts for physical language. Specific combinations of movement and gestures, generally arrived at in rehearsal exercises, become fixed images that appear as identifying "trademarks". Encapsulating a particular vision —of political repression, personal liberation, group solidarity, etc.— they are felt to express the essential nature of those performance groups. In the

---

5 Cit. Jan Kott, TDR 14, 1, 23.

6 *We, the Living Theater,* New York 1970, 24; Judith Malina and Julian Beck, *Paradise Now,* New York 1971, 77.

case of the Living Theatre, perhaps the most representative "physical nexus" of this sort was a sequence of "flying". A culminating moment in *Paradise Now,* this was a simple acrobatic display: each of the actors in turn launching themselves off a platform some fifteen feet above the stage, as if diving upwards, to fall safely into the interlaced arms of the rest of the group lined up below. As well as both a demonstration of individual trust and of the strength in community, it was also intended to signify a visionary "expansion of human potential. This could lead to flying... freed from the constraint and injury brought down on us by the errors of past civilisation, we will be free to expand and alter the nature of our being".[7] Members of the audience were also invited to participate, to experience a foretaste of this liberated transcendence and as a sign of willingness to join the group whom they relied on to catch them. This deliberate bridging of the barrier between actor and spectator —which worked both ways in Living Theatre productions, with the group moving out into the audience to act as cheerleaders or provocateurs, as well as the audience invading the stage at various points during the action, in particular to join the copulation of "Universal Intercourse" when all distinction between the actors and spectators was obliterated— is also integral to many performance groups.

The symbolic associations of "flying" were immediately apparent, even to the uninitiated; but however effective, the range of meanings such an action contained were necessarily very general. The political aims of *Paradise Now* required a more detailed level of communication to portray sequences like:

BOLIVIA: A GROUP OF REVOLUTIONARIES PLOT THEIR STRATEGY —
THE REVOLUTION OF REVELATION
THE DESTINY MUST BE MADE CLEAR ...

PARIS: TIME FUTURE
THE NON-VIOLENT ANARCHIST REVOLUTION ...
THE VISION OF THE LANDING ON MARS.[8]

The references are highly specific: geographic locations, time frames and projections into imagined futures, even subtle ideological variants of a single political activity. How might these be expressed through gesture?

One solution was to model groupings and postures on pre-existing cultural symbols —Icarus or the Minotaur from Greek mythology,

---

7 *Paradise Now,* 127

8 Scenes designated in the chart outlining the structure of the performance, Programme for *Paradise Now,* 1968.

Amerindian totem-poles, the crucifixion and Michaelangelo's *Pietà*—another was to copy images from the news media, the most successful of these being Edward Adams, 1968 award-winning photo of the Saigon Police Chief shooting a kneeling Vietcong prisoner in the head. Paired off actors took up the same positions in a line across the stage, and "in unison... the executioners fire, the victims fall". In each of these cases the visual impact was determined by the shared connotations with which the images were already loaded. In a sense this corresponded to the physical language of "precise and immediately readable symbols" that Artaud had envisaged[9]. However, almost all these images could only be "read" in the form of tableaus, requiring stasis, and were limited to a sort of cultural Lowest Common Denominator in depending on the widest possible public familiarity with the source image for understanding.

There was also a degree of literalness in many of the Living Theatre scenes, where the actors' bodies were not so much Artaudian hieroglyphs communicating in a pre-verbal mode, as substitutes for missing speech. At times this was even explicit, as when the group took up positions for the letters to visually spell out the word "Anarchism", which then was transformed with a shout of "Now!" into the word "Paradise". In short, despite the ideological value placed on pre-textual, physical theatre, the performance of *Paradise Now* was still linguistically determined — reduced in fact to the level of visual slogans, which corresponded to the type of dialogue that remained. Much of this was not so much speeches as spoken stage directions, either interpretative glosses on what the actors were portraying

— Be the heart. Act. Find the pain. Feel it. Make the sound of it.
— The heart of Africa.

or cues for action by the spectators:

— Free theater. The theater is yours. Act. Speak. Do whatever you want
— Free theater. Because in the society we envisage, everyone is free.
— Free theater. Free being. Free life. Do anything. Do nothing. Be.
— Breathe.
— Expand consciousness.[10]

The physical basis of performance was thus retained, but codified in a way that led back to text — indeed the development of the actions is

9 *Paradise Now*, 75; *The Theater and its Double*, 94.
10 *Paradise Now*, 27, 63, 111.

evolved through verbal association. And ironically, given the Living Theatre's reliance on improvisation and their belief in performance as on-going process, both of which denied any validity to theatre as a fixed product, after the group split up in 1970 Malina and Beck indeed published a printed text of *Paradise Now.*

At first glance, this seems to be far from a conventional dramatic text, since it reveals that less than a quarter of the performance time was actually scripted, in order to allow spontaneous actions (either by members of the group, or by the audience) to be incorporated. In addition, over twenty percent of the pages are taken up by photographs, which give visual definition to each of the scenes except two: an omission explained by a note that "no photographs are available for The Rite of New Possibilities and The Vision of Landing on Mars (Rung VII) since they are performed in total darkness". In the first of these, the "action" was purely vocal, with the group creating a free-form network of "sound relationships which are, so far as [the actors] are consciously aware, not in their usual range of sounds". Unstructured, it is doubtful if this would have communicated musically, except at the most basic level of signalling something out of the ordinary. But the following sequence (the Landing on Mars) had one of the longest spoken/chanted texts in the piece, which was accompanied by representational patterns of small lights, carried by the actors inscribing circles as planets, while others grouped "in a formation arranged to resemble a Spaceship".[11]

In contrast to this simplistic show-and-tell presentation, scene-designations like "Rite and "Rung" point to a complex philosophical, even religious structure that underlay the action of *Paradise Now.* The description for each of the eight "Rungs" —the overall image for the piece being a ladder signifying "a vertical ascent toward Permanent Revolution"— contains a section of political commentary, combined with hexagrams from the I Ching (each with elaborate explication), lengthy quotations from the Hasidim and/or the Kabbalah, as well as a number of Yoga exercises (with rationales for those selected). Specifically intended as "preparation" for the actors, or as cues for the emotional states to be created at each point in the structure, there is no discernable link between these "Texts" and anything physically performed on the stage. Yet they take up over a third of the script, and are given a central function of embodying the "individual spiritual change" that is seen as the prerequisite for "exterior political change".[12]

The book is clearly designed as a documentation —with the photos recording moments from many different performances— but it is also in-

---

[11] *Ibid,* 122
[12] *Ibid,* 152, 5, 7.

tended as a script to be reproduced on the stage. Indeed it contains an announcement on the copyright page that "*Paradise Now* ...is free: for any community that wants to play it". In addition, the visual material relates to the printed words in much the same way as conventional illustrations; and the description makes clear that the physical presentation was structured by spoken language, with variations on the verbal "Free theater" exhortation being reiterated at the end of all eight sequences of action that made up the complete (but in practice often truncated) performance. As a result the printed piece is open to standard literary analysis. Ultimately the Living Theatre never managed to free themselves from text. Their abandonment of *Paradise Now,* the vehicle for theatrical renewal as well as political revolution, signals their failure to achieve a purely physical theatre — although their European exile, where the group was intentionally performing for non-English-speaking audiences, had been designed specifically "to find a way of communicating our feelings and our ideas through signs and being".[13]

Similar trajectories were followed by other performance groups. Peter Brook, having explored Artaud's ideas in an 1964 "theatre of cruelty" workshop for the RSC, experimented with non-verbal vocalization in *Orghast*, an epic piece derived "from... basic myths", searching for a universal language —still vocal, but not verbal— that could communicate "*below* the levels where differences appear, close to the inner life of what we've chosen as our material, but expressive to all people, powerfully, truly, precisely".[14] At the end of an African tour —designed to develop this "root" language through performing for native audiences without a shared speech, or even a knowledge of theatrical conventions— Brook declared:

> Our work is based on the fact that some of the deepest aspects of human experience can reveal themselves through the sounds and movements of the human body in a way that strikes a chord in any observer, whatever his cultural and racial conditioning. And therefore one can work without roots, because the body, as such, becomes a working source.[15]

Yet the material his group created out of their African experience, which evolved into an extended production, *The Conference of the Birds*, was actually far more conventional, as its title implies. Conferences, after all, are verbal; and the physical action of *The Birds*

---

[13]Julian Beck, in TDR, 13, 3, 42.
[14]Programme note (1971), cit. A.C.H.Smith, *Orghast at Persepolis,* London 1972, 50; and Ted Hughes, *Times Literary Supplement,* 1 October 1971 (my italics).
[15]Brook, in *The Drama Review,* 17, 3 (September 1973) 50.

was accompanied by extensive narration, with a full play-text being written for the 1979 Avignon Festival. In addition the performance was coded through a whole range of exotic theatrical symbols —Oriental masks, Balinese puppets, Indonesian shadow-play— which not only carry specific external significations, but (even more significantly) move away from, or abstract the body of the performer. And all Brook's subsequent pieces have not only been derived from pre-existing texts (whether Oliver Sack's *The Man who Mistook his Wife for a Hat*, or *The Mahabharata*), but also based on conventional scripts. Even if the body remains "a working source" for rehearsal exercises, in performance the sometimes extraordinary physical display of Brook's actors seldom stands alone. Instead it reinforces or expands the meaning of the speeches.

Richard Schechner, too, had attempted to create a purely physical theatre out of ritualized actions and mythic story-lines (such as *The Bacchae*), which were assumed to carry subliminal and archetypal signification. In a performance like *Dionysus in 69*, the essential meanings were intended to be transmitted by body images, even intimate body contact with the spectators, while the speeches were improvised and expressed the thoughts of the performers (as distinct from the characters). However, as with *Paradise Now*, a script of this performance piece was subsequently published — not only as a documentary record, but (like the Living Theater) as a pre-set piece for others to perform, "professionals and amateurs" being "warned that *Dionysus in 69*" was "fully protected under the copyright laws" and "subject to royalty. All rights... are strictly preserved..." Indeed, barely four years later Schechner had returned to text-based theatre, explaining that "We have moved beyond the point when actors acted with their faces, hands and voices. The rebirth of the whole performer demands the reintegration of the writer into the theater"[16].

The acting exercises out of which Joe Chaikin's Open Theater pieces grew were direct explorations in non-verbal expression of somatic experience, based on Viola Spolin's physical "theater games" or derived from Chinese theatre. Yet by contrast with Schechner, who either developed fixed texts out of improvised group work around classical "pre-texts" or used pre-existing, published texts, Chaikin collaborated closely with playwrights as an integral part of the Open Theater creative process. *America Hurrah* was written by Claude van Itallie specifically for the group; and for their most famous full-length piece, *The Serpent*, a full verbal text was evolved, using a team of writers: Megan Terry, Patricia Cooper, as well as van Itallie. The physical im-

---

[16]Schechner, *Environmental Theater*, New York 1973, 242

ages, developed through improvisation were the most immediately striking element of the performance: the keynote embodiment of the serpent itself as the Tree of Life (five intertwined actors, with flickering tongues and sinuous arms, offering apples in their hands), animals in the Garden of Eden, or the assassination of President Kennedy (based on frames from the Zapruder film of the actual event). Yet the piece was structured by the words, with a chorus of women providing narration that orchestrated the changing tone and linked the different segments. Even *The Mutation Show* —the only real ensemble piece of the Open Theatre, for which all the dialogue was created through improvisation by the actors— credited writers in the programme; and Chaikin's commitment to verbal language can be illustrated by *Tongues*. A piece for solo voice and percussion, co-written by Chaikin and Shepard, this monologue was performed by Chaikin, seated facing front and motionless, with Shepard hidden behind his chair providing the musical accompaniment. Although a major theme in the speeches is the inadequacy of words, the stasis of this performance made it a demonstration of the communicative power of verbal expression.

In short, the avant-garde performance groups of the Sixties and Seventies mark the limitations of strictly physical theatre. Inspired by Artaud, they experimented in varying degrees with a purely physical, participatory mode of communication. But like Artaud himself, whose performances were all based on scripts, even their most unconventional works were codified as texts, and all returned to the staging of extended, even literary dramatic scripts, where the primary meaning was carried by words. Although they expanded the non-naturalistic vocabulary of standard acting, the implication of their work would seem to be that at best the physical performance stands as a sub-text for speeches; and that what is spoken needs to be fixed in writing if the intention is to communicate anything more than personal cliches.

*York University*

# RECEPTION AND REALISM: THE CASE OF MAMET'S *OLEANNA*

Ann Wilson

*Oleanna* is David Mamet's controversial —perhaps by now even infamous— play about a female student, Carol, who is failing a course and approaches the male professor, John, for help. Carol, who initially appears diffident, takes offense at John's response to her plea for help, and confidently employs the resources of the university to launch charges of sexual harassment against him. William A Henry III, writing for *Time,* suggests that "by the end, the professor resembles the broken-spirited figures in anti-communist plays by Pinter or Havel, ready to comply with just about anything to end the humiliation and pain" (79).

The premiere production divided audiences, which either felt that John was the victim of a woman's false accusations, upheld by the University that has bought into "political correctness"; or, felt that the play manipulated audiences into siding with John by making Carol an implausible character. By the time the play opened at London's Royal Court Theatre in June, 1993 (in a production directed by Harold Pinter), reviewers were ready to take sides in what was seen as an issue-driven play that was likened to Brecht's *Galileo* (Wardle), Hellman's *The Children's Hour* (Morley), Miller's *The Crucible* (Morley, Nightingale, P. Taylor, Wardle), or the plays of Granville Barker (Rutherford).[1] The impulse of the critics to situate *Oleanna* within a theatrical heritage signals a key aspect of the play: *Oleanna,* a play which engages with an issue contested in contemporary society, has the characteristics of a realist drama, made evident through the comments of reviewers like John Gross who writes that "judged by ordinary realistic standards, the play contains two major impossibilities"; or Clive Hirschborn who notes "Mamet's 'realistic', staccato speech patterns —with repetitions and incomplete sentences— are mesmeric as ever...." While Gross's comment suggests that the standards of "realistic" drama are common knowledge, the stylistic range of the plays invoked

[1] The reviews for the production of *Oleanna* at the Royal Court can be found in: *Theatre Record* 18 June - 1 July 1993, 740-747.

to create a theatrical lineage for *Oleanna* indicates that "realism" is not a single coherent style, but a range of styles with the common project of representing truthfully human experience in a way which corresponds to the lived actuality. In this paper, I want to address two problematic aspects of realism. First, realism is "representation" and hence governed by the complex economies of representation. This leads to my second concern in this paper: what is the relation between what is represented on-stage and what an audience imagines to be corresponding actuality? Given that actuality cannot be reproduced exactly, what are the implications of the slippage? I want to consider two aspects of realism: the representation on stage of a milieu which corresponds to a plausible actuality and its attendant representation of characters with a coherent individualized subjectivity; and the moments when realism exceeds this project, and represents an mythic or imaginary level which engages the political unconscious. I want to argue that there is a tension between the depiction of a world which is perceived through observation and the unconscious. In considering the case of *Oleanna*, I want to tease out the tension which I think characterizes all realist projects. I do not however want to suggest that Mamet, in *Oleanna*, uses the tension for what I might term a progressive political project (and which he might see as abetting a political project aligned with political correctness); rather, I will argue that although Mamet uses the empirical aspects of realism and its excesses, which gesture to the political unconscious to advance what is an avowedly masculinist perspective that supports patriarchy, the tension between these two aspects of realism —a tension noted by many reviewers and dismissed as a dramaturgical flaw in the work— opens a space for a reconsideration of the possibilities of (theatrical) realism as potentially subverting hegemonic discourses. The paper is in three parts: a brief discussion of theatrical realism which serves as the context for the second part of the paper, a reading of *Oleanna*; the paper concludes with a consideration of the ways that *Oleanna* challenges conventional understandings of theatrical realism.

Realism emerges as a theatrical project in the latter part of the nineteenth century with the work of playwrights like Henrick Ibsen. As realism begins to take hold in the theatre, critics and playwrights being to offer commentary on its impact. For example, the American critic William Dean Howells, writing in *Harper's Weekly*, comments on plays which he has seen on a recent trip to England. He writes:

> In the plays ... there is distinctly a disposition on the part of the author to grapple with actualities of several kinds, and especially to wrestle with problems and struggle with motives. Their scene is always a recogniz-

> able semblance of the world; if I do not find it a good portrait, I am willing to suppose it is because I do not know the world very well; and in any case I perceive in their work the interests and motives that impel people in life. The persons are something like, the love is something like, the hate is something like, the vice is something like... To the inward truth, or measure of the truth, there is a pleasing response of outward truth; the plays have good form; they are at their best artistic achievements, and at their worst they are artistic intentions. (55, 56)

Several aspect of Howells' description of the new dramatic project are worth noting. Realism demands that scenes stage a "recognizable semblance of the world": what appears on stage must correspond to what might be seen in life. If realism demands the creation of a semblance of the actuality's appearance, the focus of realism is not on superficial appearance but on people, their "interests and motives." As a consequence, realism is concerned with the inner lives and, significantly, the "inner truth" of the characters. There is a tension in realism between a faithful reproduction of the social milieu of the play and the psychologies of characters who are perceived to have "inner truths" which presumably can be discerned.

Howells' use of "truth" in the context of writing about realism warrants consideration because "truth" pervades writing about realism. Theatrical realism begins when some plays tired of melodrama and the well-made play. The "exponents [realism] aimed to rid theatre of histrionics in acting and the too-evident artifice of the sub-Sardou well-made play, replacing them with a more natural-seeming acting and with plays, which, while still carefully constructed, depended less on contrived *coups de théâtre* and a mechanical snapping of pieces into place" (J. Taylor 231). While realism, as Taylor notes, offers characters who behave as people might in day-to-day life, the attempt to create a theatrical world which corresponds to the actualities of life does not preclude the shaping force of the playwright, as Howells notes in his comment that the plays must have good form and be artistic achievements. The use of the word "truth" in Howells' comments signals two other features which are aspects of realism. Realism depends on a particular understanding of subjectivity. A character has a rich, coherent inner life —or, truth— which determines his or her behaviour. A key characteristic of realism is this relation between character's interiority and external the manifestation of that interiority as behaviour which an audience can see. The use of "truth" in discussions of realism signals another important element of the realist project. "Truth" is a word which carries moral value and indicates that the realist playwright, through the "truthful rendering" of characters in situations, operates under a moral imperative. Realism, certainly historically through the issue-driven plays of Ibsen, Shaw, Galsworthy and O'Neill (to name but a few) is a theatre which is socially engaged and a such, implicitly, self-consciously political.

One of the influential contemporary discussion of realism occurs in Catherine Belsey's 1980 study *Critical Practice*, a book which sorts through a range of theories which address the complexity of representation; but, her discussion of "classic" realism, which Jill Dolan parallels in *The Feminist Critic as Spectator*, simplifies, and stabilizes, the power of realism. There is no small degree of irony that two critics (Belsey and Dolan), who are notably adept not only at making the nuances of contemporary theory intelligible to their readers, manage to over-simplify realism. I say ironic, because many of the commentators of realism in the late nineteenth and early twentieth centuries signal the complex operation of realism within economies of representation. Indeed, as my references to reviews of the Royal Court's production of *Oleanna* will indicate, both reviewers and those who were commissioned to offer commentaries have some sense of the complexity of realism which academic critics seem to want to ignore, instead positing realism as a stable, conservative entity.

In many ways, Belsey's critique does not seem inconsistent with that forwarded by Howells. Her discussion begins, in passing, with the comment that "realism is plausible not because it reflects the world, but because it is constructed out of what is (discursively) familiar" (47). In a later section, she notes:

> Classic realism, still the dominant popular mode in literature, film and television drama, roughly coincides chronologically with the epoch of industrial capitalism. It performs, I wish to suggest, the work of ideology, not only in its representation of a world of consistent subjects who are the origin of meaning, knowledge and action, but also in offering the reader, as the position from which the text is most readily intelligible, the position of subject as the origin both of understanding and of action in accordance with that understanding. (67)

At this juncture, I want to make only two comments on Belsey's formulation. In her contention that "classic realism, still the dominant popular mode in literature, film and television drama, roughly coincides chronologically with the epoch of industrial capitalism," she does not indicate the role of realism in the theatre, but identifies realism as a dominat perspective on the action which can create a single point of narration — in the case of the novel, the narrative voice; and in the case of film and television, the perspective which is controlled by what the camera allows the audience to see. Secondly, while she correctly asserts that the rise of realism corresponds to the epoch of industrial capital, it is worth remembering that rise of realism within a complex range of forces, including Darwinism and the privileging of observation as a mode for acquiring scientific knowledge and, slightly later, the emergence of psychoanalysis and commensurate concern with ideologies of human subjectivity.

Later, Belsey writes:

> Classic realism presents individuals whose traits of character, understood as essential and predominantly given, constrain the choices they make, and who potential for development depends on what is given. Human nature is thus seen as a system of character-differences existing in the world, but on which nonetheless permits the reader to share the hopes and fears of a wide range of kinds character. This contradiction —that readers, like the central figures of fiction, are unique and that so many readers can identify with so many protaganists— is accommodated in ideology is a paradox. (74)

Is the identification of an audience of readers with a range of characters really such a paradox? Perhaps the resolution of the seeming paradox lies with the desire of an audience that a work of art has meaning. The first strategy of making a work meaningful may be to enter into the imaginative world created by the artist through identification with character. What Belsey doesn't consider is the degree to which members of an audience, in their identification with characters, implicitly acknowledge their differences from those characters.

Jill Dolan, in *The Feminist Critic as Spectator*, writes:

> realist theatre imposes a conservative sense of order by delivering its ideology as normative. The transcendent pose of illusionist theatre makes the society it reflects appear to be incapable of change. Realism naturalizes social relations imposed by dominant ideology and mystifies its own authorship. (106)

Dolan's critique doesn't indicate the ways in which theatre inevitably exceeds its obvious project of mimetically reproducing a recognizable world on stage. Using the case of *Oleanna* I will suggest that Mamet violates what critics tend to see as a hallmark of realism, consistent characterization. Without jumping the gun, inasmuch as my reading of *Oleanna* remains to be presented, I will argue that one of the two characters in the play, Carol, by the second act, bears little resemblance to the woman she appeared to be in Act One. John, the other character, remains consistent. In his representation of Carol, Mamet seems to violate the contract of realism as a form, but as I will suggest, this violation, achieved through the use of the interval or intermission, allows the political unconscious of the play to overtake the representation of a credible actuality. The play is no less a realist drama for this seeming violation of dramatic convention, particularly when measured in terms of Mamet's discussion of realism reprinted in the Royal Court's program for its production of *Oleanna*.

Mamet's *Oleanna*, in taking up the problem of "political correctness," is within a tradition of realist dramas with narratives driven by social issues. The audiences of the New York production of *Oleanna* were so engaged with Mamet's representation of political correctness that they left theatre animatedly arguing over the play. Indeed, in New York, members of the audience cheered or jeered particular moments in the play. Michael Billington reports, the response of the audience in London was sedate:

> The first night of David Mamet's *Oleanna* ... was greeted with a rapt attentiveness which is a tribute to the power of the acting, the writing and, not least, to Harold Pinter's production ... which releases the mythic quality under the realistic surface.

Later in his review, Billington commends Mamet for having created "a superb mythic drama about the breaking of of (sic) the social contract that makes all education possible.... Mamet's point is that once people resort to ideological jargon or legalistic devices, then the whole idea of intellectual freedom breaks down."

Many of the reviewers agree with Billington's contention that Mamet's portrayal of three interactions between the professor, John, and the student, Carol, condemns political correctness as excessive and destructive. Like the realist drama of the late nineteenth and early twentieth-centuries, the social issue in the play is staged through the interaction of character who, as noted earlier, the playwright understands as having an "internal" or psychological truth. The question with which I want to begin my discussion of *Oleanna* revolves around character: is it accidental that Mamet stages his condemnation of "political correctness" through exchanges between a man and woman? Why not, for example, stage his position through exchanges between a white male professor and a male Afro-American student?[2]

---

2 Aleks Sierz, writing in the *Tribune* makes same point, writing, After so much hype, David's Mamet's play *Oleanna* turns out to be the least controversial play of the year, simply because, in the conflict between a professor, John, and his student, Carol, Mamet's sympathies lie so clearly with the male: in fact, the drama might have worked better if both its characters were men. In Mamet's hands, the questions of political correctness and feminism tend to muddle rather than clarify the central issue which is about power and learning."

The answer, I think, is that the "mythic" drama played out in *Oleanna* depends on gender because what is staged is a fear of Woman as inherently duplicitous and treacherous. Beneath the veneer of realism, *Oleanna* stages masculine fears of Woman as castrating. I want to present the case for this reading of the play, consider how the "realistic surface" of the play suppresses the misogyny, and conclude by suggesting that the tension in *Oleanna* between the realism and misogynistic fantasy churning beneath the surface may be symptomatic of a tension between inside and out, between inner "truth" and appearance, which characterizes theatrical realism and is avoided by a number of contemporary commentators who insist that politically, realism is inherently conservative.

As is the case with most Mamet plays, the narrative of the *Oleanna* is simple, with the dramatic action occurring through the verbal exchanges between characters. Carol, who is failing a course, approaches John for help; in the second and third acts, she returns to negotiate with him over her accusation that in their initial encounter, he has harassed her sexually. She has pursued this accusation by laying a complaint. For John, the seriousness of the charge is heightened by the fact that he is at the end of the tenure process, awaiting to hear formally that tenure has been granted. On the basis of his anticipated tenure, he is in the process of buying a house for which he has made a deposit.

Initially, Carol appears diffident and inarticulate. Her speech is fragmented, marked by ellipsis as she gropes to understand the meaning of words, beginning with the phrase "'a term of art.'" (2) We learn by Act Two that she has taken offense at John's response to her plea for help, and confidently employs the resources of the university to launch charges of sexual harassment against him. The audience witnesses the incident which prompts the complaint, an incident which eventually Carol describes as "rape." This naming is an inappropriate categorization inasmuch as it implies a physical violation which did not occur; indeed, what transpires between student and teacher may not even warrant formal action as sexual harassment. Consequently, the denial of John's tenure, the university's disciplinary action against him, seems unduly harsh.

Mamet's point is that "political correctness" cannot accommodate the "truth" and denies freedom. Implicitly, the vexing term "political correctness" is defined through the dramatic action of *Oleanna* as the accounts of the marginalized having greater credence than those of individuals in power. Mamet seems to imply that the underlying supposition of political correctness is that the marginalized are always right. Consequently, the playwright posits that John —not Carol— is the victim, thereby displacing sexual harassment as an issue in the play. What is at stake in *Oleanna* is power — the exercise of power upon which John's sense of his masculinity is predicated and the power of the victim's testimony when experience is the unproblematic locus of truth.

Importantly, for Mamet's indictment of political correctness to be convincing, the audience must accept the underlying premise of the play, that the power differential between men and women is natural and so men have an inherent right to power because it is a constituent element of masculinity. Given this assumption about gender and power, Carol's challenge has implication beyond the specifics of her complaint: her action results in John losing his source of economic security because he is denied tenure, an action which emasculates him within the specific terms of Mamet's dramas.

The play begins with John in the throes of a telephone conversation in which he is completing a real estate transaction (1). As he talks with his wife, Grace, Carol sits across from him without his acknowledging her presence; she simply waits for the conversation to end. The opening not only provides a clear cue about John's dismissive attitude towards his student, but allows the audience a brief glimpse into the world of real estate which Mamet explored in *Glengarry Glen Ross*. In contrast to that earlier play, the perspective in *Oleanna* is that of a buyer. It would seem that in order to be a successful buyer, one must be conversant in the masculine codes which, for Mamet, define business. John suggests that his wife contact "Jerry," as if he were a surrogate who might ably guide Grace through the macho world of real estate so tellingly created in *Glengarry* by the complete absence of female characters. In that earlier play, women figure only in male conversation as the phantasmic other against which men define themselves. Gender, in that play, is constructed with stunningly simple logic: to be a man is not to be a woman; all characteristics associated with women are not masculine and hence, when associated with men, become terms of denigration implying homosexual inclinations, for the homosexual is perceived as a feminized man. Take, for example, the moment in *Glengarry Glen Ross* when Roma castigates Williamson for blowing a deal:

> You stupid fucking *cunt*. You *idiot*. Whoever told you you could work with *men*? ... I don't care ... whose dick you're sucking on. You're going *out*.... What you're hired for is to *help* us — does that seem clear to you? To *help* us. *Not* to fuck us up ... to help *men* who are going *out* there to try to earn a *living*. You *fairy*.... You fucking child.... (96-97)

In Roma's configuration of masculinity, the terms "woman," "homosexual" and "child" are equivalent and interchangeable, marking unmanly "otherness."

The academic milieu pretends to be too refined to sanction an expression of masculinity which is as transparently homophobic and misogynistic as Ricky Roma's; but John's politely expressed middle-class values suggest that his sense of masculinity is compatible with Roma's. Tenure, John tells Carol, brings "security, and yes, *comfort*" (44). He tells her that on basis of the imminent granting of his tenure, he has bought a house: "Now, as you don't have your own family, at this point, you may not know what that means. But to me, it is important. A home. A Good Home. To raise my family" (44). He pleads that the complaint will stall the finalizing of his tenure and he won't be able to the close the deal on his house. "I will lose my *deposit*, and the home I'd picked out for my wife and son will go by the boards," he says (45).

John perceives the impact of the complaint to be financial —the loss of the deposit— which undermines his role as the provider for the family. Success in business, Mamet suggested in his essay "In the Company of Men," is tied to a man's role as "breadwinner, as provider, as paterfamilias, as vestigial and outmoded as you may feel those roles to be" (*Freaks* 90). Clearly John sees himself in these roles which, to him, are inextricably tied to his job as tenured member of faculty. That there is a conflation between his role as head of the family and his position in the classroom is not surprising, for he sees them a compatible aspects of his masculinity. Further, the conflation lends credibility to Carol's contention that he plays the role of patriarch, particularly given that after Carol tells him that she has done everything he asked and still can't manage the course, he responds "I'm not your *father*" (9). "What? ... Did I say you were my father?" she responds (10). It is John, not Carol, who assumes a relation between the role of father and professor, a point further evinced when he tells her, "I'm talking to you as I'd talk to my son" (19).

What occurs in this conflation of personal and professional roles is a confusion of them. John, by suggesting that he is talking to Carol as he would to his son, implies a concern which is appropriate to a family situation, but not necessarily to a professional one. When she queries the terms of this concern, he replies, "I like you," prompting his student to ask "Why?" (21). He replies, "Perhaps we're similar" (21). John's dissolution of difference is an attempt to be empathetic, a vital component of communication; but the danger of projecting oneself into the situation of another is that the imagined response sometimes can be taken as the other person's actual response, a slippage that amounts to "this is what I imagine you to be feeling therefore this is what you are feeling." At that point, the slippage is no longer empathetic but is an appropriation of the other person's response. Whether deliberate or not, whether well-intentioned or not, this appropriation makes it difficult, if not impossible, for the other to express herself. The effect is to silence.

Carol comes to John because she is frustrated by her inability to succeed in his course. Her problems, she says, are the result of her coming from a different social and economic background, a comment that implies a comparison between her and others in which she finds herself to be inadequate (8). John asks her, "What do you want me to do? We are two people, all right? Both of whom have subscribed to ... certain arbitrary ... certain institutional ... you tell me what you want me to do.... You tell me what you want me to do..." (10). Her reply is simple: "*Teach* me. *Teach* me" (11).

John's fragmented syntax omits the noun which I assume to be "rules" or "codes," creating a gap in the dialogue which allows subtext to play: why doesn't John say "rules"? Whatever interpretation might be given to his elision of the noun, there is a clear —albeit unspoken— acknowledgement that rules do govern this situation. John's inability to say "rules" initially seems an indication of a compassionate desire to save Carol from the humiliation of being told that she in a losing player in the academic game; but at the same time, the omission opens the possibility that he cannot say "rules" because he flouts them. Carol is emphatically clear about what she wants: she wants to be taught. She consistently refers to John as "professor," never allowing that he has a relation to her other than his professional one. Rather than begin to work through her problems with the course, John sympathizes with her situation, using it as an occasion to talk about how he, too, once felt inadequate and defeated by the educational system. He projects his remembered feelings onto her: "And you will think: Why was I born to be the laughing stock of a world in which everyone is better than I?" (19). Unclear about whether their situations are analogous, she asks "Is that ... (*Pause*) Is that what I have...?" (19).

In the comparison between his feelings of failure and hers, John does not provide Carol with what she sees as the solution to her problem —tutoring— but uses the situation as an opportunity, operating on the guise of sympathy, to talk about himself. He confides that he does not know how to help her, "other than to be *personal...*" (19). Moments later, he tells Carol that he is staying rather than leaving her to discuss the purchase of the house with his wife, an inversion of the opening moment of the play when he completely ignored her as he talked with his wife (21). The implication of his staying is that now she is more important to him than his wife. His ascription of her importance carries a sexual innuendo which he maintains. Carol asks him if he has problems; he answers affirmatively, saying "If we're going to take off the Artificial *Stricture*, of 'Teacher,' and 'Student,' why should *my* problems be any more a mystery than your own?" (21). With that, John feels licensed to talk about himself, only interrupted when Carol reminds him that she is in his office to talk about her academic performance (24). His solution to her problems is to grant her an "A" for the term

> [i]f you will come back and meet with me. A few more times. Your grade's an "A." Forget about the paper. You didn't like writing it. It's not important. What's important is that I awake your interest, if I can, and that I answer your questions. Let's start over. (26)

Certainly John's comment allows a reading of this moment as harassment because the sort of attention which the professor pays the student is unwanted: she insists on maintaining the professional nature of their relation by referring to him as "professor" and by directing him to return to the issue of her grade. He offers her a solution which does not address her need to learn; rather he will give her the sign of success in learning, an "A," conditional that she comes back and meet with him. Although John's expectations are unclear, given that they are outside the normal terms of a professor/student relationship, it is not unreasonable to assume the ambiguity opens the possibility of his making sexual advances. The insinuation of the personal and its ambivalence suits him, not her; it is for his pleasure, not hers. Simply, the shifts in the terms of the professor/student relationship are not consensual.

Although John is in a position of power in relation to Carol, Mamet tries to suggest that this power is something of a sham. In the exclusively male-environments which Mamet presented in many of his earlier plays, particularly in *Glengarry Glen Ross*, men present themselves as hyper-macho because there are no women to challenge this posturing (see: Zeifman). In *Oleanna*, the possibility of a female character exposing the fragile terms of John's masculinity is not realized. Whatever nascent critique of gender might be suggested by Mamet in Act One, by Act Two that possibility dissolves when Carol appears as a woman who has lost all tentativeness and now is fully confident of the political power which she wields within the university. She has filed a complaint of sexual harassment, telling John that "Whatever you have done to me — to the extent that you've done it to *me*, do you know rather than to me as a *student*, and, so, to the student body, is contained in my report. To the tenure committee" (47).

The change in Carol's character lacks dramaturgical credibility. John, however, retains the psychological coherence which is associated with theatrical realism; consequently, he seems "real" while she seems to be a "fiction." I would note, too, that in the English production, the interval occurred between Acts One and Two. Returning after a break from the action, Carol is a changed woman who bears little resemblance to the woman in Act One. This shift renders Carol unrealistic. As John Gross, writing for the *Sunday Telegraph*, notes:

> Judged by ordinary realistic standards, the play contains two major implausibilities. It is almost inconceivable that someone accused of harassment would risk letting his alleged victim come back to his room, by herself, without witnesses. And, the transformation of Carol from mumbling lost soul to fluent ideologue is too rapid and extreme.

The first of these departures from probability doesn't matter: we simply accept it as dramatic convention. The second is a little less easy to ignore. We can go along with it for the sake of artistic compactness, but not all the way: the play would be even more compelling than it is if Mamet had prepared the ground for Carol's transformation a bit more thoroughly in his opening scene. The professor, on the other hand, is convincing from first to last.

In effect, Mamet shifts the terms of the depiction of Carol who is no longer a psychologically coherent, individuated character, but now seems to personify John's worst nightmare about femininity. The contrast between the Carol of Act One and that of Acts Two and Three suggests she has a split nature, as if the woman whom we saw in Act One is a ruse behind which the "true" (or, ironically enough, "real") Carol hides.

The misogynistic rendering of Carol as a woman who presents herself as uncertain, a strategy used with calculation by her to mask the true force of her personality, suggests that *Oleanna* finally amounts to a castration fantasy: John is duped by a conniving woman who draws him into a situation which destroys him. Part of her strategy is to provide an account of their meeting which dissolves all the ambiguities. John reads from the report:

> "He said he 'liked' me. That he 'liked being with me.' He'd let me write my examination paper over, if I could come back oftener to see him in his office." (*Pause*) (*To* CAROL:) It's *ludicrous*. Don't you know that? It's not *necessary*. It going to *humiliate* you, and its going to cost me my *house*, and... (48)

John's comment, that the price which he will pay if found guilty of Carol's accusations will be his house, is less callously materialistic if we remember the degree to which he is a man invested in his role as provider. Carol's actions emasculate him by stripping him of his ability to provide for his family.

*Oleanna* is a play about masculine power — or more precisely, the loss of it. John initially believes that Carol is powerless but, she proves him wrong when she marshals the resources of the university and then the law to support her claims of harassment and of rape. The charge of rape comes after the charge of harassment, as if Carol is a much more adept player in the games of the university than is John and is upping the stakes in the contestation for control in which the two are engaged. If in Act One he underestimated her power, she takes advantage of his miscalculation by providing the ultimate demonstration of her power: she will destroy his career and, in effect, him because his identity is inextricably tied to his professional role.

The culmination of the battle for power is the moment in which John lashes out by knocking Carol to the floor which, in some performances, prompted members of the audience to cheer. This response, cunningly orchestrated in the play, is an ironic rehearsal of the duplicity which Mamet suggested is to be feared in women: *Oleanna*'s exploration of political correctness is a pretence for the dramatist's project of justifying a man assaulting a woman: like the Sphinx of Greek mythology, Carol, the feminine devourer of men, must be destroyed; but unlike Oedipus, John is no hero and is defeated by a system which does not recognize the danger which this woman, and feminists like her, pose. Duped by "political correctness," the "system" now supports the terrible enemy —Woman— which will destroy society.

In the surge of emotion which the audience feels watching John, near defeat but able to rally enough of his strength to attack Carol, it is easy to lose sight of what triggers John's rage. As Carol rises to leave towards the end of Act Three, she says to John, "... and don't call your wife 'baby'" which prompts him to respond, "You vicious little bitch. You think you can come in here with your political correctness and destroy my life?" (79). He knocks her to the floor and raises a chair over his head, as if to hit her, saying "... *Rape you*...? Are you kidding me...? ... I wouldn't touch you with a ten-foot pole. You little *cunt*..." (79). The veneer of politeness shatters and John states, in terms as blunt as those of Ricky Roma in *Glengarry Glen Ross,* what he believes to the prerogative of masculinity: a man's right to power over a woman, to infantalize one woman by calling her "baby" and to dismember another, at least verbally, by calling her a "cunt."

As my citing of reviewers' responses suggests, the British premiere of *Oleanna* was met with somewhat mixed response to the script. For the most part, reviewers praised Pinter's deft, understated direction, and the performances of David Suchet as John and Lia Williams as Carol. In commenting about the play, which had caused such a sensation when it premiered in New York on October 11 1982 (in a production directed by the playwright and starring his new wife, Rebecca Pidgeon), reviewers focus on Mamet's success in critiquing "political correctness."

Discussion of character circulates around whether the two characters, John and Carol, are credible. What is curious is that while a number of reviewers see Mamet's depiction of Carol as misogynistic, none is interested in the implications of such a depiction for the narrative, other than to note that Mamet, by depicting Carol as a "monstrous" figure, skews —and hence, undermines— the debate about political correctness. None of reviewers entertains the possibility that the "monstrous" Carol might be symptomatic of the castration fantasy which is the sub-text of *Oleanna*. This fantasy, lurking beneath the narrative but too horrific to be voiced overtly, is kept at bay in the play through structural ploys such as parallels between the two characters, and inversions in the positions of characters.

As Louise Chunn, the women's page editor for the *Guardian*, in a guest review for *Independent on Sunday*, notes: "The male lecturer is a recognisable type — he's ambitious, self-centred, domineering. But he's not a monster." Or, as Carol says of John, "You feel yourself empowered...you say so yourself. To *strut*. To *posture*. To 'perform'" (51). Certainly, John seems infatuated with the sound of his own voice, and only reluctantly stops long enough to let Carol speak. As he pontificates on the value of post-secondary education, he is so enchanted with his own thoughts that he pauses to make notes (33).

To some degree, John is a pathetic figure whose only forum for exercising power seems to be his teaching where he has an audience of students who need to pass the course and consequently seem bound to attend to his musings. The pathos of the character is heightened by his apparent lack of self-awareness which results in his inability to recognize the contradictions in his position. Consequently, when Carol tells him that she feels that she is stupid and will never learn (14), John responds "I'll tell you a story about myself. (*Pause*) Do you mind? (*Pause*) I was raised to think myself stupid. That's what I want to tell you" (15). The text provides no reason for the moment not to be read as John attempting to be sympathetic, but his apparent lack of awareness of the terms under which he offers sympathy are startling. For a professor, who has achieved a level of professional success, to confess to a student in his office (that is, within his space) that he was raised to think of himself as stupid carries none of the risk that her earlier disclosure does.

John's apparent lack of awareness of the power differential between himself and Carol leads him to make what is a patently false assertion that they are "similar" (21). The naivete of the claim is evident in other moments in the first act when, for example, he constructs his review before the tenure committee as a test akin to her being evaluated in classes within the university. Confident that the granting of his tenure is a mere formality, he denigrates the value of tenure process saying,

> The Tenure Committee. Come to judge me. The Bad Tenure Committee.
>
> The "Test." Do you see? They put me to the test. Why, they had people voting on me I wouldn't employ to wax my car. And yet, I go before the Great Tenure Committee, and I have an urge, to *vomit*, to, to, to puke my *badness* on the table, to show them: "I'm no good. Why would you pick *me*?" (23)

Carol calls his bluff, pointing out "They granted you tenure" (23). John protests, "Oh no, they announced it, but they haven't *signed*. Do you see? 'At any moment...'" (23).

The first act ends with John receiving yet another phone call which, like the others, punctuates the intense exchanges between the two characters. The audience gathers from his responses that he is about to lose the house for which has put a deposit. His response, in the face of losing what he values —the house, which I suggested earlier is tied to his sense of his masculinity— is to have recourse to the law. "You listen: I want you to take *Grace*, you take Grace, and get out of that house. You *leave* her there. Her and her lawyer, and you *tell* them, we see them in court next..." (39). As it turns out, whatever prompted John to threaten litigation was only a ruse on the part of his wife and friends to draw him to the house where a surprise party is planned in celebration of the impending announcement of his tenure. Suffice to say, a party in a house which John and his wife don't own, celebrating tenure which has not been granted formally, smacks of hubris, to say nothing of straining credibility in terms of realism. Act One ends when Carol notes that John has to go to his party. He responds, "It seems that I do."

CAROL: (*Pause*) They're proud of you.
JOHN: Well, there are those who would say it's a form of aggression.
CAROL: What is?
JOHN: A surprise. (40, 41)

The notion that a surprise is "a form of aggression" becomes nuanced in the opening of Act Two which opens with John lecturing Carol in what seems initially to be a rehearsal of the dynamic between professor and student which we saw in Act One. Towards the end of John's speech, Mamet surprises the audience because John is not pontificating about his love of teaching, as it might seem initially, but is pleading with Carol to withdraw her complaint because it will mean that he will be denied tenure. Mamet's second surprise for the audience is the radical change in Carol's demeanour so that she is now a confident, assured woman who controls the situation. If a surprise is a form of aggression, who is the aggressor?

With the power dynamic between teacher and student inverted from what it was in Act One, John's mockery of the Tenure Committee in Act One rings hollow. Faced with the real possibility that he will be denied tenure and hence lose his means of supporting his family, he now see the tenure review as just:

> Now you don't have your own family, at this point, you may not know what it means. But to me it is important. A home. A Good Home. To raise my family. Now: The Tenure Committee will meet. This is the process, and a *good* process. Under which the school has functioned for quite a long time. They will meet, and hear your complaint — which you have the right to make; and they will dismiss it. They will *dismiss* your complaint; and, in the intervening period, I will lose my house. I will not be able to close on my house. I will lose my *deposit*, and the home I'd picked out for my wife and son will go by the boards. (44, 45)

A bit later in Act Two, John, realizing that Carol will not be swayed easily from her decision to pursue the complaint against him, pleads desperately,

> But you talk of *rights*. Don't you see? *I* have rights too. Do you see? I have a *house* ... part of the *real* world; and The Tenure Committee, Good Men and True .... Please: *Also* part of the world: you understand? This is my *life*. I am not the *bogeyman*. I don't "stand" for something, I ... (50)

I have quoted these two lengthy passages to flag several important elements in *Oleanna*. First, in Act One, John suggests that he and Carol are similar which, given their relative situations, is a misrepresentation; but by Act Two, the audience does get a glimpse of the similarity between the characters: each, when feeling imperiled and wronged, relies on official challenges for justice. When John thought that he was going to lose his house at the end of Act One, he threatened litigation; when Carol feels wronged, she launches an official complaint with the university. In a way, John has no right to feel wronged because Carol pursues justice through channels which parallel the ones which he would have chosen had he lost his house. The difference seems to be that he is worried that he will lose, that the charges brought against him will be upheld. As I indicated at the outset of the paper, by letting the audience see what transpires between professor and student, Mamet implies that the consequences of the charges being upheld are extreme to the extent of dangerously undermining justice. What is at stake in *Oleanna* is Mamet's sense of the truth of the situation which he depicts theatrically which returns us to a discussion of realism and initiates the third and final section of this paper.

The Methuen edition of *Oleanna*[3] includes selections from an essay called "Realism" which was originally published from a collection called *Life in the Theatre* by Mamet. The selection opens with the following polemic:

> Most American theatrical workers are in thrall to the idea of "realism". A very real urge to be truthful, to be "true" constrains them to judge their efforts and action against an inchoate, which is to say against an "unspecified" standard of reality. (np)

The program offers another quotation from the Mamet essay, Stanislavsky, and more notably, Vakhtangov suggested that — that to which the artist must be "true" is the aesthetic integrity of the play.... This places a huge responsibility on the artist. He or she faced with this charge —to care for the "scenic truth"— can no longer take refuge in a blanket dismissal or "endorsement" of anything on the grounds of its not being realistic.

Mamet's comments are instructive inasmuch as his reference to Stanislavsky —emended for accuracy to Vachtangov— suggests that his theatrical debts, in terms of realism, are to its early practitioners. In an interview with Esther Harriott, Mamet again makes mention of Stanislavski, saying,

> [A]s Stanislavski said, the theatre is the place we go to hear the truth. The task of the theatre worker is to bring to the stage the life of the soul. Reasoning from there to technical principles and esthetic principles, he play is a study of one single action on the part of the protagonist, and everything which contributes to that action of necessity much be included,

---

[3] The plays produced by the English Stage Company in the main theatre of the Royal Court are published by Methuen in the Royal Court's Writers' Series. The script, with added information, serves as the program for the production.

> and everything else which does not contribute to that action must of necessity be excluded. Those are a couple of really simple principles. (78)

The question which Mamet's dramaturgical principles raise, in light of a two-hander like *Oleanna* is, who is the protagonist? If the drama is seen simply as a demonstration, within the terms of realism characterized by the representation of action which corresponds to an actuality, and if *Oleanna* is read as a condemnation of "political correctness," then we can only assume that Carol is the protagonist who brings down John. The cost to the victim is high: not simply tenure and the deposit on a house, but his sense of himself as man who can provide for his family. This dynamic, as my reading of Carol as the Sphinx-like devourer of men, engages what Billington described as the "mythic" element of the play. What is evoked is a fantasy of woman as castrator, which is no less real because it is a fantasy. This is an example of a manifestation of the political unconscious which exists in relation to the conscious. In the final moments of this paper, what I want to indicate the gendered conventions of realism evident in *Oleanna* and their political potential. Mamet manipulates the audience by having Carol in Act Two appear as a much stronger, politically cognizant woman than she was in Act One; in so doing he brings to the fore the gendered dynamic which is an important ideological element of conventional modes of realism.

As my earlier references to a number of reviewers who saw the Court's production of *Oleanna* indicate, many did not accept the change of Carol between Acts One and Two as credible. In part, the play depends on the interval or intermission being held between the two acts because when the audience returns after a break, in some sense, the play which resumes isn't the play which was begun. The shift in Carol, as I and others have suggested, renders her such a radically different character in the post-interval play that she seem another person. This violates one of realism's conventions, that characters have coherence. In light of Mamet's maintaining other conventions of realism which are initiated in Act One and sustained throughout the rest of the play —the consistency of setting, of situation and of John's character— Carol can be read as simply duplicitous which is supported in the name of "political correctness." But, from another perspective, this shift in Carol's character marks something else. It is the shift from the empirical level of realism to the imaginary. That in *Oleanna*, the shift seems to result in the post-interval play being almost another play is a symptom of the always tense, problematic relation between these to aspects of realism.

As I indicated earlier, *Oleanna* only works if the audience allows the initial supposition that the *natural* relation of power between men and women has men as the primary, superior element. If you don't buy into that initial, unstated supposition (which as I would hope my reading suggests that I don't), then the play only works through dramaturgical sleights of hand. Structurally, the play works rather well, through Mamet's careful transposition of Carol as the victim to John as the victim. Mamet can make this transposition through the construction of parallels between the two characters which I have outlined earlier. But note that the case depends on Mamet's perspective on, and representation of, political correctness; Mamet's stance is not to present himself as simply documenting but as interpretting and rendering. For the play to work, he establishes and manipulates the terms of the debate by, for example, having the interval between the first and second acts. Without a break in the action, without drink from the bar, would anyone buy; the action if it played continuously? As John Gross notes, the idea that a professor charged with harassment agrees to see a student while he is alone in his office strains credibility. But the play works because by using the interval to shift modes of realism, from the empirical to the imaginary, Mamet touches the cultural fear of Woman-as-Castrator. That the play riles audiences is an index of the "reality" —however intangible— of this cultural fear.

What I have termed the "imaginary," Howells innocuously decribes as "the interests and motives that impel people in life." The point which I want to make is that realism occurs not only at the time of industrial capital, but at a point when subjectivity is under consideration, represented in the late nineteenth and early twentieth century, through work of theorists like Freud. Howells, is a contemporary of Freud. Howells, through the locution of "the interests and motives that impel people in life," gestures to the role of the unconscious which Freud makes overt through writings from 1899 and onwards. For Freud, the unconscious is individuated; but theorists, from Frederic Jameson to Louis Althusser, insist that ideology is not always lived and experienced consciously. Ideology, manifest as "myth" or collective fantasy, gestures to the political unconscious. Charting the "real" in realist drama frequently exceeds documenting the observable and enters the realm of the imaginary. Often the empirical and the imaginary are asymmetrical and are not the tidy complements of each other. This is because the realist project historically, while frequently offering a limited critique of patriarchy, ultimately is complicit in its ideologies. The tension between the empirical and imaginary levels of realism, so evident in *Oleanna* may be symptomatic of the contradiction in ideologies which support patriarchy.

Clearly, the "epoch" of capital, when as Belsey suggests, realism emerges, occurs through a confluence of patriarchal ideologies. But the emergence of notions of the unconscious also occurs as realism emerges and becomes a prevalent artistic project. In not mentioning the role of imaginary, which Mamet telling marshals in *Oleanna*, Belsey, Dolan and critics like them miss the an aspect of realism which, as Mamet's success with *Oleanna* suggests, is an active force in the culture of late capital. In the asymmetry between the empirical and imaginary levels of realism, a space opens to begin to undermine the hegemonic force of patriarchy: the asymmetry is a crack in the monolith.

*University of Guelph*

**WORKS CITED**

Belsey, Catherine. *Critical Practice.* 1980. London and New York: Routledge, 1988.

Billington, Michael. Rev. of *Oleanna* by David Mamet. *Guardian.* 1 July 1993. Rpt. *Theatre Record* 18 June - 1 July 1993. 740.

Chunn, Louise. Rev. of *Oleanna* by David Mamet. *Independent on Sunday.* 4 July 1993. Rpt. *Theatre Record* 18 June - 1 July 1993. 746.

Dolan, Jill. *The Feminist Spectator as Critic.* Ann Arbor: U of Michigan P, 1988.

Gross, John. Rev. of *Oleanna* by David Mamet. *Sunday Telegraph.* 4 July 1993. Rpt. *Theatre Record* 18 June - 1 July 1993. 745.

Henry III, William A. "Reborn Relevance." Rev. of *The Destiny of Me* by Larry Kramer; *The Sisters Rosenweig* by Wendy Wasserstein; and *Oleanna* by David Mamet. *Time.* 23 Nov. 1992. 76, 79.

Hischborn, Clive. Rev. of *Oleanna* by David Mamet. *Sunday Express.* 4 July 1993. Rpt. *Theatre Record* 18 June - 1 July 1993. 745.

Howells, William Dean. "The Play and the Problem." *A Realist in the American Theatre.* Ed. Brenda Murphy. 1895. Athens: Ohio U P, 1992. 55-62.

Mamet, David. *Glengarry Glen Ross.* New York: Grove, 1982.

____. "In the Company of Men." *Some Freaks.* Harmondsworth: Penguin, 1989. 85-91.

____. Interview with Esther Harriott. *American Voices: Five Contemporary playwrights in Essays and Interviews.* By Esther Harriott. Jefferson: McFarland & Co, 1988.

____. *Oleanna.* London: Methuen (Royal Court Writers Series) 1993.

Morley, Sheridan. Rev. of *Oleanna* by David Mamet. *Spectator.* 10 July 1993. Rpt. *Theatre Record* 18 June - 1 July 1993. 740.

Peter, John. Rev. of *Oleanna* by David Mamet. *Sunday Times.* 4 July 1993. Rpt. *Theatre Record* 18 June - 1 July 1993. 742.

Rutherford, Malcolm. Rev. of *Oleanna* by David Mamet. *Financial Times*. 2 July 1993. Rpt. *Theatre Record* 18 June - 1 July 1993. 742.

Sierz, Aleks. Rev. of *Oleanna* by David Mamet. *Tribune*. 9 July 1993. Rpt. *Theatre Record* 18 June - 1 July 1993. 740.

Taylor, Paul. Rev. of *Oleanna* by David Mamet. *Independent*. 2 July 1992. Rpt. *Theatre Record* 18 June - 1 July 1993. 743.

Taylor, John Russell."Realism." *The Penguin Dictionary of Theatre*. Harmondsworth: Penguin, 1966.

Zeifman, Hersh. "Phallus in Wonderland: Machismo and Business in David Mamet's *American Buffalo* and *Glengarry Glen Ross*." *David Mamet: A Casebook*. Ed. Leslie Kane. New York: Garland, 1992. 123-68.

# SIMULATIONS OF NATIONHOOD; SPECTACLES OF POSTCOLONIALITY: THE *SHOW BOAT* CONTROVERSY AS IMPERIAL PAGEANT*

Alan Filewod

The theatre is a platform on which we enact simulations of nationhood. This entails a homology between the theatre as a material enterprise and the textualities it produces. This productive relationship is a modelling of the discourse of nation that enables it, and which it in turn expands and renegotiates.

If nations are indeed narratives, they come into existence in the space of cultural representation. In this context, the performance text particularizes the experience of national formations in the enactment of individual crises, and generalizes it in the communal site of the theatre as a material agency of historical change. As industry and enterprise, the theatre manifests the constructedness of the community which it redefines in the process of performance.

The material theatre encloses a conceptual space in which the nation finds meaning as a formative principle of social subjectivity. The narratives which that space generates are the most common object of critical analysis. We look at dramaturgy and performance as cultural practices which circulate through the conceptual space of the theatre. But that conceptual space is materialized in an industry which replicates the social ideologies that enable and contain it.

This relationship between performance and social discourses is the point of departure for postcolonial theories. The field of postcolonialism is fruitfully diverse, because the relationship of text and power operates within various conditions of social oppression. My own point of interest in the postcolonial is the relationship of performance spectacle with the ideologies that enable it. From that perspective, postcolonialism examines the provisionality of national formations.

In this context, the theatre functions as a simulation of nationhood in two ways: as a material industry which recreates within its own changing terms the contestations of ideology, diversities, communities

* I would like to express my appreciation to Hand Fireworks Company, Milton, Ontario, for allowing me access to their archival records, to Dave Brown for pointing me to them, and to Lori Brown for guiding me through them.

and interests that produce the national state, and as an anthology of texts which embody those contestations as expressions of individual experience.

My use of the term simulation differs somewhat from Baudrillard's proposal that the simulation is a copy without an original. (Baudrillard 6) It is also useful to think of a simulation as a dislocated projection of causes without effects, and effects without causes. Or, to paraphrase Boal, the simulation is a rehearsal of the real, in which transgressions and disruptions can be staged and examined in textual modelling. But Baudrillard's formation is useful in his proposition that the simulation achieves authenticity by exposing the crisis of constructedness in the implied real. The simulation projects hypothetical nations, but the nation finds authenticity in the pluralism of the projection.

The complex of ideology, textuality and spectacle as the simulation of community is a defining principle of pageants. The popularity of the pageant form in the formative decades of Canadian nation building —the late Victorian and the Edwardian eras— provides a clear instance of this complex. I would like to construct a historical argument to address the 1993 controversy of *Show Boat* in North York, by placing it in a tradition of monumental textualities which enact totalizing ideological narratives as postcolonial simulations.

The pageant form can be defined as re-enactment offered as proof of its origin. Defined in its broadest sense, the pageant is an iconographic spectacle that enacts ideological narratives; in this sense, a Colway-style Community Play such as *The Spirit of Shivaree*, a church Nativity play and Michael Jackson's *History* tour are three typifying examples of modern theatrical pageantry.

In each case, the performances implicates the spectator in the emotional value of the iconography. The reception of the representation is the reception of the event it restages. The audience is in this way recruited as co-performers in a narrative that transforms their presence into the culmination of the historical spectacle. As W.D. King has demonstrated, in his analysis of Bernard Shaw's review of Henry Irving's production of Conan Doyle's *Waterloo*, the text in performance can be understood as a machine devised to generate specific social effects. (King 55)

The pageant form that spread throughout the British Empire through the efforts of Louis Napoleon Parker began as a kind of Pre-Raphealite theatrical invocation of pre-industrial community. It circulated a romantic myth of Englishness through the empire, and in the United States, where the widespread adoption of the Parker model articulated a myth of classical form. Parker's vocabulary was a conscious reference to a romantic construction of medieval theatre, in which the guilds are narrated as idealized communities that come together as creators of beauty under the guiding hand of the Pageant Master.

Parker's followers retained this romantic pastoralism even as they continued his precedent of placing the pageant form at the service of the state. The most successful of his disciples was Frank Lascelles, who built an international career of staging monumental pageants around the empire — including the Opening of Parliament in Cape Town in 1910 and the vast Coronation Durbar in Calcutta in 1912. In Canada, Lascelles staged the Quebec Tercentenary on the Plains of Abraham in 1908, and a production of Hardy's *The Dynasts* in Toronto at the Royal Alexandra Theatre in 1916. In contrast to the amateur medievalism of Parker, Lascelles' pageants drew on the utmost resources of the state, mobilizing army battalions, commandeering entire towns, appropriating when possible the ceremonial performances of the aristocracy. Like many empire-builders of his age, Lascelles collected honours from aboriginal peoples. The Iroquois named him Tehonikonraku, "The man of infinite resources." (*New York Times* 26 May 1934) He was in fact a man of infinite connections.

Few self-identified pageant masters attained such international distinction, but some managed to build careers in the interstice of empire and spectacle. One such was John Henderson, a London-based playwright and director who assisted Lascelles on the Quebec pageant, and whose reference in a letter to "my folks in Oakville and Toronto" suggests Canadian origin. (Henderson, 29 June 1913) Henderson's repertoire included a number of stock pageants, some military dramas set in the Canadian west, and productions of *Uncle Tom's Cabin* and *The Octaroon*.

Henderson capitalized on his military affinities at a time when the army, especially in the colonies, provided an opportunity and means for the display of social distinction. Colonial society in the Edwardian era, in Toronto, Cape Town, Calcutta and Melbourne, was marked by clearly defined registers of taste, status and power in the officer corps of the local militia regiments. The community was defined by its uniforms, and the rivalries in regimental traditions regulated a scale of acceptable social difference. The ceremony of the amateur military society transformed imperial sentiment into a social arena of power and attainment. In that sense, the pageant was not so much a production of the military, but an enactment of the militia as itself a social performance.

As an entrepreneurial producer, Henderson used his familiarity with this social environment to build his business. His letterhead carried a photo of himself in uniform, and listed numerous spectacular productions. He also wrote and produced local pageants, on a smaller scale than Lascelles, but with similar deployments of state power. In Canada, he had an ongoing relationship with the Hand and Teal Spectacular Company, the pyrotechnics firm which produced grandstand spectacles for the CNE from 1880 to 1941. Working with Hand and Teal, Henderson also wrote the 1910 *Pageant of Ontario* to celebrate the sesquicentennial of the Queen's Own Rifles, Toronto's oldest and most aristocratic militia regiment.

Henderson's own definition of a pageant, as printed in the program of the *Pageant of Ontario*, is imbued with the romantic sensibility of the Parkerian tradition:

> What is a Pageant? a Pageant is a series of historical events, regal or homely, grave or gay, heroic or simple, in a country's history, depicted by living representatives passing before us in processional review, accompanied by such music and suitable scenic embellishments as the theme of the occasion may dictate ... (QOR 15)

As an expression of the narratives that justify state power, Henderson's pageants were closely related to the vastly more grandiose spectacles staged by the military. In 1901, for example, the Grand Military Review held for the Duke and Duchess of Cornwall and York in Toronto paraded 11,000 militia troops from across the province. This was nothing in comparison to the Indian durbars, and to the most powerful of all spectacles, the annual manoeuvres of the British army at Aldershot, staged to awe the world. Perhaps the greatest pageants of all time in this vein were the Naval Reviews at Spithead, in which the entire Home Fleet of the Royal Navy performed itself.

On the local scale, Henderson replicated a similar affinity of text, performance and icon in the his Toronto pageants. The Queen's Own Rifle's pageant was nominally a depiction of Ontario history, but it was clearly presented as the province played through its essential metonym, the regiment that repelled the Fenians, thrashed Riel and sent volunteers to South Africa. The pageant was initiated by the regiment's commanding officer, Sir Henry Pellatt, who according to the regimental history, saw in the Queen's Own Rifles "the embodiment of the finest traits of Canadian character." Pellatt determined that "the interweaving of Canadian history with regimental history must be demonstrated," and so instructed the organizing committee he commanded. (Barnard 86)

The pageant displayed six "epochs" against a 650 foot painted scene. The nomenclature of the program reinforces the affinity of the military and the theatrical: Staff-Sergt. D. Collie Ross is listed as

"Chief of Staff and Stage Director." Ross was in civilian life the director of the grandstand shows of the Canadian National Exhibition, where he had worked with Hand on numerous pyrotechnic displays. Under Ross, in an organizational pyramid shared by armies and theatres, each epoch had its stage manager — all of whom were officers or warrant officers. (QOR 5)

Although the text does not appear to have survived, Henderson's program notes, written in the voice of "a spectator in the grandstand," gives a clear rendition of the scale of the show and its intended effect. In the second epoch, for example, the program tell us

> Now we see Tecumseh, that bravest of all brave warriors. How he outwitted General Harrison and is himself done to death by the incapacity of the soldiers in command. Yes, Tecumseh and the battle of the Thames will ever find a place in Canadian folk-lore. The wail of the Indian warriors, carrying off the dead chieftain, is still in my ears, when a change comes o'er the spirit of the scene, instead of battle cries and gunpowder, pretty sylvan music, that tree revolves and Laura Secord's cottage comes in view. Oh, yes, the inside of it, just as real as any house you see every day. (QOR 21)

But the pageant was more than its iconographic narrative and spectacle effects. It marked imperial allegiances both in its enactments of the community that staged it, and in the absences that such enactment must entail. The declarative enactment is vividly clear in Henderson's description of the final tableau which involved a full-scale mock of the Canada Gates at Buckingham Palace, a 40 foot statue of Queen Victoria; a parade of historic British monarchs, 400 school children, and as a grand finale, the trooping of the colours by the Queen's Own Rifles, the Royal Grenadiers and the 48th Highlanders. The program note commands the appropriate response:

> Magnificent! Everybody —from all the Epochs— comes back from the shades of long ago, and the grand chorale at the finish "Canada" —-yes, that's it, "Canada." It's here on my programme— "Canada." 1,200 people sing it and the bands accompany it. You all feel you must join in —you can't help it. And the finale grand procession— all pass in review before you to the strains of the "Maple Leaf," a fitting finish to a grand occasion. — God Save the King. (QOR 23)

You must join in. Because if you don't, you are not part of the community of response, you are not part of the empire. Even in the significantly less diverse demographic of Edwardian Toronto this was a problematic position, because the pageant was more than a celebration of the fact of the empire; it was also a deeply ethnocentric celebration of Britishness, which ranked English tradition (the QOR) higher than the Scottish and Irish regiments in the Toronto militia. Beyond the British there is only absence. There is one place in the program where this absence exposes crisis. The *Pageant of Ontario*, like so much imperialist literature of the day, romanticizes aboriginality even as it contributes to the erasure of Native cultural presence.

Wherever possible in the casting of the pageant, Henderson attempted to concretise the relationship of history and spectacle by representing historic figures by appropriate performers: soldiers represented soldiers; society ladies, drawn from the Queen's Own affiliated chapter of the Imperial Order of the Daughters of the Empire (including Mrs Ambrose Small) represented high society. The program lists the names of the actors with two significant exceptions. Tecumseh and Thayandanagea (Joseph Brant) are portrayed as iconic figures who in the imaginary of the pageant embody Native enthusiasm for imperial rule. Brant is listed as played "by one of his descendants"; Tecumseh, "by one his lineal descendants." (QOR 25-26) The absence of names erases the material reality of contemporary aboriginality by stripping the actors of identity to establish genealogical authority. The inclusion of unnamed lineal descendants is in itself an act of cultural genocide. It is quite possible that these listings are in fact theatrical hype, although the pageant did include a group of 36 men from the Six Nations reserve. We are told by the regimental history that they were "very appreciative of the fact that they had been permitted to present their race according to their own interpretation." (Barnard 91) They were not however permitted to participate in the production of the fundamental terms of representation which cast them as the last heroes of a vanished race, which can step onto the stage only as a cultural memory. Their function was to perform the landscape on which empire in built, and to serve as a mythic chorus to invest old Ontario with deep meaning. This was literally the case in the first epoch, in which Simcoe takes his leave to a chorus of Indians who chant, "No go, our Father! No go a-way-way." (QOR 13)

The climax of the pageant was the Trooping of the Colours, one of the most reverent of military ceremonies. The pageant itself was the penultimate event in a week long spectacle which expanded the field of textuality. The celebrations included a garden party at the CNE which attracted 10,000 people, a reunion smoker with boxing matches, a church parade at the Anglican cathedral, the unveiling of a Memorial Window at University College, and a climactic Grand Ball at the CNE, in which Sir Henry and Lady Pellatt replicated the formal ceremony of an imperial court. The regimental history notes that the festivities were "magnificent in scope; near faultless in execution, performed by the citizens for the citizens...." (Barnard 91)

Shortly after the pageant, Pellatt took the regiment to England at his own expense as the first unit of colonial militia to participate in the annual manoeuvres of the British Army. The young Vincent Massey, whose sense of imperial mission and deep attachment to British high culture would contribute materially to the development of the Canadian theatre and drama, was a lieutenant in the Queen's Own, and participated in both the pageant and the British expedition.

If the pageant can be most usefully read in the larger context of imperial narrative enacted by the week-long celebration, Henderson's subsequent work in Toronto clearly reveals how the enactment of nation is a negotiation with an even wider construction of community. In his productions with Hand and Teal at the CNE grandstand, Henderson offered visions of imperial glory that marked the changing sentiments of empire in the years leading up the First World War. In the context of the CNE, his imperial spectacles were the culmination not of a week of solemn ceremony, but of a community excursion through the wonders of technological progress, the bounty of agricultural science, and the transgressive pleasures of the midway.

Since its founding as a pyrotechnical firm in Hamilton, Hand and Teal —renamed TW Hand Fireworks Co in 1901— had developed a national reputation for the inventiveness of its spectacular displays. Walter Teale was "blown to atoms" in a factory explosion in 1900 (*Hamilton Times*, 27 March 1900); a year later the firm's founder, "Professor" William Hand died in similar manner. (*Hamilton Times*, 12 October 1901) Hand's son, who entered the family trade by firing his first display at the age of 14, took over the company in 1888. In 1892, he hired George Penson as a scenic artist; Penson continued as the chief designer of the spectacles until 1933. Along with the CNE shows, the company produced ice palaces across Canada for winter carnivals, holiday displays, and — in perhaps its last great moment of ideological glory — a staging of "The Journey to Mecca" for an International Shriners Convention in 1930. During the second world war, the company produced flares and very lights for the military, and continues today as a manufacturer of fireworks. We have all at one time or another seen their displays, and sent off their corner-store whiz-bangs.

From the beginning, history for Hand was the opportunity to stage spectacular effects, no matter how anachronistic. John Bentley Mays observes that the first CNE grandstand show coincided in 1882 with the introduction of electric light.

Several typewritten scripts of the Hand spectacles survive. Most of them are popular reenactments of imperial history, written by Henderson, including *The Relief of Mafeking* and *The Battle of Omdurman*. A hand-written draft of a flyer for *The Siege of Louisburg* describes the effects succinctly:

> The most important Pyro-kinetic novelty of 1903. ...
> A great tableau in Canadian History Depicted in Fireworks. The extensive French Fortifications on the sea shore will be seen outlined in brilliant fire.
> The British Ships will sail on and bombard the forts from the sea, whilst upon the land, Wolfe's Cannon will tear great breaches in the walls.
> As the scene reaches its climax, an immense canopy of lurid fire, with numerous exploding points, surmounts the entire field of combat.
> *The walls of the great fortress crumble away!*
> The Great Magazines of the besieged are pierced by the red hot shot from the fleet, and explode, throwing forth great columns of fire high into the skies. As the fires fade away, the French flag is lowered, symbolizing to disappearance forever from Canadian Maritime Provinces. (sic)

As simulacra of nation, the pageants marked more than the historic passage from romantic nationalism to industrial modernism. They also mark the historical transition to a nationalism predicated on nostalgia. Even at the moment of its most grandiose spectacles, Canadian Imperialism was a bankrupt ideology, dematerialized by the British withdrawal from the dream of a global imperial military culture. The CNE pageants were spectacles of nostalgia in which imperial sentiment was reproduced as a tourist attraction that marked cultural difference within an expanding American sphere of power. By the mid-1920s, the CNE marketed itself aggressively in the United States, advertising the Ex as "an annual world fair" located at the end of "America's main paved street," where "you might see the entire Dominion at work and at play." (CNE 15) A 1926 brochure promoted the pageants as spectacular novelties:

> Usually the military theme is stressed, and before a glowing setting, picturing some great theme of Empire achievement, troops in the uniform of famous regiments, past and present, march and countermarch, blending into an unforgettable picture of glorious pageantry. ... The Exhibition spectacle sends the spectator away with a catch in his throat and a glow in his heart, treasuring memories which will remain always. (CNE 15)

As in the QOR pageant, the narrative of empire provided an ideological field in which difference can be surrendered to the pleasure of the spectacle. But by the 1920s, the community that watched was more clearly distanced from the community that performed, in keeping with the CNE's growing function as a trade show that celebrated community as industrial organization. In the CNE, military deployments served the spectacular interests of capital. John Bentley Mays has made the useful observation that the CNE pageants spoke "in their content of the empires of this world, but in their form of the coming empire of organization promised by capitalism, catalogues of battles transformed into entertainments, crisis transmogrified into the sustained dazzle of the sign."(96) This dislocation from monumental ideological affirmation to nostalgic pleasure paved the way for the grandstand shows of the 1970s and '80s which typically featured recycled American rock stars.

The movement from a nation formulated in a principle of destiny to a nation sustained by nostalgia can be outlined in Henderson's production of *Nero and the Burning of Rome*, which he produced for Hand in 1913. *Nero* is useful as the transitional stage in which a narrative of spectacular pleasure is tenuously contained by the community enactment of national sentiment.

On one level, *Nero* can be see as an apocalyptic coda to the Victorian obsession with Rome as a template of the British empire. The moment of a stage spectacle that consumes the romantic appropriation of Roman glory in a pyrotechnic fable on the eve of the First World War is seductive. It comes down to us as a final ironic comment on the curatorial logic of the British Museum, which places the viewer at the end of a genealogy of empires, on popular literature —Horatio on the bridge— and on historiography, which frequently mapped the terms and structure of the British army onto the historical depiction of the Roman legions. The popular imaginary of the Roman empire has always of course focused on its end, and if the historical irony of the 1913 *Nero* is a modern reinscription, it was nevertheless no accident that at the height of the British empire we see a morbid fascination with the notion of decline, made even more urgent and given scientific validity by post-Darwinian concepts of degeneration in the works of continental writers like Max Nordau and Oswald Spengler. The Edwardians were well aware that the study of archaeology is the study of the death of cultures; by the same token the building of empire is the founding of an archaeology for the future.

We know quite a bit about the production of *Nero* because both the script and Henderson's handwritten notes have survived. The script is a lengthy typescript description of the mise-en-scène, filled with specific archaeological directions for the scene painters. To the modern eye it reads like a film script. A typical passage reads (with Henderson's idiosyncratic punctuation):

> When lights are switched on the Scene, the entire Forum, is a moving mass of color. Groups of populae in bright costumes of many Nationalities,

> Greeks, Nubians, Indians, Egyptians, Persians, Turks, are mixed with Roman Citizens., Patrician and Plebians. — Traders and Shop-Keepers are opening their stalls and exposing their wares for sale. [...] Every description of Huxter is there. [...] Every one shouting their wares and their excellence — such a hubbub ...(2)

Henderson's several letters to Penson are detailed instructions on the specifications of the minutiae of costumes and settings, complete with marginal drawings of hats and footwear. They display a pleasure in accuracy that survives today in the culture of military reconstructions.

Henderson's instructions are also negotiations about the social construction of the pageant. He proposed that the cast of 350 be drawn from the militia and paramilitary organizations, including naval cadets and Girl Guides. His instructions even specified how the various units should be cast: the 15 principals, 80 Roman Soldiers should be cast from the QOR; the lictors, Brutus, Nubian guards, christians and slaves from the ranks of the 10th Grenadier Guards; "Citizens" from the Sons of England cadet corps. Chariots, he suggested, "should be operated by Circus men — unless you want somebody killed?" (29 June 1913) His letters outline the rehearsal process and the preparations for the "Naval and Military Patrol" that would precede *Nero*. In all of this, he advised, "The business of our show is intricate and wants lots of rehearsing to make it go with the 'snap and vim' necessary."(29 Jne 1913)

The military presence in this industrial spectacle operated on two levels: in the casting and essentially military organization of *Nero* (with sergeant majors once again acting as stage managers), and in the parade. Henderson wrote that "The Patrol will be taken on its own and will have nothing to do with our 'Nero'." (29 June 1913) This seems to have been the falling out of an acrimonious dispute between Henderson and Collie Ross, the director of the Grandstand and de facto manager of the militia marching bands. The patrol was a patriotic display of imperial sentiment that followed the evening's opening act of vaudeville acrobats. Like the Queen's Own Rifles pageant, it was a tribute to imperial power, but at the same time it was a costumed reconstruction of imperial sentiment for the tourist audience.

In the relocation of sentiment from the imperial pageantry of the QOR to the industrialized spectacle of the CNE, we see a reconstitution of the relationship of pageant to national discourse. David Glassberg has shown in his exhaustive study how the Parkerian pageant developed in the United States as an institution of local rituals that frame the state; in effect, American pageants continue to re-embody changing meanings of America as an epistemology. Glassberg suggests a line of derivation to the Miss America pageant (261-2); it might also be traced to the animatronic Presidents of Disneyworld, and in another way, to *Angels in America*.

In Canada, with the post-imperial crisis of national narrative, the development of pageantry has been marked by an evacuation of explicit state ideology from spectacle, seeking instead to stabilize the pleasure of mass spectacle in ideologies of local experience. This has been a process that can be marked in stages, in which discussion Expo 67 and the various centennial pageants figure prominently. It is also, I suggest, one of the historical sources of the contemporary circulation of the of the Colway-style community play.

The masking of state narrative does not obscure the function of spectacle as national simulation; as both the QOR pageants and the Henderson/CNE pageants demonstrate in different ways, the governing narratives of state power had always been commodified and reproduced by the narratives of private capital. In that sense, the historical consequences of the CNE pageants are not the Colway community plays, but the great consumer spectacles: monster truck rallies at the Skydome, the Santa Claus parade, *Carmen* at Canadian Opera Company, the Klingons at Canada's Wonderland. The intervention of electronic media expands the field of production, so that pageantry includes not just the enacted spectacle, but its mediatized representations — including publicity, critical response, and, in the case of *Show Boat*, public controversy.

The North York/Broadway revival of *Show Boat*, directed by Harold Prince and produced by Garth Drabinsky's Live Entertainment Corp. of Canada, exposes the contemporary relation of ideology, community and spectacle. The *Show Boat* crisis in 1993 was a contest over the control of the iconographies of the community which gives spectacle meaning and which defines the field of reception.

The production of *Show Boat* has been promoted as a triumphant coming-of-age in Canadian theatre. Drabinsky built his entire publicity campaign on this point, casting himself as the metonymic Canadian producer who dared to the Broadway dream. In the United States, in contrast, the production has promoted as the triumphant renewal of Broadway itself: the revived, cleaned-up *Show Boat* dominates the revived, cleaned-up Times Square.

In his analysis of the controversy, Robin Breon positions *Show Boat* as an opportune offshore try-out occasioned about by Drabinksy's partnership with Harold Prince, who had the rights to revise the text, and who was looking for a sponsor. This in itself was nothing new; this is how Broadway spectacles are made and marketed. The material condition that relocates this familiar history of commodification into the domain of pageantry was the actual venue and its contested relationship to the community it ostensibly reflected.

*Show Boat*'s origins in North York were the result of a grandiose taxpayer-subsidized project by the city's mayor, Mel Lastman, to create a commercial downtown core in the suburbs. In a deal that remains closed to public scrutiny, Drabinsky obtained the rights to manage and program the newly constructed North York Centre for the Performing Arts. The contract gave him the right to secure a corporate sponsor for the theatre, which is why the North York centre is now one of an international chain of Ford Centres for the Performing Arts.

As the inaugural production in the new centre, *Show Boat* was more than a pre-Broadway try-out: it was a celebration of the city's power to attract capital. In his welcoming message in the show's program, Mel Lastman reaffirmed the civic function of an arts centre in the age of corporatist culture:

> Our Ford Centre stands gloriously among the world's truly great theatres. This is the birthplace of Broadway's best ... More than beautiful, our theatre is a major boost to the Canadian arts scene and our local economy. (Ford, program 5)

Nourbese Philip has drawn the connection between venue, capital and ideology, arguing that *Show Boat* can be understood as two plays: the show itself, and "the 'play' of events around the production":

> At issue in this latter 'play' have been the following: the inappropriateness of using a racist production to open a multi-million, municipal flagship which was also publicly funded; the public and private challenges and objections to the production made by Blacks and African Canadians; and the wholeheartedly negative responses to those challenges by the producers and the media — in short, by the powerful.(104)

Nourbese Philip documents how tightly the mass media closed ranks when African Canadian voices suggested that *Show Boat*, as play and event, was a racist foregrounding of actualized white characters against a field of marginal African-Americans. When challenged, Drabinsky mobilized a stonewall media defence of *Show Boat* as a statement of racial tolerance. This included deep coverage by the *Toronto Star* —one of the investors in the production— as well as two CBC documentary specials, the Garth Drabinksy Lecture Series sponsored by the B'nai Brith, which featured Henry Louis Gates , and hired African Americans celebrities, including Harry Belafonte and James Earl Jones. (Nourbese Philip 106-117) These defenders reiterated the same set of points: that *Show Boat* is a classic that confers distinction on the producing community, that free speech must be defended vehemently, that Harold Prince had relentlessly expurgated all traces of 1920s liberal racism form the text. For his part, Prince addressed this point in his program note:

> Throughout the production and rehearsal, I was committed to eliminate any inadvertent stereotype in original material, dialogue which may seem "Uncle Tom" today. However I was determined not to rewrite history. [...] I hope it is clear that *Show Boat*'s creators (including of course, this cast and creative team) share the deepest solidarity with those who have been victims of racism." (Ford, program 14)

Along with this pre-emptive strategy, Drabinsky and his media allies successfully disallowed the terms of protest by framing the Coalition to Stop *Show Boat* as a marginal group infected by anti-semitism. Writing in *The Globe and Mail* after news surfaced that the Ontario government had given an anti-racism grant to the coalition, Michael Coren wrote that the protestors were a "small group of unelected zealots", and that Drabinsky should sue them for damaging his commercial prospects. (30 Jan. 1995)

Drabinksy himself staged the key moments in the public controversy, as he describes it in his autobiography. "Of my own volition" he writes, "I held a consultation meeting with members of Toronto's black community" in advance of the show; later, he quotes himself as saying in a meeting with the protestors, "I will not get involved in a censorship situation. We will not have our integrity impeached." (*Toronto Star* 19 March 1995)

There are several useful narratives in this story. One of them has to do with the gradual recolonization of the Canadian theatre industry by Broadway producers, who had always used Canadian sub-contractors. This was the historical condition that the nation-building project of public subsidy in the theatre was designed to redress. Another has to do with the revaluation of the sense of nation as marketplace, by which spectacle —the visible display of power— is the means by which the market is shared. This revaluation reorders in turn the structures of value circulated through the mass media, and these discourses of value are brought to bear in the field of small public theatres by critics, funding officers, corporate sponsors and audiences. But the narrative that situates *Show Boat* as a simulation of nationhood concerns the conflation of neo-colonialism and cultural diversity. Drabinsky successfully redeployed the discourses of pluralism in his counter-attack against the protestors, and the liberal mass media supported him. The protestors, in their struggle against racism and exclusion, found themselves accused of a totalizing, monolithic ideology that impedes equity and heterogeneity. Their terms of protest were not just disallowed; they were in the most literal sense of the term appropriated. This was a reiteration of the fundamental point of the protest, that Black experience had been appropriated as a marker of authenticity in a cultural text that consolidated white power. It is an historical condition captured in one of the showstopping moments of the production, as the beautiful blonde Magnolia stands centrestage, surrounded by Black supporting players, singing, "Can't Help Loving Dat Man." In the end, the protest against *Show Boat* was not that this condition is historically false, but that in the North York of the 1990s, it is critically true. In a way that Drabinsky never intended, *Show Boat* restaged the structures of power and race at work in the community.

In his autobiography, Drabinsky calls his victory over the protest "a major turning point in cultural politics in Canada." (*Toronto Star* 19 March 1995) But as the process of disallowance reveals, nothing had changed; the public spectacle of the protest, as played out in the mass media and on the *Show Boat* stage, celebrated the victory of the dominant social order over the forces of disruption — just as imperial pageants had been eight decades before.

If the pageant tradition is defined in terms of the articulation of community in the conjunction of ideological sentiment, entrepreneurial production, and spectacle, then theatrical pageantry may be best understood as a relational practice rather than an historic genre. Its formation in a given historical moment is contingent on changeable structures of theatrical and cultural organization. Particular genres and vocabularies are as historically contingent as the ideologies they express. In the ideological domain of consumer capitalism, in which the rhetorical fiction of the marketplace fills the absence evacuated by the failure of 19th century liberal nationalism, spectacular pageants celebrate the pleasure of consumption, to the extent that pervasiveness of advertising and ticket prices are perceived as the indexes of the the historical value of the event. Contemporary pageantry is marked not by the affirmative iconography of imperial ideology, but by a constructed pluralism that reflects the boundless freedom promised by the market — itself a simulation of power that displaces narratives of nation.

*University of Guelph*

### *WORKS CITED*

Barnard, Lt. Col. W.T. *The Queen's Own Rifles of Canada 1860-1960: One Hundred Years of Canada*. Toronto: The Ontario Publishing Co., 1960.

Baudrillard, Jean. *Simulacra and Simulation.* Trans. Sheila Faria Glaser. Ann Arbor: U Michigan P, 1994

Beers, Joel. "*Show Boat* Docks at the Ahmanson." *Cheers!, Pasadena Star-Pheonix.* 15 November 1996

Breon, Robin. "'*Show Boat*': The Past Revisits the Present." *Canadian Theatre Review* 79/80 (Summer/ Fall 994): 70-79.

Candian National Exhibition. *Pictorial Portfolio Facts & Figures.* Publicity brochure, 1926

Coren, Michael. "Livent court case really about government accountability." *Globe and Mail.* 30 January 1995 C3

Crew Robert and Dana Flavelle"The World According to Garth." *Toronto Star,* 13 July 1996: H1, H9, H12

Drabinsky, Garth. "Behind the Scenes at the *Show Boat* showdown." [excerpt from Drabinsky, Garth and Marq de Villiers, *Closer to the Sun*] *Toronto Star* 19 March 1995: E1, E4

____. "Musical theatre in Toronto is alive and very well." *Globe and Mail.* 29 December 1995

Ford Centre for the Performing Arts. *Show Boat* program, 1993.

Glassberg, David. *American Historical Pageantry.* Chapel Hill: U North Carolona P, 1990.

The Globe and Mail. "Drabinsky & Co. export entertainment around the world." in "WELCOME TO OUR PAIR CITY" [advertising supplement] 13 April 1995 : F2

Henry, Jeff. "*Show Boat* protest watershed for blacks." *Toronto Star* 15 November 1994

Henry, Keith S. *Black Politics in Toronto since World War 1.* Toronto: The Multicultural Historical Society of Ontario, 1981.

Henderson, John. *Nero — and the Burning of Rome.* Typescript: 1913.

Henderson, John. Correspondence with George Penson, 1913: 6 June 1913; 15 June 1913; 29 June 1913. Hands Fireworks Company archive, Milton, Ont.

W.D. King, *Henry Irving's Waterloo.* Berkely: U California P, 1993

Little Edward and Richard Paul Knowles. "The Spirit of Shivacee and the Community Pla;y; or the Unity in Community." in Per Blask, ed. *Contemporary Issues in Canadian Drama.* (Winnipeg: Blizzard, 1994) 68-85.

Lorimer, James. *The Ex: A Picture History of the Canadian National Exhibition.* Toronto: James Lewis & Samuel, 1973

Mays, John Bentley. *Emerald City: Toronto Visited.* Toronto: Viking 1994

Mietkiewicz, Henry. "Be creative! big biz tell groups looking for bucks" *Toronto Star* 19 February 1995

National Battlefields Commission (Canada). *Souvenirs du passé et livret des spectacles historiques représenté lors du Trois-Centième Anniversaire de la fondation de Quebec, l'Ancienne Capitale du Canada.* Montreal: Cambridge Corp., 1908

Nourbese Philip, M. *Showing Grit: Showboating North of the 44th Parallel.* Toronto: Poui Publications, 1993

Queen's Own Rifles of Canada. *Semi-Centennial Reunion and Historical Pageant: Official Programme.* Toronto: 1910

# MIMICRY AND HEGEMONY: FEMINIST PERFORMANCE THEORY AND APHRA BEHN

Nancy Copeland

Feminist performance theory is a relatively recent and highly diverse discipline. It emerged as a recognizable field in the late eighties in the work of American theorist-critics, notably Sue-Ellen Case's *Feminism and Theatre* and Jill Dolan's *The Feminist Spectator as Critic* (both 1988). Case, in addition to re-reading traditional theatre history through feminism and providing an account of various kinds of (largely American) twentieth-century feminist theatre practice, devoted her final chapter to what she called "a New Poetics." This new poetics included a call for the exploration of a "female form" (129) and a critical practice informed by "feminist psychosemiotics," which Case defined as "a combination of post-Lacanian psychoanalysis, semiotics and feminism" (118), originating in the film criticism of such writers as E. Ann Kaplan, Teresa De Lauretis, and Kaja Silverman. Dolan's book exemplifies the kind of analysis of theatre facilitated by this critical approach. Her final chapter, "Materialist Feminism: Apparatus-Based Theory and Practice," brings together the elements that have remained the basic components of the field: feminist psychosemiotics indebted to post-Lacanian psychoanalytic criticism; an emphasis on Brechtian forms that "foreground... and denaturalize ... the representational apparatus" (106) and on a concomitant Brechtian performance style that can denaturalize gender; and the advocacy of lesbian desire as the agent of gender deconstruction.

Elaine Aston's survey, *An Introduction to Feminism and Theatre* (1995) provides a useful overview of the field. She notes the "'stages'" by which feminism has influenced theatre studies and the leadership of American scholars, especially in the area of "feminist critical theory" (7). Her chapter on "Performing Gender: A Materialist Practice" discusses the directions the field has taken in the nineties under the influence of Judith Butler's studies of gender performativity, *Gender Trouble* (1990), which has been particularly influential for theatre studies, and *Bodies That Matter* (1993). These directions include a foregrounding of cultural and specifically theatrical constructions of the female body, with particular emphasis on cross-dressing, and an emphasis on lesbian performance that is now, although not without some concern on the part of such critics as Jill Dolan about loss of identity, extending to queer performance.[1] Aston concludes her book by calling for greater interaction between theory and practice, the strategy also advocated by Case at the end of *Feminism and Theatre* (130-132), in order to "perform" feminist criticism through feminist theatre viewed "as a medium which maps out its theoretical and critical concerns on/ through the body" (143).

This approach would seem promising for theatre history studies, as a strategy for discovering or recovering feminist performances inscribed in the theatre of the past, but in practice the relationship between feminist performance theory and theatre history has been problematic. The orientation of the former has been overwhelmingly toward modern and contemporary examples. Aston's "case studies," for example, go back no further than Susan Glaspell, whose plays date from the first third of the twentieth century. Even within these limits, the focus of this criticism, as Aston notes, has been on "interrogative" texts and performances (38). The term "interrogative" is taken from Catherine Belsey's *Critical Practice* (1980), where she applies it to texts. "The *interrogative* text...," she writes, "disrupts the unity of the reader by discouraging identification with a unified subject of the enunciation...," "invite[s] the reader to produce answers to the questions it implicitly or explicitly raises," and "refuses a single point of view, however complex and comprehensive, but brings points of view into unresolved collision or contradiction" (91-92). Such plays as Caryl Churchill's *Cloud 9,* Marguerite Duras's *India Song,* Sharon Pollock's *Blood Relations,* and the performance texts of Split Britches are favoured by such an emphasis,[2] as is the self-conscious Brechtian performance style theorized by Elin Diamond in her very influential article "Brechtian Theory/ Feminist Theory: Toward a Gestic Feminist Criticism."

On the other hand, realist texts, and the psychologically based acting methods associated with them, are rejected, notably by Case and Dolan.[3] In arguments indebted to Belsey's portrayal of the "classic realist" text as an agent of the dominant ideology (68-69), Case and Dolan have challenged realism as incompatible with feminism. This attitude has generated vigorous opposition from other feminist writers, notably Sheila Stowell and Patricia Schroeder, who critique blanket

---

[1] For Dolan's reservations see, for example, "Building a Theatrical Vernacular."

[2] See Case, "From Split Subject to Split Britches"and Diamond, "Refusing the Romanticism of Identity."

[3] Case, *Feminism and Theatre* 123-24; Dolan, *Feminist Spectator* 84-86 and "'Lesbian' Subjectivity."

dismissals of realism (including, in Stowell's case, Belsey's) not only for their broad generalizations but for their ahistoricism. In particular, both Stowell and Schroeder note the reformist aims of early realists, including turn of the century feminists, who, far from merely reproducing prevailing conditions, exposed their contradictions and shortcomings.[4]

Undifferentiated criticisms of realism participate in the historical fallacy critiqued by Gillian Beer in "Representing Women: Re-Presenting the Past" (1989): the tendency among scholars working in women's studies to read the past only in terms of the present. She argues instead for readings that foreground the "otherness of earlier literature" by "engaging with the *difference* of the past" (67). "The task of the literary historian," she writes, "is ... to revive those shifty significations which do not pay court to our concerns but are full of the meaning of that past present," through "multiple reading" that explores "both likeness and *difference*" (68-69).

The historical myopia that can be displayed by feminist performance criticism raises questions about its applicability to the early modern period, in which theatre was highly conventional. My particular area of interest is late-seventeenth-century English theatre, specifically the comedies of Aphra Behn. Late-seventeenth-century stage comedy was constructed through well-established conventions and audience expectations, which militate against counter-hegemonic forms and meanings. Paula Backscheider has observed, with particular reference to Behn's portrayal of her female characters:

> When Behn began to write, she faced a limited number of roles, plot lines, interpretations, and resolutions for women's lives and experiences. These limitations came not only from the conventions, expectations and beliefs of the culture and its literature but also from the tendency consumers have to impose meaning on a text or production.... (85)

The constrictions of this theatrical environment and Behn's adaptations to it have led at least one critic to question the visibility of feminism in Behn's drama. Katharine Rogers has asserted that the feminism of Behn's prefaces does not appear in her plays, which, she claims, "show values and perceptions hardly distinguishable from the male writers with whom she competed" because their author "followed literary forms that provided no scope for feminine perceptions or feminine experience" (98, 100).

---

4 Stowell 82-84; Schroeder 17, 35-40; see also Diamond, "Mimesis, Mimicry" 376-79.

Nevertheless, a number of studies have applied feminist performance analysis to Behn's plays. Elin Diamond, in "*Gestus* and Signature in Aphra Behn's *The Rover*," reads Behn's play metatheatrically in terms of the relationship between the theatrical apparatus and the commodification of women, within both the plot of the play and the late-seventeenth century theatre. Laura Rosenthal, in "'Counterfeit Scrubbado': Women Actors in the Restoration," traces Behn's use of the actress's "double identity as 'whore' and the marriageable lady she often represented..." in a number of plays, including *The Rover* (15). Julie Nash applies Laura Mulvey's theory of "the gaze" in "'The sight on't would beget a warm desire': Visual Pleasure in Aphra Behn's *The Rover*." In this vein, the rest of this paper will explore a concept from feminist performance theory that I have found particularly fruitful in my work on Behn: mimicry, and the related concept of "grotesque performance," developed by Mary Russo.

Mimicry, described by Homi Bhabha in "Of Mimicry and Man" as "an *ironic* compromise" that produces a subject that is "*almost the same, but not quite*," offers a site of resistance to hegemonic discourse from within because of its simultaneous "resemblance and menace" (86). Luce Irigaray posits a similar, but more active, strategy for women within discourse: the substitution of mimicry for mimesis. In "The Power of Discourse" she advises: "One must assume the feminine role deliberately. Which means already to convert a form of subordination into an affirmation, and thus to thwart it.... To play with mimesis is thus, for a woman, to try to recover the place of her exploitation by discourse, without allowing herself to be simply reduced to it" (76). Elin Diamond, in "Mimesis, Mimicry, and the 'True-Real'" applies Irigaraian mimicry to the theatre. Her illustrations include Lois Weaver's Tammy Whynot, a mid-eighties "femme" impersonation of Tammy Wynette which both parodies the original and calls into question that original's authenticity, and Franca Rame's exploitation of her hyper-feminine appearance in *Female Parts* (373). Such performances, Diamond argues, demonstrate how mimicry "can function ... as an alienation-effect, framing the gender behaviour dictated by patriarchal models as a means of 'recover[ing] the place of her [the performer's] exploitation'" (373).

The agency attributed to the subject in the Irigaraian model of mimicry makes it more pertinent to theatre than Butler's concept of gender performativity, especially in its later form in *Bodies That Matter* as "citationality." Butler's stress on the formative power and compulsory nature of gender performance is at odds with the at least partially volitional construction of authorial self and characterization that are central to the study of a playwright such as Behn. However,

Butler's concomitant emphasis on the implication of performativity as citationality "that discourse has a history that not only precedes but conditions its contemporary usages ..." (*Bodies* 227) provides a necessary reminder that mimicry can only "work"/produce meaning in the context of normative performances of gender. Also useful is Butler's caution that drag, which was her leading example of subversively "wrong" gender performance in *Gender Trouble* (136-139), "is not unproblematically subversive" because "[h]eterosexuality can augment its hegemony *through* its denaturalization, as when we see denaturalizing parodies that reidealize heterosexual norms *without* calling them into question" (*Bodies* 231). Indeed in *Gender Trouble*, she noted that "[p]arody by itself is not subversive ... [P]arodic displacement, indeed, parodic laughter, depends on a context and reception in which subversive confusions can be fostered" (139).

The problem of reception is frequently raised in connection with mimicry. Diamond, citing as an example of gender-alienating mimicry Franca Rame's *Female Parts* monologue in which she "jokes about the asymmetry of female and male parts" while dressed in the "overcoded sex-object garb" of "a thin, black floor-length wrap, worn over a black lace chemise, black hose, and spike heels," observes that Rame's body is "on display —a fetish object— even as the terms of female objectification become available for critique" (373-74). Lynda Hart, writing in "Identity and Seduction: Lesbians in the Mainstream" about Lois Weaver's and Peggy Shaw's parody of heterosexual courtship and marriage in their *Anniversary Waltz*, notes that when a representation, intended for a sub-cultural audience, is viewed by members of the dominant group, mimicry can reify the "dominant constructions" of an oppressed group that adopts those constructions for parodic purposes, or, in cases in which "the dominant group's self-generated images" are mimicked, reinscribe the dominant image as the norm (125-126). Similarly, Marvin Carlson, writing in *Performance: A Critical Introduction* about "masquerade theory," the term which he applies to the theorization of hyperbolic mimicry, comments: "As a critical operation, masquerade performances always run the danger that Derrida cited in any deconstructive operation, which seeks to turn established structures back on themselves — that this process may also, especially for a conventional audience, simply reinscribe or reinforce those structures" (176). His example, like Diamond's, demonstrates the particular problems presented by "hyper-feminine" mimicry, in this case Monstrous Regiment's *Time Gentlemen Please* (1978), in which the attempt to "foreground the degrading sexual self-representation of women in traditional cabaret and stand-up comedy," was received by some feminist spectators as an example of the evil it intended to critique (176-77; see also Aston 94).

It is precisely the "risk" involved in this kind of mimicry that is addressed by Mary Russo's concept "grotesque performance," as it is developed in *The Female Grotesque: Risk, Excess and Modernity* (1994). She introduces the term as part of a discussion of Amelia Earhart's stunt flying. According to Russo, women stunters were "doubly suspect": marginalized within aviation because, in Earhart's words, "'they [were] ... considered guilty of incompetence until proved otherwise'" and because of the suspect status of stunt flying as "increasingly the sign of the counterfeit, exhibitionistic, unprofessional pilot" — the abjected other of professional aviation (20). Russo observes that "[t]heir status as 'already guilty' consigns them to the very activities which further their marginalization and eventual abjection from 'normal' flying" (20). She continues: "Stunt flying and similar activities, which I will characterize as 'grotesque performances,' are risky activities. On the one hand, they perpetuate the blaming, stigmatization, and marginalizing of groups and persons who occupy this self-perpetuating loop and are seen as 'high risk' groups; on the other hand, they elicit 'risk control' tactics which characterize risk as almost entirely negative ..." (22). Russo's purpose is to reclaim such easily stigmatized and prohibited "performances" for feminism (12); risk, she argues, is "a condition of possibility" (10-11).

Mimicry and the more narrowly-defined concept of "grotesque performance" provide the theoretical means to identify counter-hegemonic elements within convention-bound cultural artifacts such as Aphra Behn's comedies. They also assist in the analysis of Behn's transgressive, but still problematic, practices, especially her self-presentation as a playwright and her specialization in sex comedies. Behn's playful deployment of a stereotypically "feminine" seductiveness in some of her prologues, which has been analyzed by Jessica Munns, and her manipulation of the misogynist equation of the female writer with prostitution, which has been explored by Catherine Gallagher, are examples of "grotesque performance" in Russo's sense: they mimic misogynist constructions of women in order to critique them, but risk Behn's reinscription within those constructions.

Writing farcical sex comedy was another risky performance for Behn. In particular, her numerous bedroom scenes with their eroticized displays of the actresses' bodies (see Holland 41-42) risk reinforcing audience voyeurism and the conventional ascription of sexual incontinence to women. On the other hand, they put female desire onstage, often in the context of plots that valorize that desire. Two generically contrasting examples are provided by Lady Fancy in the farcical *Sir Patient Fancy* and Lady Julia Fulbank in the darker comedy *The Lucky Chance*.

Lady Fancy spends most of the play in which she appears attempting to accommodate the sexual demands of her adulterous lover Wittmore. In the process, she appears in a variety of shaming situations, most notably a bedroom scene in which she is revealed *in flagrante* with her step-daughter's suitor, whom she has mistaken for Wittmore in the dark. Yet, at the end of the play, when even her buffoonish husband recognizes her unfaithfulness, she avoids the fate of her prototypes, Béline in Molière's *Imaginary Invalid* and Emilia in Durfey's *A Fond Husband*, who are expelled in shame from the comic resolution. Lady Fancy retains her defiance to the end and remains onstage to dare her husband, now a publicly recognized cuckold, to recover the money she has taken to support herself and her lover.

Julia Fulbank is exposed to the audience's gaze in the last scene of *The Lucky Chance*. Her foolish, greedy husband, Sir Cautious Fulbank, has incurred a gambling debt to his wife's lover, Gayman, without knowing to whom he is indebted. Rather than pay the money, Sir Cautious has agreed to Gayman's proposal that he be paid instead by a night with Julia in the Fulbank marital bed. Julia is to be tricked into thinking that she is going to bed with her husband, on the grounds that her self-respect would not allow her to connive in this exchange. The audience sees Julia go to bed, to be followed shortly by Gayman, and then witnesses the aftermath:

> *Enter Lady Fulbank undressed; Gayman, half undressed, upon his knees, following her, holding her gown*
> LADY FULBANK Oh! You unkind — what have you made me do?

Lest we miss the point, Sir Cautious, who has been watching, comments: "Made her do? So, so, 'tis done ..." (5.7. 13-16).

This is plainly a humiliating situation for the character, but the circumstances qualify its misogyny. Julia attains further power over her lover, who has "discovered ... new worlds of charms" through this sexual experience (5.7.38). More prosaically, she uses Sir Cautious's behaviour as grounds to insist on a separation (5.7. 63-64); eventually he promises to "bequeath" her to Gayman along with his estate (5.7. 181-82). Julia's objectification in this situation is also the means of her empowerment.

"[T]ransgressive women characters and provocative plot lines" such as these are identified by Paula Backscheider as the "devices" Behn used to construct counter-hegemonic dramas by frustrating readers' "tendencies to see familiar plot patterns or archetypes" (85). But the theoretical concept of mimicry also enables us to identify subversive qualities in less conspicuously transgressive characters and situations. I will conclude by examining Behn's best known play, *The Rover*, in this light.

*The Rover*, set among the Spanish aristocracy and expatriate English soldiers during the Neapolitan Carnival, includes three major female roles: Hellena, a "wild" aristocratic young woman who evades her family's intention to put her into a convent by marrying the rake Willmore; her more conventional sister, Florinda; and the glamorous courtesan Angellica Bianca. Hellena, an expert in intrigue who talks like a libertine, pursues her man relentlessly, and disguises herself as a boy, and Angellica, who achieves an almost tragic stature through her frustrated love for Willmore, are the more obviously transgressive characters. Florinda, on the other hand, initially appears to be a normative female character. She epitomizes woman as the object of exchange between men. Both her father and her brother have chosen suitors for her; she has fallen in love with an English soldier, Belvile, but at the beginning of the play, has no means of acting on her desire. She is kept locked up at home by her brother, Pedro, and, as Belvile tells his friends, can only communicate with him by letters and "distant looks from her window," which he romantically describes as being "as soft and kind/As those which heaven sends down on penitents" (1.2. 28-30). For her part, she blushes when her sister mentions Belvile's name (1.1.16). Florinda's modest behaviour is a foil to Hellena's frankness. She gently, but frequently, reproves Hellena's outspokenness and contrasts her decorous affection for Belvile with Hellena's precipitous obsession with Willmore. "I wonder how you learned to love so easily," she asks her "rash" sister; "I had a thousand charms to meet my eyes and ears, ere I could yield; and 'twas the knowledge of Belvile's merit, not the surprising person, took my soul ..." (3.1. 49-52). Her attachment to Belvile began when he protected her from "the licensed lust of common soldiers" during the fall of Pamplona (1.1. 70-74) and it is primarily as a helpless victim who must be rescued by gallant Belvile from unwelcome marriage arrangements and attempted rapes that Florinda participates in the plot.

At first glance, then, Florinda would seem to be a straightforward example of the "serious," "noble," "pure heroines" which made up the comic line of Mary Betterton, who played the character in the original production opposite her husband Thomas as Belvile (Howe 74, 76, 104). However, analysis of how Behn deploys this conventionally "feminine" character within her complex intrigue plot suggests that she is the "hyper-feminine" vehicle for a critique of normative female behaviour, rather than a reinscription of it.

The critique begins to emerge when she ventures out of her father's house into the carnival in an attempt to get Belvile to save her from her forthcoming marriage to her brother's friend, Antonio. Her idealistic romantic relationship with Belvile is out of place in the libertine world of Carnival: in this context she is, as Belvile's friends put it, "that damned virtuous woman" who has "spoiled" him (1.2.18, 32). These romantic lovers prove incompetent at the carnival games of disguise and romantic intrigue that Hellena plays so well. Belvile, "modest[ly]" refusing to flirt (3.1.283), twice fails to recognize Florinda in her carnival disguise and therefore misses important opportunities to plot with her. Later, Florinda does not recognize Belvile, who is disguised as Antonio, and therefore misses the chance to marry him with her brother's (misplaced) blessing. When Belvile belatedly reveals his identity to her, she exclaims: "Where was my soul it could not meet thy voice,/And take this knowledge in?" (4.2. 85-86).

Such romantic ideas prove to be not only ineffectual but dangerous in the two scenes of attempted rape. The first of these is the result of Florinda's romantic solution to her dilemma: she will elope with Belvile, whom she instructs to meet her at night in the garden of her father's house, vowing "to die or make [him] ... happy" (1.2. 223). This plan places her in a more vulnerable, and titillating, situation than any in which either Hellena or Angellica appear. She enters *"in an undress,"* a loose informal gown, carrying *"a key and a little box"* of jewels (3.5.1), which, as Elin Diamond comments, is "a double metonym for dowry and genitals" (*"Gestus"* 533). She has left the garden gate open to let Belvile in, but it is the extremely drunk Willmore who arrives first and attempts to rape her. Her protests and struggling are as ineffectual as her ludicrous appeal to him as "a gentleman" (3.5.60); only Belvile's timely arrival prevents the rape. Belvile's angry question to Willmore, based on romantic assumptions about the relationship between the body and soul —"sot, hadst thou so much sense and light about thee to distinguish her woman, and couldst not see something about her face and person, to strike an awful reverence into thy soul?"— receives the matter-of-fact reply: "Faith no, I considered her as mere a woman as I could wish" (3.6. 22-27).

Florinda once again suffers from the invisibility of her virtues and of her social position when she next attempts to run away from her brother. Her masked flight through the streets, pursued by Willmore, who assumes she is a prostitute, puts her on display, as Diamond points out, "running in and out of the scenes" in a way that underlines the participation of the actress's body in the stage spectacle (534). She ends up, unwittingly, at the lodging of the Englishmen, where the embittered buffoon Ned Blunt is hiding after being robbed of his clothes and valuables by a prostitute, Lucetta. He is determined to take his revenge on the next woman he encounters, who turns out to be Florinda. Incongruously, she presents herself to the scantily clad and angry Blunt, as a damsel in distress: "Charitable sir,... I am ... a very wretched maid, forced by a strange unlucky accident, to seek a safety here, and must be ruined if you do not grant it.... I beseech you, as you seem a gentleman, pity a harmless virgin, that takes your house for a sanctuary" (4.5.27-28; 37-39). Blunt's reply —"A harmless virgin with a pox!" (41)— shows him to be as unperceptive and as single-minded as Willmore: he resolves to "kiss and beat thee all over; kiss and see they all over" and "lie" with her out of malice (48-51). His costume —"*shirt and drawers*" and "*an old rusty sword*" (4.5.6)— doubles his behaviour's grotesque combination of farce and sexual menace. Once again, as in her encounter with Willmore, Florinda is subjected to physical violence as Blunt "pulls" her "rudely" (4.5.45). Blunt is a fool, but when Frederick, a normative male character, arrives, he is equally immune to Florinda's protestations that she "entered here to save a life in danger" (91) and is quite willing to join Blunt in raping her. She finally gains a reprieve by invoking Belvile's name and bribing the men with the diamond ring he gave her. Frederick "begin[s] to suspect something" and remarks "'twould anger us vilely to be trussed up for a rape upon a maid of quality, when we only believe we ruffle a harlot" (121-23).

Florinda's "reprieve" leads to an even more outrageous situation that foregrounds her commodification. Locked up by Frederick until her status can be established, she becomes the prize in a lottery among the Englishmen and Pedro, which her brother wins by having the longest sword blade. Belvile, although he is present and aware of her identity, is prevented from revealing it by his fear of letting Pedro know the whereabouts of his sister. Incestuous rape is forestalled by the arrival of Florinda's cousin Valeria, who sends Pedro off in search of the supposedly missing Florinda. In his absence, Belvile and Florinda are married. As part of the "happy" ending, she "nobly" (5.1.189) forgives Willmore, Frederick, and Blunt for their assaults, observing to Willmore: "The friend to Belvile may command me anything" (5.1. 157).

Florinda's experiences expose not only the brutality of male libertinism and the double standard applied to women based on their class, but also the inadequacies of her kind of femininity. Her delicacy and modesty are no protection against the commodification of her body: she is the only female character who is literally manhandled. Tellingly, she is treated with less respect than either Angellica or the streetwalker Lucetta. The shortcomings of her gender performance are demonstrated not merely by throwing her into a world for which she is unequipped, but by exaggerating her "feminine" qualities —her passivity, her naiveté, her romantic ideas— to maximize the discrepancy between her resources and expectations and the often coarse and brutal carnival world. She is not parodic, but she is an example of mimicry rather than mimesis.

For Behn as a playwright, Florinda was a grotesque performance: through her Behn risked reinscribing the dominant model of female behaviour —passive, polite, and unworldly— that she more obviously called into question through her transgressive female characters, and through her own life. But the concept of mimicry makes visible the subversive potential of the character. This example also suggests the kind of connection that can be made between contemporary feminist performance theory and theatre history. "Mimicry" helps us to read Behn in the way recommended by Gillian Beer, attending to both her likeness to our concerns and to historical difference. It is this combination, finally, that gives interest to the theatre of the past: it is the responsiveness of Behn's drama, and her public persona, to our concerns that motivates our interest in her place within her historical context. Reading theatre history through feminist performance theory offers a strategy for making that vital connection.

*University of Toronto*

**WORKS CITED**

Aston, Elaine. *An Introduction to Feminism and Theatre.* London and New York: Routledge 1995.

Backscheider, Paula R. *Spectacular Politics: Theatrical Power and Mass Culture in Early Modern England.* Baltimore and London: Johns Hopkins UP 1993.

Beer, Gillian. "Representing Women: Re-presenting the Past." *The Feminist Reader: Essays in Gender and the Politics of Literary Criticism.* Ed. Catherine Belsey and Jane Moore. London: Macmillan 1989. 63-80.

Behn, Aphra. *The Rover and Other Plays.* Ed. Jane Spencer. Oxford and New York: Oxford UP 1995.

Belsey, Catherine. *Critical Practice.* London and New York: Methuen 1980.

Bhabha, Homi K. "Of Mimicry and Man: The Ambivalence of Colonial Discourse." *The Location of Culture.* London and New York: Routledge, 1994. 85-92.

Butler, Judith. *Bodies That Matter: On the Discursive Limits of "Sex".* London and New York: Routledge 1993.

____. *Gender Trouble: Feminism and the Subversion of Identity.* London and New York: Routledge 1990.

Carlson, Marvin. *Performance: A Critical Introduction.* London and New York: Routledge 1996.

Case, Sue-Ellen. *Feminism and Theatre.* London: Macmillan 1988.

____. "From Split Subject to Spilt Britches." *Feminine Focus: The New Woman Playwrights.* Ed. Enoch Brater. New York and Oxford: Oxford UP 1989. 126-46.

Diamond, Elin. "Brechtian Theory/ Feminist Theory: Toward a Gestic Feminist Criticism." *TDR* 32.1 (1988): 82-94.

____. "*Gestus* and Signature in Aphra Behn's *The Rover.*" *ELH* 56 (1989): 519-41.

____. "Mimesis. Mimicry, and the 'True-Real.'" *Acting Out: Feminist Performances.* Ed. Lynda Hart and Peggy Phelan. Ann Arbor: U of Michigan P 1993. 363-82.

____. "Refusing the Romanticism of Identity: Narrative Interventions in Churchill, Benmussa, Duras." *Performing Feminisms: Feminist Critical Theory and Theatre.* Ed. Sue-Ellen Case. Baltimore and London: Johns Hopkins UP 1990. 92-105.

Dolan, Jill. "Building a Theatrical Vernacular: Responsibility, Community, Ambivalence, and Queer Theatre." *Modern Drama* 39 (1996): 1-15.

____. *The Feminist Spectator as Critic.* Ann Arbor and London: UMI 1988.

____. "'Lesbian' Subjectivity in Realism: Dragging at the Margins of Structure and Ideology." *Performing Feminisms: Feminist Critical Theory and Theatre.* Ed. Sue-Ellen Case. Baltimore and London: Johns Hopkins UP 1990. 40-53.

Gallagher, Catherine. *Nobody's Story: The Vanishing Acts of Women Writers in the Marketplace, 1670-1820.* Berkeley and Los Angeles: U of California P 1995.

Hart, Lynda. "Identity and Seduction: Lesbians in the Mainstream." *Acting Out: Feminist Performances.* Ed. Lynda Hart and Peggy Phelan. Ann Arbor: U of Michigan P 1993. 119-37.

Holland, Peter. *The Ornament of Action: Text and Performance in Restoration Comedy.* Cambridge: CUP 1979.

Howe, Elizabeth. *The First English Actresses: Women and Drama 1660-1700.* Cambridge: Cambridge UP 1992.

Irigaray, Luce. "The Power of Discourse and the Subordination of the Feminine." *This Sex Which Is Not One.* Trans. Catherine Porter with Carolyn Burke. Ithaca: Cornell UP 1985. 68-85.

Munns, Jessica. "'Good, Sweet, Honey, Sugar-Candied Reader': Aphra Behn's Foreplay in Forewords." *Rereading Aphra Behn: History, Theory, and Criticism.* Ed. Heidi Hutner. Charlottesville and London: UP of Virginia 1993. 44-62.

Nash, Julie. "'The sight on't would beget a warm desire': Visual Pleasure in Aphra Behn's *The Rover.*" *Restoration* 18 (1994): 77-87.

Rogers, Katharine M. *Feminism in Eighteenth Century England.* Urbana, Chicago, London: U of Illinois P, 1982.

Rosenthal, Laura J. "'Counterfeit Scrubbado': Women Actors in the Restoration." *Eighteenth Century: Theory and Interpretation* 34 (1993): 3-22.

Russo, Mary. *The Female Grotesque: Risk, Excess and Modernity*. New York and London: Routledge 1994.

Schroeder. Patricia R. *The Feminist Possibilities of Dramatic Realism*. Madison, Teaneck NJ: Fairleigh Dickinson UP 1996.

Stowell, Sheila. "Rehabilitating Realism." *Journal of Dramatic Theory and Criticism* 6 (1992): 81-88.

# NARRATIVE AND PERFORMANCE IN RADIO DRAMA

Damiano Pietropaolo

I would like to speak more as a practitioner of the art of radio drama and less as a student of it. In part this is due to the fact that I have been producing and directing radio plays for over twenty years, and so I feel more in my skin speaking as a practitioner. But there is another reason: the appalling dearth of scholarly interest in the cultural role of radio, not to speak of the total neglect of an aesthetics of art forms idiomatic to radio, or dramaturgical theories of narrative and performance as they apply to radio. Aspects of narrative and performance, fundamental building blocks in the construction of radio plays, are largely ignored by scholars and critics alike; and when not ignored they are discussed in a language that is more appropriate to the theatrical presentation of plays. This lack of interest is not due to a lack of original radio plays. Even in these times of budgetary restraint original radio plays in Canada far outnumber the offerings in our theatres across the country. Indeed, often plays that first appear on radio are later presented on stage. Recent examples are John Murrel's *The Faraway Nearby*, Judith Thompson's *Lion in the Streets*, Wendy Lill's *All Fall Down*[1], as well as plays by a new generation of playwrights such as John Mighton and Jason Sherman, whose radio play based on the Old Testament Book of Job, *Patience*, recently broadcast CBC Radio (April 13/14, 1997) has just been announced by the Tarragon theatre as a world premiere for their coming season. Go figure! Timothy Findley's important and recent radio play *The Trials of Ezra Pound*[2], which was honoured at the International Radio Festival in New York and won first place in the "Drama Specials" category in the Gabriel Awards, has yet

1 John Murrel's *The Faraway Nearby* was first produced by Martie Fishman in the Calgary studios of CBC radio and Broadcast on Stereodrama on April 29, 1993; Wendy Lill's *All Fall Down* was produced by Paula Danckert in the Halifax studios of the CBC and broadcast on Januray 10, 1994; and Judith Thompson's *Lion in the Streets* under its original radio title of *Tornado*, was produced by John Juliani in Toronto and broadcast November 29, 1987.

2 *The Trials of Ezra Pound*, broadcast on CBC Stereo, March 26, 1990. Later published by Blizzard, Winnipeg, 1995.

to be noticed even though it now exists also in print form. Across the Atlantic, Tom Stoppard's celebrated play *Indian Ink*[3], which had a successful commercial run at the Aldwych in London's west end, is really the radio play *In The Native State*[4] all dressed up for the boards. Ironically, it is not until they have had a stage production that these plays receive critical attention, even though the audience they reach in a single broadcast would probably fill a medium-sized theatre such as the Tarragon in Toronto for an extended run of at least couple of years.

In a short essay on radio drama, the American playwright David Mamet, who cut his dramaturgical teeth writing radio plays, maintains that the radio play is not simply a stage play stripped of its props, costumes and settings. Appealing to our primal need for participatory narrative, Mamet maintains that:

> The essential task of the drama (as of the fairy tale) is to offer a solution to a problem which is nonsusceptible to reason. To be effective, the drama must induce us to suspend our rational judgement and to follow the *internal logic* of the piece, so that our *pleasure* (our "cure") is the release at the end of the story. We enjoy the happiness of being a participant in the process of *solution*, rather than the intellectual achievement of having observed the process of construction.
>
> And the best model for this drama is the Story around the campfire.
>
> We hear "...a windswept moor" and immediately supply the perfect imaginary moor. And the moor we supply is not perfect "in general", but perfect according to our subconscious understanding of the significance of the moor *to the story*.
>
> This is why radio is a great training ground for dramatists. More than any other dramatic medium it teaches the writer to concentrate on the essentials, because it throws into immediate relief that to *characterize* the people or scene is to take time from the story — to weaken the story. Working for radio I learned the way *all* great drama works: by leaving the *endowment* of characters, place and especially action up to the audience. Only by eschewing the desire to *characterize* can one begin to understand the model of the perfect play.[5]

In Mamet's view, then, narrative, understood in its primal form of "storytelling around the campfire..." and its direct access to our subconscious perception, is the proper domain of radio. The history of radio drama is by and large the history of popular narrative forms — the mystery genre, the soap opera, the serial. In the so-called golden age of

---

3 *Indian Ink,* by Tom Stoppard, Faber & Faber, London, 1995.
4 Produced by John Tydeman and Broadcast on *BBC Radio 4,* 1992.
5 David Mamet, *Writing in Restaurants,* Penguin Books, 1986, pp. 13-14.

radio (before the invention of television) the family gathered around the wireless receiver to listen to popular storytelling in dramatic form with much the same rapt attention that we associate with the campfire. The *popularity* of popular art forms is due, more often than not, to the *purity* of narrative approach: the dramaturgical scaffolding of the mystery play or detective story, which has been such a staple of radio drama, rests solidly on an unquestioning acceptance of pure storytelling.

If, as the genesis of stage plays mentioned above, and David Mamet's own experience demonstrates, radio drama is an essential rite of passage in the evolution of play writing, why then is radio drama of such marginal interest as a field critical inquiry?

The marginalization of radio drama in scholarly and critical studies is in large part due to the role of radio in the modern world of electronic and performance media. Ours is, to use the fashionable term, a *retinally* dominated culture, and visual literacy permeates every aspect of performance we may encounter. Unlike the stage or the concert hall, unlike the tv screen or the silver screen, radio does not have a public performance space. Even the radio broadcast of a musical performance has a semiotic reference to the hall in which it was recorded. We can *see* the hall because we may have been there, or if not that particular hall, then an iconic echo of a concert hall is present in our mind's eye.

The question is often asked: what do we see when listen to a radio play? But the real question is why we continue to ask this question of radio drama. Because the radio performance occurs in a purely private aural cyberspace, because it has no retinally accessible public space in which to unfold, the answer has been that a radio narrative unfolds in the richest performance space of all: our imagination. According to this view, we the listeners, supply the richest costumes, the most extravagant sets, the most beautiful lighting effects... and son...and so on.

This descriptive language is borrowed from an aesthetics that is more appropriate to plays presented on the stage and merely points out that we have failed to develop a critical language for the medium of radio drama. And so we continue to borrow from an aesthetics of performance whose destination is primarily ocular, to try to fill in what we perceive are the absences of an experience that is primarily auricular. Visual presence and audio presence are thus confused, because we assume that they originate in a common performance space.

The most illustrious, though ill-fated attempt, to create a radio play exploiting the possibilities of the medium to their fullest is Antonin Artaud's *Pour en finir avec le jugement de dieu*.[6] The text for this radio performance was commissioned from Artaud in 1946, just after his release from the psychiatric asylum at Rodez where he had undergone massive electroshock therapy. His theories for a theatre of cruelty now behind him, Artaud accepted this opportunity to put flesh on his dramaturgical skeleton by means of a phonographic capture of a personal performance of an original text written specifically for the medium of radio. This last utterance from the tortured Artaud is readily available as a printed text, but to fully appreciate Artaud's radiophonic dramaturgy, we should listen to his own performance of that text.

> [At this point in the presentation of the paper, those present in the auditorium listened to a three minute excerpt from Artaud's performance of *"Pour en finir avec le jugement de dieu"*][7]

Artaud's performance was never broadcast. The then director of French radio suppressed the broadcast by arguing that the people of France should be spared Artaud's vicious, scatological and obscene anti-catholicism and anti-americanism. Artaud was not the only artist to resort to the power of radio to rant against what he perceived to be the evils let lose in the world by religious and political conspiracies. Ezra Pound's broadcasts were not suppressed, nor was his ranting any less dependent on performance values to convey his rage. But I am not here to discuss the political content of Artaud's play; my purpose is to discuss performance values that are idiomatic to the medium of radio.

I believe Artaud is on David Mamet's side: defending the essential nature of radio to make primal utterances, unadorned by the distractions of spectacle, resting solely on the purity of form. Mamet focused our attention on the purity of narrative: Artaud's radio play focuses our attention on the purity of performance.

In its chant-like articulation of a tortured personal scatology, in its stringing together of poetic/onomatopoeic utterances, tumbling musically one into the other; in the relentless rhythmic repetition of glossolalia; in its automatic, trance like vocal ululations; in its dynamic range, which cradles within it the most childlike whisper and metahuman screeching, Artaud gave us a final statement on his own inner devils. He also gave us a statement about the syntax and rhythms of radio dramaturgy, which he understood to have direct resonance with

---

6 See *Watchfiends and Rack Screams: Work from the Final Period --Antonin Artaud*, ed. & Trans. by Clayton Ashleman with Bernard Bador, Exact Change, Boston 1995, pp. 281-307.

7 From an audio tape of the play in my personal archive.

the art of making music. On leaving the studio after the sound effects were recorded Artaud, said: "Well, until now I was only a writer, actor, director, sketcher; now I am a musician. "[8]

The syntax and rhythms of a radio performance are bound by a temporality. In this respect the experience of radio drama has more in common with the rhythmic structures of music and the narrative flow of fiction than with the spatial and visual demands of stage performance. Hence the question of what we see when we listen to a radio play is sure to lead us to a further marginalization of this form. In our post-literate, visually dominated culture, the radio performance is a private event. There is no public ritual surrounding the broadcast of a radio play. People listen to the radio by themselves: the relationship between actor and listener is one on one, and the aural perception of a radio play collapses the distance between spectator and performance .

Let me try an illustrate this with two examples from recent radio plays: Tom Stoppard's *In the Native State* and Timothy Findley's *The Trials of Ezra Pound.*

Stoppard's play has two settings: part of the action takes place in the 1930s in India and part of it in the 1990s in London. The dramaturgical requirements of radio, determined by its temporality, led Stoppard to a dramatic structure heavily dependent on flashbacks. And the play is, in many respects, a memory play—retrieving the past into the present in temporally sequenced scenes rhythmically building to a resolution of the narrative, much like a large musical structure moves forward through its reprise of leitmotifs. In the stage version of Stoppard's play, the two settings are simultaneously visible. Temporality, in typical Stoppard fashion, collapses into a theatrical historical present.

The contrast between the two media is a contrast between the primarily auricular demands radio and the temporality of its syntax; and the primarily ocular destination of stage performance. The former is a private, intimate experience; the latter a public ritual.

In Timothy Findley's *The Trials of Ezra Pound* there are also two settings. The court room in which Pound was tried for treason in 1946; and the inside of Pound's mind. Radio dramaturgy allows the listener to enter into the private, inner world of the protagonist by simply abolishing the separation between private and public utterance. And lest you mistake this technique for a radio version of the stage *aside,* which momentarily breaks through the fourth wall, bear in mind that radio has no fourth wall. By its very nature radio allows us entry into the

[8] Quoted in *Wireless Imagination: Sound, Radio and the Avant-Garde,* ed. by Douglas Khan & Gregory Whitehead, The MIT press, Cambridge Massachusettes, 1992, P. 295.

subconscious life of *characters* in the play because the characters inhabit the same space as the listeners. Dramaturgically the radio dramatist can collapse the private and the public into a simultaneous presence.

There is no social ritual surrounding the broadcast of an original radio play, regardless of the fame of the author or the actors. As a medium for the creation and dissemination of art, radio is caught between two polarities that have marginalized critical and scholarly interest in its cultural role.

On the one hand, the radio on top of your refrigerator is nothing more than a simple transmission device fulfilling Marconi's dream of collapsing geographic distances in the distribution of messages and/or signals that are independent of radio as a medium in its own right: the radio as tool, disguised as a piece of furniture or fashion accessory. On the other hand, the overwhelming ubiquitousness of radio in our lives —your clock radio, your refrigerator radio, your jogging walkman radio, your sports walkman, your car radio etc etc.— tends to give radio the status of sonic wallpaper and to make it subservient to its surroundings rather than the focal point of our attention, say like television. We are semi-aware of it. In the industry this is referred to as background listening. At best it is companionable listening, at worst a kind of sonic pollution. Let me try and hint at an aesthetic of *foreground* listening: the listening that takes place around David Mamet's campfire.

The few studies that have looked at the aesthetics of the cultural role of radio as a medium in its own right have tended to focus on phonography, the recording of sound for reproduction or *wireless transmission*. Phonography and radio were essential in the futurist attack on the hegemony of the written text. Both Filippo Marinetti and Alberto Savinio in Italy, and Tziga Vertov in pre-revolutionary Russia, favoured audio performances in which the word was subservient to noise: textual narrative, story, was discarded in favour of collage and juxtaposition.

A recent volume, *Wireless Imagination: Sound, Radio and the Avant Garde*,[9] is a systematic attempt at a full investigation into the relationship between the art of sound recording and twentieth century performance. And in keeping with this stated purpose, the volume maps the evolution of theories of sound first developed by Marinetti and Savinio. They were, above all, interested in developing an iconoclastic poetics of noise and the aesthetic manipulation of unstructured *found sound* to strike terror, if not pity, into the modern soul, which was in line with their militaristic pursuit of machine induced catharsis.

---

9 See above.

Their pioneering work was later advanced by the Russian constructivists, and was embraced by the surrealist movement, but even these developments were grounded in a politics intent on rebellion against the hegemony of traditional forms of artistic expression, and less by a need to develop a dramaturgy for a new medium: the radio; a medium whose power everyone understood and appreciated, particularly its ability to disseminate to the masses rhetorical exhortations in the style of Ezra Pound or Antonin Artaud. This power of the radio performance to spur the masses into action or hysteria was largely limited to the political, not the artistic sphere. Consider Hitler's and Mussolini's (not to mention Chruchhill's) use of Radio to stir up the primitive emotions. Never mind Hitler and Mussolini — just think of Howard Stern's or Rush Limbaugh's meteoric rise to celebrity status through their Artaudian use of the radio performance. These stars of radio represent the triumph of *orality* over *literacy*: of the concrete power of immediate oratorical performance, the electric *here-and-now-ness* of radio, over the abstract and mediated forms of print narrative, rehearsed stage performance, or even filmed performance.

As a form idiomatic to the medium, radio drama evolved during those years of experimentation with new media that are such a trademark of the Weimar Republic. At first the *horspiele* (sound plays) were largely adaptations from the stage, but as the popularity of radio increased *horspiele* were created specifically for the medium. But, other than this short-lived *horspiel* tradition in the Weimar Republic, few thought of radio as a venue for serious artistic presentation of spoken word art. Indeed, the level of auricular literacy was so unsophisticated that Orson Welles' famous broadcast of H.G. Welles' *War of the Worlds* was mistaken for a news broadcast — for actuality rather than fiction.[10]

Research into the aesthetic possibilities of radio did continue, but it was largely dominated by the invention of audio tape and the possibility of an artistic manipulation of pre-recorded sound. The audio tape experiments of Marcel Duchamp, John Cage, William Burroughs or the documentaries of Glenn Gould, for example. But even these failed to reach beyond their stated objective of overthrowing the hegemony of tradition with its moribund forms and dead genres.[11] In answering Ezra Pound's clarion call to *Make it New*, priests presiding at the birth of the avant garde chose to reject the narrative structures of storytelling.

---

[10]For a discussion of the relevance of this broadcast to the topic of performance values as they apply to radio see my *The Use of Drama in Information Programming*, in *CTR*, Fall, 1982.

[11]For a discussion see, see *Wireless Imagination*, pp. 373ff.

In radio, this led to disastrous consequences. The stubborn persistence of traditional forms of storytelling tells us that there is an aesthetic contract that binds author and reader, performer and listener: and narrative is its building block. Reject narrative and you will reap only one reward: the *displeasure of the text*, to coin a phrase.

Unlike its sisters in the performing arts, the dance, music or theatre, radio drama continues to be the Cinderella, stuck in the kitchen; her dramaturgical utterances emanating from the insignificant looking little box that sits on top of the refrigerator, competing for attention with all the household noises, particularly the loud clatter made by her step-sisters as they go through the ritualized preparations of donning their masks as spectators on their way to the theatre or the movies, the dance or the concert. Radio listening demands no such rituals: it does not require evening gowns, or make up, or taxis and limos. As spectators to a stage play, or a concert, we assume a public persona in a community of like-minded people and we wear our masks in order to conspire with the playwright, director and actors in the creation of the performance as a public ritual. Radio requires no masks, no community, no ritualistic preparations. And in my view it is largely because of this absence of ritual —no opening night with all the anticipation and paraphernalia that make it a community and media event— that there is no history or serious scholarly study of radio drama. It is my hope that serious inquiry into the private, intimate, nature of the radio experience, which is closer to the pleasure of reading rather than that of watching, will eventually be undertaken.

*Head, CBC Radio Performance,*
*Canadian Broadcasting Corporation*

# PAST THE DOCUMENTS, TO THE DANCE: THE WITNESS TO JUBA IN 1848

Stephen Johnson

Domenico Pietropaolo, in a recent talk at the Festival of Original Theatre (Toronto, Ontario 7 March 1997), drew a distinction between History and Historiography. He said that the use of the word "History" as applied to that which historians create is a confusing misnomer. "There is only one history," he said. If I remember correctly, he said that history is that which occurs during the passage of time. And that is all that it is. Everything the historian does should be called "historio-graphy," with the emphasis on the "graphic" or written character of the creation. History is the unexamined brute event, historiography the definition and interpretation of the event by an individual mind to some imposed significance. This may seem self-evident; it is the basis of post-modern historiography, and its subspecies that focuses on performance (see White, Burke, Postlewait, as general references). I find, however, that even in the halls of academe this distinction requires frequent repetition. I add that my own (no doubt) gross misinterpretation of what Professor Pietropaolo actually said is evidence of what he said — if I am even close to what he said. It is all quite postmodern.

This is not, however, the complete process of creating "historiography." The brute event that is the subject of the historian's study exists in the infinitessimal present. It happens, but it does not persist, even in part. The event manifests itself, as far as the historian is concerned, only through its physical artifacts, including buildings, borders, crowns, and the dead. Such artifacts include, to my purpose, what historians usually refer to as "documents" — anything recorded through language or iconography as a result of the event ("Documents" is the term I will use in the balance of this essay). It is no secret, these are what historians use as the raw material of their creative work. They are thus once removed from their intended subject — the event.

These documents are, furthermore, the result of a human intervention that colours, interprets the event during their creation. The witnesses of and participants in the event are affected by it, and in the documents record their responses to it. In effect, what the historian does is to read a text (the document) that is itself a translation of and commentary on another text (the event). In this sense, then, historians are twice removed from their intended subject.

Historians are even further removed, because the subject-event is manifested to us (if we are fortunate) in a wide array of documents, representing a diversity of individual accounting, interpretation, commentary and translation. The view of the source-event is diffracted through many kinds of lenses, and we as historians typically perform two actions. We interpret the documents as subjective responses to an event, in an attempt to understand the effects of the source event. And we attempt (however vain) to "get past" the documents and to "get to" the event. We do this because we want to interpret the event ourselves. We want to read it ourselves. In my case certainly, I want to have been there, as witness. To this end, historians spend a great deal of time negotiating agreement in the diversity of opinion displayed by the documents, explaining the contradictions, seeking a cohesive, unified picture of the original event. In the balance of this paper, I propose to look briefly at a single example of this attempt — my own efforts to "get to" the dance of Master Juba.

Juba was an American dancer who flourished during the 1840s in the variety houses of New York City, in a successful British tour with a minstrel troupe in 1848, and as a solo act in Britain until his (alledged) death around 1852. Why I would wish to understand how he danced is not the focus of this essay; but some context is required. Briefly, Juba was the subject of a very influential 1947 article by dance historian Marian Hannah Winter. She created out of the documents a seminal importance in the development of a distinctly American dance idiom. To Winter, Juba invented "tap" dance, and introduced "African" rhythms into western dance. She manufactured a "historio-graphy" of rising prominence, success against the odds of racism, integrity of performance based on direct links with African-American folk culture. Juba, by this re-reading and re-writing, re-appropriates for black culture what is otherwise generally seen as racist theft. Winter created an important place for Juba; such importance always begs re-examination.

Juba's dance invites other questions. He was written about far more than the usual touring act during his 1848 British tour, and one wonders why. He appears to have been the only performer of colour in the intensely racist and segregated business of negro minstrelsy, and one wonders why. The descriptions of him are at once thorough, precise, and incomprehensibly contradictory — and one wonders what it was about his performance that was indescribable. He danced in men's and in women's costume, for middle-class and saloon audiences, was "lionized" and despised — and, by one report, his skeleton was on exhibition shortly after his death. One wonders why. At the center of all this wondering is the single brute event — the dance.

There is no written choreography of Juba's dance. He was not a part of a culture that would think or want to record, preserve and reproduce. He was a part of a popular culture that was oral-performative, and improvisatory. This culture did not produce its own documents, except in the form of playbills and puffery. With the exception of one graphic image, that appears to show Juba performing a jig, the records that we have of his dance are all of one kind. They are the eyewitness reports written by middle-class white British men for middle-class newspaper readers, based on their personal experience of the event. These are clear examples of the artifacts used by historians, representing as they do a physical remnant of the event, the effect of the event on the witness, and the attempted translation of the event into the written word.

## *Reading Individual Documents*

As an historian, I read each document for the writer's attitude toward the dance, and for clues as to the character of the dance itself. I would like to briefly consider a few examples. Number one:

> The effort baffles description. It is certainly original, and like nothing that we have ever seen before. It is a combination of almost every quality in art —from the graceful movement of the 'minuet' to the highest pitch of terpsichorean illustration— and something more. There is such energy, such rapidity, as is quite novel in the annals of dancing. We are impressed with the notion that he is the identical black who 'danced himself clean out of sight.' Yet all is in character, all in keeping, and in exquisite time; there is both light and shade. With a consummation of art and tack he will 'bring you jump' from his most frenzied movement to the most subdued demeanour possible, and with so much quaintness and grace that the beholder is fairly puzzled which to admire most. [*Birmingham Journal*, 16 December 1848; this part of the notice is an alledged quotation from a Brighton newspaper, unconfirmed. It is consistent with the variety of notices Juba received.]

There is nothing here that would allow us to close our eyes and see or hear Juba, or that would allow a dancer to re-create a single movement. But there is something here. There is an admission of incompetence — "the effort baffles description." There is an expression of originality — that the writer has not seen anything like this dance before. The writer appears to recognize other dances in this dance — "every quality in art" from the "minuet," and so on. Another feature is extreme speed, another control, and another the sudden change from "frenzied" to "subdued."

Some of this is common rhetoric; if the dance cannot be described on paper, then the reader will simply have to pay to see it. Nevertheless, I do read into this description two sets of contradictory characteristics — indescribability opposed to recognizability, frenzy opposed to control.

A second example:

> His pedal execution is a thing to wonder at, if his flexibility of muscle did not confound us. He jumps, he capers, he crosses his legs, he stamps his heels, he dances on his knees, on his ankles, he ties his limbs into double knots, and untwists them as one might a skein of silk, and all these marvels are done in strict time and appropriate rhythm — each note has its corresponding step and action. Now he languishes, now burns, now love seems to sway his motions, and anon rage seems to impel his steps. Juba's plantation dance is a sort of terpsichorean illustration of Collin's "Ode on the Passions." One feat which he achieves with his feet excites our especial wonder; he absolutely dances with one foot on the ground and the other one never off it. [*Sterling Journal and Advertiser*, 31 August 1849, quoting a London review from *The Morning Post*, unconfirmed. The reviewer describes Juba in similar language; the London review is quoted as corroboration.]

Some of the same characteristics are evident in this description as in the last — the variety of styles, the sudden changes ("now he languishes, now burns.)" By my reading, this writer attempts to capture a sense of the dance in the speed and rhythm of the writing — "he jumps, he capers, he crosses his legs." There is also here a description of the impossible, and in the last line the nonsensical; although one could treat this line as a reference to the percussive "tap" element of Juba's dance, which of course wouldn't exist unless he had both feet on the ground.

A third example:

> The dances he introduced were distinguished for eccentricity, rapidity of motion, and the accuracy of the time kept. They approximated, in some respects, to those wild dances that may be witnessed sometimes in the remoter parts of the Highlands, including the sword dance, as there known; besides having the same idea of clanking the heels, as pervades the Polka. But it is not the office of the legs alone to do all this; the head, arms, and body generally take full share of duty, and assume such extraordinary positions, that only a being possessed of the power of Proteus could calculate upon taking. [*The Manchester Courier and Lancashire General Advertiser*, 18 October 1848]

The qualities of speed, rhythmic control, extreme gestures and frequent change are obvious. Added to this are attempts to identify features from other dances—the highland fling and the Polka. An emphasis is placed on the use of the upper body, head and arms, as if this was unusual.

Finally, I offer part of a lengthy description from Juba's first Manchester appearance:

> [Manchester Guardian, 18th October 1848] FREE-TRADE HALL. — "Juba" and the Serenaders.
>
> A party of serenaders, under the leadership of Mr. G. W. Pell, late of St. James's Theatre, gave one of their peculiar exhibitions on Monday evening in the Free-trade Hall. They are six in number, and are mostly happy in the possession of nigger-like physiognomies. The "making up" of their leader was extremely ludicrous. With literally a yard of shirt collar and frill, it was scarcely possible to witness his extravagant grimaces, without a most undignified unbending of the facial muscles, and many were the handkerchiefs employed to conceal the smothered laughter of their fair owners. The party have some good voices among them, and they harmonize well together; indeed, the melody of several of the chants, and other concerted pieces, was so pleasing to the ear, that they were loudly encored. But the great feature of the entertainment, and that which we imagine attracted the large and respectable audience present, was undoubtedly "Master Juba," the immortalized of Boz. This "phenomenon" (as the bills describe him) is a copper-coloured votary of Terpsichore, — the Monsieur Perrot of Negro life in the southern states; and possesses the additional attaction of being a "real nigger," and not a "sham," like his vocal associates. He is apparently about eighteen years of age; about 5 feet 3 inches in height; of slender make, yet possessing great muscular activity. His head is very small, and his countenance, when at rest, has a rather mild, sedate, and far from unpleasing expression. His first performance was "Miss Lucy Long, in character." With a most bewitching bonnet and veil, a *very* pink dress, beflounced to the waist, lace-fringed trousers of the most spotless purity, and red leather boots, — the ensemble completed by the green parasol and white cambric pocket handkerchief, — Master Juba certainly looked the black demoiselle of the first ton to the greatest advantage. The playing and singing by the serenaders of a version of the well-known negro ditty, furnished the music to Juba's performance, which was after this fashion: — Promenading in a circle to the left for a few bars, till again facing the audience, he then commenced a series of steps, which altogether baffle description, from their number, oddity, and the rapidity with which they were executed. The highland fling, the sailor's hornpipe, and other European dances, seemed to have been laid under contribution, and intermixed with a number of steps which we may call "Juba's own," for surely their like was never before seen for grotesque agility, not altogether unmixed with grace. The promenade was then repeated; then more dancing; and so on, to the end of the song. His other performances were called the "marriage festival" and "plantation

dances," in which, in male costume, he illustrated the dances of his own simple people on festive occasions. They were even more extraordinary than the first, — the grotesque element, in the character of the steps, largely predominating, and the physical exertion apparently much greater. The same peculiarity, of the alternate promenade and dance, was observable in both. To us, the most interesting part of the performance was the exact time, which, even in the most complicated and difficult steps, the dancer kept to the music. He appears to be quite an enthusiast in his art, and every round of applause he received seemed to stimulate him to fresh exertion. Altogether, Master Juba's Terpsichorean performances are well worth a visit.

There are a good many statements here about the dance, its performative context, and its reception. The characters were grotesquely dressed, and excited laughter from the audience. There was some embarrassment at the extent of this laughter among the more genteel members of the audience. The performers were highly skilled harmonic singers — a contrast, it seems to me, to the grotesque costume and humour. Juba himself is described in detail; I know of no other popular performers from this period who have their height and head size divulged. The costume for his role as "Lucy Long" is described in all its mismatched colour scheme. The general structure of this dance is described — a slow promenade interrupted by fast (and indescribable) solos. There are references to recognizable dances, and Juba's "authenticity" — his colour, and the assumption that he is performing his culture.

## *Reading the Group of Documents*

So goes the work of the historian, reading and re-reading individual documents, extrapolating and categorizing from the individual texts, in search of some agreement among the witnesses. In this case, I read the categories as a series of contradictions, as follows:

1. On the one hand, there is a unanimous emphasis on the precision of the sounds made, and the control that Juba had over that sound, which certainly argues for Juba's place in the tradition of "tap" dancing. However, by way of contradiction there is an emphasis on wild abandon in the dance, on frenzy, the extremes of speed and gesture, and on sudden and violent changes of position and tone.
2. On the one hand, there is a near-obsessive scientific detail in some of the physical description, unusual in the vagaries and puffery of popular criticism. On the other hand, there are examples of description that manifest the impossibility of his dance. Such descriptions are a kind of mockery of this other, more precise description.

3. On the one hand there are references to recognizable dances, apparently an attempt to describe by analogy. These include the highland fling, the Lancashire clog, the sailor's hornpipe, and the polka, but reference is also made to the "whirling dervish" and the "willis" of Romantic ballet [*The Era*, 18 June 1848]. And, of course, to Juba's "authentic" dance of southern plantation life. On the other hand, I note that these dances are all taken from the exotic margins of the British Isles or empire, and from folk and rural dance idioms. We have to wonder just how many of these dances the audience might have seen, especially anything from the southern plantation. The only reference to dance from the western theatre is to the "willis", a popular example of the relatively new and contentious Romantic ballet.

Such contradictions represent radically different readings of the same dance-text — different readings by the same reader, in most cases. Sometimes he (always a "he") heard a precise rhythm, sometimes saw a frenzied movement. Sometimes "he" read similarity, sometimes difference. Part of the historian's job is to assimilate, to resolve these contradictions, in that attempt to "get to" the performance text. This is the text, after all, out of which the writers of the documents (the "he") derived significance — or upon which they imposed significance. We cannot begin to understand the prejudices of the documents without struggling to get past them to the source.

## *Provisional Historio-graphies*

I offer, by way of a very open conclusion, some possible glimpses of Juba's dance. I make no claims for finality; all "historio-graphies" are provisional.

1. There is something unusual about the precise descriptions of Juba in the accounts. I wonder if this predilection was a manifestation of race. The Science of Anthropology was quite new, and advocated theories of biologically defined races, and the evolutionary defence of racial superiority (Bolt, passim). There was, at the same time, a pedagogical fascination with the exhibition of exotic cultures in London, including groups of Bushmen and Kaffir Zulus (see Altick, passim). I suspect that Juba was in part read as an exhibition of exotica, as if in a museum or a sideshow. If so, this might explain reports of his continued exhibition, after his death.

2. I wonder if the more extreme descriptions of indescribable movements might be analogous to descriptions of the acrobatic clowns of English

pantomime, the French foire, and the commedia dell' arte. The use of the word "grotesque" indicates this, although more contextual documentation is needed. If true, then such descriptions consitute another example of description by analogy, and another kind of theatrical dance besides ballet. This strengthens the argument for Juba's use of recognizable dance idioms.

3. Marian Hannah Winter argued vehemently that the "indescribable" in Juba's dance was an "African" idiom. I understand the liberal political desire to believe this. Is there evidence? Eyewitness reference to Juba exhibiting southern plantation slave dances is certainly not evidence; what British critic could distinguish such a thing? However, the eyewitnesses describe frequent, violent changes of rhythm. I wonder if we might read into the idea of frequent change an attempt to describe the complex syncopations of the African percussive idiom. In the contortions of the upper torso, likewise, we might read the African choreographic preference for a body low to the ground, in contradistinction to the Western vertical forms. We might.

4. Scholars such as Eric Lott, in *Love and Theft*, and the musicologist Robert Winans in his work on the banjo, have emphasized the parodic imperative of the early minstrel show. Parody is an important feature of postmodern criticism; just for our present purpose, call it "imitation with difference" (Hutcheon, 37, passim; Rose, passim). It manifests itself along a continuum from the grotesque exaggeration of the subject, to a precise impersonation. This variety is manifest in the early minstrel show, which claimed precise imitation of a culture, but offered extreme stereotype, which identified the southern slave with the northern white "wage slave," but then dehumanized one group.

   Juba may have been black; but he was also a minstrel and therefore a parodist, whether by choice or not. One American reference has him performing exact impersonations of all the other minstrel dancers on the New York stage (Winter, 33). Because he was a young boy at this time, his exact imitation would already be an exaggeration, a parodic imitation with difference. We might still explain the reference to the whirling dervish, the willis and the highland fling as attempts to describe by analogy; but it is also possible that Juba danced these dances accurately in imitation, based on exhibitions in London of Arab culture, British folk culture, and Romantic ballet (did Juba dance *en pointe*?). If this is true, then I wonder if we can ever determine to what extent he exaggerated the original.

   This difficulty manifests itself in Juba's exercise in drag, "Lucy Long." "Wench" dancing was common in the early minstrel show; indeed, it was the star turn (Lott 53-5, 162-78, passim). But the literature of this period is contradictory concerning the portrayal of the character. In some respects, it appears to have been female impersonation. In other instances, it appears to have been an obvious grotesquerie, like the "dame" of English Panto. There is no evidence of the form Juba's impersonation took. Since his dance alternated between slow promenade and fast dance, perhaps he alternated between the two extremes of drag.

5. Finally, some historians, in this (vain) effort to "get to" the subject-event, attempt re-constructions of the performance from the documents. One class of Shakespearean scholar does this, and it is a particularly strong practice among dance historians. I have been researching this, along with a dancer, with respect to Juba, and offer, as one last provisional historio-graphy, the sight of one contemporary body imitating (reading) graphic images that are themselves imitations (readings) of another body dancing (Figures 1-8). I add that this means of "getting to" the dance is predicated on the assumption that the images are based on firsthand viewing, and the intention of accurate recording; this assumption is questionable. Does the imitation help? I cannot answer that. But as imitation with difference, it may be a kind of useful parody. At the very least, imitation with the "difference" of modern dress may draw analogies with contemporary dance styles. Such similarities may be serendipitous, the result of the limits and tendencies of the human body in motion. However, they may also manifest the legacy of an oral-performative tradition — the main tenet of which is imitation with difference.

## *Two Propositions*

I would like to close with two propositions, one emanating from Juba's dance, and one from myself as historian.

The first concerns the initial reception of the products of popular performative culture. John Fiske, in *Understanding Popular Culture*, emphasizes how a popular audience can read a text in ways startlingly at variance with any authorized or authorial intention, and at variance with other members of the audience. The popular text/performance may appear to be closed; but the popular culture tends to be participatory, tends to read everything in an open and undisciplined manner. He postulates a "Producerly" text, one that

> "does not impose laws of its own construction that readers have to decipher in order to read it on terms of its, rather than their, choosing. ... it

> offers itself up to popular production; it exposes, however reluctantly, the vulnerabilities, limitations, and weaknesses of its preferred meanings; it contains, while attempting to repress them, voices that contradict the ones it prefers; it has loose ends that escape its control, its meanings exceed its own power to discipline them, its gaps are wide enough for whole new texts to be produced in them — it is, in a very real sense, beyond its own control. (103-104)

The idea of the producerly "text" helps to describe the extraordinary variance in the reception of the early minstrel show, and of Juba's dance. The form of the dance may have been quite simple in intention; but popular consumers were nevertheless encouraged to read the dance in any way they wanted. Even taken as an act of rebellion, the customer has paid. And those customers have been encouraged to bring to the performance all their own intentions, expectations, and concerns, and to "write" their own product as they watch. The historian, then, is presented with the task of assembling and interpreting a variety of documents that disagree about an event that has encouraged disagreement. By this model Juba has encouraged his own indescribability.

My second proposition is based on Fiske's source-model for the "producerly" text, Roland Barthes' *S/Z*. This model — that texts and readers can be "readerly" and "writerly," "open" and "closed" to interpretation — is now a hoary old theory. But Barthes does postulate the idea of polysemic, writerly texts that encourage the reader to produce meaning, and the idea of writerly readers who produce new meanings from old texts, whatever their intentions. The "writerly reader" does this, he says, by two means. The first is re-reading, an activity "contrary to the commercial and ideological habits of our society," and "tolerated only in certain marginal categories of readers (children, old people, and professors)...." (115-116). The second feature of his "writerly" attitude is "de-composition":

> If we want to remain attentive to the plural of a text (however limited it may be), we must renounce structuring this text in large masses, as was done by classical rhetoric and by secondary-school explication: ... everything signifies ceaselessly and several times, but without being delegated to a great final ensemble, to an ultimate structure. (11-12)

In these two terms Barthes establishes the activities most important in the art of the historian, and the resulting tensions between the parts and the whole, the intention and reception. Historians are aggresive re-readers and de-composers. The irony is that the results of their work — the "historio-graphy" — is, finally, just another artifact, like Marian Hannah Winter's work, soon to be re-read and de-composed, and added to the body of disparate texts.

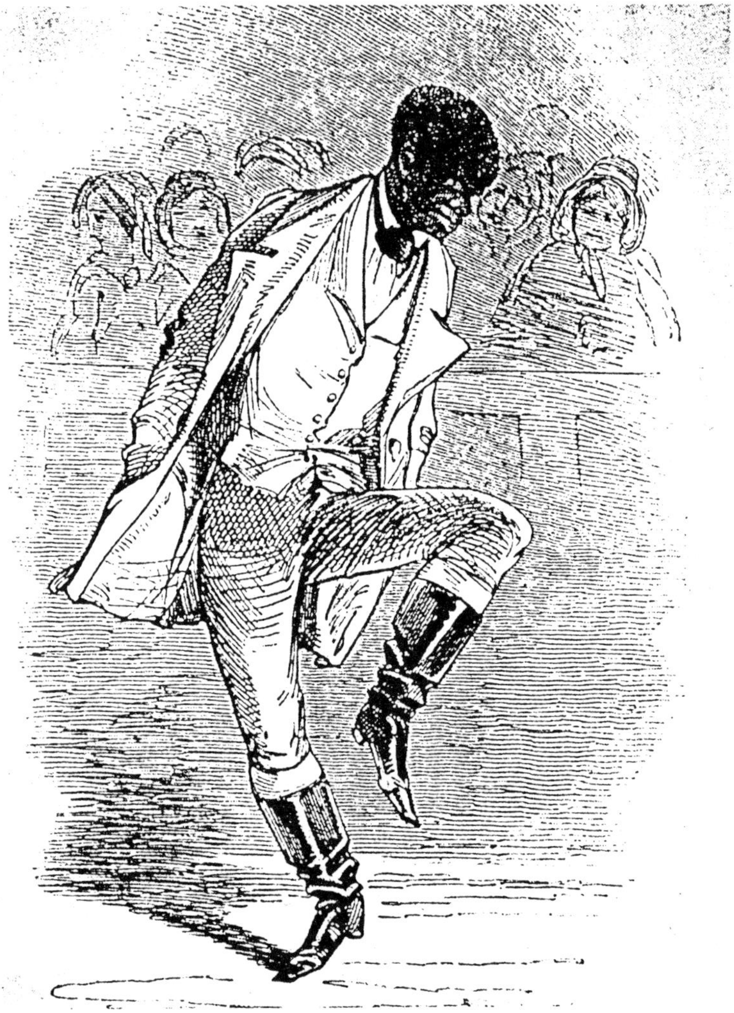

Figure 1. *"Boz's Juba" from The Illustrated London News, 5 August 1848.*

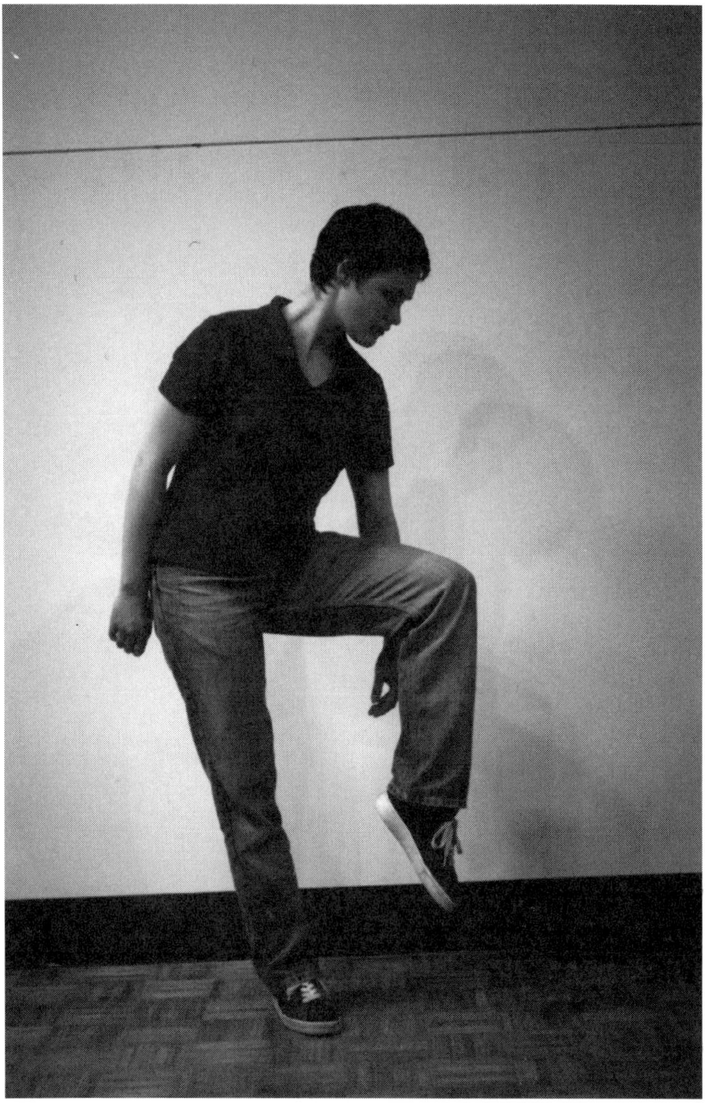

Figure 2. *Dancer Jennifer Johnson imitating Figure 1.*

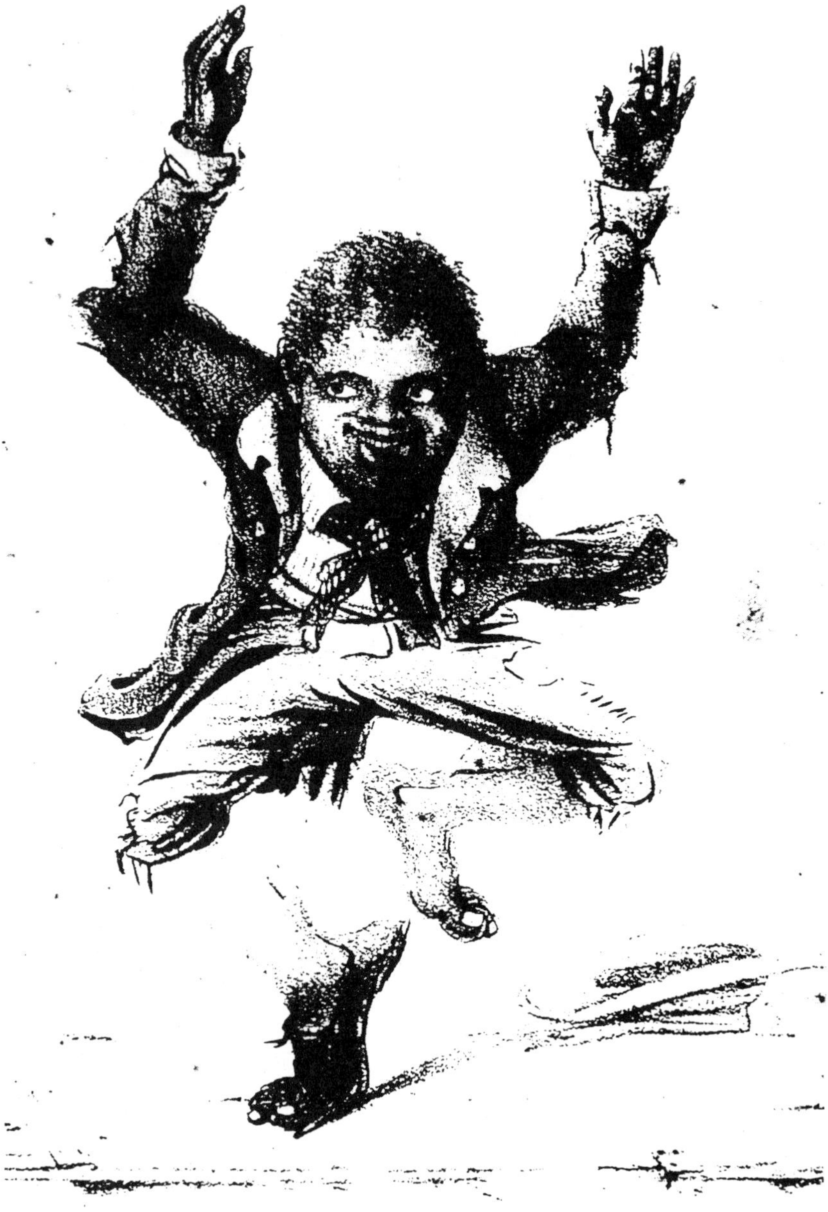

Figure 3. *Dancer John N. Smith, from a sheet music cover, 1840.*

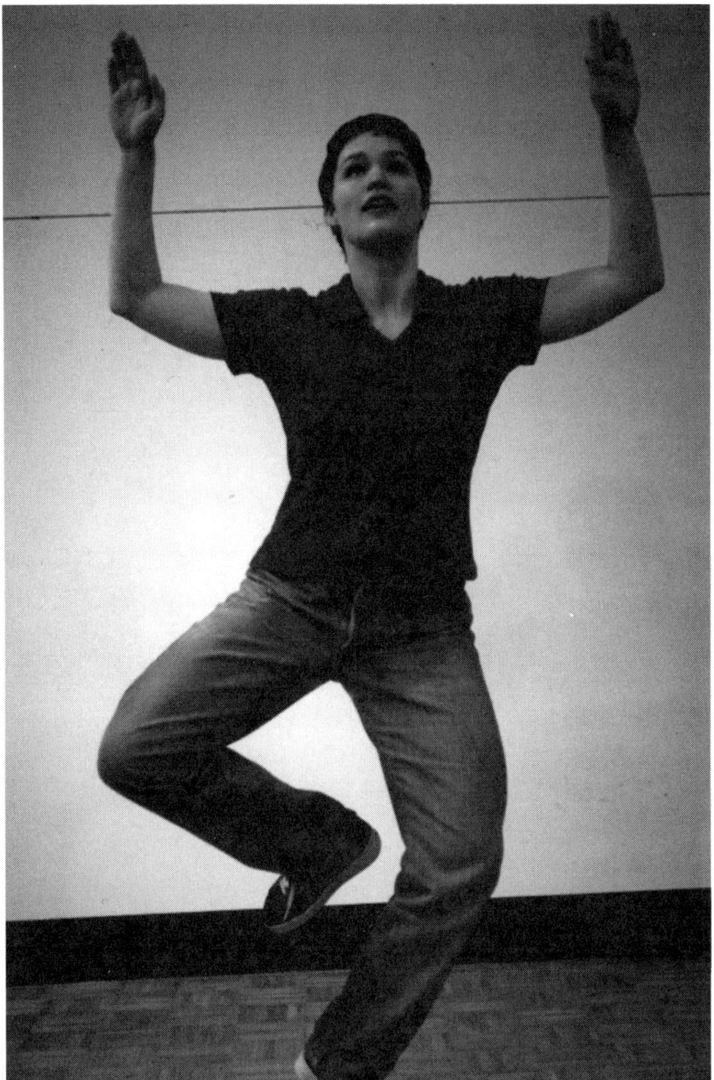

Figure 4. *Jennifer Johnson imitating Figure 3.*

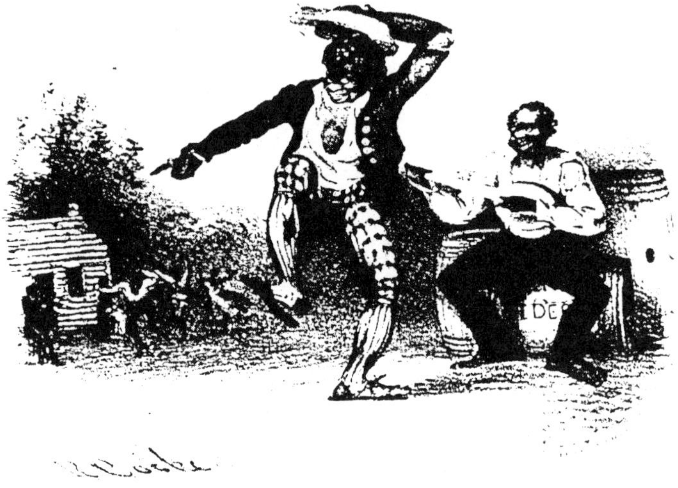

Figure 5. *From a sheet music cover, 1840.*

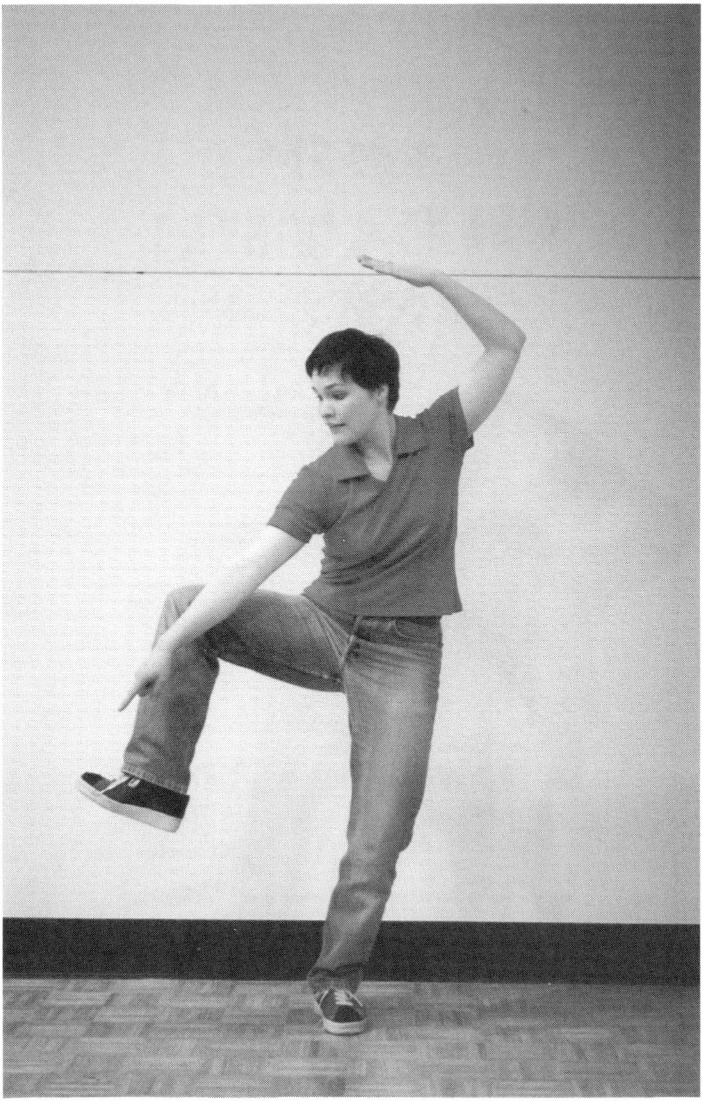

Figure 6. *Jennifer Johnson imitating Figure 5.*

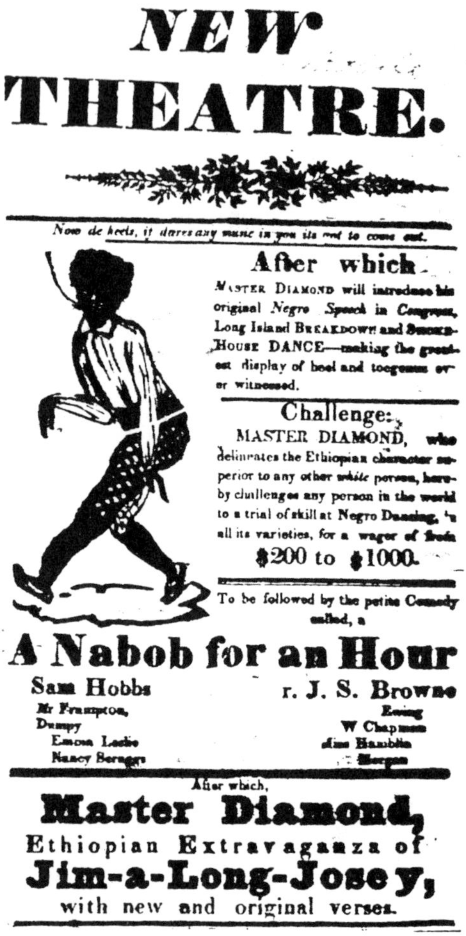


Figure 7. *Playbill dated 1841, showing dancer John Diamond.*

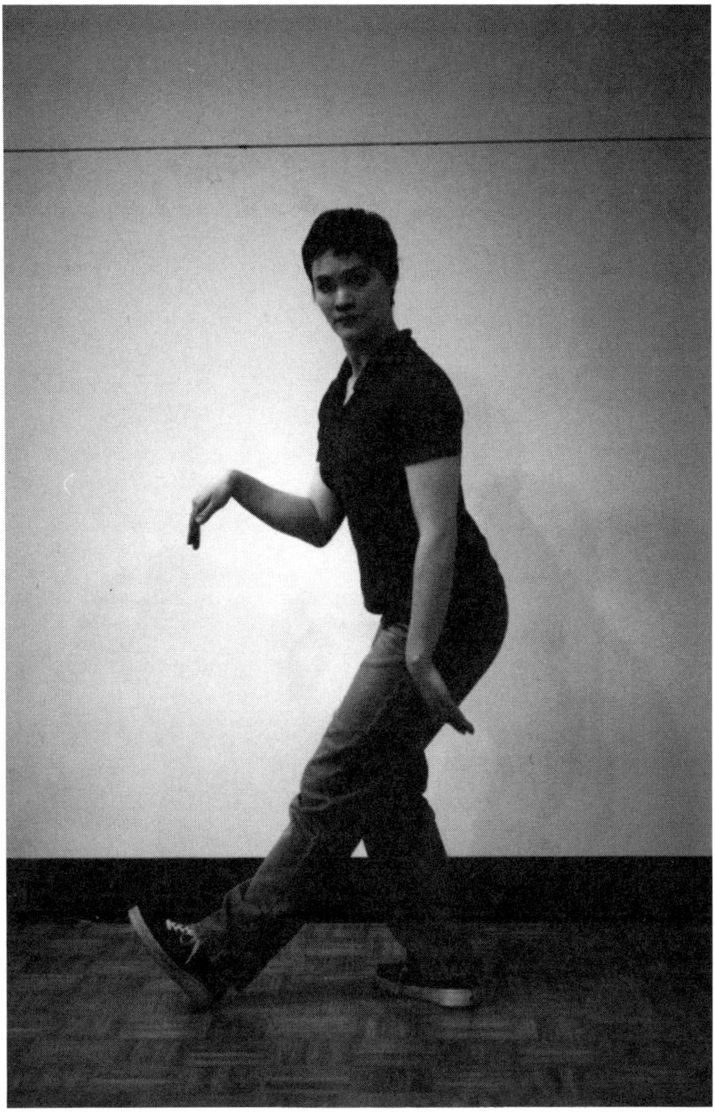

Figure 8. *Jennifer Johnson imitating Figure 7.*

## *Final Statement*

This was a long way around to Juba's dance; but it is a long way around to Juba's dance. The documents carry a chaos of conflicting readings, both within and between. Historians nevertheless tend to insist on reading the artifacts as if they were one unified text. Or, rather, we rewrite a non-existent unity into the documents. There was a unifying feature, once. It was and is not the body of documents. It was the dancing body of Juba.

*McMaster University*

### WORKS CITED

Altick, Richard. *The Shows of London.* Cambridge, MA: Harvard UP, 1978.

Barthes, Roland. *S/Z.* Translated by Richard Miller. London: Jonathan Cape, 1975.

Bolt, Christine. *Victorian Attitudes to Race.* Toronto: University of Toronto Press, 1971.

Burke, Peter. *History and Social Theory.* Ithaca: Cornell University Press, 1992.

Burke, Peter, ed. *New Perspectives on Historical Writing.* Cambridge: Cambridge University Press, 1991.

Fiske, John. *Understanding Popular Culture.* London and New York: Routledge, 1989.

Hutcheon, Linda. *A Theory of Parody: The Teachings of Twentieth-Century Art Forms.* New York and London: Routledge, 1991.

Lott, Eric. *Love and Theft: Blackface Minstrelsy and the American Working Class.* New York: OUP, 1993.

Postlewait, Thomas and Bruce A. McConachie, eds. *Interpreting the Theatrical Past: Essays in the Historiography of Performance.* Iowa City: Iowa University Press, 1989.

Rose, Margaret A. *Parody: Ancient, Modern, and Post-Modern.* Cambridge: Cambridge University Press, 1993.

White, Hayden. *Tropics of Discourse: Essays in Cultural Criticism.* Baltimore: Johns Hopkins University Press, 1978.

Winans, Robert B. "Early Minstrel Show Music, 1843-1852," in Glenn Loney ed., *Musical Theatre in America.* Westport, CT: Greenwood Press, 1984.

Winter, Marian Hannah, "Juba and American Minstrelsy, *Dance Index* 6.2, Feb 1947. pp 28-47.

# AUTHORIZATIONS OF THE PERFORMATIVE: WHOSE PERFORMANCES OF WHAT, AND FOR WHOM?

Michael Sidnell

It was only five years ago that the journal *Canadian Literature* cut the word "performativity" in a review I wrote, even though I was able to supply a few appropriate and fairly respectable citations.[1] But in a recent article for *Modern Drama* I insinuated the word without inciting any editorial intervention, as, no doubt, many other contributors have.[2] These different receptions may be partly attributable differences between the conventional discourses of the two journals but partly, also, to the temporality of usage, since it was in the interim that the term "performative" became not only widely used but almost indispensable in discourses of the arts. There is no other that so well differentiates certain potentialities and constraints within performance as this borrowing from the speech act theory of J. L. Austin.[3]

What, precisely, the specific linguistic and pragmatic attributes of a speech act performative might be, is contested. A fairly uncontroversial example would be "I warn you ..." when it is actually a warning. In this case, the utterance not only performs an action but denominates precisely what it is doing. This denominational-performative reflexivity is critical — though not, in Austin, definitive, since the speech act performative may take less obvious forms.[4] It is partly this unobviousness that allows the "special theory" of the "explicit performative" to be rather overshadowed by the general law of speech act theory that "to

1 The Associate Editor, Eva-Marie Kröller, wrote to me, on 13 April 1992, "And could you tells [sic] what 'performativeness' is? 'Performability,' 'theatricality', 'stage potential'?" Probably the most convincing of several citations I offered was to Schechner & Appel 1990:44. The review never appeared.

2 Sidnell 1996.

3 Especially from his influential William James Lectures delivered at Harvard University in 1955 and published as *How To Do Things with Words* in 1962.

4 Benveniste: F274/E237. Benveniste insists that the act must be explicitly denominated not just implied, as Austin would allow. So "Shut the door" is a performative for Austin because it is equivalent to "I order you to shut the door" but Benveniste distinguishes between the imperative, which does not name itself, and the true performative.

say something is in the full normal sense to do something".[5] But it is the explicit performative's attribute of self-realization that has charged the term with a special and necessary signification in discourse of performance. After some hesitation, the term I have adopted for this signification is Coleridge's "ipseity" (from the Latin "ipse" meaning "he himself"). "Ipseity" has the advantages of being relatively unmarked in contemporary discourse and of belonging, in Coleridge, to a set of three terms, which is specially apt for the present purpose. Coleridge's other two terms are "alterity" and "community" and the whole triad will constitute for me a paradigm of attributes of performance, though Coleridge himself had a rather different use for it .[6]

In performance theory —still in its incipience— the performative, in the given sense, is what is never merely rehearsed, even in rehearsal; the quality which, in its ingenuous form, actor-training seeks to sublimate; that is, the kind of ipseity that the rude mechanicals of *A Midsummer Night's Dream* cannot but enact in all its uniqueness. In speech act theory, in the words of Benveniste, the performative utterance,

> is an event because it creates the event. Being an act that is individual and historical, a performative utterance cannot be repeated. Each reproduction is a new act, which is carried out by someone who is authorized.[7]

The notion of a unique *act* which is not a repetition and cannot be repeated is strongly countered, though it is not denied, by Derrida's insistence that the utterance in the so-called performative of Austin's speech act theory is embedded in its inescapable iterability.[8] For Derrida, these utterances retain, in the linguistic realm, their citational form (which also, in his understanding, characterizes theatre). Even

---

5 Austin 1975:94.

6 Coleridge, 1990:77. "In the Trinity there is the 1. Ipseity. 2. Alterity. 3. Community ...".

7 Benveniste: F273/236. My translation of : "il est événment parce qu'il crée l'événment. Étant acte individuel et historique, un énoncé performatif ne peut être répété. Toute reproduction est un nouvel acte qu'accomplit celui qui a qualité."

8 In "Signature événment contexte", an address to the Congrès international des Sociétés de philosophie de langue français (Montreal, August 1971), reprinted in Derrida 1972(F). One of the translations of this essay appears in Derrida 1988(E) (along with a synopsis of John R. Searle's response and a translation of Derrida's rejoinder to Searle). References to both (F) and (E) are given in the text. The translations are my own.

more pertinently, because it takes *us* beyond speech act theory, Derrida insists that before one could investigate performatives associated with utterances —the existence of which he acknowledges— one would have to be clear about,

> what it is that is supposed to "self-manifest" or the eventness of an event that, in its supposed present and unique ocurrence, posits the involvement of an utterance that in itself cannot but be repetitive or citational or, rather —these two latter words being potentially confusing— iterable (F388/E17).[9]

Derrida himself does not attempt any such clarification of the eventness of such an event. How could he? As Derrida is intimating, the phenomenon is not, *in the first place,* a linguistic one and is therefore not purely linguistic at all.

Austin does indeed find it necessary to take account of para-linguistic circumstances of performative utterances, including their authorization, which sharply differentiates serious examples from the parasitism, as he sees it, of fictional, theatrical and poetic citationality. For him, linguistic force is critically determined by social context. And, as Derrida observes, the bearing of theatrical performance on his views of the performative is considerable. Indeed, the account of theatre that each of them gives is most revealing — though not of theatre, except in their divergence, which illuminates theatre and may be partly explained in terms of theatrical performance.

From a specifically non-theatrical stance, Judith Butler, in her *Bodies that Matter* attempts something of a compromise between Austin's performative act and Derrida's citationally decentered utterance. Citation, she posits, "accumulates the force of authority" (227) and, by concealing its discursive character, acts performatively, though only in a provisional way. I shall return to Butler's argument by way of a conclusion to these remarks. At present I pass on to another problematic requirement for the speech act performative, which is associated, as has been mentioned, with its being a unique act.

This requirement is that it must be, in Benveniste's phrase, an "an act of authority" (F273/E236). So, uttered by the croupier in the casino, "les jeux sont faits" is a performative, but not in the mouth of a bettor or in another place. The criterion of authorization is used to distinguish

---

[9] "Il faut d'abord s'entendre ici sur ce qu'il en est du "se produire" ou de l'événementialité d'un évenement qui suppose dans son surgissement prétendument présent et singulier l'intervention d'un énoncé qui en lui-même ne peut être que de structure répétitive ou citationelle ou plutôt, ces deux derniers mots prêtant à confusion, itérable."

true performatives from utterances in the correct linguistic form that are mere mockeries, or quotations or otherwise invalidated as unique acts; that is to say, the very usages that would dissolve a supposedly authorizing subject into discourse and textuality. Having no truck at all with the notion that there is a poetic function of naming that is truly performative, Austin rather notoriously asserted that a "peformative utterance will ... be in a peculiar way hollow or void if said by an actor on the stage, or if introduced in a poem, or spoken in soliloquy (22)." It is at this point that Austin's theory becomes so vulnerable to Derrida's critique and also remains isolated from later speech act theory, which attempts bring the Austinian balloon of hollow instances back into the shed. Did Austin, perhaps, pass through the looking-glass of linguistic theory into a realm where the behaviour — and misbehaviour — of words is decisively conditioned by the para-linguistic pragmatics of performances and their authorizations? Was he adumbrating the kind of performance theory that has found his word "performative" so compelling?

Here is Austin:

> Suppose, for example, I see a vessel on the stocks, walk up and smash the bottle hung at the stern, proclaim 'I name this ship *Mr. Stalin*' and for good measure kick away the chock: but the trouble is, I was not the person chosen to name it (whether or not —an additional complication— *Mr. Stalin* was the destined name; perhaps in a way it is even more of a shame if it was). We can all agree
>
> (1) that the ship was not thereby named;
> (2) that it is an infernal shame.
>
> One could say that I 'went through a form of' naming the vessel but that my 'action' was 'void' or 'without effect', because I was not a proper person, had not the 'capacity', to perform it: but one might also and aternatively say that, where there is not even a pretence of capacity or a colourable claim to it, then there is no conventional procedure; it is a mockery, like a marriage with a monkey (23-24).

Many readers have doubtless asked themselves what other forms of marriage Austin might regard as mockeries, and some have certainly made much of the fact that his example of choice is drawn from the Church of England marriage service, seeing this as an implicit affirmation of obligatory heterosexuality.[10] But, given the prominence in English fiction of the *mock* marriage, which uses the invalidity of a speech act performative as a mode of deception, Austin is probably in-

---

[10]See Parker & Sedwick 1995: 10-11.

timating the seriousness of fake authorization in a way that is implicitly critical of a certain heterosexual practice.

In any case, Austin is revelling in this "hollow" instance in a manner that is highly performative — to use the word in a sense that we understand well and he did not admit at all. As Shoshana Felman has emphatically demonstrated, Austin is a very playful speaker and writer, who loves to trail his coat all across the spoken/printed page. But his scientific discourse is seriously fractured, I would say, by the performative instantiations of Austinian selfhood that irrupt into it. The way in which he elaborates the hypothetical ship-naming —from which I have omitted a positively Wildean footnote on the naming of babies— is altogether in excess of the requirements of the argument. In one dimension, his imagined instance conjures the mental reality of the good ship *Mr. Stalin* and how Austin fictively named it. In another, he described an elaborate performance; one which would have had serious consequences, had it happened, and would have included what we clearly recognize as an attempt at the linguistic performative of naming. Why should it matter *from the linguistic point of view* whether the utterance was *properly* authorized or not, so long as it has an author; or what its consequences were, or even that it didn't take place in the real world? And what is the relevance of the unauthorized launching of the vessel? Is it to emphasize that the most momentous consequence does not contribute to the performativeness of the linguistic utterance if the act it denominates is not specifically authorized? Perhaps; but then the naming and launching of the *Mr Stalin* is a genuine —zany, Chaplinesque and subversive— performance which raises issues of agency and representation that are familar to the theory of performance.

Transposed into the realm that Austin designates "hollow" the performative is regularly resignified by analogy with the *valid* Austinian speech act performative, with its criteria of self-reflexivity and proper authorization. It serves to designate a special class of acts which may be said to be always authorized in the sense that their authorship is instantiated in the act. An example from literature would be the performative idiocy of Wordsworth's idiot boy, whose lips "burr, burr, burr."[11] This may be distinguished, in its ipseity, from the *performance* by Wordsworth of idiocy, in the usual acceptation of the word "performance". The performativities that poets, novelists, playwrights and performers let into their performances have always been important but perhaps never more so than at present. Robert Wilson regularly introduces the performativity of non-actors and his collabo-

[11]Wordsworth 1977:284.

rative use of the non-discursive language and perceptions of the autistic youth, Christopher Knowles, has been controverted on ethical and artistic grounds; the relation between the personal identities of actors and their roles, especially in matters of race, is a common issue of performativity; gender identities are everywhere the subject of performative experiment; but with respect to age-identities a degree of performativity is conventional. Juliet is rarely played by an actor over fifty, and even a thirty-year-old in the role is remarkable.

But, to confound terminological tidiness, the signification of "performative", as used in performance theory, has been modified by its association with the cognate term "performance" in its common acceptation of a rehearsed representation by actors playing roles. Using the second of Coleridge's three terms I shall call this the marking of alterity (rather than, for instance, "representation of otherness") in order to stress the inherence in theatrical performance of the marvellous potentiality for making, in Todorov's words, "an affirmation of the other's exteriority which goes hand in hand with the recognition of the other as subject".[12] Such a "recognition of the other as subject" I take to be necessary to the excellent playing of most roles, but to be lacking when the playing assumes and represents only the exteriority of the other — though this is normal in satire. But such a marking of alterity is made impossible insofar as the player and the played constitute a performative ipseity, as is common in performance art.

When the word "performative", through its etymological link with "performance", is used to signify the potential for representation, the consequence is a certain terminological confusion that rather hinders analysis, though it corresponds with an ambivalence inherent in theatre practice. So there is much to be said for reserving the term "performative" for the instantiation of ipseity (by analogy with the speech act performative) and it is certain that without careful definition, the term "performative" inevitably gets caught up in the ambivalences of ipseity and alterity that are fundamental to acting.

I shall return to the "performative" and its authorizations after taking the established term "performance" more fully into account, for it, too, has undergone modifications of connotation and usage of late. In this respect, the recent history of the word "performance" is comparable with the long, exceedingly varied and revealing history of the word "art", in its theatrical and other applications.[13] Indeed, bringing

---

[12]Todorov 1987:250.

[13]See Williams1989:40-43; and Williams1958:30-48. The use of the term "arte" by Lope de Vega marks an interesting re-signification from the point of view of dramatic theory, for which see Sidnell 1991:4, 183.

the two terms together, it might almost be said that the "art theatre" of the early twentieth century has been displaced by the "performance theatre" of the present.

"Art" is one of Raymond Williams' carefully-selected "keywords" — "art" being, in his account, closely associated with his germinal keyword, "culture". For this latter word, Williams observed (shortly after the Second World War) a range of significations modulating from the "teashop" usage, which asseverates a certain level of refinement and acquaintance with the fine arts, to the anthropological term for the complex phenomena of a society's "way of life".[14] From Williams' preoccupation with these usages of "culture" emerged his study *Culture and Society* and, later, a set of keywords, every one of which, he said, had "forced itself upon my attention because the problems of its meanings seemed to me inextricably bound up with the problems it was being used to discuss."[15] Even in 1983, when Williams added a few more keywords to his original set, "performance" did not make the cut, but it is hard to imagine that it would not do so in 1997, considering the myriad applications of the term to all kinds of human and mechanical effort and output; and considering also that performance may be seen in a reciprocal relation with culture, making and being made by it.

The recent proliferation of the term "performance" is an instance of a problematic that was not addressed by Williams; for, though he was alert to the connotations that new English usages brought with them —or left behind— when (as commonly) they were imported from other languages, he did not consider what has since become so evident: that the protean vocabularies of English can hardly be matched or withstood by the cultures that it colonises. The difficulty that "performance" and its cognates constitute for translation is symptomatic of this linguistic and conceptual dominance. And within English-speaking cultures, also, a similar situation prevails. Powerful communication technologies have not only accelerated the acceptance of neologisms and carried them into the remotest communities, but have also mediated the passage of keywords between discourses. Such exchanges help constitute the meta-discourses that develop from, and consolidate, overarching cultural practices. A rather obvious example is the economic, legal, and idiomatic overarching of the McDonalds Corporation, whereby the prefix of the Gaelic eponym has been appropriated; and a poignant example of futile resistance to such linguistic colonization is the Scottish clan McDonald's struggle to retain its rights to its patronymic amid the welter of "Mac-words". But these are as nothing

[14] Williams 1989: 11-26.
[15] Williams 1989: 15.

in comparison with the range of practices and phenomena falling underneath the arches of "performance".

Narrowing the perspective to the field in which we have a special interest, consider this sampling of books concerned with theatre and performance published between 1990 and now:

*Performing Feminisms: Feminist Critical Theory and Theatre;*

*Performance as a Political Act: the Embodied Self;*

*The Secret Art of the Performer* — this is a translation in which the word "Performer" is offered as the equivalent to the word *Teatro* in the original;

*The Performance of Power: Theatrical Discourse and Politics*

*Critical Theory and Performance;*

*The Politics of Performance: Radical Theatre as Cultural Intervention;*

*The Semiotics of Performance* — another translation, in which the word"performance" conflates the words "teatro" and"spettaculo" of the original title; Theatre and the World;

*Performance and the Politics of Culture;*

*Performance at the End of the Twentieth Century;*

*On Edge: Bodied Spaces Phenomenology and Performance in Contemporary Drama;*

*Performativity and Performance;*

*Performance and Cultural Politics;*

*Performance: a Critical Introduction;*

*The Explicit Body in Performance;*

*Performing Nostalgia: Shifting Shakespeare and the Contemporary Past;*

*From Acting to Performance.*

That this concentration of "performance" cognates is not just Routledge's corporate jargon is revealed by a review of the articles published in the same period, which are just as busy with "performance" and in which it is consorting with the same partners — the body, theory, feminism, politics and culture. A distinctive recent usage, shading off into the performative, opposes "performance" to "theatre," and though this "performance" is often situated within theatre, its primary site is so-called performance art, where it signifies something like acting minus roles. Of this kind of "performance," Josette Féral has said, "Performance is the absence of meaning. ... Performance is the death of the subject (173)." This important set of significations I am bracketing on the present occasion, with a view to taking it up in a later article. I am also going to no more than mention the honorific usage of the term "performance" whereby, like "art" formerly, it confers and claims a certain *cachet*.[16]

The immense range of extra-theatrical usages of the term is also relevant, and staggering to contemplate. In such contexts as athletics, government, manufacturing, motor racing and surgery, "performance" both signifies the relevant practices and their outputs. "Performance" is a measurement of such pragmatic or material results as legislation, sales, speed and ratings. The intrinsic forms and motivations of these practices, and the esthetic and conceptual responses to them are not seriously at issue, but their productivity is. That is to say, the criteria for these non-artistic performances tend to be different from those traditionally —though insecurely— associated with artistic ones.[17] But pragmatic and material outputs (and inputs) are by no means disregarded in artistic performances while, in non-artistic ones, the esthetic and conceptual aspects are also discernible, though frequently deemed irrelevant. And, saliently, there are tensions between the pragmatic/material and the esthetic/conceptual in both artistic and non-artistic performances.

The clearest examples of conflicting valuations seem to occur in athletic spectacles, in which the efficient and the esthetic are often contrary indicators. Here is an example from an account of a world championship boxing match of about fifty years ago:

> The entire orthodox world owes a debt to Benny Leonard. In all the other arts, philosophies, and what nots conservatism seems to be crum-

[16]In this context, it may be worth mentioning the particular usage that has been rather misleading attributed to "antitheatrical prejudice." An example readily to hand is Wole Soyinka's comment on recent treason charges against democracy activists in Nigeria. The outcome is already decided, he is reported as saying, but the Nigerian government will put on "an elaborate charade, a performance" (*Globe and Mail*, 17 March 1997, p. A7). As in many such usages, the negative valuation is not applied to theatre as such but to a theatrical invasion of what should be a distinct social practice. This will be found to be the case with many supposedly antitheatrical usages, which bring home the importance of theatre rather than antagonism to it. They carry their negative charge when applied to inappropriate objects just as religious terminology does. When worship, for instance, is extended beyond the accepted linguistic and social norms —to money or art, for example— it also encounters checks. But the linguistic constraints on the *performances* of, say, brokers and teachers are much weaker at present than those on the *worship* of dividends and learning.

[17]But this situation is complicated in an obvious and less obvious way. The less obvious is that the term "performance" itself elides the non-artistic and artistic phenomena; the more obvious that both kinds of criteria are used in both kinds of performance.

> bling before the attacks of the radicals. A stylist may generally be identified today by his bloody nose.
>
> Benny Leonard remains the white hope of the orthodox. No performer in any art has ever been more correct. He follows closely all the best traditions of the past. His left-hand jab could stand without revision in any textbook. The manner in which he feints, ducks, sidesteps, and hooks is unimpeachable. The crouch contributed by some modernists is not in the repertoire of Leonard. He stands up straight like a gentleman and a champion and is always ready to hit with either hand.
>
> Rocky Kansas does nothing according to rule. His fighting style is as formless as the prose of Gertrude Stein. One finds a delightfully impromptu quality in Rocky's boxing. Most of the blows which he tries are experimental. There is no particular target. Like the young poet who shot an arrow into the air, Rocky Kansas tosses off a right-hand swing every once and so often and hopes that it will land on somebody's jaw. But with the opening gong Rocky Kansas tore into Leonard ...

... and so on to the knockout. Perhaps you already know, or guess, who won. It was Leonard, with a beautifully-placed, highly-orthodox blow to the point of the jaw. "There's still a kick in style and tradition carries a nasty wallop," jubilated the aesthetically-inclined reporter.[18] What particularly makes for identifiable unease in such situations is the incontrovertible self-evidence of the scoring system when its results

[18]Heywood Broun. I thank my colleague Professor Bruce Kidd for drawing this passage to my attention and supplying the text, which is from "Three two-fisted sportswriters", his undated script for a CBL-CBC radio broadcast.
An opposite outcome of conflict between efficiency and style occurred in the Henley Regatta of 1950, in which the Harvard eight won the Grand Challenge Cup. Apart from the superstitious fears associated with a third Harvard victory following those of 1914 and 1939 —fears that were fulfilled by the outbreak of the Korean War— the remarkable and lasting impression left on this occasion was of a disturbing discorrespondence of rhythm and power. Instead of using "the long reach and lay back" of orthodox rowing style, which was supposed to produce maximum power in the boat, Harvard "confined the stroke as much as possible to leg drive with a ... minimum of body swing." Observers found this style graceless and alarmingly mechanical, and some were driven to the unhappy conclusion that "bodyswing was for practice but sitting-up was for racing." The Harvard win remained a confusing phenomenon for rowers and their coaches for years afterwards. Actual efficiency had both contradicted kinesiological theory and defied the traditional esthetic of the sport. See Dodd 1981:151-2, and *The Times*, July 10 1950:7.

are incongruent with such subjective valuations as appreciations of style or orthodoxy.[19]

In theatrical and other artistic performances, prizes have always been given to winners but other criteria are strongly operative, and indeed, prior. The prizes are an attempt to quantify the unquantifiable, and all "scoring" systems in the arts are held to be inexact and debatable. Even the box office tally is commonly supposed to be either not necessarily or necessarily not, a measure of excellence. But there are nevertheless all kinds of pragmatic, material and quantifiable features to which value and meaning will be ascribed: concrete aspects of the design; the ages, genders and races of the players; the economics of the production; the use or adaptation of a particular written text; the number of spectators walking out; the number of curtain calls; and the fact of a police presence.

From the discussion so far of performance and the performative I wish to draw two pairs of antinomies. One is "performative" ipseity as opposed to the marking of alterity in performance; the other is the reception of the performance according to either pragmatic/material or esthetic/conceptual criteria. Of course, these oppositions are predicated to structure discussion and are so far from being mutually exclusive in the theatre that the ways in which they are mixed will be major sources of energy and interest.

Let me give a concrete —or at least anecdotal— example of the paradigm as it was operative in a production of *A Midsummer Night's Dream* directed by Jill Dolan, a production that marked a transition in her thinking about authorizations of role-playing and indentity:

> At a public discussion of the production [Dolan relates] a lesbian from the Madison community complained that she didn't see any real "dykes" in the production, only straight women playing at it. One of the more earnest young cast members misunderstood her point and responded: "But I was gay. When I came out for the disco number, I was gay." And that's exactly the point. The young performer, probably for the first time in her life, wanted to be seen as a lesbian. Given the history of my own theorizing, I should have been unsettled by this exchange. After all, a straight woman was assuming the place I once might have insisted be saved for a "real", "live" lesbian body with its specific material, perhaps visual markings. But in the context of theatrical pedagogy my alliance was with the performer, who learned and desired to make visible somewhere on her own body a sexuality that representation usually

---

[19]Sports such as ice skating and gymnastics, in which scoring is not self-evident are, for that reason perhaps, highly politicised with respect to judging.

> elides. I learned that making these subject positions visible was more important to me than who inhabited them.[20]

The Madison lesbian, in this report, was looking for a performative ipseity within the performance and not finding it; while the young performer's criterion of performance was proficient representation of gay alterity (which, we note, is distinguishable from the real thing). Dolan sides with the actor but her alliance is qualified so as not to constitute general agreement about the performative function. In a *pedagogical* context, says Dolan, it is productive for the actor to learn to make visible "a sexuality", and this pragmatic use for the theatrical exercise now dislodges her earlier assumption about performative ipseity as authorization. Dolan also notes another definite value, which is both pragmatic and conceptual. This is that she herself has learned to be more concerned —at least in such a context as this— with the visibility of the subject position than with the identity of its agent. She now values the alterity of performance above performative ipseity and appears to be in agreement with Lessing in wanting (pedagogical) theatre "to bring back the symbolical of the moral to the visible" (as opposed to invisible abstract symbolism on the one hand and the social actualization of the moral on the other).[21] But all of this is subject to the qualification that it is specific to "pedagogical theatre" and would not necessarily apply to non-pedagogical theatre (or to non-theatrical pedagogy).

But just as my paradigm is oversimplified, so is Dolan's account of the issues involved in the production post-mortem. For one thing, it does not take into account the different subject positions and performance roles of the lesbian and the student as respectively spectator and actor; nor that what actually constituted the performance was already a negotiation between them. The elements in the question "whose performance, of what and for whom?" cannot readily be disentangled. It has become a commonplace of our discourse about theatre — one for which there are many earlier antecedents — that spectators and actors construct the performance together. And, from time to time, at least from Rousseau on, the complete mergence of the two functions has sometimes been proposed as the only foundation of a right theatre practice. Along with performative ipseity and the marking of alterity, the "community" —to employ the third Coleridgian term— of production and reception, bears strongly on authorization, which is continually be-

---

[20]Dolan 1993:157.
[21]Lessing 1962:17.

ing re-negotiated in theatre in terms of ipseity, alterity and community.

As to *what* is being performed, the Dolan anecdote is also revealing. Assuming that one of the answers is *A Midsummer Night's Dream*, this is not the given one, which is sexuality. But we would need to know much more about this production to have a good idea of what was being performed, for that was determined partly by for whom and how. Theseus observes of the mechanicals' production that "Our sport shall be to take what they mistake" (5,i,90). As the spectators always do to some degree, the mythical aristocrats of *A Midsummer Night's Dream* decide what is being performed for them.

But what is most fundamentally at issue in interrogating the *what* of the performance may be accounted for in relation to the basic disagreement of Derrida with Austin over the speech act performative. On the one hand, the *what* of the theatrical performance may be understood as an inescapably citational, decentered and discursive text (whether or not it has been scripted); on the other hand, it offers itself as a unique act (whatever its textual and discursive citationality) determined by the pragmatics of its social context, and, as such, instantiating its authors— or subjects. As between these two positions, what is chiefly at stake may be intimated by Judith Butler's attempt —as I take it to be— to reconcile them, though not in terms of theatre.

One of the motives for the essays collected in Butler's *Bodies That Matter*, and the one that most concerns me, is Butler's attempted clarification of certain misapprehensions about performativity that arose in the reception of her earlier book *Gender Trouble.* A bad reading of this book, which was also the most popular reading, went, says Butler:

> something like this: I can get up in the morning, look in my closet, and decide which gender I want to be today. I can take out a piece of clothing and change my gender, stylize it, and then that evening I can change it again and be something radically other, so that what you get is something like the commodification of gender, and the understanding of taking on gender as a kind of consumerism. ... [a volitional act] on the part of a subject who treats gender quite deliberately, as if it's an object out there, when my whole point was that the formation of subjects, the very formation of persons, *presupposes* gender in a certain way — that gender is not to be chosen and that "performativity" is not a radical choice and it's not voluntarism.[22]

It sounds almost as though Butler were distinguishing between the performance of gender and a performative ipseity of it. But if it is *perfor-*

---

[22]Butler 1992:83-4.

*mativity*, not a performance, that she wants, it is not an identity-based performativity such as that of the Madison lesbian in Dolan's anecdote. From Butler's point of view this would be an essentializing concession to a symbolic order that she does not wish to affirm.

So, though Butler makes a point of relating her performative to the speech act performative, it lacks Austin's anterior authorization, is only provisional and, like Derrida's utterance is decisively citational. Nevertheless, she claims for it a certain pragmatic value, or perhaps one should say requires it for certain pragmatic reasons.

> There are forms [she says] of citing and resignifying oppressive norms which are not necessarily theatrical; and though citation appears as an act of deference, it can be very aggressive and disconcerting. And I think Brecht understood this.[23]

In Butler's attempted reconciliation between discourse and performativity, the performative accumulates authority from previously authorized usages and thus becomes a mode of power, or force:

> If a performative [she says] provisionally succeeds (and I will suggest that "success" is always and only provisional), then it is not because an intention successfully governs the action of speech, but only because that action echoes prior actions, and *accumulates the force of authority through the repetition or citation of a prior, authoritative set of practices. ...* In this sense, no term or statement can function performatively without the accumulating and dissimulating historicity of force. [24]

In this way she has attempted to avert the threat posed by the performative of an ontological irruption into discursive constructions of meaning; but has attempted also to moderate the dissolution of the supposed subject into discursive citationality by her provisional performativity. Butler's context for this hybrid discursive-performative is a real-world that includes, as Derrida's does, the theatrical as a mode of citationality. But in the theatre, perhaps, there is no reason to introduce such a reconciliation, since the interest and pleasure so largely consist in the playing out of the ambivalences and contradictions of ipseity, alterity and community; of pragmatic and non-pragmatic receptions; and, above all, of discourse and performativity.

*University of Toronto*

---

[23]Butler 1992:89.
[24]Butler 1993:226-27.

## WORKS CITED

Auslander, Philip. 1997. *From Acting to Performance.* London and NY: Routledge.

Austin, J.L. 1975. *How to Do Things with Words,* 2nd ed., edited J.O. Urmson and Marina Sbisá. Cambridge, Mass.: Harvard University Press.

Barba, Eugenio and Nicola Savarese. 1991. *A Dictionary of Theatre Anthropology: The Secret Art of the Performer.* Translation by Richard Fowler of *Anatomia del teatro.* London and NY: Routledge.

Benveniste, Émile. 1966(F). *Problèmes de linguistique générale.* Paris: Gallimard.

Benveniste, Émile. 1971(E). *Problems in General Linguistic.* Translation by M.E. Meek. Coral Gables, Florida: University of Miami Press.

Bharucha, Rustom. 1993. *Theatre and the World: Performance and the Politics of Culture.* London & NY: Routledge.

Butler, Judith. 1990. *Gender Trouble: feminism and the subversion of identity.* London & NY: Routledge.

Butler, Judith. 1992. Interview with Liz Kotz. *Artforum,* 31:82-89.

Butler, Judith. 1993. *Bodies That Matter: on the discursive limits of "sex".* London & NY: Routledge.

Carlson, Marvin. 1996. *Performance: a critical introduction.* London & NY: Routledge.

Carr, C. 1994. *On Edge: Performance at the End of the Twentieth Century.* Middletown: Wesleyan University Press.

Case, Sue-Ellen, ed. 1990. *Performing Feminisms: Feminist Critical Theory and Theatre.* Baltimore: Johns Hopkins University Press.

Case, Sue-Ellen and Janelle Reinelt, ed. 1991. *The Performance of power: theatrical discourse and politics.* Iowa City : University of Iowa Press.

Coleridge, Samuel Taylor. 1990. *Table Talk,* Vol.1, ed. Carl Woodring. Princeton, NJ: Princeton University Press.

Derrida, Jaques. 1972(F). Signature événement contexte, in *Marges de la philosophie.* Paris: Editions de Minuit.

Derrida, Jaques. 1988 (E). *Limited Inc,* edited Gerald Graff. Northwestern University Press.

Diamond, Elin, ed. 1996. *Performance and Cultural Politics.* London& NY: Routledge.

Dodd, Christopher. 1981. *Henley Royal Regatta.* London: Stanley Paul.

Dolan, Jill. 1993. *Presence and Desire.* Ann Arbor: University of Michigan Press.

Fabian, Johannes. 1990. *Power and Performance.* Madison: University of Wisconsin Press.

Felman, Shoshana. 1980(F). *Le Scandale du corps parlant.* Paris: Editions du Seuil.

Felman, Shoshana. 1983(E). *The Literary Speech Act: Don Juan with J.L. Austin, or Seduction in Two Languages.* Translation by Catherine Porter. Ithaca, NY: Cornell University Press.

Féral, Josette. 1982. Performance and Theatricality: the Subject Demystified. *Modern Drama* 25,1:170-181.

Garner, Stanton B. jnr. 1994. *Bodied Spaces: Phenomenology and Performance in Contemporary Drama.* Ithaca: Cornell University Press.

*Globe and Mail.* March 17, 1997: A7.

Kershaw, Baz. 1992. *The Politics of Performance: radical theatre as cultural intervention.* London & NY: Routledge.

Lessing, G.E. 1962. *Hamburg Dramaturgy.* Translated by Helen Zimmern. NY: Dover.

Marinis, Marco de. 1993. *The Semiotics of Performance.* Translation by Áine O'Healy of *Semiotica del teatro: L'analisi testuale dello spettaculo.* Bloomington and Indianapolis: Indiana University Press.

Martin, Randy. 1990. *Performance as a Political Act: the Embodied Self.* NY: Bergin & Garvey.

Parker, Andrew and Eve Kofosky Sedwick. 1995. *Performativity and Performance.* London & NY: Routledge.

Reinelt, Janelle G. and Joseph R. Roach, ed. 1992. *Critical Theory and Performance.* Ann Arbor: University of Michigan Press.

Schechner, Richard and Willa Appel, ed. 1990. *By means of Performance: Intercultural Studies of Theatre and Ritual.* Cambridge: Cambridge University Press.

Sidnell, M.J. ed. 1991. *Sources of Dramatic Theory, Vol.1: Plato to Congreve.* Cambridge: Cambridge University Press.

Sidnell, Michael J. 1996. Performing Writing: Inscribing Theatre. *Modern Drama* 39:547-557.

*The Times.* July 10, 1950:7

Todorov, Tszvetzan. 1987. *The Conquest of America.* NY: Harper.

Williams, Raymond. 1958. *Culture and Society: 1780-1950* London: Chatto and Windus.

Williams, Raymond. 1989. *Keywords: a vocabulary of culture and society,* rev. and expanded. London: Fontana Press.

Wordsworth, William. 1977. *The Poems,* Vol. 1, edited John O. Hayden. Harmonsworth: Penguin Books.

# CZECH PERFORMANCE THEORY

Veronika Ambros

*[W]e cannot confuse ... the development of a given art with the history of culture or with that of ideology alone* (Mukařovský[1]

*Dedicated to the memory of František Galan (1946-1992), Miroslav Procházka (1942-1997) and Michael Quinn (1958-1994).*

"For us in the West the quality not only of the artist but also that of the audience is decisive" says one of the leading directors of the Czech avant-garde E. F. Burian in his 'Prague dramaturgy' (Burian, O, 1946: 78). Burian's concern about the audience indicates one of the key issues in the Czech theory of art that sees the work of art "as an *intermediary* (sign) between the creator and the community."

Other important questions with regard to performance theory are: the role of the text, the relationship between the dialogue and the monologue, the relationship between the actor and the dramatic character, theatrical and dramatic space, and between a human being and objects.

Although, all of them deserve a thorough examination, this presentation can only survey some of these ideas. Moreover, it will and can not offer either a national nor a singular performance theory but only several aspects of performance as examined by some theorists and practitioners of Czech drama and theater especially between the wars.

A few authors such as Herta Schmid, Keir Elam, Jiří Veltruský: František Deák, Miroslav Procházka, and Michael Quinn reviewed the theories of the Prague Linguistic Circle with respect to theater and drama.[2] Yet, none of them focused on the mutual relationship between theory and practice of the Czech avant-garde. Hence, even though the

1 Mukařovský, Jan. " An Attempt at a Structural Analysis of a Dramatic Figure" in Steiner, Peter, ed. *The Prague School. Selected Writings 1929-1946.* Austin, 1982, 171-177: 171 (LtN, 1931).

2 Quinn, Michael L., *The Semiotic Stage,* New York, Peter Lang, 1995; Veltrusk¥, Jiří, *Příspěvky k teorii divadla,* Praha, Divadelní ústav, 1994.

theoretical works serve here as a point of departure they will be complemented by case histories of directors Jindřich Honzl, Emil František Burian and Alfréd Radok.

The attempt to escape a simplifying national label has several reasons. Prague, as one of the important centers of Czech, German, and for a while Russian cultural life, was at the crossroads of traditions,[3] nations, trends,[4] and peoples. As Burian's statement indicates, in 1937 Czechoslovakia was considered to be safely rooted in the West. More specifically, during the existence of the first Czechoslovak Republic between 1918 and 1938, its art was inspired in Paris and Moscow, as well as in Berlin and Vienna.

The continuing intercultural exchange influenced both the art of that period and the thoughts about its nature as well. The Czech literary scholar Felix Vodička, speaks about two competing tendencies within the Czech cultural tradition: the "narrowing" and the "widening." *Narrowing* occurs whenever the nationalistic tendency prevails and the culture is concerned with its own tradition, the *widening* is typical of times in which the culture is responsive to a variety of external impulses.[5] The latter is characteristic of the period following the foundation of the new political construct called the I. Czechoslovak Republic in 1918.

An indication of this trend was the formation of the Prague Linguistic Circle in 1926. For instance, among the founding members was the representative of the Russian Formalism, the linguist and literary scholar Roman Jakobson. Another was his close friend "the forerunner of structural ethnography" Petr Bogatyrev,[6] who extended his examination of Russian folklore to Czech and Slovak folk theater. It was also Bogatyrev, who carried over "the concept of language phenomena to art" (Deák, 1976: 90).

The Czech writer Milada Součková remarked on the cosmopolitan quality of the Circle: "Seldom was Czech without an accent heard. The guests from abroad added to the linguistic confusion." They brought with them "the air of the great intellectual world. Semantics, semiotics and phenomenology moved in the forefront of the scientific vocabulary" (Součková in Matejka, Sound, 1976: 2n.).

---

3 Veltrusky:, Jiří, Sémiologie a avantgardní divadlo, *Příspěvky k teorii divadla,* Praha , Divadelní ústav, 25-33, 1994: 27.

4 Mukařovský, Jan "On the Current State of the Theory of Theater"in Steiner, Peter, ed. *The Prague School. Selected Writings 1929-1946*. Austin, 1982.

5 Vodička Felix. "Kategorie Kontinuity." *Plamen* 7 (1965): 47-53.

6 (Součková in Matejka, Sound, 1976: 4). i. Matejka, Ladislav, ed.: 1976. Sound, Sign and Meaning. Quinquage: 552.

While the Russian Formalists derived their theories from poetry as the dominant literary genre of the Russian avant-garde (Majakovskij and Xlebnikov in particular), their Czech colleagues paid special attention to drama and theater. The reasons for this interest were manifold. The traditional role of the Czech theater was that of a substitute for a political arena. After 1918, however, the Czech stage opened up to all kinds of artistic experiments. Just the list of the set designers, composers, choreographers reads as a version of who is who in modern Czech art (Vl. Hofman, J. Seifert, V. Nezval, K.Teige, F. Štýrský).

This is especially true of the *Osvobozené divadlo* [*The Liberated Theater*] which the avant-garde group Devětsil founded in 1925 as a playhouse of *Poetism*[7]. This distinctly Czech trend, in which elements of Dada and Surrealism were mingled, declared art for "modus vivendi."[8] According to Jarka Burian: "The Soviet influence was mainly evident in staging,[9] the French in texts."[10] In addition, the repertoire of *Osvobozené divadlo* illustrates the Czech-French connection. The theater began with an adaptation of Molière called *Circus Dandin* (1926), continued with Ribemont-Dessaignes' play the *Dumb Canary* (1926), Apollinaire's *Tieresia's Breasts* (1917; 1927) and Jarry's *Ubu Roi* (1896; 1928).

Between 1927 and 1938 the *Liberated Theater* became synonymous with the work of Jiří Voskovec and Jan Werich. The theater was unique with regard to the subject of the dramatist. Instead of a singular author there were first two and later on even three involved, since the musician Jaroslav Ježek contributed greatly to the popularity of the theater. They acted in their own revues which consisted of a blend of nonsense texts, cabaret sketches, songs and dances. Jakobson reflected on the specific character of this stage by analyzing the ways in which both leading comedians of this theater Voskovec and Werich produced 'švanda' [fun].[11]

---

[7] Michael Schoenberg wrote a lengthy study about this theater. Schoenberg, Michael. *Osvobozené divadlo*. Toronto, Sixty-Eight Publishers, !988.

[8] More to Poetism and *Osvobozené divadlo* in Ambros, Veronika, "Vest Pocket Revue" reviewed, *Zeitschrift für Slawistik*, 457-463, 1993.

[9] The first group of prominent Czech artists (J. Honzl, Jaroslav Seifert, Karel Teige, Bohumil Mathesius) travelled to Moscow in 1925. Obst, Scherl

[10] While the knowledge of Russian art was often based on hearsay, the contacts with French art emerged as direct communication between the French and Czech artists (Breton, Šíma, Kupka, Apollinaire).

[11] It originally appeared as a contribution to a collection of articles celebrating the first decade of the *Osvobozené Divadlo* [Liberated Theater]. Jakobson, Roman. "An Open Letter to Jiří Voskovec and Jan Werich on the Epistemology

Another innovation of the Czech theater is connected with the person of the composer, director, author and actor E. F. Burian. Influenced by jazz, Burian attempted to parallel the music by using human voice as an instrument. In 1928 at a festival in Sienna he successfully presented his *voice-band*, a group of actors reciting poetry, "wedding of poetic text and musical expression" (Burian, 1976: 96). The *voice-band* replaced the chorus in several plays.

From the outset of his career as a director Burian strove to create a *composite* theater which presented "a mixture of language, movement, light, and music."[12] As Piscator and Honzl before him, Burian too disrupted the theatrical illusion by projecting film clips showing for instance the charts of the unemployed. Later on, however, his use of film underscored the lyrical tendency of the performance so that paraphrasing Brecht's epic theater Burian's staging can be dubbed as lyric theater[13]. This applies in particular to the so called *Theatregraph* a combination of film and actors, a predecessor of the famous *Magic Lantern* [*Laterna Magica*] created by Burian's disciple the director Alfréd Radok in the nineteen fifties.

Jarka Burian describes Burian's invention:

> The chief technical innovation was the use of a scrim covering the entire front of the stage and serving as the primary projection surface. The technical essence of *Theatregraph* was the simultaneous vision of projected images on the frontal scrim with live action behind it. You could not tell, finally, whether the live actors were in front, behind, or simply part of the projected image, enveloped in it. The images were not simply illustrational or information (Burian, 1976: 107n).

When Burian himself claims that the: "Filmed stage projection is a spatial concern, non-illustrational and non naturalistic" he also criticizes Piscator for using film to supplement the stage scenery (Burian, 1946: 52). In contrast, Burian's use of projection was often metonymic as in the case of Wedekind's *Spring Awakening*. Wendla's eyes as a blown up detail accompanied the dialogue of her parents and a bud and flowers were shown when focusing on Wendla herself.

Both theaters served as a point of departure or means of illustration for several theoretical aspects of performance. Jan Mukařovský, for instance, is a case in point: To support his thesis that the role of the

---

and Semantics of Fun," in Quinn, "Jakobson and the Liberated Theater", *Stanford Slavic Studies*, 1, 1987.

[12]Liehm, A. J., 1972: 73.

[13]Adolf Scherl describes the 'lyrisizing' tendency of Burian's work of the late thirties in Obst, Scherl.

actor can be assumed by another component in his lecture on the present state of theater theory in 1941 Mukařovský: refers to Burian's staging of *The Barber of Seville* where "the flickering of the light and changes in its color connected with the howling of the storm expressed the people's revolt" (Mukařovský in Steiner, 1982: 208). Furthermore, Burian's adaptation of a prose work by the Czech author Viktor Dyk provoked Mukařovský's theories of dialogue and monologue. Bogatyrev on the other hand, was instrumental in E. F. Burian's staging of Czech folk plays. And Jakobson's article on semantics of fun is applicable to Poetism as well as to the theater of the absurd.[14]

Moreover, as Jiří Veltruský claims, the art of the avant-garde was created by artists for an artistic audience.[15] Yet, it was far from being elitist. On the contrary the artists and theorists shared the leftist bent[16] prevalent among the Czech intellectuals of the thirties. Burian himself opened his theater to exhibitions of young artists and public lectures by prominent actors and theorists. In fact, one of Mukařovský's most important contributions, the already mentioned lecture on the state of contemporary theater, was prepared for this occasion and drew its examples from the practice of Burian's theater.[17]

Although the Czech avant-garde theater had already begun to flourish in the twenties, the Prague Linguistic Circle turned to questions of theater and drama only in the thirties. One of the reasons for this sudden interest was the book *Estetika dramatického umění* [*Aesthetics of Dramatic Art*, 1931] in which the esthetician Otakar Zich presented a comprehensive theory of dramatic art. It inspired the theorists of the Prague Circle and provoked their ideas about drama and theater.

What Zich calls dramatic art is a sum of dramatic works (i.e., performances). According to him a dramatic work is "what we perceive (see and hear) during the performance in theater." This presentation is a "real action, performed by real people, in a real space and real time" (Zich, Estetika, 1986: 14; 62).[18]

To Zich the dramatic text is a catalogue [soupis] of speeches, to be spoken by specific *dramatis personae* (Zich, 1986: 74). Stage directions are merely seen as instructions which the author would use to secure his

---

[14]Ambros, Veronika. "Fictional World and Dramatic Text: Václav Havel's Descent and Ascent." *Style* 25.2 (1991): 310-19.

[15](Veltruský Sémiologie 1994: 27)

[16]Burian's theater, for instance, was organized as a co-op.

[17](Mukařovský Structure, 1978: 201-219)

[18]Herein Zich came close to the ideas of his Polish colleague Roman Ingarden. Although *Das literarische Kunstwerk* [The Literary Work of Art, 1931] was published in the same year as Zich's work, Ingarden's appendix on dramatic art was added only to the 1960 edition.

interior vision (Zich, 1986: 72). Zich claims that for any true playwright the dramatic art exists as a theater performance, more correctly as his vision of it. A similar process would be typical of the spectator who perceives the persona of the actor and 'creates' a dramatic persona.[19] Zich distinguishes between the actor's figure and the dramatic persona (which is formed through the perception of the observer). In view of its latent semiotic tendency the editors of Zich's book rephrase it as the difference between the sign and its reference, that is, meaning (Zich, 1986: 341). The actor's figure unites two types of expectations [představa] a technical one based on the knowledge of the actor's craft and a pictorial [imaginary] representing someone or something (Zich, 1986: 43).

Zich's analytic theory considers dramatic art a fusion of different arts into a new single art rather than a collection or synthesis of the already well known arts (Zich, 1986: 35). Zich refutes the independent status of the dramatic text as a work of art. In spite of this and the fact that Zich based his theory on exclusively realistic material, which limited the importance of his contribution, his work has been extremely stimulating especially for the younger generation. As Miroslav Procházka remarks, although Zich did not use the word sign, his work, which is essentially semiotic, Mukařovský's prepared the way for the semiotics of theater.[20]

The interest in semiotics and semantics distinguishes the Prague School from Russian Formalism. In the words of Jan Mukařovský: "structuralism superseded Formalism in conceiving the structure as a set of signs"[21] (Zich, 1986: 78). To Bogatyrev the national costume, like a house, is "not only a thing but also a sign of the nationality, the economic status, the religion, and so on, of its owner." (Matejka, 1976: 33) Mukařovský expanded this notion of the sign to art in general, when

[19](Zich, 1986: 45; 104 (The dramatic person is a result of a synthesis achieved by the audience: 2 are demonstrative 1. the static one: through appearance and dress 2. dynamic: through behaviour and speech, 2. cognitive [myšlenková] 3. textual: trough language.

[20]M. Procházka "U základů semiotiky divadla, II. Sémiotická témata v české meziválečné teatrologii." in *Wiener Slawistischer Almanach*, Bd. 5, 1980:117-144, 117.

[21]Jan Mukařovský "Structuralism in Esthetics and in Literary Studies" in Steiner, Peter, ed. *The Prague School. Selected Writings 1929-1946*. Austin: University of Texas Press, 1982: 65-82.<1941>

he said: "A work of art draws attention because it is a thing and a sign at the same time."[22]

Towards the end of the thirties the journal of the Prague School *Slovo a Slovesnost* [Word and Verbal Art] published a number of articles dealing with crucial questions of drama and performance. The budding theory of performance and drama, however, was not merely a domain of theorists. Directors Burian and Jindřich Honzl (who directed many of the plays in *Osvobozené divadlo*) challenged the traditional understanding of theater not only on stage but also in their articles.

Among the most prolific young scholars was Jiří Veltruský who entered his polemics with Zich's theories in 1941 at the age of 22. Conversely to Zich's position on the dramatic text, Veltruský: states:

> Drama is a work of literature in its own right; it does not need anything but simple reading to enter the consciousness of the public. At the same time, it is a text that can, and mostly is intended to, be used as the verbal component of theatrical performance.[23]

Furthermore, he develops Zich's idea that the stage directions introduce the vision of the author.[24] Veltruský distinguishes between the dialogical and extra-dialogical[25] part of the dramatic text. Dramatic dialogue is, according to him, both a sequence of utterances made by two or several alternating speakers and an utterance of a single speaker, the author (Veltruský, Drama, 1977). With regard to performance, the directions indicate how the action is distributed throughout a play.

In theatrical performance, these notes are eliminated, and the resulting gaps in the unity of the text are filled by other than linguistic signs. This is not an arbitrary process but essentially a matter of transposing linguistic meanings into other semiotic systems (Matejka, 1976: 96).

---

22 Jan Mukařovský "Záměrnost a nezáměrnost v umění" *Studie z estetiky*. Praha: Odeon, 1966: 92 a. 98. <1943>

23 Veltruský, "Dramatic Text as a Component of Theater"in Matejka, *Semiotics,* 1976: 94-117, 95.

24 (Veltruský, Drama, 1977) orig. in 1942 .Dramatic dialogue is both a sequence of utterances made by two or several alternating speakers and an utterance of a single speaker, the author. (Veltruský, Drama, 1977)

25 Although Veltruský was the first to emphasize this distinction as a specific quality of dramatic text, it was much later that this naming of the two parts was suggested by E.M. Dam-Havelková in her study "In Between a Play and a Story: Smoček's Piknik" in Steiner, P., Červenka, M. and R. Vroon <eds>, *The Structure of the Literary process*, Studies dedicated to the Memory of Felix Vodička, LLSEE , Amsterdam; Philadelphia, Benjamins, 8, 1982: 62-93.

[T]he author's annotations fulfill the most elementary condition of the semantic unification of the dialogue, which no drama can dispense with. It is not the direct speeches themselves nor any of their components that indicate which speech is allotted to whom, so providing information without which the reader could not follow the thread of the dialogue, but the speaker's name which the author puts before the speeches (Veltruský, Drama, 1977: 40n.).

This deictic character of the extradialogical text is one of the stable characteristics of a dramatic text. According to Jindřich Honzl "verbal deixis serves as a semantic filter that enables the dramatist to create an image of the world and of people (...). Such a semantic filter, which does not admit images undesired by the dramatist, alters the profile of those real elements out of which the representation of a human being and his behavior is created in a play."

While in a realistic play the stability of a character is questioned only in case of false or mistaken identity, in modern theater in which one sign can replace another, the notion of stability gains importance with respect to what Honzl calls "dynamics of signs in the theater" particularly typical of avant-garde performance. Honzl claims that "[t]he constancy of a structure causes theatrical signs to develop complex meaning" (Matejka, 1976: 79).

Conversely, as Karel Brušák described, the text is of "little significance" in the Chinese theater that developed a set of stable signs.[26] "The conventional *action sign* never aims at imitation of reality. An action sign ... owes its final form to a tension between the aesthetic function and other functions communicative, expressive ...." (Matejka, 1976: 67). Brušák uses the term *functions* introduced by contemporary linguists (Karl Bühler) with respect to language, thus suggesting that the signs employed in Chinese theater build a system close to a linguistic one.

The first time Mukařovský dealt with the linguistic aspects of dialogue was in a brief introduction to the Program of Burian's theater in 1937. There Mukařovský refers to Burian's remark about the contemporary resurrection of the Wagnerian concept of theater as a synthesis of different arts. According to Mukařovský modern stage works

---

[26]Based on his research of the Chinese theater Karel Brušák distinguishes between the dramatic and the action space:"The visual side of any dramatic performance apprehended by the spectator can be termed dramatic space."

The action space is "a nomaterial and transitory fictitious space conjured up by the movement of actors, by the movements and color changes of light, by the moving images of film" (Brušák, "Signs in the Chinese Theater" Matejka, 1976: 59-73; 60)

would absorb anything modern technique introduces. As a result, the old stability vanished without having been replaced by a new one. Modern dialogue plays with semantic shifts. Since it does not have a particular purpose, it becomes stage poetry. Later, when he examined Karel åapek's prose and drama Mukařovský turned to a more general analysis of the topic.[27] According to him Čapek's graphic organization, and in particular the use of dashes, indicate the intonation and therefore the relationship of the characters to one another. In some cases, however, the same grapheme may emphasize the underlying lyrical tendency of the utterances.

In another article (1941) Mukařovský discusses dialogue as the confrontation of different "contextures" and "semantic reversals...on the boundaries of the individual replies."[28] These require 1. the existence of polarity expressed in the personal deixis as 'I' and 'you' and the possessive pronouns, 2. the relationship between the interlocutors and the situation surrounding them, presented in temporal and spatial deixis such as 'here' and 'now' 3. a shared topic is necessary to achieve semantic unity. The distribution of these elements characterizes different types of dialogue such as an argument (contradiction between 'I' and 'you'), the exchange about a situation and a conversation. Abstract as these ideas might seem, they offer themselves as very useful tools for the dramaturge and the critic who compares the text with the performance. Veltruský supplemented Mukařovský's theory with an important additional feature:

> Dialogue ... differs from monologue in that it unfolds not only in time but also in space. The constantly changing 'here and now' may be called the extralinguistic situation of the dialogue. The intense relationship between the dialogue and the extralinguistic situation is reflected in the vocabulary of the dialogue (Matejka, 1976: 129).

In addition to the abovementioned graphic separation into a dialogical and an extradialogical part of the text, the distinction between the audience and dramatic space is yet another constant with regard to the theatrical performance. According to Honzl what separates theater

---

[27]Mukařovský, Jan, "K. Čapek's Prose as Lyrical Melody and as Dialogue", Garvin, Paul L., *A Prague school Reader on Esthetics, Literary Structure, and Style,* Georgetown, Georgetown UP, 133-149, 1964 <1939>.

[28] Pfister, Manfred, *The Theory and Analysis of Drama,* Cambridge, Cambridge UP, 1991: 128 <1977; 1988>.

from ritual is the fact that a ritual has participants and no spectators.[29]
Based on the assumption that "all the relationships between stage figures and characters are projected into space" Veltruský sees as dramatic space "a set of immaterial relations that constantly changes in time as these relations themselves change." (Matejka, 1976: 97)[30] Unlike Zich who sees the stage as the place "where plays and operas are performed" Honzl states that "the stage can be represented by any real space." Moreover, he introduces the sound of axes cutting down the *Cherry Orchard* (Matejka, 1976: 76) as an example of an acoustic, non spatial denotation of the stage.

Referring to contemporary Russian directors Honzl claims that their constructivist arrangement often "failed to create an unambiguous sign." Describing a performance directed by Tairov in which the props denote different spaces, Honzl arrives at the following conclusion: "The sign (representative) function of the scenery and props is determined solely by the movements of the actor and by the manner he uses them..." (Matejka, 1976: 78). Hence a practicable can denote a boat on the lake or a swing in the park, an ornament replaces the furniture of a salon. In Burian's presentation of the classical Czech romantic poem *May* the changed light denoted a different space.

The interchangeability between the object and human beings is a recurrent topic of some authors which echoes some of the current stage experiments. Comparable to Burian who tested the musical quality of speech, Honzl used human bodies to present the text. For instance in *Tieresia's Breasts* by Apollinaire (1927) he transformed actors into letters. The different combinations of the letters created different verses" (Matejka, 1976: 85).

The fact that René Wellek and Roman Jakobson had to leave the country after 1938 foreshadowed the devastating effects of the German occupation on Czech culture. The Prague Linguistic Circle that continued its activity throughout the war, ceased to exist after 1948 when Czechoslovakia became a part of the so called Eastern Bloc.[31] Although the tenets of the Circle were repeatedly attacked in Czechoslovakia, its influence on the Czech post-war theater as much

---

[29]"Ritual and Theater" in Steiner, Peter, ed. *The Prague School. Selected Writings 1929-1946.* Austin, 1982: 135-173.

[30]According to Honzl "a stage can equally well be represented by any real space" (Matejka, 1976: 76).

[31]This notion was contested in the eighties by three authors and thinkers representing the idea and tradition of Central Europe — György Konrád, Czesław Miłosz and Milan Kundera.

as that of the avant-garde was palpable. This is particularly true of the scenographer Josef Svoboda and Burian's pupils, the directors Otomar Krejča and Alfred Radok.[32] While Krejča managed to create his theater, Radok had to move from stage to stage. After 1968 Krejča directed either abroad or in small town theaters. Radok emigrated to Sweden, where his experiments were subject to hard criticism. Of the three only Svoboda's works received critical acclaim both in Prague and abroad. In contrast, Radok, who put first Czech film, then theater back on the map of European stage, seems to be falling into oblivion.

The work of the Prague Linguistic Circle was 'resurrected' by a new generation of scholars[33] in Prague in the sixties and suppressed again after 1968. In the newly defined 'West,' Prague School theories served as a base for semiotics of drama and theater as presented by Herta Schmid,[34] Keir Elam and Patrice Pavis. Other theorists, however, though they call themselves structuralists, seem to be oblivious to the history. Their use of the term structuralism is limited exclusively to the ideas of the French theorists of the sixties. This is particularly true of Richard Hornby's and Susan Melrose's[35] works. In her book on semiotics of dramatic text Melrose dismisses Mukařovský's notion of sign, because he is "Theater critics and teachers might protest — not telling us anything new at all."

In contrast, Michael Quinn's book *The Semiotic Stage,* accentuates the need to look at Czech performance practice and theory as an important phase in the development of theater studies.[36] Moreover, it reveals that along with their contributions to the general theory of aesthetics and to literary history, their thoughts on theater and drama are among the most important accomplishments of the Circle.

Admittedly, the reception of the Prague Linguistic Circle has been impeded by the fact that some of the works such as Zich's groundbreak-

---

[32]"Experiment is a duty" Svoboda, Josef. "Mošnosti potřeby", *Divadlo,* 7, 7-11, 1967: 8.

[33]Among the most important were M. Červenka, L. Doležel, M. Jankovič, J. Levý.

[34]The collection of theories of drama compiled by the German scholar Herta Schmid together with her Dutch colleague Aloysius van Kesteren included studies by Mukařovský Veltruský and Honzl. Schmid herself drew attention to the Prague school contribution in her introductory study. Kesteren, Aloysius van, Schmid, Herta <eds>, *Moderne Dramentheorie.* Kronberg /Ts.München, Scriptor, 1975.

[35]It is her only reference to the Prague School. Melrose, Susan. *A Semiotics of the Dramatic Text,* Houndmills, Macmillan, 1994.

[36]In the English speaking word his work fulfills a similar function as Herta Schid's had in Germany of the seventies.

ing book have not been translated into English.[37] Other texts were scattered in several publications. As a result, their terminology is often inconsistent and volatile.

In his review of Structuralism in theater, František Deák is certainly right when he arrives at the conclusion that there are "no examples of structuralist analysis of actual performance." Yet, as I attempted to illustrate, the works of the Prague School refer to each other as much as to the practice of the theaters. Even if they do not propose a comprehensive performance and drama theory, the dispersed articles, essays, and certain elements of the staging itself point to a system of thoughts about theater. In this regard the title of this article should read: Czech Performance and Theory — Mutual Attraction.

*University of Toronto*

## WORKS CITED

Ambros, Veronika. "Vest Pocket Revue" reviewed, *Zeitschrift für Slawistik*, 457-463, 1993.

____. "Fictional World and Dramatic Text: Václav Havel's Descent and Ascent." *Style* 25.2 (1991): 310-19.

Burian E. F. "Příspěvek k problému jevištní mluvy" *Slovo a Slovesnost*, 5, 24-32)

____. *O nové divadlo. 1930-1940.* Praha, ústav pro učebné pomuæcky prů æmyslový:ch a odbornych škol v Praze, sv. 6, 1946.

Burian, Jarka. "E. F. Burian: D34-D4" *The Drama Review*, 20, 4, December, 95-116, 1976.

Deák, František. "Structuralism in Theatre: The Prague School Contribution." *The Drama Review*, 20, 4, December, 83-94, 1976.

Dam-Havelková, E.M. "In Between a Play and a Story: Smoček's Piknik" in Steiner, P., Červenka, M. and R. Vroon <eds>, *The Structure of the Literary process*, Studies dedicated to the Memory of Felix Vodička, LLSEE, Amsterdam; Philadelphia, Benjamins, 8, 1982: 62-93.

Hedbávný, Z. *Alfréd Radok.* Praha, 1995.

Honzl, J. "Herecká postava", *Slovo a slovesnost*, 145 -150, 1939.

____ ."Ritual and Theater" in Steiner, Peter, ed. *The Prague School. Selected Writings 1929-1946.* Austin, 1982: 135-173.

---

[37]This is for instance the case of E.F. Burian's "Contribution to to the problem of stage discourse" (Burian, E. F."Příspěvek k problému jevišní mluvy" *Slovo a Slovesnost*, 5, 24-32) and Honzl's "The Actor's Figure" (Honzl, Jindřich, Herecká postava , *Slovo a slovesnost*, 145 -150, 1939).

Jakobson, Roman. "An Open Letter to Jiří Voskovec and Jan Werich on the Epistemology and Semantics of Fun," in Quinn, "Jakobson and the Liberated Theater", *Stanford Slavic Studies*, 1, 1987: 155-162.

Kesteren, Aloysius van, Schmid, Herta <eds>. *Moderne Dramentheorie*. Kronberg /Ts.München, Scriptor, 1975.

Liehm, A. J. "Theatre in Czechoslovakia." *Theatre Quarterly*:» 2 (Apr.-June 1972: 72-79.

Matejka, Ladislav, and Irwin R. Titunik, eds. *Semiotics of Art: Prague School Contributions*. Cambridge, Mass.: MIT P, 1976.

Mukařovský Jan. *Kapitoly z české poetiky*, Praha, Svoboda, 1948.

____. "Záměrnost a nezáměrnost v umění" in *Studie z estetiky*. Praha: Odeon, 1966: 92- 98. <1943>

____. "K. Čapek's Prose as Lyrical Melody and as Dialogue" in, Garvin, Paul L., *A Prague School Reader on Esthetics, Literary Structure, and Style*, Georgetown, Georgetown UP, 133-149, 1964 <1939>.

____. *Structure, Sign and Function. Selected Essays by Jan Mukařovský*:. Burbank, John, Peter Steiner, ed. New Haven: Yale UP, 1977.

____. "Dialog a Monolog." *Studie z poetiky*. Praha: Odeon, 1982. 208-29.

Obst, Milan and Scherl, Adolf. *K dějinám české divadelní avantgardy. Jindřich Honzl - E.F. Burian*. Praha, Nakladatelství Československé akademie věd, 1962.

Pfister, Manfred. *The Theory and Analysis of Drama*, Cambridge, Cambridge UP, 1991 <1977; 1988>.

Procházka, M. "U základů semiotiky divadla, II. Sémiotická témata v české meziválečné teatrologii." *Wiener Slawistischer Almanach*, Bd. 5, 1980:117-144.

____. *Znaky dramatu a divadla*. Prague, Panorama, 1988.

Quinn, Michael L. *The Semiotic Stage*, New York, Peter Lang, 1995.

____. "Jakobson and the Liberated Theater", *Stanford Slavic Studies*, 1, 1987: 153-155.

Scherl, Adolf. *Emil František Burian*. Berlin: Henschelverlag, 1966.

Schoenberg, Michael. *Osvobozené divadlo*. Toronto, Sixty-Eight Publishers, !988.

Steiner, Peter, ed. *The Prague School. Selected Writings 1929-1946*. Austin, 1982.

Svoboda, Josef. "Mošnosti potřeby", *Divadlo*, 7, 1967: 7-11.

Veltruský, Jiří. *Příspĭčvky k teorii divadla*, Praha, Divadelní ústav, 1994.

____. "Dramatic Text as a Component of Theater" in Matejka, Semiotics, 1976: 94-117.

____. "Theatre In the Corridor," *The Drama Review*, 84, 4, 67-80, 1979.

Vodička Felix. "Kategorie Kontinuity." *Plamen* 7 (1965): 47-53.

Zich, Otakar. *Estetika dramatického umìní*. Praha: Panorama, 1986.

# JIKKAN, ANOTHER WAY OF SEEING: PERFORMANCE ETHNOGRAPHY IN JAPAN[1]

Frank Hoff

An alumnus of Waseda University, Honda Yasuji returned in 1949 to teach. In the meantime, he had been a secondary school teacher for twenty years in the northeastern (Tohoku) area of Honshu close to many of the performing arts discussed below. On his return to Waseda, he met Gunji Masakatsu (1913 - ), a specialist in kabuki. By sharing the first-hand knowledge of what he was seeing in the countryside, Honda directed the younger scholar's eye to current rural folk performance. These revealed a striking number of characteristics shared with noh and kabuki, connections that were only beginning to be understood at the time. Gunji acknowledges his indebtedness to Honda in the afterword of his *Kabuki: Styles and Tradition* (1954).[2] The Honda-Gunji friendship (the two lived as neighbors in Tokyo for a while) could be regarded as responsible in part for a new departure in kabuki scholarship in the postwar period.

---

[1] Originally the second chapter of a book manuscript, this article has been prepared for independent publication here and material on Orikuchi Shinobu (1887 - 1953) [Japanese personal names throughout are given in the traditional way, last name first] has been added. About the performance ethnography of Honda Yasuji (1906 - ), the book includes, as well as background material, a translation of selections from his travel diaries to give a concrete example of what travel and research in the countryside was like in the 1930s.

'Jikkan' (*jitsu*, real, true, actual; *kan*, feeling, sensation) is defined by one Japanese dictionary as the feeling, sensation, that arises when one comes into contact with the real thing, as opposed to imagining or speculating about it from a distance, as a scholar might in his study for example. Orikuchi and scholars writing about him tend to give this word —widely used in normal speech and writing without much precision, one imagines— a special meaning. My essay emphasizes jikkan as the sensation that arises from a particular experience, seeing performance. But there were other ways, as well, in which Orikuchi felt he came into direct awareness of the actual thoughts and feelings of people of the past, in particular, the 'early period' (*kodai*). He believed that these experiences, as well, had the potential of elucidating or verifying his scholarly speculations.

[2] Gunji Masakatsu, *Kabuki: yoshiki to densho* (Tokyo: Nara Shobo, 1954).

The two looked at performance in different ways, however. In his scholarship of the period, Gunji sought an indigenous prototype for the performing arts of Japan. From festive parades through folk theater, kabuki, noh and even the Imperial enthronement ceremony, he traced a thread to what he then regarded as uniquely Japanese characteristics, beliefs and practices in everyday life. Honda, on the other hand, aimed to study the histories of specific countryside performance traditions that had survived into the early part of the twentieth century; he also found links between these and noh and kabuki. Much of his work involved collecting traditional texts, closely documenting performance, and questioning performers and other members of local communities. A predecessor, Orikuchi Shinobu relied with a passion on the actual experience of seeing performance to bring to life his research and writing on folklore, including countryside performance. In part, he aimed to understand, through his own —often quite physical— experiences, what, in fact, the ancient period (*kodai*) was really like. The different ways these three had of looking led to differences in their practice of performance ethnography.

* * *

On 23 July 1954, Honda and Gunji saw kagura at the Takuhi Shrine on the island of Oki, off the coast of Shimane Prefecture. Within three months, a brief report of the visit written by Gunji appeared in print.[3] Honda's account is included in a published description of a longer trip of his own, 15 to 29 July.[4] Worked up from field notes and first published in November 1954 in the periodical *Performing Arts Revived*, the latter includes an account of the Gion festival and other performances. Honda describes the climax of his visit to Oki:

> Finally, we climb to the top of the mountain.... A spectacular view spreads out below Mount Takuhi. It is justly praised, for from the shrine a single glance encompasses mountains and the sea beyond. Breath-takingly it opens out from a room in the shrine building used for kagura. Sacred decorations are nearly in place, a canopy hangs above the center of the room, and wooden shelving, on which *kami* [power] will be invoked, is set up on all four sides. Food offerings are made in the *gakuya* [place for preparation or where drums are placed]. This is the setting for the

3 'Oki no hitoyo,' insertion, in eds. Honda Yasuji and Gunji Masakatsu, *Minzoku geino* (*Dento geijutsu koza IV*) (Tokyo: Kawade Shobo, 1954) pp. 4-7.

4 Honda Yasuji, *Minzoku geino saihoroku* (Tokyo: Nihon hoso shuppan kyokai, 1971) (hereafter, abbreviated as *Saihoroku*) pp. 212-27.

> great *shime kagura*, which goes on from evening until the next morning. Instead of electric lights, acetylene gas is used. Some sixty or seventy worshippers, drowsing or gazing intently at what is going on, huddle together in a room next to the one used for kagura. It reminds me of kagura at Horohayama.[5]
>
> Meanwhile, in a separate shrine there is a ritual held for the vigil of the festival. Here, too, older performers dance. To me the whole ceremony, over at dawn, seems like a dream. Had I only one observation to make, I would say that bobbing up and down in the miko [shamaness] dances and techniques used in noh here are very much like Yamabushi kagura.[6] Without a doubt, ancient noh was performed at Oki even before sacred noh were seen at Sada.[7] After the drinking and eating that conclude the ceremony, performers go down the mountain again.[8]

Gunji's account of the same visit includes these comments:

> As night deepens, the excitement of people gathering together grows. Cries of praise from spectators, like *iro-otoko* [you sexy man], increasingly rain down on the dancers ... People on all sides clap hands rhythmically, singing together what sounds like kagura songs. Young men's hips sway like jazz dancers. Two eddies of dance begin, one in the kagura-den [building or place where kagura is performed], another among onlookers. I am bewildered. It is uncanny, the sense alive here that kagura is an occasion of mutual camaraderie between uproarious gods and life, what is expressed, in a verse of ancient Japanese, as '*ana tanoshi sasa*' [Ah, how joyful. *Sasa*]. Yes, performance does suddenly take flight, leaving behind the ordinary dimensions of space and time within which we normally live. The sudden wonder of it all wings us beyond boundaries of space

---

5 'Kagura' is a popular name for many rural performances. As a term in Honda's classification system it is one of several major performance types. Frank Hoff, 'Kagura', *Encyclopedia of Japan* (Tokyo: Kodansha, 1983) vol. 4, pp. 106-8. Horohayama is a place in the Tohoku. Kagura performed there is an example of a type known, in Honda's system, as 'shimotsuki kagura.'

6 'Yamabushi kagura,' performed extensively in several provinces of the Tohoku, is a sub-type of kagura in Honda's classification system. Irit Averbuch, *The Gods Come Dancing: A Study of the Japanese Ritual Dance of Yamabushi Kagura*, (Ithaca, New York: Cornell University East Asia Program, 1995). The format taken when the findings of Honda's extensive study of Yamabushi kagura in the 1930s were published is discussed in the book manuscript mentioned in note #1.

7 'Sacred noh at Sada' refers to a part of the repertory of kagura at the Sada Shrine, Shimane Prefecture, Yotsuka-gun, Kashima machi. *Nihon minzoku geino jiten*, Ed. Bunkacho and Nihon Nashonaru Torasuto (Tokyo: Daiichi Hoki shuppan, 1976) pp. 665-7.

8 *Saihoroku*, pp. 220-1.

and time that separate the present from once-upon-a-time. And so will it always be, so long as human kind survives, so long as there is art.

The hour when drowsiness overtakes the place is, as one would imagine, the time when a miko begins to address nocturnal gods. Suddenly the canopy, hanging from the ceiling and decorated with sacred five-colored paper streamers, descends and covers her head. She sets off on the same journey as one's own indwelling spirit. Flower-like, pieces of five-colored paper flutter noiselessly down, like the three-cornered snow of kabuki. 'We are covered. We are covered. By a round moon we are covered.' At last, together with the words of this kagura song and the sound of the *daidoro* drums, the miko begin to be filled with the remembrance of that ancient day on which gods came to them.

At this moment I realized that the daidoro sound heard in kabuki at the appearance of spirits of the living and the dead is the noisy clamor of kagura.[9] It was then, too, that I felt, with genuine emotion, that this is the ancestral home of those cries uttered when Japanese instrumentalists perform ... But, above all, it is through miko possessed by gods beneath a canopy that, with joy, I read down to its very essence and understood the noh play 'Dojoji.' For when the *shite*[10] in the play goes under the on-stage bell prop and is transformed into the shite of the second half, it is a vestige (*omokage*) of miko possessed by gods under this canopy. Transmitted here is one of the expressive forms [*hasso*][11] of the theatrical arts of the Japanese people. It is true that noh may well have survived because it was filled out as literature at the hands of the great artists of the Middle Ages. But what I have seen here today testifies to the road along which it travelled on the way toward survival.

Dawn broke slowly over the sea of Oki. In its faint glimmer, reflected on the water, I woke with a start from sleep on the summit of Mount Takuhi, rising steeply 452 metres above sea level. At the sound of the large drum which the modoki [term for a performer] beats during 'Kiribe,' the finale of Dawn Kagura, as it is called, I surrendered myself, bit by bit, to the satisfaction that the soul feels on its joyful return once more to the world of men.

---

[9] The first of many references to a relationship, proposed by Gunji and discussed below, between a classical theater type, here kabuki, and a countryside performance.

[10] The principal performer/character in noh. Relevance of the two-part division of noh to folkloric studies is mentioned below on p. 140.

[11] Gunji may not have intended to use the term hasso in the sense in which Orikuchi had used it before him. 'Hasso,' (Nakano Naomi) *Orikuchi Shinobu jiten* (hereafter abbreviated as *Jiten*), ed. Nishimura Toru (Tokyo: Daishukan, 1988) pp. 358-65. The term was productive in Gunji's writing about theatrical forms as late as 1970: 'Geino no hasso to bungaku,' *Bungaku*, 38/2, 1970. 'Michiyuki no hasso,' *Kabuki no bigaku* (Tokyo: Engeki Shuppansha, 1963).

July 1954, the month of this visit with Honda to the Takuhi shrine on Oki Island, saw the publication of Gunji's *Kabuki: Styles and Tradition*, the collection of essays mentioned above. One of the earliest dates to 1946[12]. In another of them, 'The Origin of the Aragoto Style in Kabuki' (1953), Gunji's new approach to kabuki studies can be sampled. Standard histories of kabuki identify a great actor, the first Danjuro (1684-1740), as the creator of this bravado style of acting. But Gunji credits an older performance tradition as its ultimate source, one that can still be seen, studied and enjoyed in the countryside of Japan.

Two essays —both reprinted in another collection (1959) of Gunji's, 'Expressive Forms [*hasso*] in Kabuki'— first acquainted readers with a proposal of his for rewriting performance history so that it would take into account what he was then seeing in the countryside. The first, 'The Question of Countryside Traditions for the Study of Kabuki,' appeared in the January 1956 issue of the periodical *Literature*; the other, 'Kabuki and Folklore,' in its November 1956 issue. In this periodical Gunji's ideas reached a wider readership than they would have done in specialty journals for which he also wrote. In the first, he mentions the daidoro drumming of Takuhi kagura, described above as a style that marks the appearance of the supernatural in both countryside festivals and on kabuki stages. In the second he mentions Ayako-mai, a dance form Gunji and Honda saw at the end of August 1956. His views on countryside performance as a key to the question of origins were rapidly coming together and Gunji also rushed into print, for the November issue, comment on performances he had seen perhaps only a month or so earlier.

'Kabuki and Folklore' emphasizes the need for a personal experience of countryside performance if one is to understand kabuki history. The performance ethnographer writes to give an account of outward aspects of what he sees. But, Gunji argues, in looking at Ayako-mai one needs to intuit an older tradition behind the performance. This alone leads to the true significance of the dance for kabuki history. Wherever village culture still makes possible such performances, the essence of theater and of dance is alive even in our own century. As he looks at something like this, the ethnographer/historian should respond with

[12]'Saruwaka no kenkyu' (a study of the role 'saruwaka, in countryside dance and its relation to the same term in kabuki) pp. 174-237, shows Gunji's use of evidence from countryside performance already published by others. It begins with three short sections: a summary of previous scholarly opinion on the meaning of 'saruwaka' in older documents; visual evidence for the role of saruwaka; references to the 'discovery' of saruwaka in folk dance. Quotations from Kodera Yukichi's [1895-1945] writing on countryside dance are used and and reference is made to two of Honda's books.

feelings that older generations of indigenous spectators once would have had.

From what he writes in the January essay we understand how Gunji, active as scholar and theater-goer in the mid to late 20th century, might be said to have experienced a traditional way of seeing performance. He describes what it felt like in the summer of 1955 to see an outdoor Buddhist procession at the Taima Temple in Nara, as a line of monks, masked as twenty-five Bodhisattva, crossed a bridgeway in the late afternoon sunlight. As they moved, symbolically at least, from the other world to this and back again, Gunji experienced a 'living version of antiquity.'[13] And it was then that Gunji had his insight: The *hanamichi*, a unique acting area in kabuki, and the *roppo*, a movement technique performed there, were 'later stagings' [*butaika*] of the processional form he was seeing in Nara that day. He discovered an archetype (he notes a similar runway, the *hashigakari*, in noh) for a type of physical expression in the performing arts of Japan: showing off the way a performer walks, the art of walking he calls it. On that day 'I had, indeed, a direct experience [*jikkan*] of a deep ethnic performance technique passed down to kabuki.'

* * *

Jikkan, the term Gunji uses for the insight, was used earlier by Orikuchi Shinobu. He also originated the term hasso —'an expressive form in the theatrical arts of the Japanese people'— used by Gunji in his passage about the Takuhi festival. Ultimately, one can identify what Orikuchi means by either of these terms only within the context of the extensive system of his thought[14]. But a passage in a talk (1949) of his on folklore and performance tells the reader about the role jikkan played at

---

[13]James A. Fujii, *Complicit Fictions* (Berkeley: University of California Press, 1993), pp. 250ff. The festival in Nara is discussed in: Elizabeth ten Grotenhuis, 'Chujohime: The Weaving of Her Legend,' *Flowing Traces: Buddhism in the Literary and Visual Arts of Japan*, ed. James H. Sanford, William R. LaFleur, and Masatoshi Nagatomi (Princeton, New Jersey: Princeton University Press, 1992) pp. 198ff. *Nihon rekishi to geino* (Tokyo: Heibonsha, 1990) v.2, pp. 215ff; its video clip (#5) shows a portion of the procession.

[14]Hirosue Tamotsu, 'Kaisetsu' (Commentary), in *Orikuchi Shinobushu (Kindai Nihon shiso taikei* 22), ed. Hirosue Tamotsu (Tokyo: Chikuma Shobo, 1975) pp. 367-403.

the historical moment in the early 1930s when a study of performance ethnography in Japan was emerging.[15]

> Mr. Hayakawa [Kotaro] said one could see both the festival at Niino and a representative flower festival in the Shitara area on the same visit and urged me to come along with him ... Choosing a day for the performance of a flower festival that corresponded closely to that for the festival at Niino, happily, we were able to see both ... Until then, I had never seen a festival with so large a performance component and was deeply impressed. I thought I would try to study these festivals systematically. And whenever I talked about the impression I had in seeing them, a certain structure did, in fact, come to mind. In the meantime, a group with shared interests gathered. As personality types, Kodera Yukichi and Kitano were different from one another but they made a good combination and we got along well together. One or two years after I began lecturing [at Keio University in 1928] on the performing arts, we decided to publish the journal *Folk Arts*.
>
> Until then, the way it was with people who wanted to study the performing arts was just to leap in. If an amateur could perform something on his own, he would try to become a scholar. Of course, this was not so simple in the case of kabuki, but amateur performers on the samisen or who sang just jumped in. When it came to articles in *Folk Arts*, on the other hand, we tried to create an objective attitude: to look at performance with the feelings performers have. I would say at the time: 'Jikkan is essential.' Jikkan was the ideology of the period. What point was there if one did not go out to see these things? The main thing was to go out to see performances. Everyone agreed ... Researching performance in books was important but it was by seeing them that we fleshed out book knowledge ...

Published in 1929, a brief account of an incident that occurred in 1925 on the visit Orikuchi and Hayakawa paid to the Niino Snow Festival casts light on the sort of impression that could inflame Orikuchi's imagination during a research trip such as this. He and Hayakawa were fortunate enough to be allowed to take part, along with the hereditary local performers of its roles, in the period of preparation and strenuous ritual taboos that precede the main festival. On the day before its principal event, they were present when masks to be used during the festival were refurbished and repainted. The performers had no practical explanation to give their visitors about what they were doing. Orikuchi describes his own way of understanding what he saw:

---

15 'Shoki minzokugaku kenkyu no kaiko,' *Orikuchi Shinobu Zenshu: Noto-hen Tsuiho* v.3 (Tokyo: Chuokoronsha, 1987) p. 282ff. The published version of the talks was reconstructed from notes and the remembrance of listeners.

> It is possible to think of the custom as left over from a belief that renovating the masks had the same effect as remaking them year after year. But there was something older still — something that perhaps went beyond how old it was or how uniquely Japanese was the custom. I had a feeling that —however faintly— here is the skill that once bestowed life anew each year to masks of the dead. A flicker of candle light led me to imagine something so ancient —one cannot even say how old— as to be older than the ancient period (*kodai*) itself.

Orikuchi tells us that the masks before his eyes were quite new, as a matter of fact. Sometime after his first visit to the area, in the summer of 1920, fire destroyed the storage place of the masks and other festival paraphernalia. Nothing could be saved. So older men among those who were responsible for the festival gathered together to make a new set. At the ceremony described above, everyone —even those who presumably had a hand in making them— said that the masks were absolutely the living image of those that had been burned. Realizing that this was clearly not true, Orikuchi speculates that they would have said this only because on the eve of a festival they had to believe it to be so.

The inaugural issue (January 1928) of the periodical *Folk Arts* published an installment of Orikuchi's lecture on 'Okina,' that he had delivered at a meeting of the Folk Art Society. He writes here of the 'origin' (*hassei*)[16] of this type of performance for a single person masked as an old man (i.e. okina). Versions of 'Okina' were being performed on classical stages (as they still are) and in many types of dance. What Orikuchi believed were related performances are widespread in the countryside. During visits to Okinawa (the summers of 1921 and 1923) he saw, or people there spoke to him about, performances or rituals that in time would allow him to formulate an hypothesis about the origin of 'Okina.' But before discussing what he had seen in Okinawa he made a short methodological statement. This includes his own explanation of the importance of jikkan to his scholarship and thought.[17]

---

[16] *Jiten*, pp. 346-57.

[17] Orikuchi mentions other performances that contributed to his understanding of the form of 'Okina.' These include what he and Hayakawa saw on their visit (1926) to see the flower and Niino festivals. The period between his folkloric studies in Okinawa and the trip with Hayakawa was crucial to the development of Orikuchi's thought. Performances he saw then seemed to him to confirm his emerging concept of the visit of a 'stranger god' (Orikuchi's English translation of the term *marebito*). The hypothesis was that marebito comes periodically (seasonally) for community festivals in this world from a far away place (the 'other world'). The term 'marebito' [mare: rarely; hito (bito): for Orikuchi in

> Experience is key to the way I do research. Gathering documentation, making notes of what I read in my study — the purpose behind all of this is to obtain a direct experience [jikkan] of the past.[18] Let me call my method one of 'historical anthropology based on jikkan.' In addition to understanding forms of 'Okina' still found in the contemporary performing arts, like dengaku, kagura, kabuki etc. —in addition, also, to an understanding of the structure of 'Okina' in rituals, dances and theater dating to a time before jushi-dengaku— one needs the direct intuition [*chokkan*] of how these are performed today that comes with study in the field. Intuition here lies close to personal experience.

---

this context, a form of life midway between kami and human] is one he seems to have chosen for the idea as he returned by ship, in the summer of 1923, from research in Okinawa. The idea was soon inseparably linked to another that also took shape at the same time: a single origin (hassei) that gave rise simultaneously to both literature and the performing arts. For what marebito said and what he did at these festivals was the origin both of literature and of performance. A series of four articles on the origin of 'Japanese literature' (literally, *kokubungaku*, our country's literature) appeared independently of one another in journals between April 1924 and January 1929. The background to the separate publication of each is complex. But ultimately the publication of *Kodai Kenkyu* brought them together into a single volume. In order to accommodate these articles that had been independently published, titles were adjusted and, in some cases, texts themselves were divided into subsections and subtitled. In this way, each of the four articles, that either mentioned marebito in passing or dealt in detail with the idea, was known as one part (#1 - #4) of a single series, a study of the origin of Japanese literature. Looking at these works and the published version of Orikuchi's lecture on the origin of 'Okina,' one realizes how great was the influence of the two summers spent in field work on Okinawa and the visit with Hayakawa to see the Niino festival and a representative flower festival. In other words, what was eventually destined to become an essential part of Orikuchi's system of thought grew up hand-in-hand with performances Orikuchi saw —in fact, heavily depended upon his seeing them — and with the experience of travel itself to reach the distant places where they could be seen. Jikkan —in this case, a special way of seeing performance that put Orikuchi in personal touch with the ancient period and with 'origin'— was integral to the process that led to discoveries just mentioned, marebito and the hassei of literature and performance.

[18]In 1912 Orikuchi made a trip to the Ise, Shima and Kumano area, during which he had an intuitive experience (jikkan) of a world beyond the sea. He stood on a promontory looking toward the horizon beyond 'waves sparkling in the sun.' At that moment he believed that he experienced the same deep sense of longing for the other world that people in the ancient period had felt. Thereafter, the 'other world' become a primary concern for Orikuchi's scholarship and thought.

In the quotation below from the same series of talks, Orikuchi discusses the skills that are needed by the collector of folkloric material; how to train the eye to see and how to train it to document performance. Questions such as these remained of interest to Gunji, Honda and others who, in postwar generations, have had their own role to play in the performance ethnography movement whose beginnings are discussed below by Orikuchi. Of special interest are details about how he came to make his first visit to see the winter festival of Niino and a representative flower festival. The many 'Okina' and *oni* (demon) rituals/performances in the repertories of these festivals became one model for his concept of an annual visit by the 'stranger god' who comes from the other world for seasonal festivals. Later in his writing, he elevated what he had seen with his own eyes into evidence for what he called the origin (hassei) of Japanese literature and performance. Orikuchi would go with students to see the same festivals year after year. At a personal level they had somehow become an annual event that was needful in his own life.

> After various discussions, Professor Yanagita's folkloric study came to stand on its own. Some young scholars turned to ethnography; we remained steadfastly in the area of folklore. Then the periodicals *Folkloric Studies* and *Ethnology* began to be published. With their appearance came a split in our group too. Some specialized in the folk arts but with a primary emphasis on performance. In short, there were two groups then. For one, objects were the main concern. Performance was paramount for the other. Quite independently of us, the aim of yet another group was the countryside arts (kyodo geijutsu = visual arts) as understood by people like Yanagi Soetsu. In terms of scholarship, the work of those whose main emphasis was performance prospered and grew in the direction of the 'folk arts' (minzoku geijutsu) until a periodical by that name began to be published ...
>
> There was a particular reason why this kind of fashion (passion it was too) was stirred up. We made trips into the countryside to see performances. The very first things we saw were, of course, dance festivals in Shitara-gun called the 'flower festival.' Their repertories were varied and a festival went on all night. We began to go and see them. Had it not been for our visits to see these, the folk arts movement, very likely, would not have succeeded. Traveling was useful because it stirred up a spirit of study and research in performance.
>
> You might call the artist Hayakawa Kotaro a student in the first phase of Professor Yanagita's career. He drew pictures and had a talent for making local people talk to him. His representative publication is 'The Flower Festival.' He was suited to be a collector of folklore. There was another person, Sasaki Kizen, a native of Tono Village in the Rikuchu

area, who was older than me. He told Professor Yanagita legends that were then published as 'The Legends of Tono' and later furnished materials for its sequel. Sasaki gathered folkloric materials. A superstitious person, he felt at home with transmitters of folklore. He was a great collector of material in Eastern Japan while Hayakawa was a great collector living in Tokyo.

Mr. Hayakawa first lit the fire ... He said to me once: 'Performers from flower festivals far back in the countryside come down to the area around Nagashino to visit the homes of sick people where they dance. One performer looks like a demon wielding a huge ax. Ritually he steps on afflicted parts of the sick. I cannot recall where this is.' As a matter of fact, some ten years earlier [1920, as noted in the chronology of *Jiten*, p. 716], I myself had gone to the village of Niino. I got there by going eastward from the Nakazugawa station on the central rail trunk line. Though planning to go to Toei, by chance I passed through Niino. I learned, from what I was told at the time, that a 'Snow Festival' was performed there. The village is almost the last one on the southeastern boundary of the Shinshu area. Cross another range and you come out deep in the mountains of Shitara.

Adding this information to what I already knew from Hayakawa, it was clear that a single mountain separates flower festivals, performed in the Mikawa area, from the Snow Festival. Before long, Mr. Hayakawa made inquiries for me and found out that flower festivals are performed at the time of the solar new year. We said we would plan to set out for Niino. Just then young Goto, a student at Waseda University and a member of a family of sake makers in Niino, came to see me. He urged me to come to Niino. I learned the schedule —times and places— of every festival that year. And so I decided to go with Mr. Hayakawa. This time, we went by way of Iida City. We arrived at Niino in advance of the Snow Festival and saw various of its rituals. Then we crossed over to Mikawa, went to see the flower festival at Tone Village, deep in the mountains to the northeast, returned to Niino the next day and saw the Snow Festival.

This was the beginning. This is how the study of the folk arts started. This is how it began and the next year the entire folk arts group turned out to see flower festivals. It used to be said of me that: 'At the beginning of the new year, Orikuchi leads his friends into the mountains of the San-Shin-En area. They follow in his wake like shit floating after gold fish.' So started research into performance. I have seen about everything there is in the mountains on the border between the three older provinces. There must be things I have not seen as well; there must be festivals I have not put my hands on. Evidently Mr. Kitano's student, young Arai Tsuneyasu, has walked around and seen almost everything there is to be seen no matter how small.

We had a great deal of experience in making records of this kind of performance. We were incredibly active in that sense. Making written records of performance is not easy. It is important to have some code system of one's own. To some degree one must be able to use musical notation as well and one must record dance patterns. And so clever people did well to let the sound of a flute, for example, somehow become part of themselves. One has to devise dance symbols to take down dance movements. Some people did it with diagrams that look like wire-work dolls. The young Kitano and Nishitsunoi made records but their work was not thorough enough. At least you must make as much preparation as they did. But if you cannot do so, anyway you must go and look at things. And I looked as much as I could. It was a point on which I could not compromise with the record-making type of researcher. One has to activate, in some concrete way, the knowledge one has. For there is understanding that is latent in documents and records. Even by just going and looking you acquire a concrete type of understanding. When you see things that look alike you gain the power of embodying what you know. As you look, comparisons leap to mind from what you have already seen. But, of course, there are mistakes too. Most people think through associations with what they already know. Generally, when there is no apparent relationship, one's attention rapidly springs to life. Instantaneously one combines the two: one's understanding and what one is looking at. Usually there are mistakes. Take, for example, something unusual. Right off one associates this with aboriginals in the south seas or with the Ainu. But when it comes to a scholarly theory, it is a sin to emphasize these associations. The first gleam of scholarship is a mind and a heart that spring to life. Looking itself has value.

There were others, too, standing beside me who could make the most of my understanding. It was enough, then, if I merely looked at what I saw. But it is a good idea to make records of performance if one wants to prevent looking from becoming ineffectual. Actually, however, at first one goes to look at what is there; the next time one goes is in order to make a record. This is probably the right way. At any rate, first of all, lay hold of what you have when you feel your heart dancing. When a researcher's heart and mind are not dancing his attention is unfocused and results are not interesting.

Documenting performance in the Tokyo area is generally a failure. What you see may be unusual but it is also under the influence of city life. One looks but is unmoved. There is no novelty to the object of one's research. What you need to do is to go out and look for something that is unusual but also something that is far away from what normally surrounds us. The further away it is, the more rapidly one's powers of observation begin to work. It is valuable to have some understanding of dance, theater or music as a background to one's interest. Kodera went prepared in this way. However, it is also true that one can get too involved with special

> knowledge so that one is not much stimulated by what one sees. Training the eye is everything.

* * *

Along with evidence of the sort that dominated standard theatrical studies at the time — documents, pictorial and historical evidence — arguments made in Gunji's 'The Origin of the Aragoto Style in Kabuki' (1953) are supported by comment on costume, movement, religious practices, customs, beliefs etc. already reported by researchers of countryside performance. Then by 1956 Gunji was asking more, asking not only that the researcher observe such details but that, from what he sees, he draw a direct intuition of an ethnic tradition standing outside of history. In addition, 'Kabuki and Folklore' (1956) asks for a new approach to the writing of theater history. The article notes the contribution of Yanagita Kunio to folkloric studies and Orikuchi Shinobu's scholarship on countryside performance. The importance of the latter's concept of jikkan is acknowledged but his approach to studies in the field is faulted. Not being 'scientific' enough is its weakness, an approach that will not characterize folk performance studies in the postwar period, Gunji speculates. In the future a scholar will apply methodologies and principles borrowed from sociology and historical studies and show concern, for example, for performance as an integral part of village lifestyles. All are approaches already found in folkloric studies. Gunji acknowledges the progress made by contemporaries in documenting performance in the countryside. However, what is really needed is the equivalent of an archeologist's hands-on experience at a work site. Conventional literary studies of theater analyze the dramaturgy of plays but do not set out to understand them in performance. What Gunji requires is the personal experience that comes only to a spectator in the countryside at the very place and during the very time of performance.

What can be learned from seeing a performance like Ayako-mai? Gunji's reflection (Section #6 of 'Kabuki and Folklore') on conventional body language in a countryside version of kyogen is an example. He speculates on how to interpret a fixed pattern of movement whenever Taro Kaja —the name for the conventional role of the servant in the classical theater of kyogen as well— faces and interacts with his master. During performances of Ayako-mai a fixed pattern (*kata*) is used over-and-over in what the spectator may tend see as independent dramatic situations. Audience laughter each time the performer repeated the kata was Gunji's clue. He was puzzled at first. Words the servant spoke —what Taro Kaja says whenever he moved in this way— made it clear that distinct situations were being played out between master and servant even though audiences saw an identical movement repeated each time.

Gunji's commentary runs something like this: a kata in this tradition can be used in different situations. This is paralleled by what goes on in the everyday life of the village when villagers use simple, repetitive movements in their daily life. Beneath both types of recurring patterns —what performers use in festivals and what members of a community employ in everyday life— flows a single, unceasing spiritual energy. This contrasts to the way performers in cities approach their craft. Actors in Tokyo, for example, use what they call 'art' —'a weak and sickly individuality' is Gunji's gloss in the mid-1950s— to create something for a one-time-only performance. Movement in the repertory of countryside performers, on the other hand, was very likely derived from the use of gesture to cause rainfall, for example, or from what was intended to prevent natural disasters, subjugate malignant spirits or invoke life's blessings.

In short, the power behind a countryside performance, such as Ayako-mai's, is its ability to set in motion invisible forces. With this in mind, Gunji suggests that there may be no point whatsoever to interpreting the meaning of a kata, like that of Taro Kaja before his master, in the context of a particular dramatic situation. The meaning of each such physical expression of the human body has already been sanctioned by life in a community over the ages. The type of meaning that Gunji, himself a sophisticated urban spectator, expected to find when seeing or reflecting on such performances can be sampled as we reconsider his comment on seeing kagura at the Takuhi Shrine.

During the festival, a canopy is slowly lowered over two priestesses, as five-colored pieces of paper rain down from above.[19] Gunji associated the ritual transformation that came to his mind at this moment with a change in the identity of the noh performer/character in the dance-drama 'Dojoji.' On the noh stage, the performer positions himself below a large stage-prop bell, suspended from above, which is then precipitously lowered over him. When it is raised again, the bell reveals the manic power of a transformed person.

The same suggestion, that the play 'Dojoji' can be understood folklorically through the concept of transformation under a large on-stage

---

[19]Yamaji Kozo, 'Oki Dozen kagura no miko-mai,' *Nihon rekishi to geino*, v.1, pp. 192-5. A video tape that accompanies the book includes scenes of the festival. 'Oki Dozen kagura' (Yamaji Kozo), *Nihon minzoku geino jiten*, pp. 658-60. Honda Yasuji, *Kagura (Nihon no minzoku geino* 1) (Tokyo, Mokujisha: 1966) pp. 518ff.

prop lowered over the performer, is found in an earlier essay of Honda's. In 'The Sacredness of the Mirror Room' (1937) the act of covering —being hidden or in ritual seclusion (*komoru*)— is postulated as a technique of transformation.[20] Honda supports this argument with observations drawn from his research in the countryside. It develops like this. At the far end of the runway that leads to the noh stage is a curtain through which the main performer makes an appearance. The off-stage space beyond (seen from the auditorium) is called the mirror room. Within this special area, the performer puts on a mask before coming down the runway to the stage. In many noh plays, the performer later returns to the mirror room, from which he emerges a second time, after a costume and mask change, to begin the latter half of the play. Honda proposes a folkloric understanding of this room at the far end of a runway and of a change of costume and mask there: The mirror room is a place of concealment and of transformation. He associates noh's characteristically two-part structure with the change that occurs in this enclosed space. For Honda, noh dramaturgy is one of transformation.[21]

Another place of concealment in noh is a temporary and portable on-stage structure —free-standing as opposed to the suspended bell in 'Dojoji'— made of bamboo and in the form of a temple or tomb, for example, placed on stage. Into it the shite disappears and out of it he reappears, perhaps after a change of costume or mask within. Honda asks the reader to understand this temporary hiding place (itself almost a portable 'mirror room') through examples, discussed elsewhere in his article, of an unusual use of auxiliary performance areas in countryside performances.

One was documented by Hayakawa Kotaro in his study of the flower festival. A structure called the mountain (*yama* or white mountain, *shira-yama*) was part of a rare large-scale performance of kagura

---

[20] A series of Orikuchi's lectures, addressed to the Countryside Study Group at Kokugakuin University in 1939, were recorded in student notes and published in 1971. The sixth, '*umare-kiyomari*' (transformation, rebirth), mentions the play 'Dojoji' and shirayama (white mountain, see below). *Orikuchi Shinobu Zenshu: Noto-hen*, v.7 (Tokyo: Chuokoron, 1971) pp. 530, 538. It also discusses the relationship between komoru and transformation. Student notes of Orikuchi's 1946-7 lecture series on Shinto were later published. *Orikuchi Shinobu Zenshu: Noto-hen Tsuiho*, v.1 (Tokyo: Chuokoron, 1987). The subject is the soul (*tamashii* or *reikon*). Here komoru is discussed in the context of Japanese religous thought. Honda and Gunji address the idea of komoru and of umare-kiyomari within the performing arts.

[21] Frank Hoff, Willi Flindt. 'The Life Structure of Noh: An English Version of Yokomichi Mario's Analysis of the Structure of Noh,' *Concerned Theater Japan*, v.2, no. 3-4, pp. 209-56, esp. pp. 255-6.

in the flower festival area. Though no longer performed at the time of his visit, Hayakawa learned about the white mountain and its use through interviews with the few older villagers who could still remember it or recalled what others once told them about what it was like to be inside.[22] A group of older villagers dressed in white, the color of death, proceeded along a passageway and then passed within the constructed mountain. They seem to have understood it to be a place of seclusion, of eclipse before rebirth. After a period of time —during which various rituals/performances took place there— they emerged reborn.

In 'The Sacredness of the Mirror Room,' Honda proposes a relationship among the yama in this type of kagura, on-stage props in noh (these are also places of transformation and rebirth) and other unique spatial arrangements that were used in performances he had once seen in the countryside.[23] He also associates the mirror room of the noh stage with aspects of the enthronement ceremony (Daijosai), the central transformative rite —making a man into the emperor— of the Imperial Court.[24] Noh shares with the Daijosai a mechanism of concealment, change, rebirth and eventual manifestation of power. 'Dojoji,' the Daijosai, the mirror room — each includes a physical place of (or space for) transformation, where life forms, or identity reforms, within a chrysalis-like structure. In his 1937 essay, Honda associates, as Gunji was to later, the mirror room of the noh, the mountain of the older kagura performances and the bell shaped stage prop of 'Dojoji.' He aims to understand what lies behind each —what they share— through research he made in the countryside when he observed the use of areas that are auxiliary to the main 'stage.'

By relating kabuki performance techniques to an underlying tradition of Japanese ways of thought and feeling Gunji hoped to clarify

---

[22]Yamamoto Hiroko, '"Jodo-iri" no doramachyurgii — Oku-Mikawa no shimotsuki kagura o megutte,' *Nihon rekishi to geino*, v. 8, pp. 26-98, is an example of how a scholar writing in the early 1990s understood the festival. Takei Shogu's writing on kagura in the Mikawa area, ibid. p. 98 bibliography, is another example.

[23]Honda writes about spatial arrangements used by groups of Hoin kagura as clues to a relationship between the mirror room in Noh and rebirth rituals of kagura. *Rikuzenhama no hoin kagura* (Ishinomaki City: Kyodosha Shobo, 1934) p. 10, pp. 62ff; especially p. 63 note #3.

[24]Daijosai' (Stanley Weinstein), *Encyclopedia of Japan*, v.2, p. 59. D.C. Holtom, *The Japanese Enthronement Ceremonies* (1928), Robert S. Ellwood, *The Feast of Kinship: Accession Ceremonies in Ancient Japan* (1973). Orikuchi wrote extensively on the Daijosai and the imperial system. See article on 'Daijosai' in *Jiten*.

Japanese theatrical form in general, not just that of kabuki.[25] An example of his way of thinking at the time is found in the 1955 essay 'Form that Leads to Creativity.'[26] According to Gunji, the curtain in kabuki does not necessarily mark scenic breaks in the dramaturgy of plays as it is thought to do in modern theater. It is more than a scene-marker, a temporary interposition between the spectator and the stage. For as he is about to step on stage in a role, the performer uses the curtain as a source of power. Even before he appears before an audience, the performer has already made his appearance (*shutsugen*) behind the curtain. A ritual rope (*shimenawa*), continues the argument, is the prototype of the curtain in Japan. The shimenawa demarks a zone for performance by setting it apart from the ordinary world. It alerts viewers that someone —or something— secluded or hidden within or beyond is waiting to appear.

Though discussing modes of appearing in Japanese performance Gunji writes, one might say, about a universal issue, theatricality. Yet he clearly intended his argument to be read as an exploration of the deeper meaning of arrival in theater —manifestation, epiphany, appearance or whatever— in relation to a specific culture. He explains the essence of Japanese theater as transformation, manifestation and display, just as he had experienced these in various performances in the countryside. Paralleling the use of the stage curtain, Gunji cites visual evidence from an early period in the history of kabuki to illustrate how spectators once entered the theater under a curtain that was suspended above a small entranceway. Coming into a theater in this way qualified the spectator to become a participant in performance, an event shared between performer and spectator. The curtain, in the equation, is a border, a marker, both spatially and temporally.

Gunji then goes on to equate the effect of the appearance of certain large and moveable scenic elements in kabuki with that of an actor. His description of a building or temple gate that rises slowly to view, as it is elevated by a stage device called *seri-age*, is compelling. Seeing the on-stage operation of a technique of manifestation, the astonished viewer enjoys a power and an excitement —in this contrivance to animate the 'inanimate'— similar to what he or she feels at the first appearance of the human actor.

---

[25]For Orikuchi, an archetype that Gunji understands folklorically as standing outside (or beyond) historical change is responsible for various specific historical innovations.

[26]'Sozo e no keishiki: enshutsu to engi no hasso' (first published in the periodical *Engeki hyoron*, no. 21, June 1955 with the subtitle 'Kabuki no shuhen 1'), republished in *Kabuki no hasso*, pp. 54-67.

Gunji writes that the trembling of stage sets as they rumble into view, raised aloft from pits below the stage until they ride high above it, once recalled to kabuki audiences great wheeled floats creaking slowly down city streets at festival time, whether of the Gion-e in Kyoto or of Sanno and Kanda Myojin festivals in Edo.[27] Even at festivals today, the movement of decorated wagons setting out along crowded streets toward a shrine —like those in Kakunodate, Akita Prefecture— is accompanied by music from instrumentalists who ride high aloft on the floats.[28] Music at a festival marks the appearance of kami, and can be a striking folkloric parallel to the special type of theater music, technically called *seri no aikata,* that accompanies the lifting into view of large props on the kabuki stage. Sounding (*hayashi*) is a natural concomitant of manifestation; it signals the appearance of kami, whether object or actor comes into view. In short, the music of floats in a festival suggested to Gunji what might have been the original expressive function (hasso) of today's stage technique of seri-age in Kabuki.

The following quotation harmonizes several ideas in 'Form that Leads to Creativity.' Techniques of appearance, enumerated in the discussion above, are associated here with the *Hyo no yama.*[29] Hyo no yama were structures on wheels (originally carried on poles) that were once transported from remote areas of the countryside to the imperial court in Kyoto as part of the imperial enthronement ceremony. *Hikidai,* mentioned below, can still be seen today in a very few Kabuki plays.[30] A performer stands on a platform (-dai) mounted on wheels that is then pulled (hiki-) into view. Typically, an actor who is mounted on these moving platforms sways back and forth trying to keep his balance. Awkward as this older technique was for making, or 'showing,' an appearance, requiring that the actor be pulled into the presence of his audience, it further exemplifies Gunji's understanding of revelation as the

---

[27]*Nihon rekishi to geino,* v. 10, has essays on city festivals such as these. Hattori Yukio, 'Toshi no shukusai fukei,' is a discussion of the Sanno festival, p. 15ff; Hattori Yukio, 'Eizo kaisetsu,' comments on the Gion festival, pp. 186-94. The video tape that accompanies the book shows scenes of floats like those described below by Gunji.

[28]Fred S. Thompson, 'Manifestation of the Japanese Sense of Space in Matsuri,' *Fudo: An Introduction,* ed. Anthony V. Liman and Fred S. Thompson (Waterloo, Ontario: University of Waterloo Press, 1986) pp. 23 ff.

[29]Honda Yasuji, *Dengaku, furyu 1 (Nihon no minzoku geino II),* p. 578 note #1 is Honda's interpretation of the origin of hyo no yama. Frontispiece to Honda Yasuji, *Katarimono, furyu 2 (Nihon no minzoku geino IV),* p. 6, speculates on whether hyo no yama were wheeled or stationary.

[30]Soga Juro's appearance to his younger brother, Goro, in a dream sequence of the play *Yanone* is an example.

essence of performance. Associating the enthronement ceremony of an emperor —itself the ultimate manifestation of political and religious power— with a portable or moveable yama, the following is a complex conclusion to an essay about the essence of theater: a hidden source of power, raised, poised and on the verge of making its appearance.

> What is the meaning of the on-stage prop in noh, the techniques of hikidai and seri-age in kabuki? What is the significance of purposely exposing such devices by drawing them forth before the public's eyes? Everything —absolutely everything— about the marvel, the miracle, of rebirth must take place before the eyes. For the performance technique of drawing something forth has an emotional effect of its own. Take the fact that long ago, at the time of the Daijosai, the Hyo no yama was transported, at a prearranged time, from the headquarters of the governors of [two representative] provinces [selected each year]. The point of doing this was to respectfully present before the court this yama in which the spiritual essence of each local district governed by the Emperor [*sumira mikoto*] had been temporarily lodged. This was done in order to congratulate Him and pray for His continuing prosperity and long life. Now, the significance of the ceremony of drawing the Hyo no yama along the road was to expose —to show openly to all— subtle perturbations of life hidden within and to convey to viewers along the way a living impression [of the vitality lodged there] over the entire of the ceremonial route of the yama as it made its way to the capital.

* * *

The primary focus of Honda's scholarship over a lifetime has been performance traditions in the countryside. In part, he was concerned lest some would no longer be performed in the new Japan that was emerging. While it was still possible to do so, he wanted to investigate and document them. The basis of Gunji's expertise was kabuki history, though his writing and lecturing extended to many other Japanese performance types, classical and contemporary as well as countryside. (His viewing experience has had an amazing range.) Because of these individual concerns, each scholar had his own way of looking at and reflecting on what he saw in the 1950s. Still, they traveled together, talking to one another —one has to imagine— about the marvellous things they were seeing at a time when many fine performers with training from the prewar period were still active. We have to believe that there was great vitality in these traditions at that time.

Honda and Gunji arrived at Nihonmatsu station, Fukushima Prefecture, on Saturday afternoon 25 February 1956 (the 14th of the lunar first month that year, and the vigil of the celebratory New Year's

Day). They took a bus bound for Suzuishi and got off at the Akaizawa stop.[31] After dining with a farm family, they saw a performance of local dance at their host's home. It began around 5:30 and lasted for an hour or so. The itinerary of the journey, published in 1967, details other visits the same evening during which they saw the same two types of dance, (shichi-fukujin and taue-odori) at other farm houses in the neighborhood. And until late that evening, they had the opportunity of questioning older performers about the dances. Honda notes that he enjoyed the evening, sharing the warm and joyous mood of a truly rural New Year's Day celebration. The next morning, the pair set off to see a performance of kagura at the Suzuishi Shrine; in the afternoon they returned to Nihonmatsu City, saw a film about a local festival and heard a live performance of festival music.

Some ten years earlier, 2 April 1944, Honda had paid his first visit —this time on his own— to the same area to investigate these dances. Later, in publishing his report in *Dengaku, furyu 1* (1967), he supplemented what he learned in 1944 with observations made in 1956. Included are representative songs and speeches recited during the performance. These were written out for him —in local pronunciation, he notes— by performers during the visit of 1956, when Honda, taking advantage of the New Year's festival, was able to observe more than one performance of the same dance style.

The report on dances at Ishii Village takes up twenty-three pages of *Dengaku, furyu 1*, the majority of which reproduce texts of what was recited or sung. The section of the book in which it is included is one of more than twenty reports on transplanting dance in the Tohoku. Organized geographically, from north to south, altogether they cover some two-hundred and forty-eight pages. A brief introduction describes characteristics of this dance type as performed in the six prefectures of the Tohoku (Aomori, Iwate, Akita, Yamagata, Miyagi and Fukushima). The length of the reports differs, as did specific conditions, also described, under which each visit took place. From these nearly two-hundred and fifty pages, the reader gains a sense of the local quality of transplanting dances —what Honda calls the 'wit, humor and sentiment of farming communities in the Tohoku'— as well as information about times, places, ways of performing and details about the dancers, their costumes, movements, how performance space was used etc.

---

[31] Honda's report on two dance types, shichi-fukujin (seven gods of good fortune) and taue-odori (transplanting dances), at Ishii Village was published in *Dengaku, furyu 1*, pp. 464-487; itinerary p. 484.

At the conclusion of the article on the dances of Ishii Village, Honda notes the two separate occasions on which he visited, saw performances and gathered information and documentation. When publishing, his practice was to date a report and name the people in the community who had assisted him. Returning to a site is evidence of his carefulness as a performance ethnographer. The entire last page of a published report (some ninety-one pages in length) on an entirely different performance type documents the dates and the purpose of each of several study trips to research the Ogi (fan) festival of Kurokawa after his first visit, 13 August 1933. This single page, then, is a chronicle of Honda's investigation of a major countryside tradition.[32] Along with Horohayama, 'Zaido,' Yamabushi kagura and bangaku[33], the Ogi fes-

---

[32]Honda Yasuji, *Ennen (Nihon minzoku geino 3)* (Tokyo: Mokujisha, 1969), p. 851. A summary of steps in the process of Honda's investigation of the festival include: 13 August 1933, visits Kurokawa Village where he learns about its festival for the first time. 15 August 1933, sees a performance of Kurokawa noh at a shrine in nearby Tsuruoka City. His detailed documentation of a dance, 'Shiki-sanban,' seen that day, is reprinted in *Ennen* (pp. 844-51). Taking advantage of their plans to make a pilgrimage, Honda arranges for members of one of the two performance guilds from Kurokawa to perform, 2 December 1933, at a theater in Ishinomaki City, where Honda teaches. Visiting Kurokawa at the time of the Ogi Festival, 1-2 February 1936, he makes the detailed field notes that will serve as the basis of his published article. 27 July 1936, Honda visits Kurokawa to observe the annual summer airing of costumes etc. He is now able to see at close range the costumes, masks and props of both guilds and to meet and talk with older members of the community. He works rapidly to bring his rough notes, memories and documentation into final form for publication. The finished article is dated 'New Year's Day 1937.' ('New Year's Day' is often chosen to mark a propitious conclusion to an article, irrespective of whether writing was actually brought to a close on the first of January or not.)

[33]Honda wished readers of *Yamabushi Kagura, Bangaku* (Sendai: Saito Hoonkai, 1942) to know something of the process by which his investigation of Yamabushi kagura and bangaku evolved over nearly a decade. For that reason, he included an addendum to the book. Hoping that readers would be able the better, thereby, to understand both the way he conducted research and the fact that, even in a single coherent tradition, separate performance groups may each have its own unique characteristics, he included an abridged travel account of repeated visits he made to investigate kagura. He hoped that this approach would balance the survey, in the book's introductory matter, of general characteristics of Yamabushi kagura and bangaku as an integral performance type. Honda recognized the importance of Hayakawa Kotaro's work on the flower festival but faulted (in conversation with me) the format Hayakawa had chosen in which to publish the results of his investigation. In Honda's opinion, Hayakawa placed too much emphasis on shared features —the 'least common denominator' as Honda called it— of this family of kagura. As a result, the uniqueness of local

tival of Kurokawa is one of several large-scale festivals and traditions researched by Honda in the 1930s. As such, each merited repeated visits and the kind of concentrated attention shown by the dates noted on the final page of the lengthy report published on the Ogi festival.

Particular circumstances determined with what degree of detail Honda would record what he saw in the field and, later, how much of this he would care to keep in his published report. His personal development as a scholar was one such factor. For example, he made a meticulous record of its choreography when he saw the lion dance of Kobama Village toward the end of his vacation in September 1928.[34] (Like his report on Ishii Village, this early choreographic record is included in the 1967 volume.) In a note, Honda explains that he was able to see the same style of dance, performed by different groups, more than once and hear experienced dancers explain it.[35] A young man in 1928, he was still learning how to document dance. As a result he made a full choreographic record and so an early step in Honda's technical development as a performance ethnographer has been preserved. A report on the transplanting dances of Mirumae Village is included in *Dengaku, furyu 1*.[36] It relies on Honda's performance record of 20 March 1933 and on what he learned from talking with dancers and older members of the community. At the end of this lengthy record, Honda cites their names along with those who later allowed him to use their personal written notes on the dances. Acknowledging such contributions in print was part of the code of folkloric studies.

Occasionally a published travel account may specify a conceptual discovery made on a field trip. One such methodological insight arose under unusual circumstances. The report in question was first published in installments (between 23 and 28 January 1949) in a local newspaper. Gathered together, these were later reprinted as a single article, entitled 'A Recording Trip' in Honda's collection of travel accounts, *Reports on Folk Performance from the Field* (1971).[37] It tells of an early postwar visit (13-15 January 1949) to several villages in the area of Honda's birthplace in the company of members of the Sendai Broadcasting

---

performances are lost sight of. Honda aimed to overcome this defect by the format he chose for his own study: by including an addendum with travel accounts and comment on individual performance groups in addition to a collection of texts, annotated with indications of movement and costume.

34 *Dengaku, furyu 1*, pp. 861-72.

35 *Ibid.* p. 865.

36 *Ibid.* pp. 359-82. This performance is a splendid example of one in a rural setting and Honda's report on it is a model of how documentation can bring such to life even for the reader many years later.

37 *Saihoroku*, pp. 167-74.

Station led by a personal friend, Takeda Chuichiro.[38] After a certain session of recording songs, he asked Takeda —the question was as much to confirm Honda's own impression— what kind of music seemed to be most like that of the lion dance of Kobama Village they had just finished listening to and recording.[39] The exchange gives us an insight into the give-and-take of a cooperative research project.

> From what you hear on the radio [writes Honda], there seems little doubt but that music for the lion dance in the Shirakawa area seems to use the music of *daidai* kagura without any change at all. On the other hand, there is nothing special about music for the deer dance; it is found everywhere throughout the Rikuzen and Rikuchu areas. But the music of the lion dance at Kobama is different. And yet, it is not the music of dengaku. Mr. Takeda thought a while before answering, "It is like bugaku." Without a moment's hesitation, I slapped my knee in agreement. Clearly, it is really difficult to detect in this music the melodies of bugaku. And yet certainly I myself had acknowledged the fact that dancers in the dance "Yamagakari," that we had just recorded, use hand movements that share something with what is used in the bugaku dances "Nasori" and "Ryuo." I told Mr. Takeda that I had, in fact, just finished writing down this very point in my notes. Then I asked him another question: "Well, if the music is like bugaku, which particular dance of bugaku is it like? What do you think?" "'Nasori' and 'Bato,' of course." was his answer.
>
> I cannot go into details here. But certainly the most important discovery I made on the trip was to find elements of bugaku style in lion dance. As a result, I now have to reconsider lion dance as it is currently performed in and around Tokyo. Do elements of bugaku still remain in these performances? Might they prove useful in looking for a yet older type of lion dance?

Before he took up a teaching post in the prewar period at Ishinomaki City, Miyagi Prefecture, Honda visited his birthplace. It was not too far away, Fukushima Prefecture, Adachi-gun, Motomiya Village. On 1 May 1929, he saw a performance of kagura at Motomiya's Adatara

---

[38]Two texts, representative of what Honda used as a radio lecturer in a series of broadcasts from Sendai on aspects of the performing arts of the Tohoku are reprinted, Honda, *Rikuzenhama no hoin kagura* pp. 535-79. One (on shimotsuki kagura and miscellaneous festivals and performances) was broadcast for thirty minutes, at five o'clock in the evening of 18 December 1933; the other (on summertime dances) at 11:10 in the morning, 8 July 1934. The text of another broadcast from the Sendai studio (19 April 1938) on the subject of song traditions was republished, *Nihon matsuri to geino* (Tokyo: Kinseisha, 1974) pp. 185-95 (originally published in the journal *Oncho* nos. 9-10, May 1938). A selection of recordings of song and music was also included in the live broadcasts.

[39]*Saihoroku*, p. 171.

Shrine; and on another visit (19-20 October) he saw kagura at the autumn festival of the neighboring Ukishima Shrine. In May he had the good fortune to meet Kokubun Jihachi, then a man of sixty-six years and the leader of the group that performed at both shrines. As a result of the meeting, Jihachi became a primary informant in Honda's investigation of kagura in the area. Within a few days after the autumn festival, Honda wrote up both what Jihachi told him and what he himself saw, and submitted this detailed report on kagura as performed here to the periodical *Folk Arts*. It was published over four installments, beginning with vol. 3, no. 4 (April 1930).[40]

Kokubun Jihachi first began to learn kagura in 1881 at the age of eighteen. When Honda met him in 1929 he had already been performing some forty-eight years. A story circulated about why Jihachi had begun to study kagura. As a soldier, his father's life was in danger when he found himself embroiled in one of the battles that marked the turmoil surrounding the Meiji Restoration.[41] To escape certain death, he slipped within the precinct of the Ukishima Shrine. To thank its tutelary divinity for saving his life, the father committed his son to learning kagura — its drumming, flute playing and dance. Jihachi was an unusually dedicated and talented student. Even at the time of Honda's visit, many years later, stories were still circulating about his almost superhuman efforts in learning kagura as a boy and about his mature skill as a musician.

Before the Meiji Restoration, kagura was performed by shrine priests in the area. Ten or twenty would gather together to perform at a shrine. A certain priest might be known for his special talents, perhaps as a drummer of a particular dance or as the dancer. With the Meiji Restoration came social and religious turmoil that undermined the position of shrine priests throughout Japan. As a result, priests in the area of Motomiya were no longer permitted to perform kagura. Rather than allowing their inherited traditions simply to expire, however, they chose to teach performance skills to lay members of the community.

As part of the transition to a younger generation of performers in a radically new age, certain changes were sometimes made to kagura's music and dance traditions. For example, Komatsu Sazen (1837-1917), also a priest of the Nagaya Shrine, made some adjustments to his shrine group's dancing and musical styles. In 1873 he began to teach a revised version to local people. Kokubun Jihachi was one of Komatsu's students. As a result, at the time of Honda's visit, the style of the group

---

[40]Reprinted in *Kagura*, pp. 971-1003; p. 1002 identifies time and place where the documentation was made.

[41]*Ibid.* p. 1002.

at Shiraiwa Village was what Jihachi had learned from his teacher, Komatsu Sazen. In time Jihachi himself led both the group at Shiraiwa and the one that performed at the Adatara Shrine festival of neighboring Motomiya. In fact, the young performers Honda saw in 1929 had been, in their turn, Jihachi's students. Jihachi was conservative, notes Honda, and did not take liberties with what he had learned, though performers elsewhere may have followed a model of innovation in a period of transition and modernization in Japan.

On 15 January 1949, the crew from Sendai's radio station recorded a performance by the kagura group from Shiraiwa Village.[42] In fact, that recording was the main reason the trip had been arranged. Ever since his visit in 1929, Honda had looked forward to the day when he would be able to make an audio recording of this music.[43] But the experience came as a surprise. The group no longer sounded like what he remembered hearing some twenty years earlier. To Honda, who could still recall the once beautiful drumming of Kokubun Jihachi, kagura music at Shiraiwa Village now sounded somehow old fashioned, as if 'a once fine piece of art work had begun to show signs of age and decay.'

> But even the masterpiece "Yotsubyoshi" [four beats] was, unfortunately, beginning to change for the worst. The musicians had left out something, perhaps because there were too few present and no one to play the *dai-byoshi*. The parishioners [Honda's way of referring to the performers] had better devise some scheme or other. If they don't, kagura itself —once performed to the refined and sonorous style of music that was played exclusively by shrine priests before the Meji Restoration— will decline. Then the group's performance will become commonplace and amateurish. Two or three dance numbers is all they will be able to play. As things stand now, collapse is inevitable.

Over the twenty years between 1929, when he first heard Jihachi, and 1949, the date of the recording session, Honda had become familiar with the quality of performance throughout the countryside of Japan. In addition, whenever possible he asked performers whether there were written documents or an oral tradition that might explain the history of their tradition. For, an often complex network of human relationships can explain who learned what from whom and, in some cases, even suggest how changes had taken place in the process. When possi-

---

[42]'Rokuon-ko,' *Saihoroku*, pp. 167-74.

[43]A voice recording of songs from Horohayama's Shimotsuki kagura was broadcast on Akita radio, 8 November 1937. Honda asked Takeda Chuichiro to make a western staff musical transcription (performers are identified in a brief note) of two of these and reproduced this on five gravure pages inserted between pp. 50-1 of his *Shimotsuki kagura no kenkyu* (Tokyo: Meizendo Shoten, 1954).

ble, the materials Honda wished to publish included documents clarifying the fate of often fragile traditions of performance in a period of breathtaking cultural change and innovation. Honda was sensitive to change in the performing arts. He understood the need for it. But during the recording session just mentioned, it is likely that he felt a chill of apprehension: Might a tradition he had first known through the interpretations of a very fine performer, Kokubun Jihachi, now face extinction?

*University of Toronto*

# OUTSIDE SHAKESPEARE / INSIDE QUÉBEC: PAULA DE VASCONCELOS'S METONYMIC PERFORMANCE TEXT *LE MAKING OF DE MACBETH*

Denis Salter

*"We don't 'do' plays, we '(re)make' them"*
Paula de Vasconcelos.[1]

## *The Current Status of the Shakespearean Performance Text*

In 1996, I ended my essay, "Acting Shakespeare in Postcolonial Space," with the modest proposal / obnoxious polemic that Shakespeare should no longer be produced in postcolonial cultures. Reason: doing so *always* places the autonomy of the postcolonial actor in jeopardy —within a network of discursive relations over which and through which he or she has no substantive control— and nothing can be done to minimise that risk. I implied, moreover, that Shakespeare's world-wide cultural capital is so large, so widely dispersed, and yet so discursively centralised that it is difficult, perhaps impossible, not only for the postcolonial actor but for the postcolonial *spectator* to experience Shakespeare otherwise.[2] It seems that all the interpretive possibilities have already been pitched and optioned and that taking ownership of an imaginative space to call y/our own either costs too much or is unthinkable since there is, in effect, precious little Shakespearean cultural capital actually available for purchase in the discursive market place. What else can the postcolonial actor and spectator do, I speculated, except refuse to let themselves be coopted by Shakespeare through the strategies of withholding their labour, their money, and

[1] Quoted in Denis Salter, "Blood ... Sex ... Death ... Birth: Paula de Vasconcelos's *Le Making of de Macbeth*: an interview," *Australasian Drama Studies* 29 (October 1996): 75.

[2] Denis Salter, "Acting Shakespeare in Postcolonial Space," in *Shakespeare, Theory, and Performance*, ed. James C. Bulman (London and New York: Routledge, 1996), p. 129.

their perceptual and imaginative resources and indeed their acquiescence to his (capitalistic) authority?

I suspected then, however, and I think even more urgently now, that this is a defeatist position, perhaps even a cop-out, and I have often wondered *if* my cultural diagnosis were not overstated, *if* alternative models for theorising and performing Shakespeare *might* be possible, *if* a return to the rehearsal hall *might* lead to practical discoveries about how to overcome the alienated condition of the postcolonial actor, a condition that likewise afflicts the spectator, and *if* it *might* be worth trying to conceptualise a performance text in which Shakespeare —as originating authority and as producer of primary cultural capital— could be effectively disabled, allowed to function as nothing more than a, admittedly legitimating, pretext that can ultimately be subjected to erasure. *The* question was / is: how? especially without setting up a situation in which Shakespeare continues to exercise his authority as a spectral trace within the system of imperialising textual representation.

I myself have no answers —and I can't get answers from directors, actors, playwrights, audiences, even critics and colleagues when I buttonhole them at parties— and, worst of all, I have discovered that, for many people, the problem I have tried to diagnose isn't a real problem anyway. "So what's wrong with Branagh?" is often the slightly hostile, if misprized and tangential, response as the person edges towards the canapes. I, too, have lapsed into uneasy silence, as I watch Baz Luhrmann's film *Romeo + Juliet*, which I love for all the wrong, postcolonially-incorrect reasons, and as I listen to the audio CD —which I bought at a store with the fitting name of Phantasmagoria— over and over again with my prebuscent daughter. (Luhrmann's film *Strictly Ballroom*, however, is a pathos-driven investigation of the punishing ways in which traditional aesthetic protocols school, contain, destroy / and give birth in the struggle to rewrite postcolonial identities.) Meanwhile, intellectually speaking, I have moved on —or so I thought— to other matters. One of them, as it turns out, is that hoary trope, metaphor, the other is that other hoary trope, metonymy, both aptly described by Gérard Genette as "the irreplaceable bookends of our own modern rhetoric."[3]

As I studied both of them against the backdrop of a self-set course of reading in the politics of inter- / intra-cultural performance, I discovered that the paradoxes of how to enact / interpret Shakespeare from embattled postcolonial subject-positions insistently reasserted

3 Gérard Genette, *Figures of Literary Discourse*, trans. Alan Sheridan (New York: Columbia UP, 1982), p. 107.

themselves while they led me to a reconsideration of some of the problematics of Shakespearean performance-textuality not just anywhere / everywhere but specifically in my own time, my own place. Last April [1996], when I went to see Paul de Vasconcelos's production of *Le Making of de Macbeth* at the Musée d'art contemporain, it turned out that I had lucked in to an unusually intelligent rendering of a highly aestheticised, almost art-for-art's sake, postcolonial *and* postmodern(ised), inter- *and* intra-cultural, meta-performative agon between these two foundational tropes. I think, in the end, that it was metaphor —and *not*, alas, metonymy— that emerged victorious, a result that confirms my suspicion that Shakespeare, fundamentally, is *not* contestable, at least not from a fraught postcolonial condition. (It also gave rise to wisecracks from colleagues who reminded me that that is what 'meta is for.') None the less, because of the incommensurability of metaphor, on the one hand, and metonymy, on the other, not only as literary tropes, but, even more important, as ways of being in the world —as phenomenological mediators— I have come to recognise that metonymy *is* indeed a part(ial) solution —an *emergent* performative strategy— if not for subverting and traducing Shakespeare, then at least for interrogating his place within the (sub)cultures of Québec / Canada and, in turn, our place outside / within his canonical authority. Note: a part(ial) solution but not, I am in fact happy to report, a definitive answer.

Before I discuss some key scenes in which Vasconcelos's *Making* played out the metaphor / metonymy dyad and its complications in relation to a much-revised written text, acting style, *mise-en-scène*, and the critical, social, ideological surround, I want to make a brief excursion into some of the traditional literature about, first, metaphor, and second, metonymy, and then I want to glance at a few issues in current debates about inter- and intra-cultural performance as they bear upon these particular tropological compass points.

## *What is Metaphor? Then. Now*

Historically, metaphor has usually been deployed, I think, to establish a resemblance or similarity between one thing, idea, or action and another; a process articulated by its etymological origins in the ancient Greek word for "transfer" (OED). Metaphor has been designed to articulate shared qualities and traits; to reify a common ground; to colonise and then to aggrandise a common/wealth of cultural, ideological, and figurative knowledge. As Roman Jakobson observes, metaphor tends to be preoccupied with symbolical identifications and with the careful ordering, perhaps the ranking, of cognitive and imaginative categories of value.[4] Jakobson's intellectual heir is partly Aristotle who argues, in the *Poetics*, that "metaphor is the transfer of a name that belongs to something else either from the genus to the species, or from the species to the genus, or from one species to another, or according to analogy." Further, Aristotle insists that "to use metaphors well is to see resemblance."[5] As Genette explains, in examining the historical evolution of metaphor, "[w]e know that the term metaphor tends increasingly to cover the whole of the analogical field; whereas the classical ethos saw in metaphor an implicit comparison, modern thinking would tend to treat comparison as an explicit or motivated metaphor."[6] It seems to me, to generalise, that from antiquity to modern and contemporary times, metaphor has functioned as a trope that (perhaps inevitably) seeks to yoke together, often with epistemic violence, marked differences; the final object has been to create what Northrop Frye calls, in the *Anatomy*, "the concrete universal," one that is meant to bring about "a unity of various things."[7] Thus, as a transfer-mechanism —i.e. as an instrument by which to circulate and affirm (traditional?) values— metaphor, especially in modern and contemporary times, has had inseparable and perhaps irreducible tropological and ideological functions.

In the writing of Western(ised) theatre history, metaphor's unifying power, classically-privileged genealogy, and protocols of surveillance and visibility have legitimated its use-value in supporting a totalising, Euro-inflected, teleological, relentlessly developmental, progress-narrative of macro-history in which the objective, wittingly or otherwise, has been the effacement of cultural difference to position *all* of us in the narrative register of the One and the Same.[8] As Bert O. States reminds us, quoting James L. Calderwood on Shakespeare, although a metaphor is *initially* a source of "'creative insight and for a time gives off a spark of aesthetic pleasure,'" it eventually wears out, "'collapses into an inert name — or more familiarly 'dies.'"[9] In writing

---

4 Roman Jakobson and Morris Halle, *Fundamentals of Language*, 2nd rev. edn. (The Hague and Paris: Mouton, 1971), passim.

5 "The Poetics," trans. Alfred Gudeman, in *Literary Criticism: Plato to Dryden*, ed. Allan H. Gilbert (Detroit: Wayne State UP, 1962), pp. 99 and 103.

6 *Figures*, p. 110.

7 *Anatomy of Criticism: Four Essays* (Princeton: Princeton UP, 1957), pp. 124-5.

8 I develop this argument at greater length in my seminar paper, "Metonymic Tensions and the Restaging of Theatre Historiography," annual meeting of the American Society for Theatre Research, New York, 14 November 1994.

9 James L. Calderwood, *Metadrama in Shakespeare's Henriad: Richard II to Henry V* (Berkeley and Los Angeles: U of California P, 1979), p. 14 as quoted in Bert

(theatre) history, the death of metaphorical modes of cognition often goes unnoticed, however, or un(re)marked; the metaphor continues to function as a lifeless epistemological corpse / corpus that we none the less take for granted as it brings a kind of hidden collective death to the cultural and intellectual ideologies from which it once originated and for which it now serves as a kind of unauthorised undertaker.

For postcolonial cultures —Canada, Québec, and many others elsewhere— the preoccupation with metaphor as an instrument of synopsis, enclosure, and death has been nothing short of devastating.[10] These cultures have often been written out of the historical record through metaphors of exclusion or treated *en passant* through metaphors of marginalisation / peripheralisation. Meanwhile, they have been assimilated and naturalised within larger narrative patterns through metaphors of diachronous domination — for, as States has recently put it, citing Walker Percy, metaphor "is a big thing happening in a small place."[11] Postcolonial cultures have also been literally and figuratively imprisoned within a dated and arguably reductive, but none the less still potent and deeply inscribed, centre / margins binary in which their own values have been radically diminished and in some cases, alas, demonised. Whenever —and I can't think of any single exception to this historical process— hegemonic cultures have brought their own metaphorical patterns and expectations to bear on the Other, they have routinely sought to elide differential properties. As Juan Villegas has argued, for example, 'Latin American culture' —which has tended to be read as a totalising entity— has often been patronised as "negative or grotesque," marked by a distinct "lack of originality," and positioned as a (mere) derivation of diachronous European paradigms.[12] Repeatedly, in Latin America (so-called), metaphor has func-

---

O. States, *Great Reckonings in Little Rooms: On the Phenomenology of Theater* (Berkeley and Los Angeles: U of California P, 1987), p. 12, n. 9.

[10]The critical literature on this subject is still in its infancy. For some preliminary formations, see Eric Cheyfitz, *The Poetics of Imperialism: Translation and Colonization from 'The Tempest' to 'Tarzan'* (New York and Oxford: Oxford UP, 1991), passim; You-Me Park, "Against Metaphor: Gender, Violence, and Decolonization in Korean Nationalist Literature," in *In Pursuit of Contemporary East Asian Culture*, eds. Xiaobing Tang and Stephen Snyder (Boulder: Westview P, 1996), pp. 33-47; Keyan G. Tomaselli and Johan Muller, "Class, Race and Oppression: Metaphor and Metonymy in 'Black' South African Theatre," *Critical Arts* 4.3 (1987): 40-57; and Juan Villegas, "Toward a Model for the History of Theater," in *The States of 'Theory': History, Art, and Critical Discourse*, ed. David Carroll (New York: Columbia UP, 1990), pp. 255-79.

[11]*The Pleasure of the Play* (Ithaca and London: Cornell UP, 1994), p. 88.

[12]"Toward a Model," pp. 258-59.

tioned, like allegory, as an ideologically-regulated strategy of appropriation and articulation achieving its ends through the linguistic violence of the transposition of Eurocentric paradigms. In this context and others like it, allegory, once completely out of fashion, has, like the return of the repressed, come back to do the coercive ideological work for which it was originally designed; as Stephen Slemon argues, it "allows the coloniser always to read the 'other' in the ideological mirror of his own metaphysical system and to rationalise real cultural difference as a factor of the permanent hierarchical difference inscribed in the manichaean master code."[13] If we 'transfer' (as in substitute) metaphor for allegory, the epistemological validity of Slemon's argument is in fact enhanced through the principle of rhetorical complementarity and magnification. Big things do indeed happen inside —and in the ongoing territorialisation of— small places.

The link between the genealogy of metaphor and the history of Shakespearean production provides primary evidence of the double process of enclosure and exclusion. Turn to *any* major work on stage history in general and Shakespearean performance practices in particular published over the last few years and try to locate, on the totalising maps that they draw up, even the briefest mention of a *tradition* of postcolonial rereadings and restagings of Shakespeare; a *tradition* that, having existed *for over a century*, could itself make a claim, *if* it were inclined to do so, for having metaphorical stability and comprehensiveness.[14] All these studies subscribe (again wittingly or otherwise), to the principles of linear narratives, of centre and margins nomenclature, of definitive interpretations / summaries of unproblematised empirical evidence and of unproblematised period and geopolitical categories. They seldom, if ever, examine the troubled relationship between pictorial evidence, on the one hand, and verbal descriptions, on the other; indeed, they tend to take pictorial material —its origins, its kinds, its viewing protocols— at (universalising) face value and take perverse pride, not in decoding ways of seeing but in providing examples of so-called 'new' pictorial evidence. Moreover, Shakespeare's cultural capital —how, why, and to what ends it has been amassed, how it functions in variously defined ideological constituencies— is never even glanced at, let alone granted systematic analysis. Despite an occasional, anxiety-ridden, gesture towards the influence of cultural materialism, there is a general reluctance to explore the shifting ground be-

---

13"Post-Colonial Allegory and the Transformation of History," *Journal of Commonwealth Literature* 23.1 (1988): 161-62.

14I detail the trajectory of this (counter-)tradition in "The End(s) of Shakespeare," *Essays in Theatre* 15.1 (November 1996): [1]-14.

tween the performance of culture and the culture of performance; with one or two exceptions, the emphasis is resolutely on theatre within conventional, metaphorically-sanctioned, temporal and spatial categories.

Reading these works, you could be forgiven for thinking that Russian formalism, structuralism, semiotics, poststructuralism, deconstruction, hermeneutics, phenomenology, cultural critique, Marxist criticism, feminist criticism, gender theory, and postcolonial theory *and* practice were all waiting to be invented; you could also be forgiven for thinking that most of the world, apart from Britain, selected parts of Europe, and the U.S., does not exist except as occasional sightings on a CNN-manipulated global teleprompter. On the evidence of these books, where *is* metaphor? Alive and well, apparently, flourishing in the groves of academe, in the editorial practices at Cambridge and Oxford, and, if these books are to be believed, in the ways that certain (select) directors, designers, actors, critics and audiences have constructed / authorised Shakespeare by means of (reductive) concept-driven productions.[15] It is not surprising that States should end up describing metaphor as "work[ing] like a secret password or handshake known only to insiders."[16]

## *The Recuperation of Metonymy. Now*

As nearly as I can tell, apart from the thinking of a small number of scholars —among them, Hayden White, Homi K. Bhabha, Paul Ricoeur, Paul De Man, Jacques Derrida, Kenneth Burke, David Lodge, Genette of course, and, most famously, Jakobson— metonymy has been neglected, perhaps even suppressed, as an historiographic strategy.[17]

---

[15]See Jonathan Bate and Russell Jackson, eds., *Shakespeare: An Illustrated History* (Oxford UP, 1996); John Russell Brown, ed., *The Oxford Illustrated History of Theatre* (Oxford UP, 1995), Dennis Kennedy, *Looking at Shakespeare* (Cambridge UP, 1993); J. L. Styan, *The English Stage* (Cambridge UP, 1996) and Simon Trussler, *The Cambridge Illustrated History of British Theatre* (Cambridge UP, 1994).

[16]*Great Reckonings in Little Rooms*, p. 114.

[17]See Hayden V. White, *Tropics of Discourse* (Baltimore: Johns Hopkins UP 1978), Jacques Derrida, *Dissemination*, trans. Barbara Johnson (Chicago: U of Chicago P, 1981) and *Margins of Philosophy* (Chicago: U of Chicago P, 1982), Paul De Man, *Allegories of Reading* (New Haven: Yale UP, 1979), Homi K. Bhabha, *The Location of Culture* (New York and London: Routledge, 1994), Paul Ricoeur, *The Rule of Metaphor*, trans. Robert Czerny et al. (Toronto: U of Toronto P, 1975), Kenneth Burke, *A Grammar of Motives* (Berkeley and Los Angeles: U of California P, 1969), David Lodge, *The Modes of Modern Writing* (Ithaca: Cornell

In traditional classical models going at least as far back as Aristotle, and developed over the centuries of the Western rhetorical and tropological tradition by eighteenth-century French grammarians like Nicolas Beauzée, metonymy has tended to be designated as literary trope that is always subservient to the longstanding authority of metaphor.[18] It is mainly Jakobson's seminal 1956 essay, "The metaphoric and metonymic poles" (published in his *Fundamentals of Language* with Morris Halle) that has been responsible for modernist preoccupations with their bookend status, to gloss Genette, in contemporary rhetorical theory and practice. Despite the widespread influence of Jakobson's essay, however, metonymy's form, function, and value, and its possibilities for revised historiographic and interpretive methods in theatrical, cultural, and literary studies, remain largely unexplored. Indeed in many quarters of the Anglo-American academy, metonymy is *still* regarded with suspicion, not as a bookend or polarising opposite, but rather as a perhaps inferior subspecies of metaphor, and as a cognitive / tropological mode that only has use-value for feminist theorists indebted to Lacan (for example, Kaja Silverman, Jane Gallop, Naomi Schor, and Peggy Phelan)[19] and for postcolonial provocateurs (for example, Bhabha and, more recently, Salman Rushdie who, in *The Moor's Last Sigh*, simultaneously parodies, subverts, contains, and *celebrates* Bhabha especially in relation to metonymic narrative configurations).[20]

---

UP, 1977), Genette, *Figures of Literary Discourse* and Jakobson, *Fundamentals of Language*. See also Lodge's novel, *Nice Work* (London: Secker & Warburg, 1988) which investigates the metaphorical / metonymic 'poles' in the making of meaning, value, and sex.

[18]*Grammaire générale; ou, Exposition raisonée des éléments nécessaires du langage, pour servir de fondement à l'étude de toutes les langues* (Paris: J. Barbou, 1767).

[19]Kaja Silverman, *The Subject of Semiotics* (New York: Oxford UP, 1983), Jane Gallop, *Reading Lacan* (Ithaca: Cornell UP, 1985) and *Thinking Through the Body* (New York: Columbia UP, 1988), Peggy Phelan, *Unmarked* (London and New York: Routledge, 1993), and Naomi Schor, *Breaking the Chain* (New York: Columbia UP, 1985). See also Luce Irigaray, *This Sex Which Is Not One* (Ithaca: Cornell UP, 1985).

[20]Bhabha, *The Location of Culture* and Salman Rushdie, *The Moor's Last Sigh* (Toronto: Vintage Canada, 1996): the Bhabha 'connection' is literalised / parodied on p. 329; I would propose that the entire novel is an exploration of the metonymically-configured subject- and narrative-position.

I am grateful to Proma Tagore and Priya Kumar for helping me to understand the connection between Bhabha, Rushdie, and metonymy.

Metonymy has good reason to be in bad odour, for it does have a shit-disturbing agenda. It is not merely a polar opposite, but is frankly antagonistic towards the high, class-conscious status of metaphor. Hence the inherent attraction of metonymy for postcolonial theory as that theory seeks to develop an anti-hegemonic critical vocabulary to oppose, and perhaps eventually to supplant, metaphor, and as it works to interrogate and dismantle a variety of ontological impasses regulated by metaphorical appropriation and containment. Historically, metonymy has been instrumental in establishing not uni- but rather poly-valent relationships based on the principle of contiguity between one thing, idea, action, or another; as David Lodge succinctly puts it, it functions in such a way that "an attribute or cause or effect of a thing signifies the thing,"[21] a process of part / whole substitution that rhetoricians often call metalepsis. Unlike the unifying, wholesale, transfer strategies of metaphor, however, metonymy foregrounds interrelated *dis*similar properties, to open up not a common/wealth but an *un*common ground, one in which the geography of part(s) / whole, margins / centre is radically problematised, placed on a discontinuous differential continuum, and in which correspondences, connections, affiliations, and attributes *in-between* things, ideas, actions, and indeed people are exposed not simply as causal or linear, but rather as multifactorial and synchronous, perhaps marked by the (dissident) potential for condensing, disrupting, and eventually displacing the sign-systems that are totalised by metaphorical domination.

Metonymy, as its etymological origin in the ancient Greek for "change of name" demonstrates, is indeed dedicated, first, to the *un*- and, second, to the *re*-naming of the linguistic register and the epistemological world-view that the linguistic order has sought to shape and legitimise. As an act of tropological *resistance*, metonymy is a device that allows us to see or *re*see what has been sublimated by the dead hand of cultural — ideological traditions and of ontological habits. As States concisely puts it, apropos the avant-garde potential of nineteenth-century realism, both metonymy and its cognate form, synecdoche, can be used as "devices for reducing states, or qualities, or attributes, or whole entities like societies to visible things in which they somehow inhere."[22] Metonymy, in this sense, is a poetics of (material) perception, one in which the gaze is turned back upon itself in an act of (self)-refreshment, readied to see what it could not see before; it is not, however, a colonising gaze, moving outward, seeking to imperialise

---

[21]Lodge, ed., *Modern Criticism and Theory: A Reader* (London and New York: Longman, 1988), p. 57, n. a.

[22]*Great Reckonings*, p. 65.

worlds elsewhere, for that form and function are of course reserved for metaphor and its coercive protocols.

Although the metonymic yearns for autonomy, in the final analysis it is often denied the right to possess itself fully to achieve self-determi(nation), a phenomenon that incites frequent bouts of existential trauma inside the reiterative sites of enunciation. Indeed, I would argue, following not only Ricoeur but also Pierre Fontanier's work on tropes early in the nineteenth century, that metonymy, paradoxically, is not only a matter of contiguity —an idea that tends to reduce it to its materialising or reifying function— but also a matter of correspondence, connection, and contingency in which "two objects [or more] *'form an ensemble, a physical or metaphysical whole, the existence or idea of one being included in the existence of the other'*" [emphasis in original]; and that as a result of the kind of horizontal symbiosis that this ensemble produces, "a relationship that brings together two objects each of which constitutes 'an absolutely separate whole'" comes into (fragile) existence.[23] In this mutually reinforcing ensemble, this conflicted hybrid of interdependent or contingent, metaphysical relationships, coloniser *and* colonised, original *and* copy, whole *and* part, centre *and* margins, same *and* different, in brief, metaphor *and* metonymy, not only encounter but, ontologically and tropologically speaking, *require* each other to form an imbricated, anxiety-provoking, historical continuum in which every kind and category of value is called, perhaps permanently, into question.

To put it another way, once metonymy, through its attributive, ensemble functions, manages to contaminate and estrange metaphorical authority, it is no longer a simple matter of the coloniser seeking to take absolute control over the colonised. In their conflicted will to power, each of them is reconfigured: the original is disrupted by the copy, the whole is fragmented by the partial, the dystopian is found wanting in the presence of the utopian, and the metaphorical is written (over) —to a degree— by the metonymic. From these polarising phenomena, and others like them, emerge not only the condition of hybridity but also the figure of the double who turns up, with uncanny frequency, as a spectre within a whole range of postcolonial texts. This figure of the double is the character who lives to inhabit two or more spaces (especially outside / inside) *simultaneously*, who is and is not him- / herself, who occupies both the 'real' and the 'imaginary,' who acts out, and is marked by, both roles of coloniser / colonised in a series of endlessly reconstituting significations of thwarted physically- and metaphysically-inflected forms of desire. The central metaphorical /

---

[23]Fontanier is quoted in Ricoeur, *The Rule of Metaphor*, p. 56.

metonymic text in these cases is the palimpsestic multi-performance-text of the suffering, seemingly deformed, postcolonised body, inscribed by, through, and in-between the interstitial values of the seen / not seen, the visible / invisible, the normative / grotesque, and the here / elsewhere.

## *Metaphor / Metonymy & Inter- Intra-Cultural Performance*

For a short period in the late eighties, early nineties, the critical, theoretical, and historical literature on inter- and intra-cultural performance practices provided a way of thinking about the ways in which hitherto delegitimated and suppressed differences might serve to disrupt authorised and repressive hegemonies. The chief difficulty, however, is that most (perhaps all) of this work has been produced by metropolitan authorities, including Patrice Pavis, Erika Fischer-Lichte, and Bonnie Marranca (and Gautam Dasgupta); the work of Rustom Bharucha has been perversely positioned both without and within these discursive formations.[24] In all cases, without exception I would argue, differences of various types have been constructed as *relational phenomena*, marked by their positionality towards dominant Western theatrical practices. This, I believe, is itself a strategy for containment — inadvertent perhaps but none the less coercive and producing an unresolved tension between macro and micro models of cognition and reaffirming the reductive dangers of *the* centre and margins model. As has often been remarked, but not remarked often enough, heated debates about the death of the subject brought about by various postmodern, metropolitan-controlled doubts about the desireability, status, and ontological truth-claims of autonomy have had the effect, in postcolonial sites of contestation, of robbing them of their epistemological quest for the stabilisation of identity; for finding a way out of the dilemma of being always already *post*.

Much of the critical literature on both inter- and intra-cultural performance seems to believe, whatever the ontological evidence to the contrary, that despite the death of the sovereign subject, identity-posi-

---

[24]Bonnie Marranca and Gautam Dasgupta, eds., *Interculturalism and Performance: Writings from PAJ* (New York: PAJ Publications, 1991), Patrice Pavis, ed., *The Intercultural Performance Reader* (London and New York: Routledge, 1996), Rustom Bharucha, *Theatre and the World: Performance and Politics of Culture* (London and New York: Routledge, 1993), and Erika Fischer-Lichte, ed., *The Dramatic Touch of Difference: Theatre, Own and Foreign* (Tübingen: Gunter Narr Verlag, 1990).

tions *are* recuperable, realizable, and knowable; and that performance itself —in the sense of enabling restored behaviour, of (re)presenting the actualising experience of being different, of perhaps overcoming the dangerous paradoxes of double-agency and of licensing cultural promiscuity, and of resisting dominant modes of inscription and codes of representation— is *the* instrument of choice for those people who none the less remain disenfranchised. But for the postcolonial subject, articulated through the differential protocols of metonymy, none of these things are in fact assured. Practically, postcolonial subjects might not have, or might not be able to create for themselves, actual theatres where the performance of their identity-politics is in fact welcome and productive. Theoretically, postcolonial subjects are rightly wary of the phenomenological uncertainty of performance itself. It is seductive to imagine that you *might* be able to perform your invisible self into visible existence by taking over the instruments of the master's / father's house. But how confident do you feel, surrendering yourself to this *possibility*, when you know from real-life, hard-won experiences, that metaphorical entrapment awaits you, that the codes of metaphorical representation all/ways seem to have pre-emptive authority, and that your own subject-position is tenuous in the extreme? To be a permanently postcolonialised metonymic subject, after all, is to be subject to a world of shifting and slippery *differential* relations in which nothing, absolutely nothing —'your self' as self-authorising performance-text least of all— is guaranteed as being *yours*. What, then, can the postcolonial director/actor actually do, especially when face to face / mask to mask with the single BIGGEST metaphor of them all: Shakespeare....? What is revealed? what is concealed? How? and why?

## *'We don't 'do' plays, we (re)make them:'*

Paula de Vasconcelos

Directors, I think, don't really choose plays to direct; instead, plays choose them, with the choice a function of the mostly invisible discursive preoccupations, neuroses, obsessions of a particular historical moment. In the entire Shakespearean canon, I can't think of a play better suited than *Macbeth* to an investigation of the functions, forms, and values enabled by the conflictual will to power between metaphor, on the one hand, and metonymy, on the other. Just as these tropes are effectively about struggles over the ownership of the categories of cognition, *Macbeth* is a play about the possession, dispossession, and repossession of, pun intended, relentlessly gendered *sovereign authority* within a visible / invisible discursive economy of witchcraft and demonology, crime, punishment, and redemption, psychic imbalance and restoration, and blood, purgation, trauma, and healing, in which Shakespeare traces multiple disturbed and disturbing affiliations among the body private, the body public, and the body politic. In the primary, if often glossed over, conflict that the play embodies between England, on the one hand, and Scotland, on the other, questions are implicitly raised not only about the intertwined processes of colonisation and (potential) *de*colonisation, but also about the kinds of tropes in which these historically-rooted violations of both the body private and the body politic take place.

Questions are also raised, as a consequence of these linguistically-based and ontologically-determined struggles, about the politics of personal and public identity; the play seems to suggest that the cost of (self-) betrayal will either be a descent into the chthonic, into witchery, into bloodshed (Macbeth) and / or a descent into blood and madness (Lady Macbeth). The play, then, maps the recurrent preoccupations of divided (post)colonial subjects, in Québec as elsewhere, who cannot live within traditional, monarchically-(or capitalistically- ) determined, hierarchies of power, but, who, at the same time, cannot live outside those hierarchies except by becoming victims of historical forces that are much more powerful than they can ever be. Denied agency, historically (in)stalled in the victim position, postcolonial subjects, like their exemplars of Macbeth and Lady Macbeth, seem to exist for one purpose only: to be excluded, through death and madness, from a renewed, normative, stable, hierarchically-intact social order.

To put this schema into national terms, one could say that just as 'Scotland' is effaced / purged by 'England', Shakespeare's *Macbeth* is a profoundly preservative / conservative affirmation of the need to ensure the stabilisation of an untroubled narrative of monarchical succession. In the Québec context, the play has therefore tended to function as a complexly received and produced multitext, in which the transgressive, alienated, unstable Other of Québec (tenuously represented by the Macbeths as perverse couple) itself has to be literally and figuratively demonised, driven mad, and killed off if the fiction of political continuity, at the symbolical level, is to be sustained; and if the trauma inflicted by the Conquest is to be laid to rest or, at the very least, forced underground, rendered invisible. The very decision to perform the play *now*, in the midst of continuing post-referendum *angst*, is, in effect, a dangerous move, for it could force one to become complicit with the ongoing, metaphorically-driven project to legitimate the violations of imperialism / federalism: that is, unless (an)Other text, metonymically-positioned and therefore vulnerable, can be tellingly created / performed, at the same time and within the same space of enactment, to contest Shakespeare's controlling apologia for the inherent naturalness and inalienability of monarchical succession.

Attempting to produce this counter-text is the task that Paula de Vasconcelos, together with the writer, Jean-Frédéric Messier, has set for herself in the aptly named, *Le Making of de Macbeth,* a title that registers both the continuous process of (re)making Shakespeare —moving outside of his canonical status so as to go inside the politics of Québec— *and* the split subject-position, the doubled condition (*of* / *de*) that inevitably destabilises the postcolonial (re)writing of identity at its very moment of inception. Saying, as Vasconcelos does, that she doesn't 'do' plays, that she (re)makes them, seems to ensure that the struggle for (textual) autonomy will succeed, to a degree; it will only succeed, however, *if* a useful way can be found to register difference (away) from the originating, parental text.

I know no one, however —Vasconcelos herself included— who has fully succeeded in doing so; performance (always) seems to lead, as though by means of a hidden ontological trap, to the reinscription of the very value-systems that it seeks to challenge and perhaps subvert: metonymic dis / placement has yet to find a way to resist the seductive power of metaphorical conflation. The making is none the less useful in disclosing why, how, and to what ends, metonymic strategies are invoked, and provides a case study, in microcosm, of the current state of play within *one* postcolonial condition.

## *Character and the Lateral Play of Difference*

*Le Making*[25] is preoccupied with character as a polyvalent multitext, in pain, perhaps impotent yet potentially procreative, glimpsed / tableaued in different sites across time, through space. The ever-shifting nominal centre is the director, Elizabeth, whose *angst*-ridden dilemmas in producing *Macbeth* form the met*o*-text out of and on top of which, as in a palimpsest, the text of *Le Making* is conjured ... In the leaking / bleeding categories of identity that the production envisions, Elizabeth is a function of diversely-situated affiliations. Elizabeth I is her main antecedent, except to say it this way is to suppose that their relationship is linear, when in fact the production is at pains to situate them both as coextensive, their relationship produced by an historical

[25]All comments on the text, *Le Making of de Macbeth,* come from the photocopied version —Mise en texte de Jean-Frédéric Messier; d'après une idée de Paula de Vasconcelos— kindly lent to me by Paula de Vasconcelos and Pigeons International. Other comments on the production are based on my own observations of it on several occasions during its run.

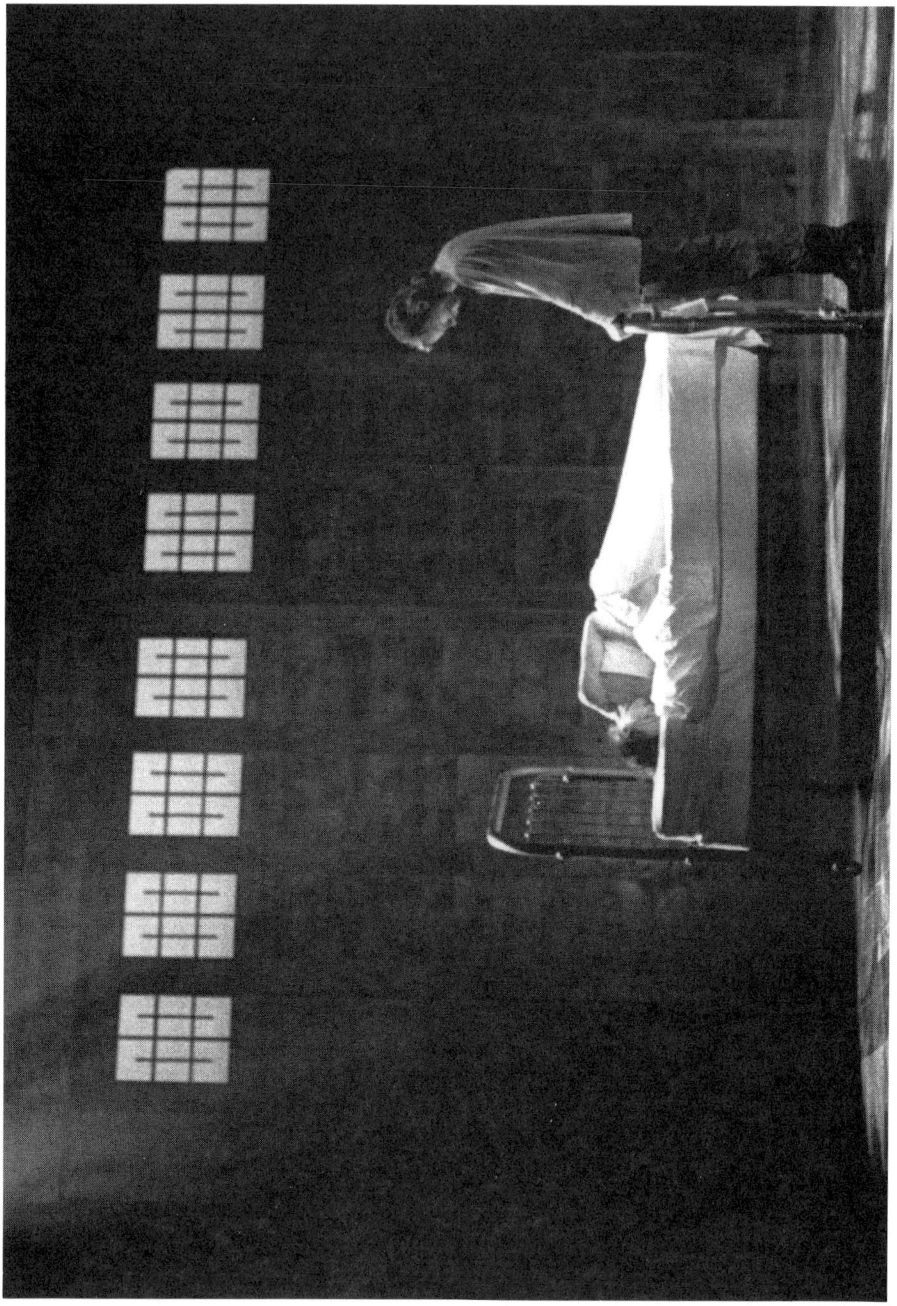

Fig.1. *Elizabeth in a coma.*
Photo courtesy Louis Taillefer.

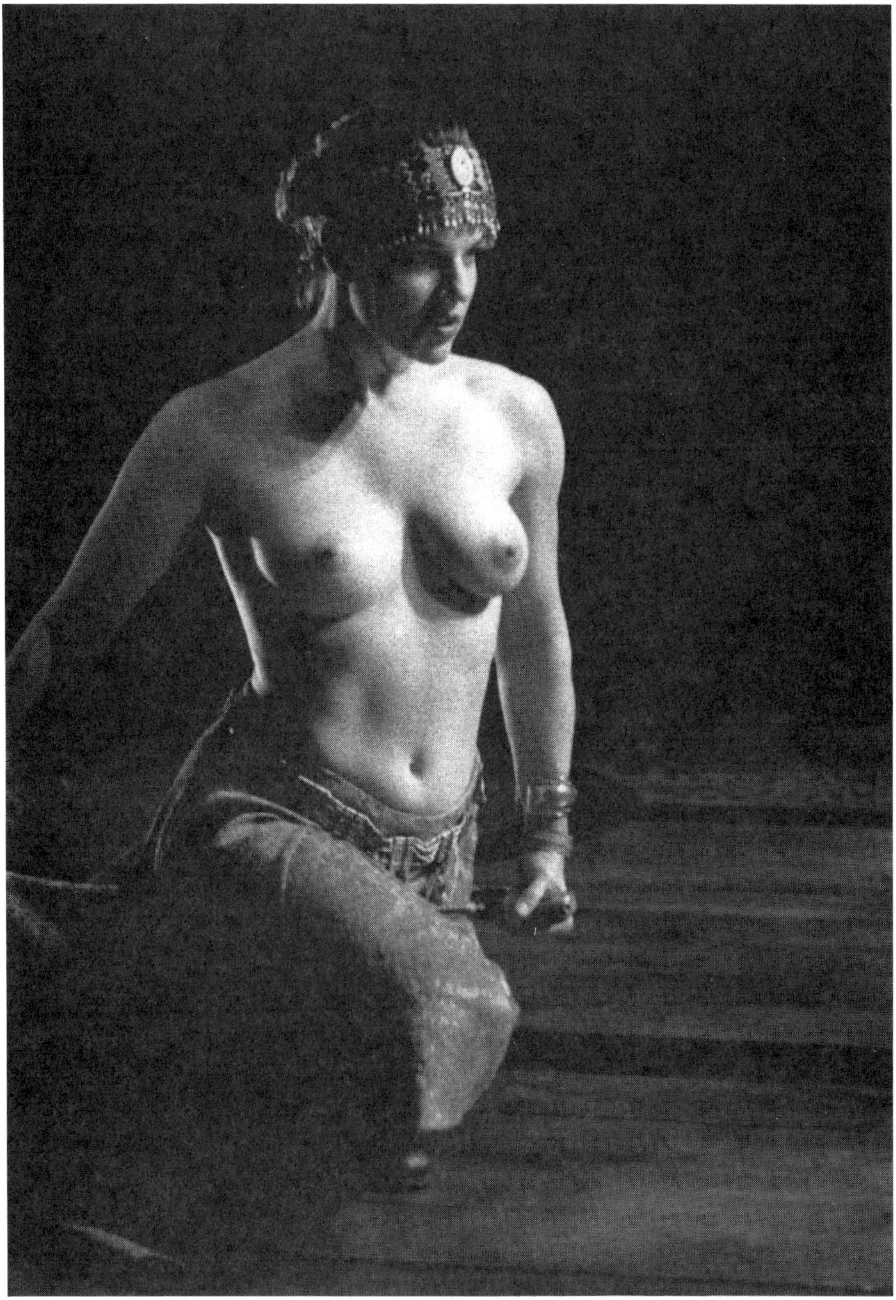

Fig. 2. *Sylvie Moreau as Lady Macbeth.*
Photo courtesy Louis Taillefer

process of prodigious doubling. Mary, Queen of Scots, is the self-assured, rooted Other against which Elizabeth's own descent into madness is defined through the principle of opposition. Catherine, Elizabeth the I's lady-in-waiting, is played by Sylvie Moreau, the actress who *also* plays Lady Macbeth, and so in the master / servant relationship, with Catherine as liminoid, as intermediary, Elizabeth the director, Elizabeth I, Catherine, and Lady Macbeth are experienced as iconic projections within a same / similar time / space continuum. Sylvie Moreau / Lady Macbeth also plays one of the Witches, and so 'witchery' / bedevilment are projected or deflected into the depths of Elizabeth's 'character.' Character here is not centred and centering but dispersed across a discursive field; it is not vertically, but horizontally, positioned; it is not one but many; it is not precise and knowable but diffuse and elusive.

Elizabeth, as director, has reached an impasse which is the ostensible inciting incident of the entire play. Afraid of blood, of the messy fluidity of procreation, and afraid, without really understanding why, by her art yet so bewitched by it that she has no time for 'life,' Elizabeth none the less wants / needs to become pregnant. At a moment of crisis, brought about the protracted impasse, by her inability to live across the art / life divide, she (like Lady Macbeth, a textual spectre who guides and contra-defines some of her actions) faints and enters into a deep coma. Elizabeth, as a site of multiple identities, embodying but by no means reconciling time past, time present, and time future, is the postcolonialised body in pain, at once outside / inside virtually everything that might confer a fixed identity upon her. Her coma eventually has a therapeutic function, setting her free of her daemons, allowing her to return, purged, to her life, where she now has the *courage,* as a *woman,* to abandon the directing of *Macbeth* — meanwhile allowing her company to decide whether they themselves want to continue with it — and to become pregnant by her lover, Robert. The pregnancy, like her omnidirectional, attributive 'character,' also provides her with a bloodline to Elizabeth I: Robert is named *after* Robert, Elizabeth I's lover, the *first* of two Roberts in her life; meanwhile, Paul-Antoine Taillefer, Vasconcelos's husband, plays both Robert *and* Macbeth, so 'real' life and 'fictional' embodiment are conjoined, in such a way that blood, crime, guilt, and (possibly) liberation are registered through multiple frames of reference.

In the (in)visible moral pattern of both *Macbeth* and *Le Making,* good comes from bad, light from dark, life from death; history, however, is not constructed in such a relentlessly linear model, but, by means of the multiple character-affiliations, seems ultimately to exist

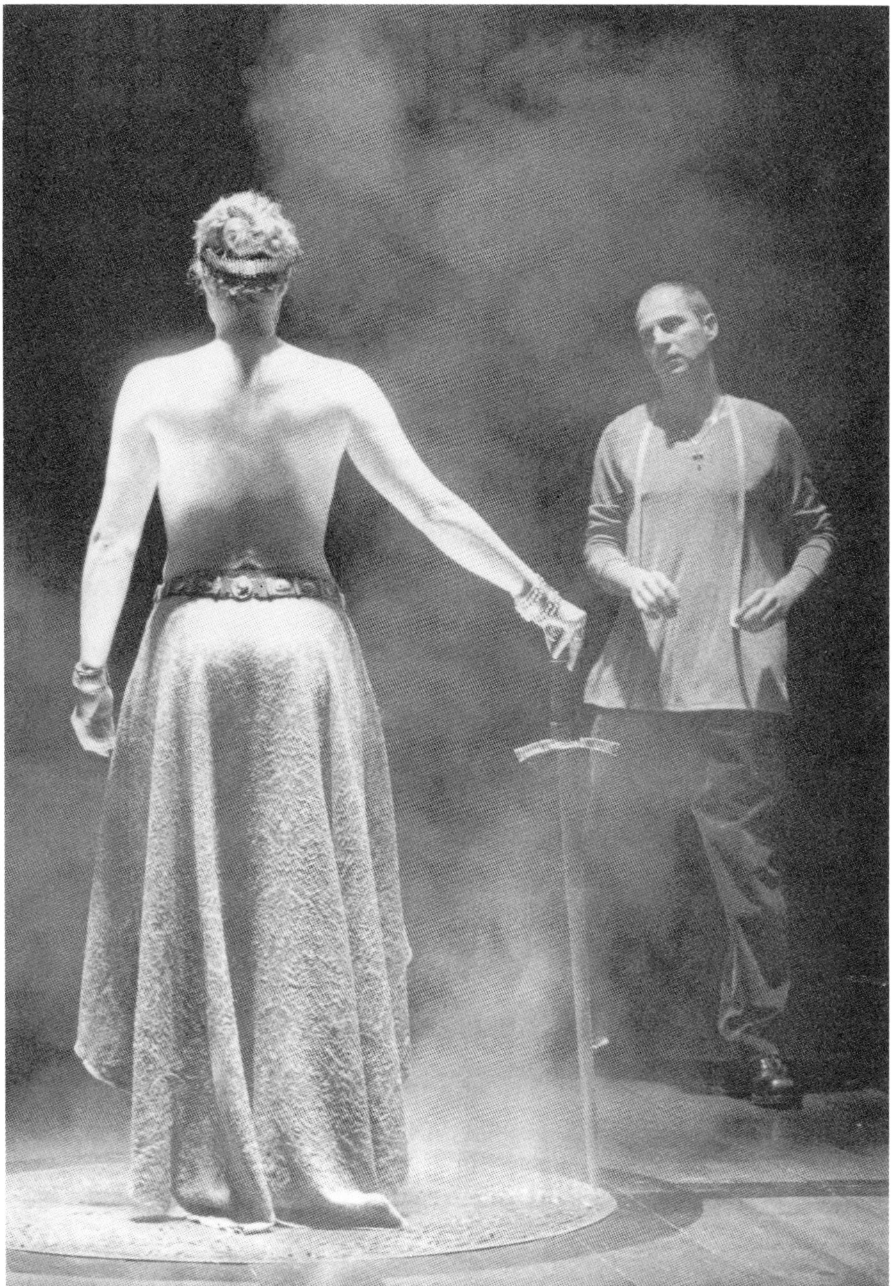

Fig. 3. *Sylvie Moreau as Lady Macbeth.*
Photo courtesy Raymond-Marius Boucher

within the *paradox* of an atemporal, eternal present, one in which, as Vasconcelos herself has put it, she can attempt to situate herself and her company as *contemporary* artists providing their reading of a mélange of historical source materials, Shakespeare's play being only one of many among them ("What *I* and our whole company try to do is to experience the play — elaborate it, if necessary, as in *The Making of Macbeth* — from who we are at any given time in history").[26]

These layered narratives and palimpsestic characterisations are not, I think, (merely) exercises in rapacious postmodernised / (postcolonial) eclecticism in which differences, temporal, spatial, and cultural, are blithely erased. Rather, they are indeed exercises, as Vasconcelos herself acknowledges, in seekinging to get a purchase on (historical) locations of meaning; a kind of naive assertion of who you are, where you stand, and what you might become (hence the preoccupation with blood, desire, and impotence / fertility) and, at the same *time*, a way of *making* clear, especially through imagistic means, uncontaminated by verbal language, the confluence of forces, myths, legends, narratives, images, and desires that have enabled your existence. The question, however, is what kind(s) of identity *can* be purchased in this shifting field of (re)presentational possibilities?

Elizabeth *does* escape from the madness of her art; she *does* become pregnant and therefore succeeds where both Elizabeth I and Lady Macbeth had failed. She *does*, then, create the future for herself, in a way that they couldn't, apart, that is, from acquiring what perhaps is even more permanent and powerful than what Vasconcelos's Elizabeth acquires: enduring status as dominant icons in the formation of the Western unconscious. Elizabeth is, ultimately, a paradigmatic metonymically-configured subject: formed not by and for herself but by forces Other than: by a dense conflation of historical and literary figures; by a play, *Shakespeare's Macbeth*, which she must renounce in order to survive, but by means of which she acquires an oppositional identity; by a clichéd pop culture narrative about madness and the price of going on; and by being situated, situating herself, in an atemporal present which reveals her as the self-in-flux, authorised not so much by and for herself but rather by an inherited network of discursive practices that effectively rob her of a capacity for agency and individuation.

There is intense utopian-driven pathos in all of this. Existentially, Elizabeth yearns to *be* Elizabeth, but her art, and its multiple, culturally-specific, sources thwart this ambition; sovereignty — personal and political — does not, ultimately, belong to her, but rather to Elizabeth I, the primary template in relation to which Elizabeth's own identity

---

[26]Quoted in Salter, "Blood," p. 75.

can function as nothing more — or less — than as a diminished copy of a (barren) power that once *was*.

## *Blood*

Elizabeth: a body in pain ... undergoing trauma ... seeking to heal herself outside of the gendered / colonialised codes of representation ... succeeding in giving birth (to herself) but only by relinquishing art, theatre, Shakespeare and *his* universalised Queen. Despite her initial rejection of the dominant image of blood, Vasconcelos came to recognise that Shakespeare's *Macbeth* and therefore her *Le Making* had to become preoccupied with this image as theme and variation ("you can't get around it: bloodshed, bloodlines, blood images, bloody battles — blood is everywhere").[27] What kind of blood was / is it? In a conventional reading, it might have (simply) been blood as violation and guilt made manifest. But in this production the symbolical and metaphorical were always being contested by metonymic displacements and reconfigurations of meaning. Thus, in a key scene ("Le Sang 2") — forming a *dis*continuous correspondence between acts one and two, and providing a kind of visual performance score that shadowed the verbal performance score on the theme of the wounds of battle ("so they / Doubly redoubled strokes upon the foe: / Except they meant to bathe in reeking wounds" [11]) from earlier in the play —the actors— not as characters but as themselves —*playfully* and *violently*— covered themselves and one another in buckets and buckets of red paint. Later in the play, the multiplying images of actors as blood leaked over / seeped through into the (primary) image of Elizabeth, waking from her coma, being helped, as though a marionette, by Robert as she walked slowly across the stage, before gradually pulling a long red ribbon from between her legs — an evocation of death / madness / sleep / destruction; of life / clarity / wakefulness / (re)birth; and of the visceral mess by which Elizabeth was / is both repelled and attracted...

These dispersed images, poeticised embodiments of the umbilical cord, had, in my view, many effects / affects. They imparted poeticised density to both the verbal and visual performance-texts; in the project of interrogative re-naming, they murdered and then recovered the urtext, Shakespeare's *Macbeth*, from its status as a metaphorical corpse / corpus, allowing us to see it, as if for the first time, as a source of enabling desire; and they served to underscore the production's primal

---

[27] *Ibid.*, p. 68.

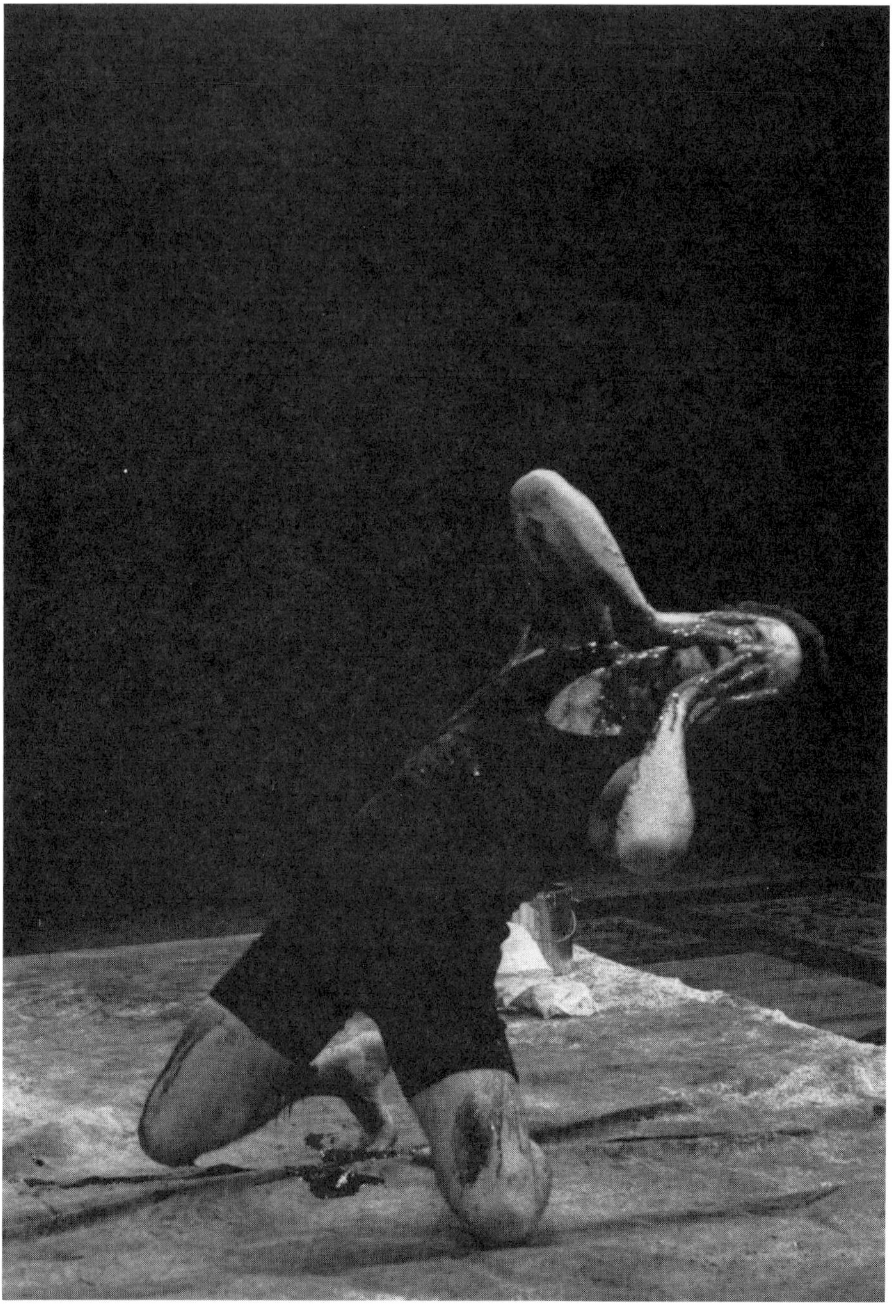

Fig. 4. *Mario Saint-Aman a Henri during the body-painting scene.*
Photo courtesy Pigeons International

Utopian yearning to re/vision, to reveal, to tease us with a kind of poetics of in/visibility, to enhance the protocols of perception, and to urge us to reconsider and perhaps reinstall the Feminine as *the* site of origin — desire embodied here within and beyond the moment of trauma. In particular, this impression of the (bloody) fecundity of the Feminine drew from and inspired multiple affiliations between and among the figures of Elizabeth, one the one hand, and Lady Macbeth, on the other. The production was at pains to present Lady Macbeth, not as a hysterical, PMS-tormented, contemporary woman, not as a semi-divine maenad, not as a Siddonian criminal virago, not as a Terryian cooing dove, but as an empowered hybridisation of personified and empowering Beauty, Strength, and Sexuality, irradiated by the iconic authority of Diana, India, the Orient, and Amazonia. Yet this heightened poetics of hybridisation did not have a homogenising function —collapsing all these sources into a single metaphorical register— but rather insisted on the heterogeneous, the fractured, and the non-referential constitution of being; allowed Lady Macbeth —and therefore Woman for whom she served as a metonymy— to exist outside conventional modes of representation; and, most of all, imparted visceral immediacy to Elizabeth's protean identitities (artist / madwoman; wife; mother-to-be).

## *Of Puppetry and Puppets*

In seeking to represent the unspeakable, *Macbeth* infects its performers with preternatural dread, with premonitions of disaster. It is itself an object lesson in awful *re*naming: superstition has it that if we call the play by its real name, we court disaster; so we allay our anxieties by renaming it as something different: as the *Scottish* play. Difference, then, as in metonymy's proliferating agenda, reduces metaphysical stress, resists trauma; it is the Oneness of metaphor that continues to evoke terror (especially on 'opening' *night*). In the performance of *Le Making*, fear was indeed pervasive: towards *Macbeth*, towards art —the source of Elizabeth's primary trauma— and, perhaps most of all, towards Shakespeare himself as the textual arbiter whose unifying presence could not (ultimately) be resisted even through the metonymic protocols of reinscription. In addition to the displacing functions of renaming, the performance sought in numerous ways to cut Shakespeare down to size, a process that I think of as a metonymic condensation; a way of liberating the postcolonial subject from Shakespeare's all-encompassing magnitude by deliberately (re)making him partial, not whole, contained, not expansive, 'provincial,' not metropolitan.

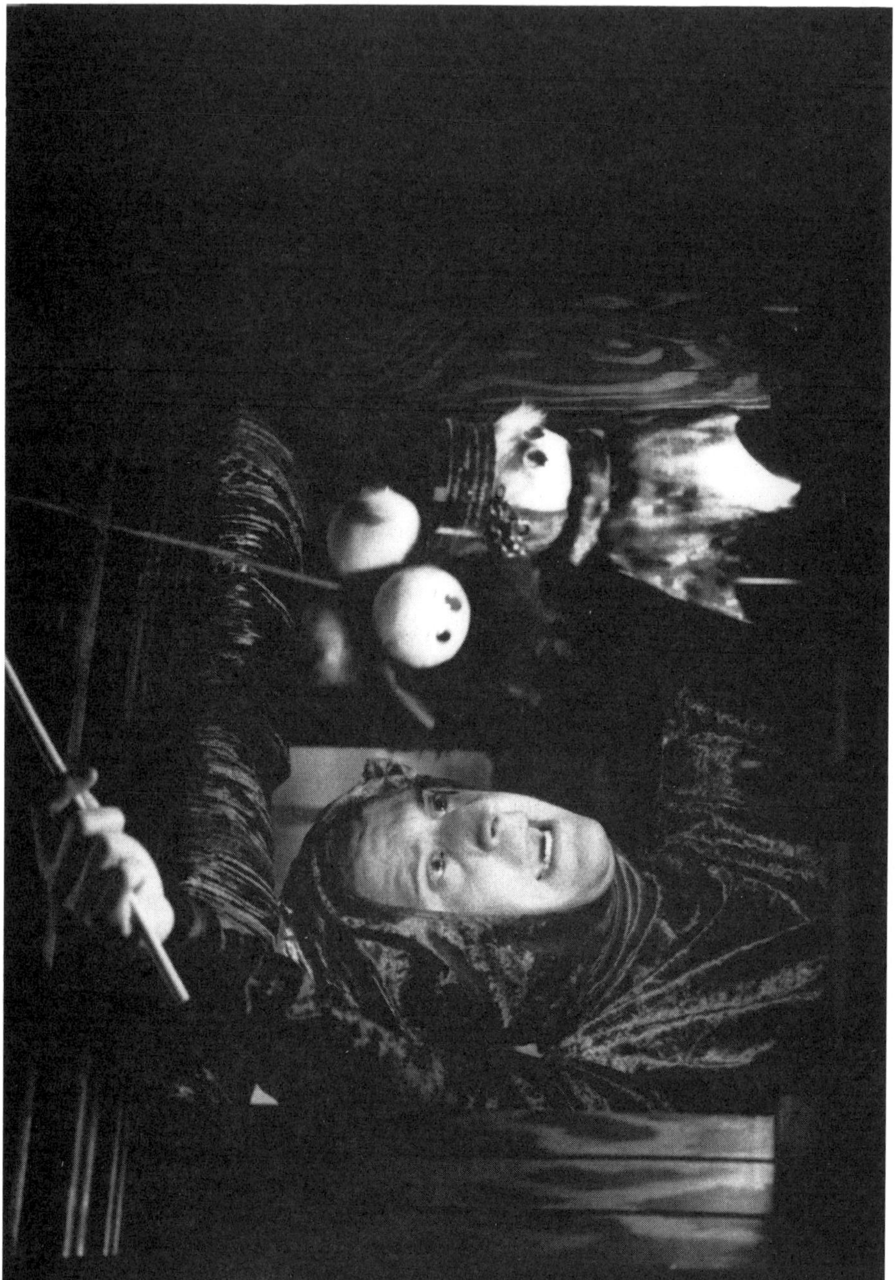

Fig. 5. *François Papineau as Pierre the Puppeteer.*
Photo courtesy Pigeons International

Vasconcelos's production worked through this process in the figure of Pierre, the puppet master in a red fool's cap, who appeared three different times, with his own perambulating mini proscenium arch stage complete with green baize curtain, to retell the story of Macbeth and Lady Macbeth as a serio-comic brutal struggle between Punch and Judy. As Vasconcelos has remarked, Pierre intervened in Messier's text as a blasphemous commentator on Shakespeare, traducing his authority; as a clear way of encapsulating the main story in English for a francophone audience, decoding it, as it were, to make its meaning transparent; and as a device for demythologising and debunking the Macbeths, allowing us to see them as people just like us.[28]

In addition, however, it seems to me that Pierre, as puppet master, managed to *re*frame the Macbeths, circumscribing their power in the world at large and revealing them as puppets that could be manipulated, not solely by the supernatural force of destiny, as they are in *Shakespeare's Macbeth*, but through Pierre's own (and therefore *our*) reimagining of them. In this new micro-narrative, the so-called normal order of things was inverted: power was now in the hands of a so-called fool, the 'witchery' of his art was demystified as a skilful performance, and he himself was gradually revealed to be, not foolish, but wise. Indeed, within the revisionist moral trajectory of *Le Making*, Pierre —in contradistinction to Elizabeth— could readily separate his art from life; whereas she was always in danger of being destroyed by her single-minded absorption within the art of (Shakespearean) performance, he knew how to make them divisible, a strategy that protected his sanity and allowed him to present his art not as a tragic infection but as a generous gift to his daughter, yet another of the production's (in)visible sources of Feminine renewal.

## *Making Metonymy*

The challenge, I would provisionally remark, for Shakespearean performance and for ways of thinking about it, is to de-metaphorise cognitive modes, categories, tropes, and narratives. Yet this is an extraordinary challenge, if for no other reason than because so many of us have had our minds and imaginations conditioned by the protocols of metaphor; they are second nature to us, hence invisible, hence all-powerful. Shakespeare, moreover, as cultural capital —and as pedagogical and performative institution— himself exists largely as a function of metaphorical modes of interpellation. Now, however, that I myself,

---

[28]*Ibid.*, pp. 81-82.

partly in response to Vasconcelos's *Le Making*, have at least begun to imagine Shakespeare otherwise through the protocols of metonymy, I am beginning to see traces, incipient formations, resistant sites, of metonymy in all kinds of unexpected places. Could it be that metaphor is reaching a point of exhaustion as *the* dominant trope of Western rhetoric? I doubt this. But I note, in the autumn 1995 issue of *Brick*, that the U.S. poet Carolyn Forché, who has dedicated much of her career to writing committed, political poetry in self-imposed exile *outside* of the U.S. in (especially) El Salvador, observes in an interview with Eleanor Wachtel that she is now engaged with a self-conscious "resistance to metaphor." Forché says that instead she has "been exploring a different tributary of language, which is its tendency toward metonymy... In metonymy you explore all the things associated with a given word, the way in which that word slips and moves around and through the language and back through its history, and picks up meanings along the way and sheds others." Later, Forché remarks, with reference to Pablo Neruda, that at certain points, "many things can't be a metaphor for anything, and serve no metaphorical purpose." Many things, Forché implies, just are themselves—no metaphor is *adequate*, as a mode of transfer / translation into something *other than*, in rendering these things exactly as they *are*.[29] Quite apart from a U.S. poet in exile, trying to clear away an imaginative space to call *her* own, for the postcolonial subject in a state of (tropological) siege, metaphor clearly no longer has any real epistemological validity, except as an unthinking reflex action of the mind / imagination. To be in the world metonymically, however, as I have suggested, is to make oneself vulnerable not only to the continuing authority of metaphor but to the embattled politics of the inter- and the intra-: the very interstitial sites where you might normally expect the postcolonial subject to 'belong.'

I almost feel compelled to conclude, as I did in "Acting Shakespeare in Postcolonial Space," that postcolonial cultures should continue to avoid doing Shakespeare at all costs. But, if they none the less feel compelled to remake him, then, as in Vasconcelos's *Le Making*, it seems to me that perhaps the only way to proceed, however fraught, is through an exploration of what the metonymically-configured subject-position enables. Doing so, however, has many consequences: among them, the recognition that art of this kind requires that the postcolonial spectator, critic, theorist, historian, and historiographer must also learn to exist otherwise, becoming engaged, with Forché and others, in

[29]Eleanor Wachtel, "An Interview with Carolyn Forché," *Brick* 52 (Fall 1995): 48.

the collective act of "resistance to metaphor." Frankly, I have difficulty imagining what a completely de-metaphorised world would be like. But trying to think this way serves to remind me, as does Forché's observation about the place of metonymy in contemporary poetry, at least from Neruda onwards, that there has indeed been, since the nineteenth century, a mostly *hidden* modernist tradition of metonymically-driven Shakespearean theorisation, criticism, and performance that has mostly existed outside / in exile from, metropolitan centres. "Shakespeare and Modernism's Other" — but that is a title for another essay, for another time, another place.

*Mc Gill University*

# RUNNING TIME: SCENOGRAPHY AND TEMPORALITY IN PERFORMANCE

Natalie Rewa

> And now is the thing seen or the thing heard the thing that makes most of its impression upon you at the theatre, and does as the scene on the theatre proceeds does the hearing take place of seeing as perhaps it does when something real is being most exciting, or does seeing take the place of hearing as it perhaps does when anything real is happening or does the mixture get to be more mixed seeing and hearing as perhaps it does when anything really exciting is really happening. (Stein 65)

In this section taken from her lecture *Plays* written in 1934 Gertrude Stein asks questions that are very useful to the study of scenography. She proceeds through questions that seem to test spectator response in general and at very specific moments —those when emotional engagement is the strongest. She sets up her discussion of emotional response in terms of the consciousness of being able to differentiate between the impact of seeing or hearing, which, in the theatre are often considered simultaneous. In her first question she asks simply whether there is a hierarchical order, in terms of reception, of hearing and seeing. As she makes her question more precise she adds in, not only the concept of narration, but also the complexity of the artificiality of performance — in opposition to life. She likens these moments in the theatre to similar moments in life when something exciting is happening and hearing takes over from seeing. Alternately she muses whether seeing replaces hearing when "anything" real is happening. She ends this round of questions by mixing these categories so that she asks about moments when the real excitement is really strong, whether the senses are mixed and indistinguishable. As she ties the visual and verbal to the emotional she seems to situate theatre somewhere between the visual arts and the literary arts. The way in which she probes performance encouraged me to consider how scenographic design might benefit from an interdisciplinary exploration of space and time for the emotional response.

When Gertrude Stein asks, "Does the thing seen replace the thing heard or does it help or does it interfere with it." (Stein 65) these questions have in them reverberation of the way in which verbal and visual arts have been thought of as either one or the other. Lessing's analysis of space and time in artistic expression is particularly interesting in this context. He encourages artists to stay within their disciplines. He cautions painters not to depict allegories because they unfold in temporal sequences which cannot be accommodated in single image, and poets are cautioned against the static and pictorial rather than bringing forth the image in temporal terms. The metonymies of postmodern scenography seem to be able to create the significant images sought after by Stein and develop visual narratives that are multifaceted. It is this that is the topic of my exploration. Contemporary design appears to appreciate Stein's understanding of the spectator's subjectivity "from the standpoint of sight and sound and its relation to emotion and time, rather than in relation to story and action" (Stein 66) as well as Lessing's understanding of temporality of poetry.

Hence, the running time of my title refers to space-time revealed by the scenographic design that is apparently separate from the narrative of a verbal text. My interest is in the way scenography provides a place to accommodate the emotions. This exploration is still concerned with some of the questions posed by Stein in the thirties but, I would like to ask them in terms of the way anticipation, memory, and physical perspective are part of individual designs. Consequently my consideration of scenography does not consider time and space as consistent and independent, rather scenographic design is being considered here as that which allows movement (action), but also place as pause in time. It is this pause in which movement is to be transformed into place.

The shift in thinking of the metaphysical space-time into the theatre, since it is not derived from literariness might benefit from reference to the evolution of art history over the last two decades — where Michael Fried, WJT Mitchell, Griselda Pollock, Rosalind Krauss and Mieke Bal take on the iconicity of visual art and the writing of art history. A useful point of departure is Erwin Panofsky's categorization of iconographic analysis and iconological interpretation. Panofsky draws attention to areas of slippage in knowledge between the epistemology of the spectator interpreting, and the cultures of representation. He offers a useful caution in his "corrective principles of interpretation" when looking at paintings. He differentiates between iconographic analysis, which draws on literary sources and allegories, as distinct from iconologic interpretation which points to the "symbolical values," the meaning of content. He suggests that, in the case of interpreting paintings, it is as, "impossible to give a correct iconographical analysis by indiscriminately applying our literary knowledge to the motifs, as it is for us to give a correct pre-iconographical description by indiscriminately applying our practical experience to the forms" (Panofsky 36). So too, in the study scenography looking only through the literary lens of the dramatic text is limiting, it is much more helpful to introduce the modes of representation and the cultures of the representations.

It is not surprising to find that following Panofsky's discussion, scholars such as Michael Fried and Svetlana Alpers began to question the performativity within the composition and how one might transfer into language the way in which a picture "works". Fried's work in the early 80s is helpful because it begins to consider how the picture holds the attention of the viewer. His binary opposition between the absorption which maintains all energy within the frame is contrasted with the theatricality which acknowledges presence outside the frame. Alpers, when looking at Dutch art of the 17th century characterized it as descriptive rather than narrative as Italian painting of the same period. When feminist scholars as Mieke Bal discuss paintings in the 1990s it is in consideration of getting beyond the word-image opposition. Her analysis of Rembrandt's *Susanna Surprised by the Elders* cuts through "the realist illusion that promotes the enjoyment of the represented body without further ado" (Bal 43). She chooses an interdisciplinary approach drawing on narratology, ideology, and history. It is this combination of strategies adopted by the art historian that is perhaps most helpful in finding a new path in discussing scenographic design.

Recently WJT Mitchell asked "What do pictures *really* want?" While his question is posed of art history and the interpretive strategies or rhetorical positions of art historians, it has been helpful in clarifying my own thinking. He seeks to shift the aim of the inquiry from what pictures do, made famous by his study *Iconology* where he looked at verbal-visual co-relations, to reclassifying pictures into a minority speaker position of the subaltern which has been open to the dialectics of "power and desire in our relations with [them]" (Mitchell, 1996, 74). He guides the reader through a shift away from pictures as "vehicles for the interpretation of meaning or instruments of power" (Mitchell, 1996, 76) where they are feminized, and treated as being looked at but not necessarily expressing any desire in themselves or being aware of being beheld. His conclusions are an appeal not to annex the picture into other discourses but valorize vision "as important as language in mediating social relations" (Mitchell, 1996, 82).

This work by art historians which looks at the picture as an artifact is also helpful for the study of scenography. One cannot, however, use the term scenographer interchangeably with scenography, as one would painter in relation to painting, since in the production of performance the number of people involved varies as do the circumstances of the design created, but this in itself would make a fascinating study. Moreover, scenography which projects images beyond a simple geometric grid into the fourth dimension of time, cannot easily, be held as a two dimensional image. Contemporary CAD programs although still working on a grid, can, when using animation, begin to accommodate the fourth dimension. The result, still on a two dimensional screen, although helpful in some ways, returns the documentation of such a moment to a painting. My recourse is to use several slides of a production, when they have been available, to indicate, how a single set design, regraphs space-time in performance as part of the sculptural evidence of volume and direction of motion. In elementary terms the concern might be with sightlines, making sure that every one can see, and the geometric models which consider the performance space as a cube into which a human figure can be accommodated. The preliminary sketches of a designer's ground plan and scale drawings might maintain the concept of proportion with a human figure at the centre. Or do they? Postmodern design challenges this notion in resoundingly interesting manner. Similarly, approaching the question of scenography and temporality probes stage space and cognition. That is, the concept for the spectator of "where is here" of the performance in direct relation, very often, to the precise theatre, which governs focal distances and proportionality within the performance. Thus during the running time of the play the spectator considers the manipulation or use of the scenographic materials, as stilled out of chaos, for observation.

I would like to spend the remainder of the paper proposing four examples of the way in which scenography might be studied for "what it wants" and how certain instances of scenography challenge stable images of time and space. My examples have to do with the way in which the scenographic design pairs up with another media — music in opera and dance, and the spoken word in that latter two examples. The productions under consideration are *Salome* by the Canadian Opera Company (October 1996); *Prélude à l'Après-midi d'un faune* and *The Rite of Spring* by La Compagnie Marie Chouinard (January-February, 1997); *Glenn* by Necessary Angel (September 1992); *Froth, a Spectacle about Shopping and Hysteria* by the Froth Collective (December 1996).

The first that I will discuss is the production of *Salome* by the Canadian Opera Company. The reason that I have chosen this production is because it does not naturalize the environment of Herod's castle, rather it reconfigures space so that the spectator is encouraged to look not in straight lines, but to rotate the stage in the imagination. The scenography for *Salome* was constituted of Derek McLane's set, Philip Barker's film and videos and Michael Whitfield's lighting. The artists explored space as a kind of patchwork that was dependant on drawing attention to the perception of borders of solid forms.

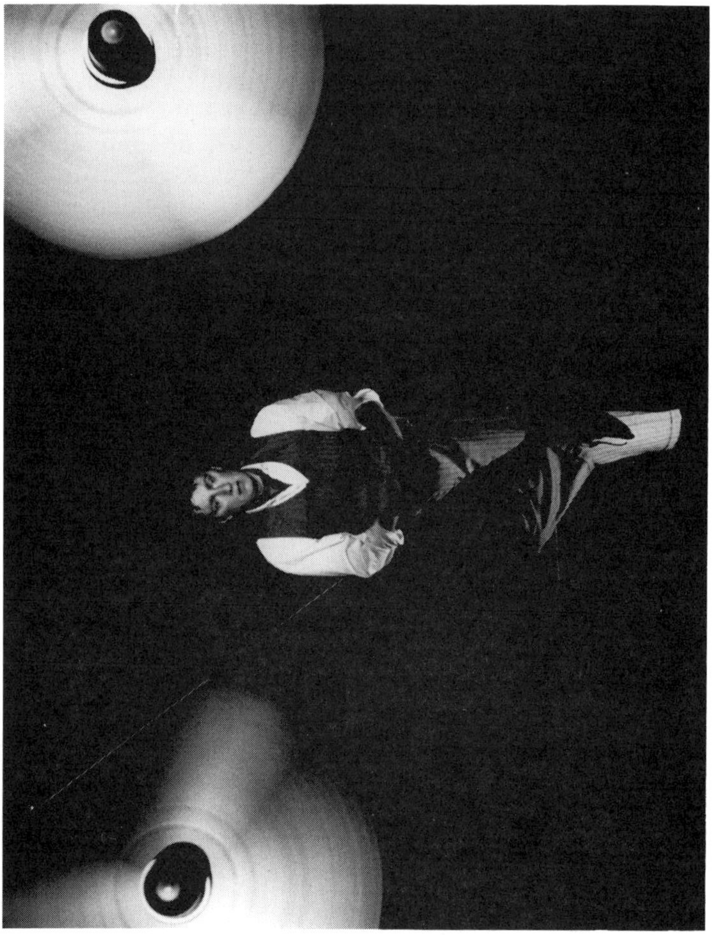

Fig. 1. *Robert Lepage in* Needles and Opium. *Lepage's scenographic design in performance challenges the traditional orientation of the horizontal and vertical axes of the stage floor and proscenium opening. In this instance the proportions of the human performer in relation to the stage set tests the spectator's understanding of Humans as the crucial unit of measure.*

Photo: Claude Huot. Courtesy of ExMachina.

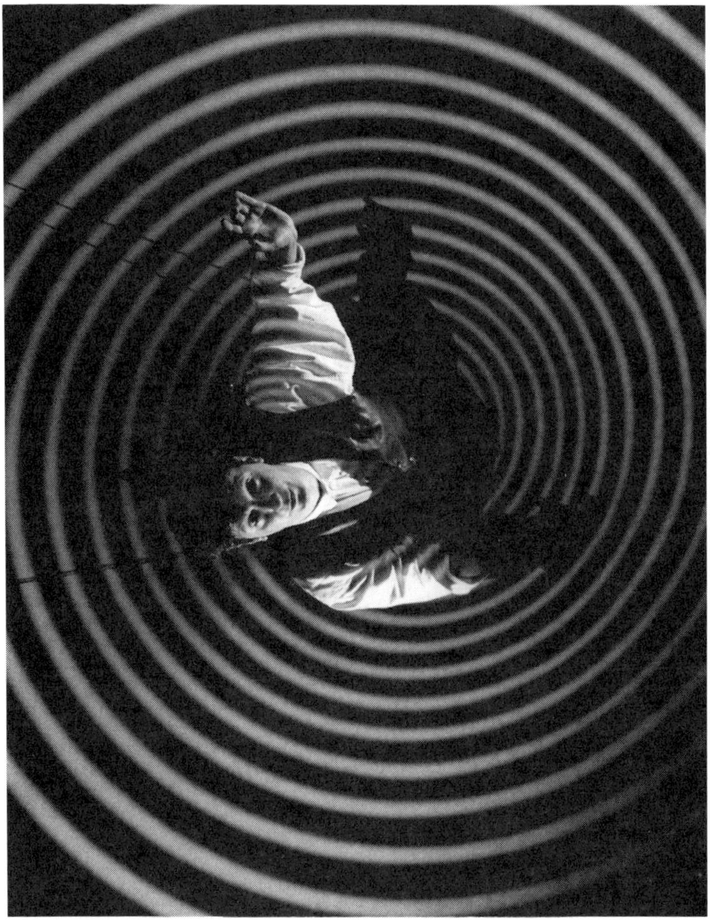

Fig. 2. *In his production of* Needles and Opium *Robert Lepage invites the spectator to consider very thoroughly how scenography can can defy geometric orientation. At this moment in performance the spectator's perspective is put into question, by the disorientation accomplished by slide projections and realignment of the actor's body in space. The spectator is invited to reread what is seen and to sort through the possible positions of the human figure as falling into a vortex, rising out of it, or floating through a tunnel. The regular signs of a body in space, guided by gravity and defined by the feet on the floor is denied.*

Photo: Claude Huot. Courtesy of ExMachina.

The COC, and opera internationally for that matter, has been venturing into the question posed by Stein so many years ago. In the late seventies Christopher Newton directed a stunning *Madame Butterfly*, but in a traditional set. More recently Robert Lepage and Michael Levine reconceived Bela Bartók's *Bluebeard's Castle* and Arnold Schoenberg's *Erwartung* (January-February, 1993). The opening sequence of Bartók's opera presented Laurie-Shawn Borzovoy's projection of miniature of a castle, a hologram projected into the blackness of the proscenium frame rotating, as if in a filmic panorama shot. Michael Levine's set confronted the spectator with seven doors in a receding perspective in a velvety blackness. The doors were defined by a thin red line of light seeping between each door and its framing. The consciousness of the physical rake of the stage, was not immediately evident in the darkness of Robert Thomson's lighting design, but was made explicit when hundreds of pearls rolled down the stage. The sound of the pearls hitting the ground and rolling across the floor elicited a strong consciousness of gravity in the imagination of the spectator. This gravitation pull was defied in the final moments when the singer, having slipped into the trough of water at the edge of the stage, was absorbed by the water and disappeared from view. Moreover, the iconography of the rooms behind the seven portals, mentioned earlier, were defined by solid blocks of light when the doors were opened. When the light was forced through the door it changed from solid colour, almost tangible by its volume, into a beam as it was dispersed into the blackness of the stage. The magnificence of the scenes invited the spectator to check whether what they were seeing was actually plausible in a physical world.

The scenographic design for *Salome* similarly encouraged the spectator to explore the environment of the stage checking the logic of what is actually seen. While Michael Levine's designs maintain the "face on" perspective and developed depth and defied gravity, the scenography for *Salome* subverted the way in which a proscenium arch might suggest a "geometral vision." McLane's set presented the spectator with a series of interlocking perspectives which at first seem incompatible. Michael Whitfield's lighting then picked features of each perspective to provide various configurations, that did not initially seem to exist.

The visually clever set created two vanishing points which crossed at right angles. The first perspective that one notices is framed along the upper and lower edges of the Hummingbird Centre's stage by two elongated triangular structures which stretch the width of the proscenium opening. Both of them have the high end at the left side of the stage. During performance it becomes clear that they are not of identical size, since the upper one can accommodate and did, a figure at full

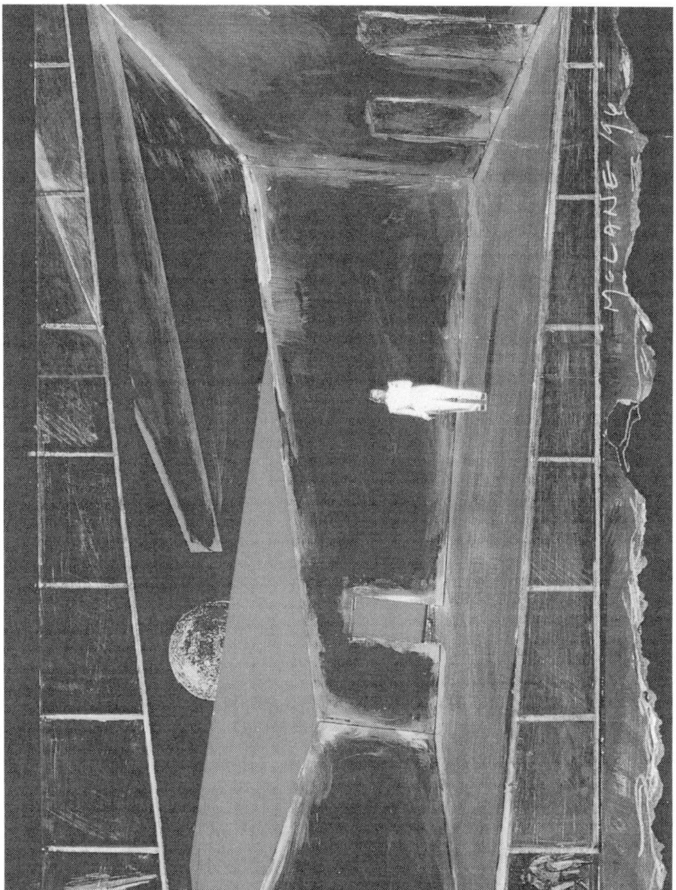

Fig. 3. *Drawing of the set for Salome for the production by the Canadian Opera Company at the Hummingbird Centre. The geometry of Derek McLane's set, with the attention to the borders where solid planes meet allowed Michael Whitfield the opportunity to pick out two separate perspectives for the spectator.*

Drawing: Derek McLane. Photo: Courtesy of the Canadian Opera Company.

height and thus was given the connotation of a catwalk-cum-observation post. This same structure, might simultaneously be understood as the cross-section of the other perspective — the raked stage which rises from right to left across the proscenium frame. Intriguing is the way either of these perspectives was accommodated depending which lines were used to substantiate the desire for perspective.

This double perspective was used to extremely good effect by *metteur en scène* Atom Egoyan. The design encouraged chronology to be replaced by the spatial temporal distribution of the figures within the frames. When Salome is observed from the catwalk, or when Salome traces the edge of the bottom wedge the arias seem to be in counterpoint to the "precarious" positions of the human figures. This design makes the concept of "now" very much like Gertrude Stein's questions about seeing and hearing mentioned at the beginning of this paper. This scenographic design also accommodated Jokanaan's off stage presence.

He was incarcerated in the "crawl space" closest to the audience, but his "narrative" prison in a cistern, was signalled by the light in this lower triangle that was actually also the underside of the raked stage — which accommodated Herod. Jokanaan's space-time coordinates as seen by the spectator, became those of the point where the two orientations of the stage intersected. Moreover, his physical presence was presented metonymically by live video projection of his lips while singing. As Jokanaan prophesies from his prison cell, his lips appear on the screen at the back as a video projection and assume a role in the perspective of the raked stage. Philip Barker's video projections shift the perspective of the spectator abruptly, even more so as the "paintbrush" used to draw them on the back wall is Salome's hand as she wipes the blood from the dead Narraboth. The voice is no longer "off" since paradoxically the mechanism for expression, the mouth, is "on" stage.

Particularly fascinating in this design was the handling of the *Dance of the Seven Veils* since it sets up yet another perspective to the exclusion of the first two. As Salome is about to dance she sits upon a swing, and Herod settles into a large chair upstage of her. As her dance begins the swing is drawn up into the flies and her skirt becomes a projection screen. The film projected on her skirt is initially a film of a forest. Very soon the purely telluric image is replaced by the image of a woman walking in a moving-filmed forest. For the spectator the film is highly disorienting, because there is very little encoding to explain the temporal orientation of this forest, or identify the imagination that calls it up, all that is known is that it overwhelms the pre-existing concept of space. The forest might be utopian, the desired landscape of the body which we are not seeing. In any case the image has an eeriness

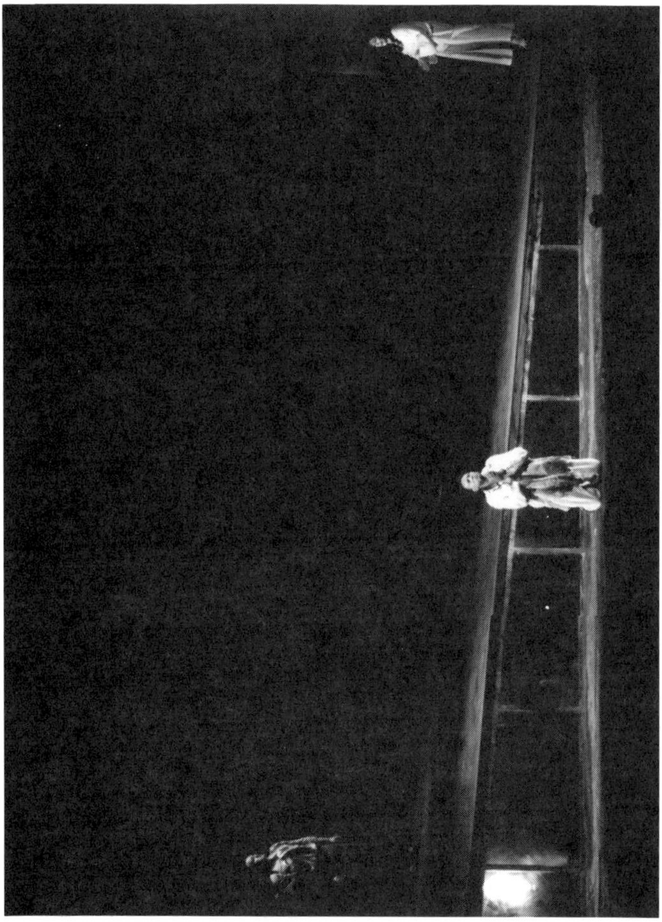

Fig. 4. *The set in performance. Using the raked stage for the definition of Herod's territory, Michael Whitfield's lighting picks out the lower triangle created by the incline as performance space for Jokanaan which is both on and off stage. Seen here from Left to right: Jon Villars as Narraboth, Simon Estes as Jokanaan and Ljuba Kazaranovskaya as Salome.*

Photo: Courtesy of the Canadian Opera Company.

about it for the Toronto spectators, as if they were certain of having been there or were willing to go there, which was confirmed by the guesses in the reviews of it being a Muskoka forest. The syntagmatic imagination of the spectator "no longer sees the sign in perspective, it *foresees* it in its extension ... it is, then, a strictly fabricative or even *functional* imagination" (Barthes 217). The film denies Salome's existence for the spectator as a stable artefact of the story, since she has become, in this case literally, a projection. The final images of a dancer who is assaulted by several fully-dressed male attendants is tremendously disturbing, but not noted beyond the silhouettes on the screen. When the dancer/Salome is finally discovered, she simply lies on the floor. All of this and never a stop in the music, just a reorientation of time and space. No explanation, no links. Only the inexorable progress of the musical score.

The guidance of music as keeping time is even more interesting when one turns to scenography and its place in contemporary dance. While some modern dance insists on narrative structures, reaching beyond the decorative presence of the dancer in motion, choreographer Marie Chouinard questions kineaesthetics of dances from the past in this particular program. Chouinard works as both a choreographer and scenographer and encounters time and space as highly gendered. She created the choreography to Debussy's *Prélude à l'Après midi d'un faune,* as a solo piece for herself in 1987 (in 1994 she entrusted this solo piece to another dancer), and a company piece to Igor Stravinsky's *The Rite of Spring* in 1993. Both have toured extensively and thus ought not to be seen as geared to a specific theatre. Marie Chouinard's choreography to this music is made the more interesting because Vaslav Nijinsky set the choreography to the same pieces in 1912 and 1913 for the Ballets Russes. The original designs for the Ballets Russes were by Léon Bakst who had already designed such sumptuous visual extravaganzas as *Cléopâtre* and *Schéhérazade.* For the second event on the programme Chouinard totally departed from masculinist modernism by adding an exciting prelude of Robert Racine's *Sound Signature* to Stravinsky's twenty eight minute composition.

Her choice of Debussy's eleven minute *Prélude à l'Après-midi d'un faune* is particularly striking and filled with cultural reverberations. In the first instance she brought together the historical choreography, but changed the image of the dance. Along with lighting designer Alain Lortie, Chouinard demonstrates an iconoclastic attitude to the modernist tradition. Chouinard has chosen to quote, but only partially, Vaslav Nijinsky's original performance from 1912. With true bravura strokes Chouinard choreographed a solo performance of what Nijinsky had presented himself as an eight person ballet. The earlier version

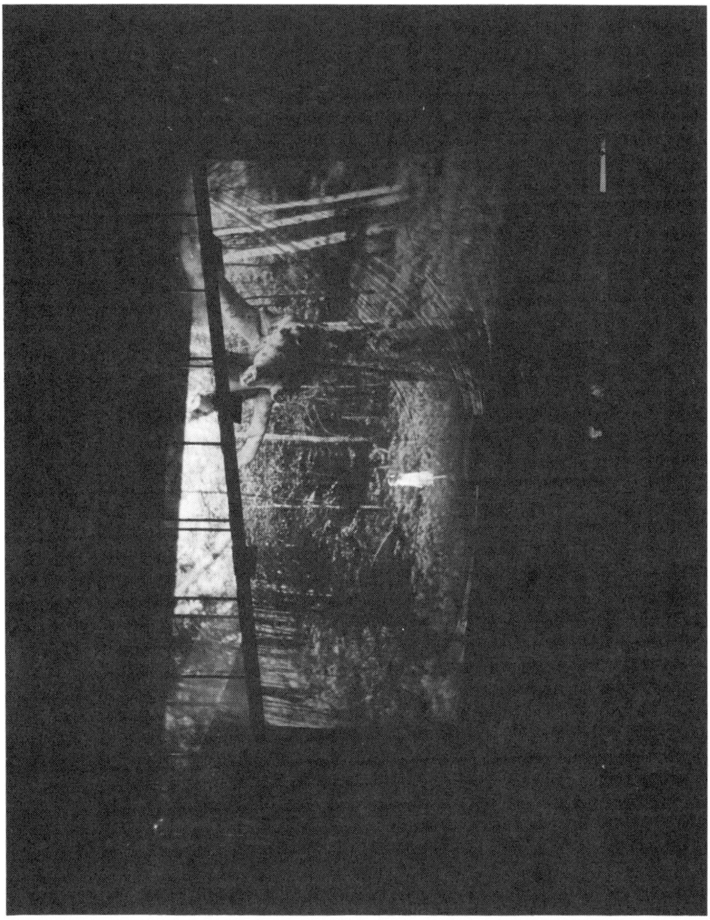

Fig. 5. *The screening of the film on Salome's skirt, obliterates the earlier perspective of the stage and creates a third performance place. Philip Barker's film raises significant questions of perspective.*

Photo: Courtesy of the Canadian Opera Company.

was succinctly summarized in the original programme note: A faun dozes, Nymphs tease him, A forgotten scarf satisfies his dream. The curtain descends so that the poem can begin in everyone's memory. Nijinsky danced the faun and his sister Bronislava the role of the main Nymph. Chouinard maintained Nijinsky's choreography, derived from the Egyptian friezes in the Louvre (de Meyer 65-95). The dancer Pamela Newell performed keeping her torso turned out to the spectators, while holding her head in profile. She also kept the style of the dance: flat foot, with the knees slightly bent. But whereas Nijinsky's faun was dressed in coffee-coloured tights on which the brown patches overlapped from tights to flesh so that the general effect was to merge the human with the animal, Chouinard elaborated this original concept — possibly because latterly it would have looked too much like a contemporary Milk commercial. Her costume featured padding at the patches, making one thigh seem disproportionately larger than the other and she drew attention to the bodiness of the dancer by adding onto them rubber protrusions which resembled thick individual animal hairs. As for the faun's ears, she eschewed Nijinsky's wax flesh-coloured elongations and instead of the wig with two horns peeping out from among the golden curls the dancer wore a set of wonderfully celebratory curled horns. Moreover, rather than a discrete garland of leaves around her hips Chouinard's dancer removed the tip of one of the horns and attached it with some little ceremony as an emblematic celebratory phallus.

Chouinard further played with the spectator's expectations of the masculinist view of the interaction between the faun and nymphs by performing the effective presence of the nymphs by a different medium. Rather than the corporeal presence of nymphs in long pleated cream tunics decorated with geometric motifs in green and blue or with stylized leaf patterns, Chouinard reconstituted them by sharply focussed beams of light. As Chouinard's faun encounters the nymphs it is done without the actual presence of female dancers on stage — the faun extends his hand into the beams of light and observes the light upon the limb. This faun is emboldened and thrusts his animated pelvis into the beams of light with an increasing mischieveness. As Debussy's music guides the listener through Mallarmé's symbolist and masculine faun, Chouinard removes the heterosexual narrative visually.

Furthermore, instead of Nijinsky's final frieze pose of the faun on the scarf, Chouinard breaks the constrictions of the two dimensionality of the "frieze' and in the final moments allows the faun to revel fully, with head thrown back in the gentle foil shower of climax blurring the sequential constraints of ordered time. This faun a exhibits feminist "jouissance." Gone is the symbolist veil surreptitiously gained, gone is the masculinist reverie.

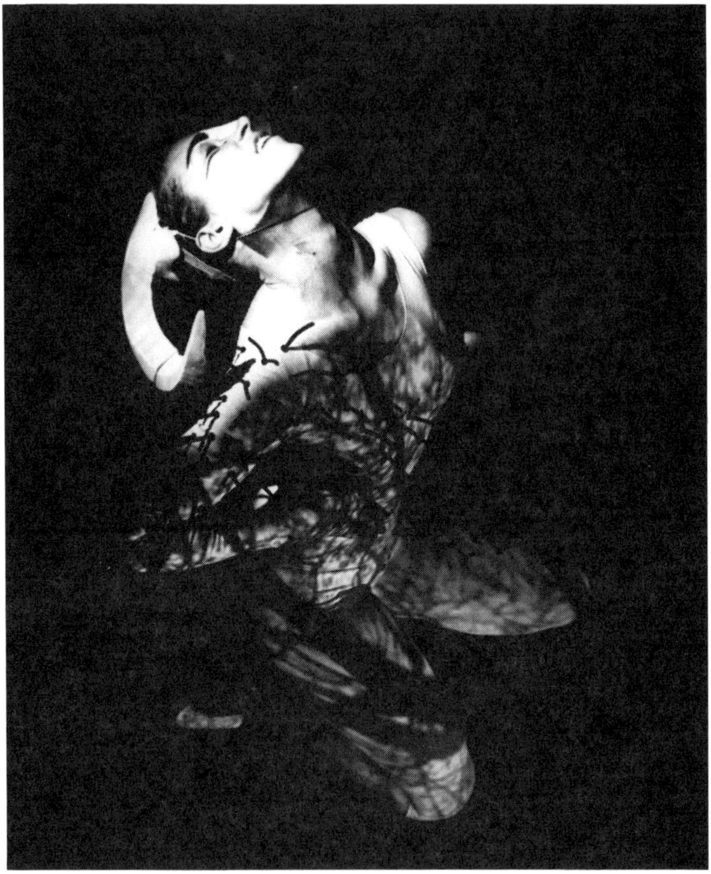

Fig. 6. *Pamela Newell as the faun in Prélude à l'Après-midi d'un faune, the choreography by Marie Chouinard to Debussy's music. Chouinard's rendering of the faun breaks from the two dimensionality of the frieze- style adopted by Vaslav Nijinsky in his choreography. This shift in perspective retunes the spectator's imagination from human experience of the frieze and Mallarmé's concept of memory to an immediate image of ecstasy.*

Photo: Stephen Hues. Courtesy of La Compagnie Marie Chouinard.

The second offering on the program was equally interesting, but here in a turn that one begins to expect from Chouinard. For the fifty minute ballet Chouinard appended Robert Racine's *Sound Signature* to Stravinsky's *The Rite of Spring*. Chouinard's wit is apparent in the choice of Racine's music as a commentary on the apparent relationship between music and dance, that one is to interpret the other, or rather to express the other in the abstractions of form in kineasethetics. Racine's composition which is literally the sound of a signature — a nibbed pen on fine paper, the kind with a very high rag content, creates a sonic environment of writing onto the stage, which has very different associations than those immediately visible. At one stunning moment the dancers lie down on their side, with their back to the audience, tucking in their head and limbs out of sight to create an image of a field of large primordial bones.

Once the music switches to Stravinsky Chouinard's choreography challenges the choric folk images of Dhiaghilev's Ballets Russes and sends her dancers on "elliptical voyages" of nuclear particles which do not know their own identity. The images she creates are those which might be glimpsed through a microscope, which confront the sense of movement trajectories, catching the dancers in carefully defined beams of light. (For the record, the sacrificial narratives of the Ballets Russes, Mary Wigman, Martha Graham and others are totally dispensed with). She characterizes her dance simply as synchronicity:

> I wanted to show the very moment of life's creation. But it cannot be done. Perhaps because I am human. Perhaps because that moment never really occurred. (program note)

Moreover, her understanding of the project leads her to bring the dancer out of the time of the music and into the timing of the dancer in space. The dancers no longer use the grid as a point of reference but appear as if made visible only by the beam of light that catches them in their trajectory through space. Each dancer dances into a kind of ecstasy, breaking up any uniformity of choral movement by the simultaneity. The eye of the spectator follows the circles and how they are inhabited by different dancers in combinations, sometimes achingly beautiful.

Whereas dance does not seek to change music into language a play such as *Glenn*, which sought to bring Glenn Gould to the stage tried at least to fill the silences between broadcasts and concerts by words. Graeme Thomson's design for the set and lighting consolidated the scenography in one imagination. The effect was stunning. With four Goulds on stage, acted by four different actors, Thomson's design sought to maintain simultaneity throughout the design.

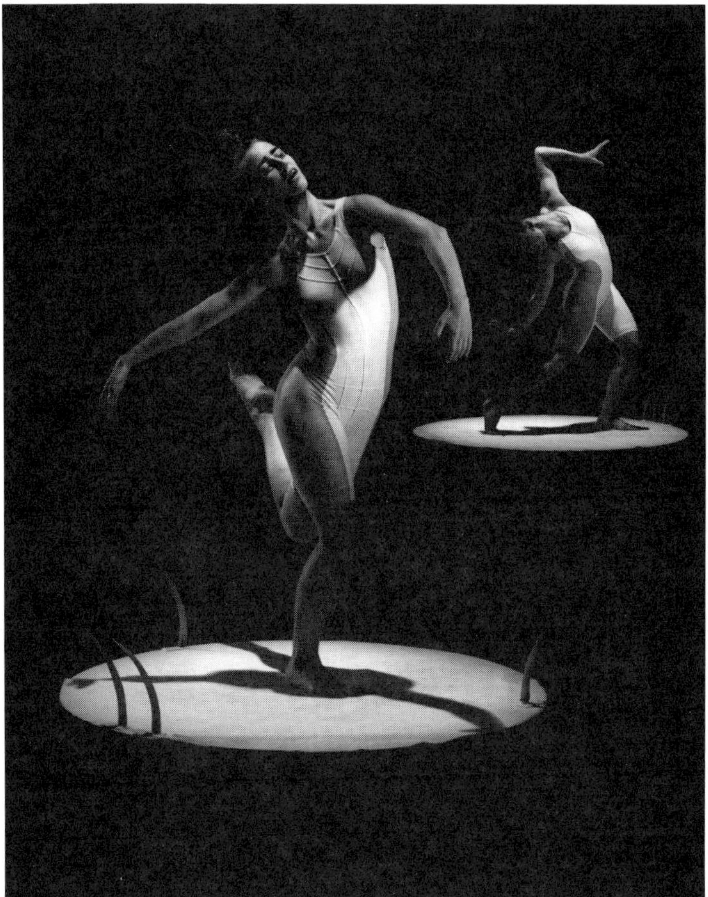

Fig. 7. *Images from* The Rite of Spring, *choreography by Marie Chouinard. Dancers are detected on the stage by carefully focused beams of light designed by Alain Lortie. Seen here Pamela Newell (front) and Mathilde Monnard (back).*
Photo: Marie Chouinard. Courtesy of La Compagnie Marie Chouinard.

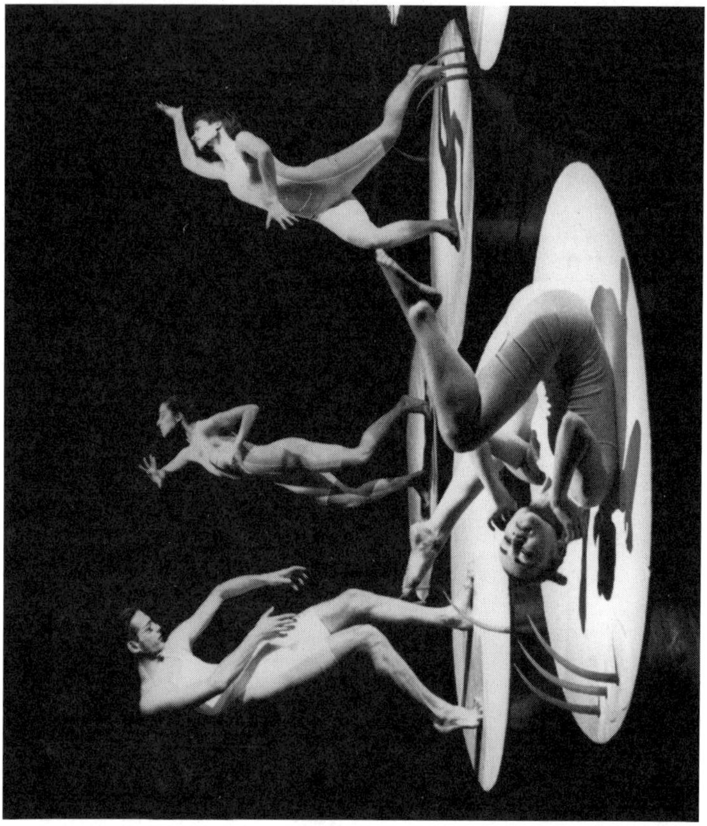

Fig. 8. *Rather than taking up choral movement the dancers recombine in front of the spectator to present images of energy caught unawares. In simultaneous time the dancers perform on individual stages created by the pools of light that pick out their place in their nuclear trajectories. Seen here Domique Porte, Daniel Éthier, Marie-Josée Paradis and Pamela Newell.*

Photo: Marie Chouinard. La Compagnie Marie Chouinard.

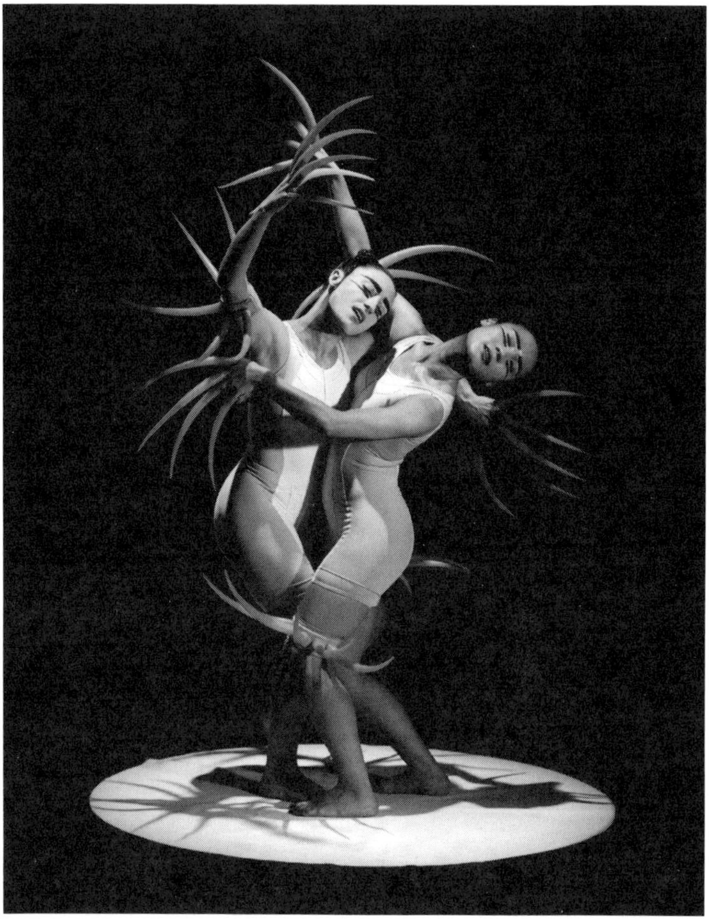

Fig. 9. *The images of primordial tensions and energy are clearly evident in the way in which Marie Chouinard combines dancers by extending limbs which together refine the concepts of the body in motion. By "catching" the movement in a beam of light the subatomic matter is stilled for an instant of observation. Lighting by Alain Lortie, dancers: Mathilde Monnard (L) and Chi-Yu Chang (R).*

Photo: Marie Chouinard. Courtesy of La Compagnie Marie Chouinard.

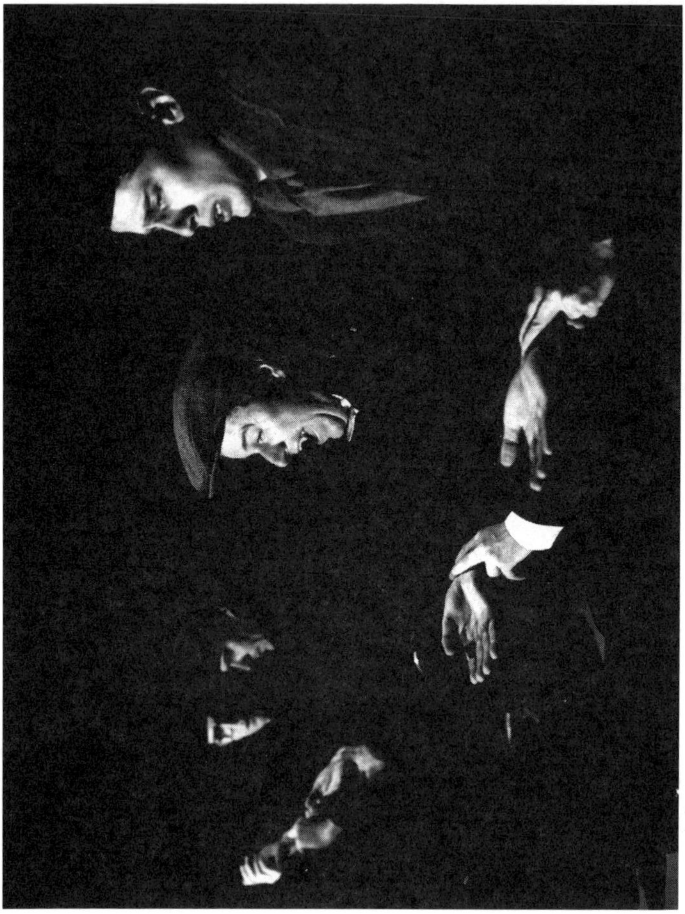

Fig. 10. *Muliple representations of Glenn Gould are presented as simultaneous in Graeme Thomson's scenography for Glenn. While the focus might be on Randy Hughson (L) and Duncan Ollerenshaw (R) in the foreground, Thomson's lighting never lost sight of the rhyming images created by the gently lit other Goulds, here seen represented by R.H Thomson (L) and Henry Czerny (R) in the distance.*

Photo: Cylla von Tiedemann. Courtesy of Necessary Angel Theatre.

Graeme Thomson's spatial and temporal disorientation might profitably be seen contrasted with the cinematography of *32 Short Films*. Both develop metonymy's of Gould's oeuvre, but the iconicity in at least one of the films provides a striking example of what I am talking about in Thomson's design. In one film, actor Colm Feore as Glenn Gould walks out to the viewer in a full screen white expanse, from the middle of what at first looks light a blank screen with only a pesky spec on it. The viewer discovers very soon that Feore/Gould is walking on the frozen Lake Simcoe.

When *Glenn*, which predates the film, was performed at the du Maurier Centre in Toronto, in September 1992, Thomson's design addressed the spectatorial perspective, much in the way of sheet music. Rather than creating one perspective for the four Goulds, Thomson set them across the stage, each with an item from biographical time. But the stage was not defined by a proscenium, nor was it set at one end of the large room. Thomson refused any one vantage point over another and seated the audience in the round and in a single tier in the galleries. The scenographic design which picked up the icons of Gould — chairs, scarf, recording studio, and piano keyboard, in this case suspended from the ceiling on wires was seen differently all the time. The four actors representing Gould were not presented in chronological sequence, and Thomson's clear stage allowed all to be attentive to any moment, while the icon of an existence was gently lit to keep the spectator aware of concurrent moments. This approach changed the perspective of the viewer from the usual vertical axis of the proscenium arch stage to the horizontal one of sheet music, where the direction of up and down is graphically represented in five line segments and divided by the bars. The suspended keyboard seemed the response to the sheet music, a crossing of perspectives to decipher the symbols on the "page." The image of time and timing was further reinforced by Thomson's introduction of a distinct technique in the lighting. Thomson, introduced lighting which seemed to suspend the actors after the final curtain. The effect was taken from photography, of an afterburn, which sears the image onto the cornea, or plate, and for me at least was the image I have kept in my mind since.

A final look at temporality on stage, that I wish to examine is that presented by the Froth Collective, for which set designer Dany Lyne collaborated with lighting designer Philip Beesley. Together these two created an environment in which to watch fashion spin its narratives. The attention to detail in this production is particularly exciting, in terms of what Michel de Certeau has noted about the distinct perspective of the perception of a city from a generalized overview, *versus* the details of a pedestrian who can only take in a limited and

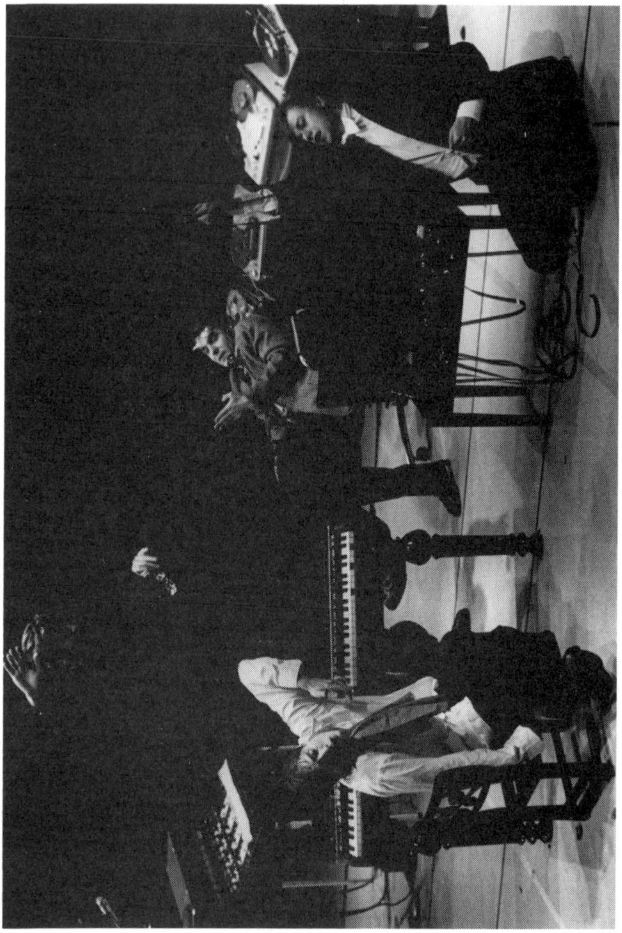

Fig 11. *The floor as sheet music supported the notes of Glenn Gould's biography. Thomson's lighting orchestrated the intensities of Gould's life picking up his presence in relation to a prop from life. Seen here from left to right: R.H. Thomson at the console, Duncan Ollerenshaw at the piano, Henry Czerny at the recording studio and Randy Hughson checking the tapes.*

Photo: Cylla von Tiedemann. Courtesy of Necessary Angel Theatre.

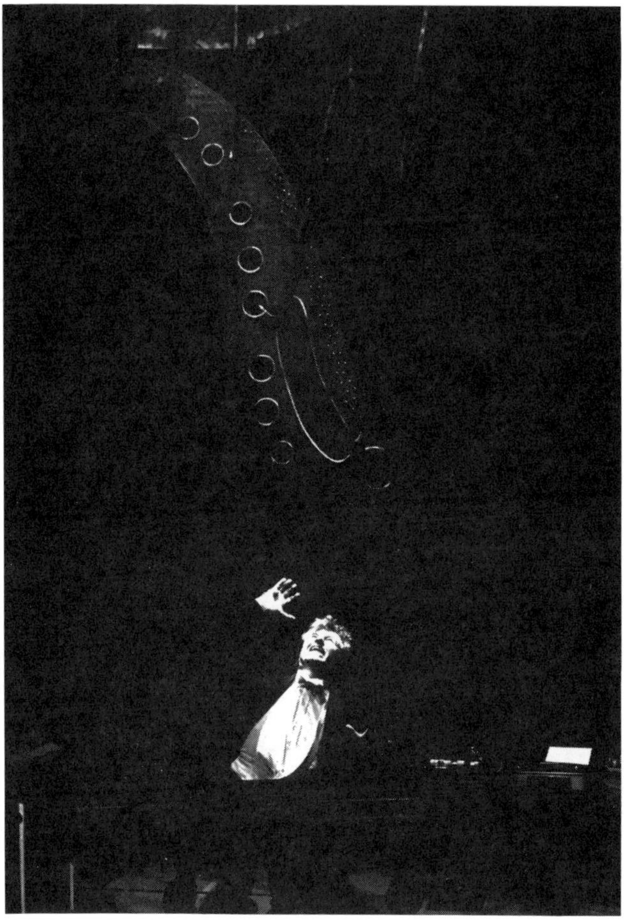

Fig. 12. *Graeme Thomson's scenography shifts the perception from the horizontal axis to the vertical when the sound board from a piano is suspended above Randy Hughson at the piano on the stage floor.*

Photo: Cylla von Tiedemann. Courtesy of Necessary Angel Theatre.

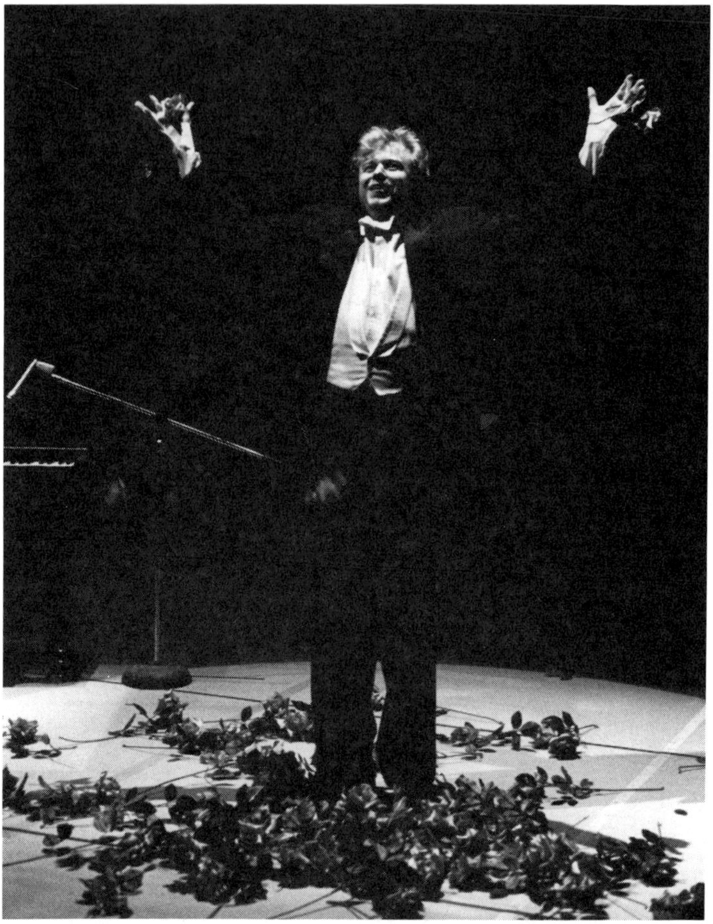

Fig. 13. *The final image after a concert cannot be captured in still photography — Graeme Thomson's afterburn effect, a photographic exposure over time, fixed the image of the glorious Gould in the imagination of the spectator. Seen here Randy Hughson as Gould amid the accolades and roses.*

Photo: Cylla von Tiedemann. Courtesy of Necessary Angel Theatre.

immediate section of the city (de Certeau 142). The production did not take place in a "proper" theatre, rather the performance was "held" in the yet-not-leased space above the Bedo store at 318 Queen Street West. The production made this already highly theatrical strip of the city self-reflexive.

The production invited the spectators to embark on a journey before settling in comfortably on the bleacher seating. The initial effect was a little like attending a performance by Théâtre de Soleil, since the company performed in a space that became a theatre, and one had to change the cultural bias for a performance space to this "unmarked" space. The audience had to wait in the lobby/front room of the empty retail space and then when let in actors and audience enacted the crossover, in this case between civilian spectators and shoppers. As much as finding the right store with the right dress the spectator in this case was invited to be held in the ambience of pre-Christmas commercialism and also leave it, participate in it, be complicitous or distanced from it. Spectators enter the boutique through the "dressing room" passage into the "store" where the great discount sale is taking place and are immediately challenged to BUY SOMETHING. The performance space is simple — raised a centre aisle defined by the seating, the cash station at one end and the dressing room, draped in silver lamé at the other. The walls of the boutique are suggested by the bleacher seating, and the racks of clothes are suspended in this high-tech fashion décor from pipes that connect the banks of seating.

The environment that is created is not unfamiliar to anyone who has shopped beyond a mall, the spatial rhetoric is of the fashion industry. What is particularly interesting in this case is the use of precise detail which is possible because of the intimacy of the created space. The runway theatre pits the Desirée dress that becomes an object fetishized, near the Visa machine and opposite the dressing room. The sequined Desirée dress rhymes, almost seductively by its texture and by the way it catches the light with the shimmery walls of the dressing cubicle. The initial geometry of the configuration is called into question during the performance as the walls seems to be tugged into various directions as clothing/costumes get removed from the racks, and characters enter through the racks of clothes. The emptiness of the centre aisle, however, seems to snap the spectator back into the rectangular geometry, when it mutates during performance into a fashion show runway. The spectator first sees the dress hanging near the cash register, but eventually it moves on a clothes-line apparatus the length of the theatre — to taunt characters as they take refuge in the silvery enclosure of the dressing room. Dany Lyne's design makes the audience confront the "other" — the presence of other spectators — since there is

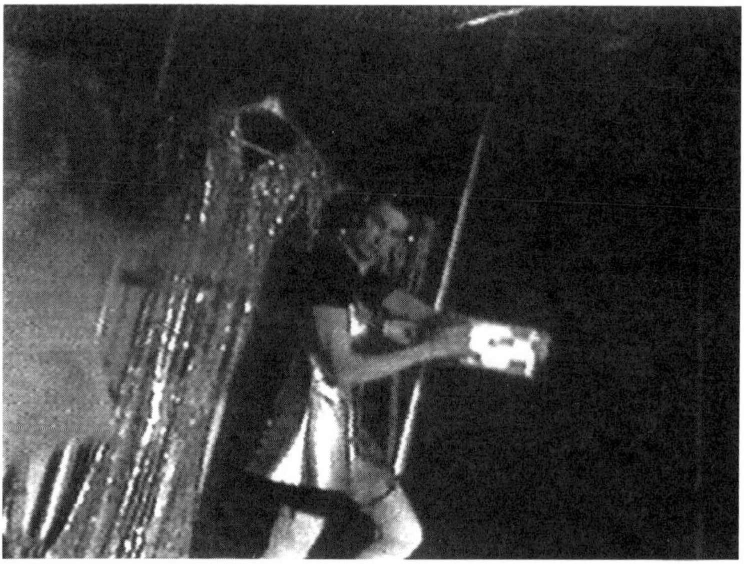

Fig. 14a. *Alisa Palmer playing the musical instrument of the fashion industry — the Visa machine, behind her — the Desirée dress;*

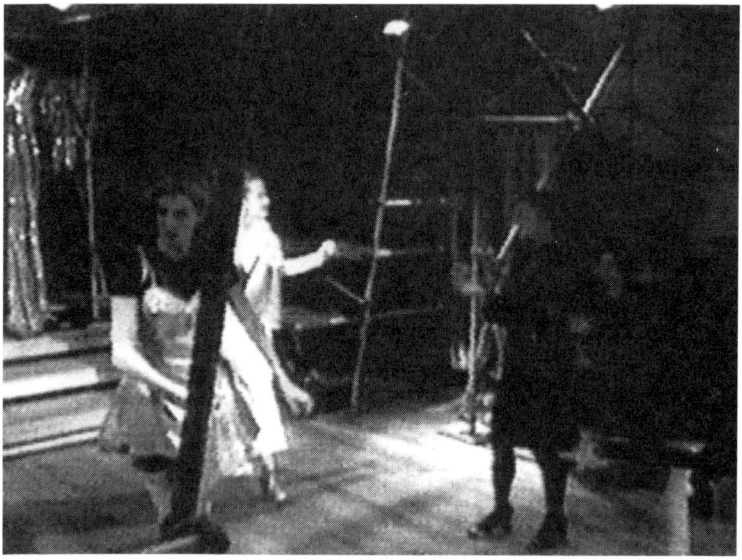

Fig. 14b.*At completion of the transaction, Janet Burke as the store manager hands the customer Bonnie Kim her purchase in a tasteful bag as Alisa Palmer the harried sales attendant goes to check on the stock;*

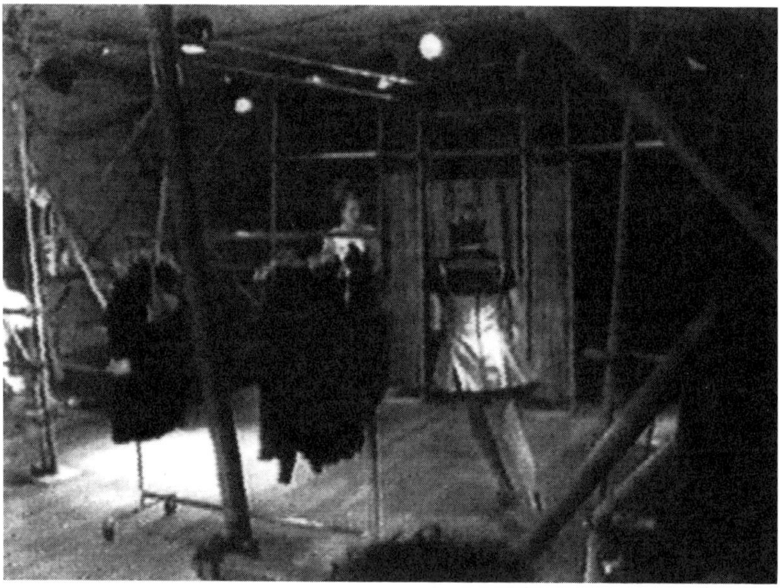

Fig. 14c. *At the other end of the store Janet Burke as the manager and Alisa Palmer as the sales attendant hover around the change room with hopes of a sale; (a-c). Redefining empty retail space as a place to perform fashion fables, designers Dany Lyne and Philip Beesley created a space in which spectators encountered watching themselves watching. The seating served as the unobtrusive wall of the boutique which proposed a structure for the floor plan. The rectangle of the store was completed by a raised platform at one end. Almost altar-like this area combined the cash station and place for the Desirée dress. The iconicity of this special place was pointed to by its opposition to the high-tech temporary dressing room for the shoppers at the other end of the centre aisle.*

Photos: Courtesy of Froth Productions.

no one place to be looking where one does not also catch the reaction of a fellow spectator, especially as the dress travels the length of the runway. As the sequins pick up the purple lighting by Philip Beesley, the dress is without a human wearer, but as it passes, it invites the spectator to consider a potential "personal relationship" with it. In this case the scenographic design not only picks up on the concept of the commercial concept of special occasion garment, the intimidation of a fashion boutique, where fashion is serious and no one ever smiles, as much as it also draws attention to the rhetoric of the feminist imagination.

To return to my initial question, that by Gertrude Stein, about seeing and hearing. Having explored these few examples of contemporary scenographic design one really must ask the question in a slightly different way — not to what does one respond, but by what means is one asked to pay visual attention in performance. If the verbal text has been theorized because there is a concept of linguistic commonality, scenographic design might be explored for its own materiality and iconicity. Analysis of encoding of space by the design might profitably be reconstituted with a greater awareness of the need for individualization of the imaging involved, and not simply derived from the dramatic narrative. Perhaps scenographic analysis involving the experiential enjoyment of variability of time, mass and length quantified by physics would liberate scenography, at least partially, from literary constraints. Scenography might be explored further for the syncopated rhythms that it encourages in the spectator as the eye comes to rest and brings together associated images. A study of the fourth dimension in design would appreciate the energy and hence performativity of what intially might have been perceived as an abstract construction. The scenography would then be understood as creating the dramatic moments not simply illustrating them.

*Queen's University*

**WORKS CONSULTED**

Alpers, Svetlana. *The Art of Describing: Dutch Art in the Seventeenth Century*. Chicago: University of Chicago Press, 1983.

Bal, Mieke. *On Meaning-Making: Essays in Semiotics*. Sonoma, California: Polebridge Press, 1994.

Barthes, Rolland. "The Imagination of the Sign." In *A Barthes Reader*. New York: Hill and Wang, 1982.

de Certeau, Michel. *L'Invention du quotidien: I, Arts de faire*. Paris: Gallimard, 1990.

de Meyer, Adolph. "Album de Meyer: *Prélude à l'Après-midi d'un faune*, 1914." In Ann Hutchinson *et al*, *Afternoon of a Faun*. New York and Paris, The Vendome Press, 1987.

Fried, Michael. *Absorption and Theatricality: Painting and the Beholder in the Age of Diderot*. Berkeley and Los Angeles: University of California Press, 1980.

Lessing, Gotthold Ephraim. *Laocoon: An essay upon the Limits of Poetry and Painting*. New York: Farrar, Straus and Giroux, 1969.

Mitchell, W.J.T. *Iconology: Image, Text, Ideology*. Chicago and London: University of Chicago Press, 1986. "What Do Pictures *Really* Want?" *October 77*, (Summer 1996), 71-82.

Panofsky, Erwin. "Iconography and Iconology: An Introduction to the Study of Renaissance Art." In *Meaning in the Visual Arts*. Garden City, N.Y., Doubleday, 1955, 26-54.

Stein, Gertrude. *Look at Me Now and Here I am: Writings and Lectures 1909-45*. Toronto, Penguin Books, 1967.

# TOWARDS A MATERIALIST PERFORMANCE ANALYSIS: THE CASE OF TARRAGON THEATRE

Richard Paul Knowles
(with Jennifer Fletcher)[1]

The principles of the type of analysis that has become known as "cultural materialism" are succinctly outlined by Jonathan Dollimore and Alan Sinfield in their brief general editors' Foreword to the 1980s series "Cultural Politics," published by Manchester University Press. Defining "cultural" in the analytical, anthropological sense as "the whole system of significations by which a society or a section of it understands itself and its relations with the world,"[2] and "materialism," in opposition to "idealism," as an insistence "that culture does not (cannot) transcend the material forces and relations of production," Dollimore and Sinfield outline an approach that "sees texts [including,

[1] I am indebted throughout this paper to the students enroled in my 1996 Graduate course at the University of Guelph, "Reading the Material Theatre in Contemporary Toronto." For research on the Factory Theatre I am indebted to Ahnes Hong and Cristiana Ziraldo. Most notably here, however, I am deeply indebted to Jennifer Fletcher, who, although she played no direct part in the writing of the paper, and therefore in producing any inaccuracies or infelicities it has, might be regarded as a collaborator. I am drawing here directly on her research at Tarragon, her interview with Mallory Gilbert, and her unpublished essay on *The Retreat* written for that graduate course, as well as on Scott Duchesne and Jennifer Fletcher's "Show, Don't Tell: Judith Thompson's *Sled* and The Tarragon Theatre's Public Workshop Program," written as part of an Independent Study graduate course at Guelph and presented as an "Occasional Paper" at the Centre for Cultural Studies/Centre d'Études sur la culture at the University of Guelph and at the Association for Canadian Theatre Research conference at Brock University, Spring 1996. Finally, I am grateful to Christine Bold for her comments and suggestions, and to Denis Salter and others for their helpful questions following the delivery of the oral version at the "Performance Text" conference in Toronto.

[2] It is important to note that, while cultural materialism in this tradition defines "culture" in its anthropological sense, it is *not* aligned with the empiricist cultural materialism that anthropologist Marvin Harris promotes in his book, *Cultural Materialism: The Struggle for a Science of Culture.*

here, performance texts] as inseparable from the conditions of their production and reception in history; as involved, necessarily in the making of cultural meanings which are always, finally, political meanings" (ix). "Cultural materialism does not pretend," they insist," to political neutrality:"

> [It] does not ... attempt to mystify its perspective as the natural or obvious interpretation of an allegedly given textual fact. On the contrary, it registers its commitment to the transformation of a social order that exploits people on the grounds of race, gender, sexuality, and class. (x)

A major part of my own research in recent years has been concerned with the development of a materialist method of performance analysis that I think of as "Reading the Material Theatre."[3] Because this involves the ideological analysis of the material conditions of theatrical production, what I am working towards is congruent with cultural materialism; because it is concerned with the production of *meaning* in the theatre, by practitioners and by audiences, it shares some of the concerns of drama and theatre semiotics. Like Marvin Carlson and others who have attempted to extend the range of application of theatre semiotics to include such things as reception, and what Carlson calls "the entire theatre experience" (*Theatre Semiotics* xiii), including, pre-eminently, theatre architecture (*Places of Performance*), I am interested in a fully contextualized interpretative approach. But unlike Carlson, my focus is explicitly on resisting interpretative discourses of the universal and individual, and in engaging in a rigorous focus on the realms of the historical and the social, which are "where," as Alan Sinfield notes, "meaning is made by people together in determinate conditions and where it might be contested" (Sinfield 141). What I am working towards, then, might best be called an applied "materialist semiotics."[4] Finally, I am interested in developing a method that

---

3 See, for example, my analyses of voice texts in "Shakespeare, Voice, and Ideology," and of the discourses, facilities, and practices of a specific theatrical organization in "Shakespeare, 1993, and the Discourses of the Stratford Festival, Ontario." For the most comprehensive introduction to "reading the material theatre" that I have published to date, however, see "Reading Material: Transfers, Remounts and the Production of Meaning in Contemporary Toronto Drama and Theatre."

4 Sue-Ellen Case and Janelle Reinelt use the term "materialist semiotics" as the title for one section of their collection of essays, *Performing Power*, but they don't explain its use, nor do the essays in the section collectively constitute a method in any explicit way. Tobin Nellhaus, whose article is subtitled "Toward a Cultural Materialist Analysis," concerns himself with hegemony as performative,

brings the analysis of the material conditions for the production of meaning to bear on the analysis of specific performances in the contemporary theatre. In doing so I am working within the assumption, made by Stuart Hall in his analysis, "Encoding, Decoding," of televisual significations, that power relations at the point of production loosely fit those at the point of consumption—reproducing, therefore, a pattern of hierarchy, but allowing some limited space for use or reading against the grain.

* * *

I would like to develop modes of analysis that consider performance texts not as the autonomous works of individual creators, products of the determinable intentions of playwrights, directors, and other theatre artists, but as the results of a more complex mode of production that is rooted, as is all cultural production, in specific and determinate social and cultural contexts. I would like to consider performances, then, as cultural productions which serve specific cultural and theatrical communities at particular moments as sites for the negotiation, transmission and transformation of cultural values. I want, that is, to look at the ways in which versions of society, history, class, race, or gender can be both instantiated and contested, in different degrees, in a given performance text, and the degrees to which the transgressive or transformative potential of a particular script functions on a continuum from radical intervention to radical containment depending, in part, on the material conditions within and through which it is produced.

My focus in this essay is on the ways in which the ideological work done by a particular production may be seen to have been mediated in complex and ongoing ways by the cultural and, particularly, *theatrical* conditions through which it has been produced by theatre workers, and through which its meaning is produced by theatre audiences. Included in this project are considerations of such things as:[5]

i) theatre and stage architecture, exterior and interior, which serves silently to inscribe specific and ideologically coded ways of working, for practitioners, and of seeing and understanding, for audiences;

---

with larger cultural *epistemes*, and with the question of "what theatre tells us about the structure and dynamics of hegemony" (4), rather than with developing a materialist reading strategy that might be applied to particular performances.

5 This listing is a close approximation of one in my article, "Reading Material," 260. For an elaboration and clarification of each of these areas as they apply to Canadian theatre see pages 260-66 of that article.

ii) the training of actors, directors, designers and other theatrical practitioners, the effects of whose naturalized assumptions about character, action, focus, and audience perception are often mystified in productions whose meanings they help to shape or subvert;

iii) the processes of new play development, which privilege particular forms and genres and often silently inscribe the conservative wisdom of received traditions;

iv) rehearsal and production processes, through which meaning is negotiated and encoded, but whose shape and duration are determined by a combination of theatrical tradition, professional regulatory structures, stage management practices, and organizational and funding structures unrelated to the specific project in question;[6]

v) organizational and funding structures themselves, which at this historical moment of "late capitalism" (Jameson) tend to be determined by the financial and ideological interests of an increasingly corporatist culture, and which in turn determine a broad range of shaping factors, from production budgets, cast sizes, and duration of rehearsal processes, to ticket prices and audience amenities;[7]

vi) the public discourse of the producing theatre as circulated through its history, mandate, programming, playbills, posters and publicity releases, each of which plays a role in determining audiences' "horizons of expectation" (Jauss), and therefore their production of meaning; and

vii) the geographical location of the performance venue, which shapes the audience's experience of what Baz Kershaw, following Richard Schechner and Victor Turner, calls the "gathering" and "dispersal" phases of performance (Kershow 24, 257; see also Bennett 133-47, 174-76).

Each of these conditions, in varying degrees in each instance, can involve its own internal contradictions, together they relate to one another in varying degrees of congruence or conflict, and these contradictions and conflicts can provide the opportunity for a range of contesta-

---

6 I will not be discussing these rehearsal processes in my analysis of Tarragon, since they are shared with most other not-for-profit theatre companies in Canada. There is, nevertheless, a great deal of work to be done in this area, on such things as the length and organization of rehearsal periods, stage-management procedures, directorial practices, union regulations, and the timing and organization of design consultations and implementation.

7 Again, I don't have space here to analyze these in detail as they relate to Tarragon, but again their impact is significant and pervasive. For an analysis of these forces at work in another theatre see my "Shakespeare, 1993, and the Discourses of the Stratford Festival, Ontario."

tory readings.

It is useful to examine briefly how some of these contextual factors play themselves out at a particular theatre, and in a particular production or productions. I have chosen here, for the purposes of clarity, to focus on the relatively straightforward and unusually homogeneous example of Toronto's Tarragon Theatre and its productions in 1996 and 1997, respectively, of Jason Sherman's new Canadian play, *The Retreat*, and Tennessee Williams's American classic, *The Glass Menagerie*. I have chosen this theatre and these productions less for their fascination as interestingly contested sites of negotiation of cultural values than for their unusual clarity as examples of the operation of containment in action. I am aware here of the dangers of inscribing as an analytical model the too simple early new-historicist binary of subversion and containment, and will try to point towards opportunities for fissures in what might otherwise appear to be a closed system. Meanwhile, however, it is important to acknowledge that a closer examination of other productions with more vexed relationships to Tarragon as an institution, or of productions at theatres with more conflicted or contested discourses, histories, and spaces, would yield more complex analyses of systems of meaning production that are never completely closed nor seamless.[8]

Tarragon Theatre began its life as one of four theatres in Toronto in the late 1960s and early 70s which set themselves up as nationalist "alternatives" to the then-established mainstream Regional Theatre network,[9] which was considered by many to be inadequately serving the needs of Canadian actors, directors, playwrights, and audiences.

---

8 For an example of what I hope is a more nuanced analysis, see my "Reading Material," 266-86.

9 By "Regional Theatre network" I mean to refer to those theatres established across the country in the wake of the Massey Commission report in 1951, most of which functioned as "branch-plant" operations, taking Art and Culture from the Centre to the supposedly culturally impoverished regions (see Czarnecki). I am not referring here to the small, lower-case regional theatres that emerged in various parts of the country and that usually functioned in a relation of real or rhetorical opposition to the large Regional Theatres. The term "alternate" was widely used in the 1970s to refer to the theatres involved in what is now most often called "the alternative theatre movement" (see Johnston 5). Most scholars, however, have in recent years become uncomfortable with a mainstream-alternative binary that may have been strategically useful for certain theatre workers in the 1970s, but that is now considered both to be (re)productive of various kinds of marginalization, and insufficiently nuanced as an analytical category. I invoke it here as part of a historical discourse that has had, and continues to have, significant material and interpretative consequences.

The mandates and practices of the so-called "alternates" —which included, in addition to Tarragon, The Factory Theatre Lab, Toronto Free Theatre, and Theatre Passe Muraille— in fact varied considerably, and Tarragon, in particular, has worn the label "alternative" with considerable discomfort. Although Tarragon has always been anxious to position itself "on the cutting edge,"[10] and although its play-development mandate and relatively small budget have set it apart from the Regional Theatre network from the beginning, the theatre has produced in its policies, procedures, physical arrangements, public profile, and production history a discourse of stability, balance, comfort, and quality that equally sets it apart from such organizations as Factory Theatre, with its discourse of excitement, adventure, and risk.[11]

Tarragon is located "on the ... edge" of, and literally across the tracks from, Toronto's fashionable Annex area, an older, residential quarter of the city made up of a mixture of formerly, recently, or soon-to-be renovated homes, largely brick, and peopled for the most part by professionals, artists, and university faculty and students. This location is to some degree liminal: the approach to the theatre by public transit involves a potentially uncomfortable walk from Bathurst Street along the poorly-lit Bridgman Avenue on the borders of a railway track, and the trains passing by during performances provide regular disturbances to the illusionistic veneer of most performances. The majority of Tarragon's audience, however, arrives at the theatre by car, and makes use of the convenient parking lot on the south side of Bridgman Avenue, and the primary effect of the positioning of the theatre at the edge of the Annex would seem to be its association with that neighborhood's demographic and economic mix, together with its participation in the comforting discourse of "neighbourhood" itself. The theatre's audience base

---

[10]I am quoting this from the theatre's 1996-7 season brochure, which in is in turn quoting from the "CBC, November, 1995." The phrase suggests that Tarragon aspires more to be *avant-garde* than alternative; that is, the theatre presents itself as doing work that is in advance of, and poised to take its place within, an evolving canon rather than work that is consciously oppositional.

[11]The Factory has traditionally been understood, in its early years as Factory Theatre Lab ("Lab" was dropped in 1984), to have been in real or imagined conflict with Tarragon, usually over questions of style and subject matter: Tarragon has typically been seen as the home of naturalistic plays on Canadian subjects, with David French seen as its paradigmatic playwright; Factory, meanwhile, is generally seen as having been a more experimental venue associated with non-realistic plays set in exotic locations, with the early work of George F. Walker serving as the preferred example. Few of these constructions venture beyond the personalities of the theatres' respective founders, Bill Glassco and Ken Gass, to examine other material and discursive differences.

is largely derived from the generally "well-off" "professional-managerial class" as defined by Barbara Ehrenreich and John Ehrenreich, with ages ranging from the 40s to the 60s, together with an admixture of University students and theatre workers.[12]

The theatre building itself is the site of a former warehouse and casting factory (Johnston 147), but its exterior over the years has become comfortably overgrown by trees, bushes, greenery, and a kind of genteel decay. In the same period the interior has evolved through a series of expansions and renovations into a virtual rabbit-warren of offices, workshops, rehearsal halls and passageways on its second level, with the ground floor devoted primarily to the main, mid-sized performance space, seating just over 200,[13] a small, variable-seating "Extra Space," and a (relatively) large lobby with front-of-house facilities and audience amenities that include a refreshment bar serving coffee, juices, bottled water, premium (Upper Canada Brewery) beers, and the theatre's trademark "big cookies." Jennifer Fletcher has characterized the working spaces at Tarragon as democratic in organization and communal in sensibility: "the financial and administrative offices mingle and overlap with the artistic directorship offices," she notes, pointing out that both Urjo Kareda, the theatre's current Artistic Director, and Mallory Gilbert, its General Manager, understand the company "as a community or family of workers where a sense of 'collaboration' governs the atmosphere" (9).[14] The lobby area is relaxed and comfortable, with well worn couches, fresh flowers, warm colours, and photographs both of previous productions and of "the Tarragon family" —including Cleo,

---

[12] According to Mallory Gilbert, "a fair number" of Tarragon's audience members are from "the Annex area." "They are a fairly well-educated audience. They're very well off." In addition to Gilbert's comments, I have drawn for my account of Tarragon's audience base partly on my experiences working at and attending the theatre, and partly on statistics gathered by the theatre in January 1995 ("Tarragon subscriber households/Tarragon single ticket buyers by address").

[13] The capacity can vary according to the audience-stage configuration. The capacity listed in "Coming on Strong: Tarragon Facts and Figures," a brochure used for fundraising purposes, is 205 (100 is the capacity listed for the Extra Space). The capacity for the March-April 1997 production of *The Glass Menagerie* was 218.

[14] The slippage between the discourses of family and those of cooperation, collaboration, and democracy, of course, masks the hierarchical structure of the patriarchal family in ways that, applied to Tarragon theatre (with its Artistic Director "father figure" [Kareda, "Director"] and female General Manager), are suggestive. Like those of cooperation and collaboration in this context, moreover, those of tolerance and liberal pluralism tend to exist within naturalized hierarchies in which agency is distributed unequally.

the family dog— lining the walls. Both theatres create and reinforce a democratic sense of comfortable fairness for both theatre workers and audiences through the use of undifferentiated seating areas, single-price general admission policies,[15] and unpretentious programs with artists' names listed alphabetically (rather than by size of role or reputation), and all workers acknowledged equally.[16]

As an organization, Tarragon Theatre has been constructed throughout its history through a discourse of stability and balance that intriguingly blends the fiscal with the philosophical. According to Denis Johnston, Bill Glassco founded Tarragon partly in reaction to what he saw as "slapdash production standards" and "offhand squalor" at Factory Theatre Lab (146), and partly as an attempt to "balance his conservative aesthetic with the experimental quality of the venture" (149). The theatre's early success was interpreted similarly as "a combination of sound management and personal commitment" (Kareda "Tarragon's Short History"). Indeed, the name Tarragon was itself chosen explicitly "to avoid anything with 'workshop,' 'studio,' or 'lab' in it" (Campau):

> The name "Tarragon" ... was a reaction against the kind of alternative theatre which promised half-realized artistic experiments. Instead, it offered the imagery of the kitchen: a bright, comfortable work place where carefully chosen ingredients are skilfully combined to bring pleasure to one's guests. It also suggested the well-bred courtesy of the Glasscos' upbringing, of a style not to be found at Passe Muraille or Factory. (Johnston 149)

The discourse of the theatre over the years, and indeed the theatre's

---

[15]In significant contrast to Tarragon's policies, Factory Theatre for the past decade has consciously differentiated between lower ticket prices for weekday performances, when audiences tend to arrive at the theatre by public transit from addresses in Parkdale and other city neighbourhoods with significant working-class, "ethnic," student, or artist populations, and higher prices for suburban and better-off weekend audiences that tend to come by car from further afield, and are prepared (and able) to pay higher prices. According to George F. Walker (in conversation), who was for a time Artistic Director at Factory, and who has premiered most of his work there, this decision was a conscious political choice, and it has resulted in the constitution of two distinct interpretative communities for the theatre's shows. Tarragon, however, like other theatres in the city, does have a pay-what-you-can matinee performance on Sundays (a certain minimum is expected).

[16]Fletcher, however, notes that the prominence of the playwright in the public discourse of the theatre is the exception to this general rule. I will return to this issue below.

organizational history since its inception in 1971, has been similarly characterized *by* and *as* a careful *balancing* of ingredients within an atmosphere of well-bred, family-style courtesy. It is a discourse and a history that sort well with a politics of liberal tolerance and fairness adopted and exercised out of a position of social stability and cultural security. Part of this security derives from the social positioning —what Johnston calls the "upper[-]crust" sensibilities (144)— of Jane and Bill Glassco, who founded the theatre, partly "for the fun of it," as "a family operation" (Johnston 144, 148). But it also derives from the stability and continuity of the operation itself. Uniquely among small Canadian theatres, Tarragon has had only two Artistic Directors over its (first) quarter-century of history, the second, Urjo Kareda, hand-picked in 1982 by the first, Glassco (who remains a board member). When Kareda was selected, moreover, he was on record as a strongly supportive reviewer of Tarragon productions since his praise was registered for the theatre's first show —in his first review as lead theatre critic for *The Toronto Star*— in 1971. Moreover Kareda later wrote of Tarragon and its founding Artistic Director that

> a theatre is a family and Glassco is certainly a father-figure at Bridgman Avenue; the pressures of balancing that with his own private family —his marvellous wife Jane (who also works at the Tarragon) and their three children— must be unimaginable. ("Director")

Similarly, the theatre's General Manager since 1975, Mallory Gilbert, has worked for Tarragon as an administrator since — again in Johnston's characterization — she joined the "founding family" in 1972 (153). Gilbert has also been constructed by the public discourse of the theatre since then as, in Kareda's words, "an extraordinarily family oriented person.... But it's a family that's not just her two kids and (ex-husband and friend) John Gilbert, but a very big theatre family within this building [Tarragon Theatre] and across the country" (quoted in Vit Wagner C5). In the same newspaper article, Vit Wagner discusses Gilbert's abilities in "balancing the books" and working to make Tarragon both "a model of stability on the uncertain landscape of alternative theatre in Toronto," and "the country's most reliable purveyor of new Canadian drama" (C5).

It may be thinking too precisely on the publicity, but one might be forgiven for wondering if the cluster of images around family, balance, stability, and sales ("purveyor of new Canadian drama"), works to construct a context within which it might be more possible theatrically to ask, or hear, some kinds of questions than others, and in which deconstructions of liberal humanist values and social structures centring on the patriarchal, capitalist economy of the family might be difficult. Indeed, the familial model of heterosexual patriarchy might even be expected to issue less in societal intervention than in an essentially *re*-productive economy that has, not surprisingly, been most frequently associated by scholars and critics in recent years with Tarragon's preferred mode, poetic naturalism, of which more below.

There is also an interesting slippage, as I have suggested, between the discourses of comfort, stability, and balance, the theatre's attempts in their productions to present balanced accounts of contemporary issues, and Tarragon's reputation for financial stability and balanced *books* — a reputation that once again sets it apart from organizations such as Factory Theatre, which prides itself on theatrical risk-taking while also always existing precariously (or perhaps failing to exist) at the edge of financial collapse. At a time when Factory has twice in one year seen its loans called in and its doors padlocked, and a time when all arts organizations in Ontario have suffered from deep federal and provincial cuts, Tarragon, according to its most recent financial statement (30 June 1995), managed in one fiscal year to increase its revenues and pay $58,640 against its accumulated deficit of $68,613. Again, however, one might be forgiven for wondering if organizational and financial balance frames a theatrical aesthetic and ideological positioning that feature a liberal-centrist political discourse of balance aligning Tarragon more closely with such public institutions as the CBC, which works within a mandated (nationalist) discourse of balance and equal representation, than with any movement in the theatre, the arts, or society that could justifiably be considered to be alternative.

* * *

How, then, do all of these geographical, architectural, organizational, and discursive conditions —together with the training of actors, directors, and designers, the processes of rehearsal and technical production and of new play development— play themselves out in the production of meaning, by practitioners and audiences, in particular performances? Quite comfortably, in the case of *The Glass Menagerie*, in 1997, and Jason Sherman's *The Retreat*, in 1996 (at least as it emerged from the rehearsal and development process at the theatre) — productions that are particularly closely fitted to Tarragon's discourse, working conditions, and methods.

Both productions were framed, of course, by the cumulative discourse and the general physical and geographical context that I have been outlining. Both were also framed directly by Tarragon's traditional interest in poetic naturalism as a style; by the dominant traditions in Canada of actor and director training and rehearsal practices; and by Tarragon's mandated privileging of the playwright and the literary script, together with, in the case of *The Retreat*, its processes of new play development.

Tarragon from the beginning has been a literary theatre, devoted primarily to the development of the playwright as writer. Both Glassco and Kareda have academic training in dramatic literature, and Glassco's 1971 manifesto, "Why Tarragon?", on the founding of the theatre, articulates a focus on the playwright. As Robert Nunn notes in his entry on the theatre in *The Oxford Companion to Canadian Theatre,*

> Tarragon's mandate has always placed the playwright at the centre.... There has been virtually no attention to collective creation nor to work in which gesture and image, not language, constitute the commanding centre. A passion for language and a dedication to the playwright define Tarragon's identity and represent its greatest strength. (518)

Within this mandate, Tarragon has always evinced a preference for a style that might best be described as poetic naturalism — a heightened naturalism best suited to explorations of human psychological motivation and interaction in recognizable settings and situations. From the beginning both Glassco as a director and dramaturge and Kareda as a reviewer and Chekhov scholar showed a deep sympathy for naturalism. In his well-known introduction to David French's first play, *Leaving Home*, produced at Tarragon in 1972, Kareda articulated the "mysterious richness of the naturalistic technique," and the strengths of a style he called "selective naturalism" — naturalism "with the detail carefully gauged and controlled for poetic resonance." "Naturalism," he argued "is an impressionistic method with strict and fascinating formal controls" (viii), and he praised Toronto's young playwrights in the 1971-2 season for turning their attention to "old-fashioned, naturalistic drama" (ix). It is not surprising, then, that the Canadian playwrights with whom the theatre is most closely associated, from David French in the 1970s to Judith Thompson in the 80s and 90s, have tended to work in styles that may stretch the boundaries of naturalism, but rarely break through them.[17] Nor is it surprising that revivals produced at

---

[17]Judith Thompson's work at Tarragon would provide a fascinating case study for more nuanced materialist analysis. Her conception of character and language, and her interest in individual character psychology, conform comfortably to the conventions of poetic naturalism, and she has described naturalistic drama as "what I love. It's what I love to watch and it's what I do best.... It's what emotionally engages me" (Duchesne and Fletcher 6). Thompson's plays,

Tarragon have tended to be selected from the naturalistic repertoire — works by Chekhov have dominated, but those of the naturalistic O'Neill, Mamet, and Shepard show up from time to time.

In 1997 it was the turn of Tennessee Williams, whose early work, *The Glass Menagerie*, felt quite at home within the Tarragon family. The production was framed in the season brochure, in familiar terms that focus on family and on balance, as an "unforgettable tragicomic story of a family —mother, son, daughter— that is both sustained and made vulnerable by its illusions." Williams himself was identified there as "the American theatre's most generous and humane poetic dramatist," but neither there nor in the lengthy program biography was any attention drawn either to the autobiographical character of the play nor to the scholarly and theatrical revival of interest in Williams as a gay playwright. Finally, the brochure drew attention to the Director, Diana Leblanc, who is currently best known as the director of the critically acclaimed Stratford Festival production of another masterpiece of American naturalism, O'Neill's *Long Day's Journey Into Night*, and to the casting of "the great Martha Henry" as Amanda. The choice of Leblanc and Henry is typical of Tarragon practices in hiring and casting from among Canada's leading actors and directors working within the country's dominant tradition.[18] Martha Henry is Canada's best and best-known naturalistic actor, trained in the tradition first developed by Stanislavski for productions of Chekhov. She is uniquely suited to and experienced in performing the major roles in classic natu-

---

nevertheless, place naturalistically-conceived characters within actions and situations that range from the extreme to the impossible, that often invoke social division and discomfort within audiences that are not homogeneously constructed, that include internal contradictions, and that evoke expressionistic dreamscapes, living memories, and ghosts that serve as sites of contestation, and that resist too simply affirmative or univocal readings.

[18]This applies, specifically, to *The Retreat* as well as to *The Glass Menagerie* and most other Tarragon mainstage productions. In fact Joe Ziegler, playing the central role in *The Retreat*, was also a graduate of NTS, and is a rightly respected Canadian actor in the naturalist tradition. It is worth noting that other contemporary and specifically Canadian acting traditions have emerged, for example, out of the Paul Thompson years at Theatre Passe Muraille, and out of Toronto's Theatre Resource Centre and the clown work of the late Richard Pochinko. It is interesting that Tarragon's focus on Canada and on "creating a distinctive kind of theatre, one which, hopefully, can make a contribution to this country's culture" (Glassco [2]) has not led it to explorations of new approaches to acting, directing, or design, but has focused exclusively on script development within a received theatrical tradition. It has focused, that is, on the production as *product* rather than on the shaping influences of the processes of production.

ralistic drama (including Chekhov), and (under the direction of Diana Leblanc) she has made something of a specialty in recent years of the female leads in productions of plays by Williams, the O'Neill of *Long Day's Journey*, and Miller, plays closely associated with the American variation on Stanislavski's System known as the American Method — a method that is not incidentally also closely associated with American schools of (normalizing) psychotherapy. In fact, both Leblanc and Henry were trained at the Canada's National Theatre Schoo —Henry is famous as its first graduate— where they would have learned, as Denis Salter has argued, an eclectic, depoliticized, culturally unlocated approach to acting rooted in a blend of the Stanislavski System and the American Method —an approach that is deeply ideologically coded and culturally affirmative, and that focuses attention on the realms of the psychological, individual, and "universal" rather than on the social and historical— and therefore the political.

> What they won't [have acquired] at the school . . . is systematic training in the kinds of interpretative and stylistic problems which the ideologically-driven theatre of Brecht, Piscator, Meyerhold, and Boal has tried to come to terms with. Nor will they [have received] extensive training in the ritualistically-explorative theatre of Artaud, Grotowski, Schechner, and Brook; nor in the post-modern "pure performance" theatre of Wilson, Foreman, the Wooster Group, and Lepage. (Salter 8)

Not surprisingly, then, Tarragon's *The Glass Menagerie* was a strong and solid production within a clearly naturalistic tradition. It contained few surprises, and those that it did contain had to do with interpretations of character and unusual delivery of lines. The play rewards this treatment, of course, but one wonders whether another theatre might have taken more care to historicize the show, to pay attention to what Tom calls, in the play's first scene, "the social background of the play": the revolution, followed by the triumph of Franco, in Spain; and "disturbances of labour" and "a dissolving economy" in 1930s America (5), not to mention Amanda's racism or the social context for, and social cost of, the rugged individualism of the "gentleman caller" (which in the Tarragon production was merely cute). Indeed, one wonders whether the Tarragon's focus on Williams as America's most generous and humane poetic dramatist *precludes*, for example, the interrogation of this autobiographical play as, potentially, a social analysis about two women left literally and figuratively powerless after being abandoned in 1930s industrial St. Louis by the play's three men.[19]

---

[19]The power fails in the middle of the play, of course, because Tom has spent the money set aside for the electric bill on his membership in the Union of Merchant

What the production did focus on, of course, was the straightforward presentation of Tennessee/Tom's justificatory autobiography, and the expression of his/their personal angst.

My questions here, I want to emphasise, are not attempts to second-guess production choices or to propose alternative interpretative readings of the script, but to examine what made those choices rather than others possible, probable, obvious, or perhaps even inevitable, to examine some of the often-neglected factors that make such choices "natural," or common sensical,[20] and that frame audiences' production of meaning, whatever production decisions are made. I want to suggest that, for most members of the Tarragon audience, *The Glass Menagerie* did, indeed, function as the self-contained but —in the usual naturalist slippage— also universalist "story of a family...that is both sustained and made vulnerable by its illusions," rather than as a play about the human, material costs of specific historical, social and political circumstances and decisions — in 1930s St. Louis, in 1944-5 Chicago and New York, where it was first produced, *or* in 1990s Toronto, where it might have had contemporary political resonances that I suggest were available at Tarragon only through a determinedly resistant reading. It is significant that none of the production's reviewers made any connections with contemporary social issues, or noticed any resonances with contemporary Ontario politics in the fact that the play is about a single mother with a disabled adult daughter who is left at the end to deal with poverty in a time of high unemployment and economic collapse. Ironically, however, an article by Kate Taylor that appeared in *The Globe and Mail* early in the run of the Tarragon production (and that also featured a National Theatre/Royal Alexandria co-production of the play), was titled "Popular Play Needs *Balancing* Act" (my emphasis), and employed other familiar Tarragon imagery: Taylor unquestioningly accepted the facts (in spite of Tom's statement to the contrary in the prologue) that the characters "should be realistic figures," and that "it is the playwright who, like a good cook, reduces a mess of human muddles to an intensely flavoured tragedy." Taylor's article never questions the common sensical presupposition that the play's intended and desirable effect is Aristotelian therapeutic catharsis through identification with "painfully real" tragic situations enacted

Seamen, to enable him to escape what the script and the Tarragon production treat as his entrapment at home (77). The power failure in the Tarragon production was treated--by Amanda and by the production--primarily as an opportunity for the use of romantic candlelight.

[20]See Catherine Belsey, 1-36, for an analysis of the relationship between common sense and dominant ideology.

by sympathetic characters. As theorists from Brecht through Boal to contemporary feminists have argued, however, catharsis is fundamentally culturally normative and affirmative, leaving audiences purged of any potentially disruptive or socially critical impulses they may have had, while naturalism creates a secure sense of order by delivering its ideology as normative.

Tarragon's production of *The Glass Menagerie*, then, represents an unusually coherent example of the operation of silent and relatively seamless ideological containment through material conditions that work together with one another and with a relatively self-contained script to keep at bay, if not entirely to banish, the view from the other side of the tracks.

* * *

Tarragon is of course best known for its production of new work, and it is perhaps useful to turn to a production of a new Canadian play written by a Playwright in Residence at the theatre, developed, in part, through the Tarragon "Playwrights Unit," and therefore shaped at the level of the generation of the script as well as the mounting of the production and its meanings, by the discourses and practices of the theatre. One might expect, in this instance, the relationship between the discursive and other frameworks and the production of meaning to be clearer, less unqualified, less nuanced — and perhaps less open to contestation or resistance — than in productions of scripts emerging from a different context.

Tarragon's commitment to language and to the playwright manifests itself in a number of play development programs and residencies at the theatre, and although Tarragon claims that its Playwrights in Residence and members of its Playwrights Unit have "complete freedom," Scott Duchesne and Jennifer Fletcher have argued convincingly that most playwrights tend to conform to the theatre's "house style" (5-6).[21] Given the material conditions of trying to make a living as a playwright in Canada, it is not surprising that writers would see membership in the Tarragon family as an opportunity to have their work produced there, or that even within Tarragon's atmosphere of genuine generosity and tolerance certain pressures would silently come into

[21]"Complete freedom" is Mallory Gilbert's phrase. See also Duchesne and Fletcher's analysis of the workshop process for Judith Thompson's *Sled* in the Winter of 1995-6, and Kathleen Flaherty's account of the typical play-development workshop in Canada.

play. Indeed, in a *Theatrum* forum focusing on Tarragon's Playwrights Unit in 1984-5, Robin Butt and David Demchuck, members of the Unit, both comment on such implicit pressures to conform to what Butt calls "a Tarragon esthetic" (Devine 14), which Demchuck identifies explicitly as "poetic naturalism" (Devine 15). Butt, moreover, notes the political impact of this on the work of the playwrights selected for production at Tarragon: the plays, "usually provocative," he argues, "never quite provoke" (Devine 14).

Jason Sherman's *The Retreat* might be considered to be one such play. At the centre of the main plot is David, a film producer in Toronto who feels that his company, represented in the play by his hard-nosed partner Jeff, is selling out. David is attracted by both the idealism and the younger female author of a screenplay that has been submitted to him as instructor of a writer's retreat in what is clearly Banff, where the central action of the play takes place. The screenplay, written by Rachel, a teacher in a Hebrew school in Toronto, is based on the story of Sabbatai Zevi, the 17th-century Jewish mystic who declared himself the Messiah and then shocked his followers by converting to Islam. *The Retreat* is the story of the affair between Rachel and David at the writers retreat, and the fallout of that affair for David's marriage, family, and business, and for Rachel's understanding of herself, her integrity, and her father, Wolf. Rachel's father as a young man had fought for the creation of a Jewish state, but has since become disillusioned with diplomatic compromise and political expediency. At the time of the play's action he is living in an old-age home in Toronto, suffering from a brain tumour, and ranting about the 1993 peace talks between Yassir Arafat and Yitzhak Rabin. Rachel's conversations with her father about Israel, in person and by phone, form a running choric commentary on the rest of the play's action.

The ingredients are available in the script for a serious examination of the intersection of the personal with the social and political, and specifically with the politics of being Jewish in Canada in the 1990s. As *The Toronto Star* review said, the play "does not shy away from tackling large, important issues, and, on occasion, even risks giving offence" (quoted in Sherman, back cover). *The Retreat* opens with a monologue by Rachel, who is on the phone defending herself against attacks by members of her school's Parents committee, who *are* offended by what she has been saying to the students in her course on "Israel Today":

Rachel: [W]hat I said was: if these men, these Palestinian men, are terrorists, then why don't we call the Jewish settlers on the West Bank terrorists too?...well, I'm sorry the Lifkin boy went home in tears ... if I knew he

> had a brother who lived on the West Bank, I...look, the only way we're gonna have peace is if ... my God, I am sick to death of people blindly following this leader and that leader and the empty promises of a better life when the end result always and forever has been and will be deception, betrayal and misery...and *that* is why it's important for me to, yes, challenge these kids to think critically... (9)

By the end of the play, Rachel is seen apologizing to her class and abandoning her course on Israel today in favour of a safer one on Jewish mysticism. Sherman, then, here and elsewhere in the script, evinces an awareness of the potential for compromise and balance to produce containment, and this opening monologue establishes the frame for what could be a provocative, self-reflexive political drama.

The play also evinces considerable and considerably sophisticated Brechtian self-consciousness about the ways in which dramatic representation, like political representation, and like religion, can defuse critical analysis and political action — self-consciousness that may be seen to open a fissure in the production's overall discursive veneer. At one point, for example, Jeff and Rachel are discussing her screenplay:

Rachel: Okay. A long time ago. The Jews, they get kicked out of Israel. They wander. They long to return. They develop the myth of the Messiah, a symbol of strength and hope. But that very symbol *prevents* them from acting, from returning to Israel.

Jeff: Like a Frank Capra film.

Rachel: Yes it — what?

Jeff: Frank Capra...Jimmy Stewart: "Fuck you, Mr. Potter." Okay, he didn't say "fuck you," but... Goes to Washington, whatever. Does the big speech to, to, the oppressor.

Rachel: Uhh...

Jeff: The hero does the speech, does it up there on the big screen and we go, we, in the audience, go, "Hooray. Give it to him." Which absolves *us*...

Rachel: Yes.

Jeff: Of, of...

Rachel: Doing the speech, of...

Jeff: *Acting*.

Rachel: Yes, yes. The Messiah acts on our behalf. It makes us weak because it says: one day *he* will come for you. And when things get desperate enough, and some guy says" "I am *he*. Follow me," you don't question it. The followers of Zevi were desperate. And the followers of Zionism were desperate. After the Holocaust, they were vulnerable to *he* who said, "Let us return to Israel." They didn't question the return. They did-

> n't question the morality of taking another people's land.

Jeff replies, "I love it. I love that journey you just took me on" (70-71).

At Tarragon, nevertheless, the play neither deconstructed its own politics nor ignored them; rather it put on display at moments such as this the *tools* for a critique of its own representations, and those of theatre in general, but within the Tarragon context it failed to push the point, or to challenge the audience to in fact *make* such a critique.[22] The play's self-reflexivity functioned at Tarragon to produce a kind of politcal catharsis, allowing the audience the pleasure and release of loving the provocative journey the play takes us on, but, in Robin Butt's terms, never quite provoking us to do anything about it. Its *verfremdungseffekt* was, as in many contemporary theatrical invocations of Brecht, merely effect.

Finally, the script includes what is a presumably critical representation of the deflection of the political by the personal, and again a potential space for resistant interpretative strategies. In an earlier conversation about the screenplay, Rachel tells David about the inspiration for her screenplay in the life of her father as an escapee from the Nazis, and as one of Menachim Begin's Betar Boys. David, however — who claims, not to be "a Jew" but to be "Jew...ish," and who doesn't "follow Israel"—fails to understand:

David: Don't get me wrong, your father's story is terrific, but what does it have to do with your screenplay?

Rachel: That's what this movie is *about*.

David: Your screenplay.

Rachel: Yes.

David: Is about...

Rachel: Israel.

---

22 As Jonathan Dollimore argues,

> Nothing can be intrinsically or essentially subversive in the sense that prior to the event subversiveness can be more than potential; in other words it cannot be guaranteed a priori, independent of articulation, context, and reception. Likewise the mere thinking of a radical idea is not what makes it subversive: typically it is the context of its articulation: to whom, how many and in what circumstances; one might go further and suggest that not only does the idea have to be conveyed, it has also actually to be used to refuse authority *or* be seen by authority as capable and likely of being so used. It is, then, somewhat misleading to speak freely and only of "subversive thought"; what we are concerned with (once again) is a *social process*. (13)

David: I don't see it. I don't get that. Explain that to me.

Rachel: Well...

David: I mean, you've written a beautiful screenplay about a *man*, the, the *inner* life, his *struggle*. This stuff about Israel, it's, I mean...

Rachel: Are you saying forget about Israel?

David: No, I mean it's up to you. All I'm saying is, don't force it to become *about* something, especially something as ephemeral as, as, a political struggle.... (44)

In spite of these potentially contestatory traces of self-consciousness, and in spite of the fact that David comes at the end of the play to a desire to research and write about Wolf's life, however, his motives for doing so, in the Tarragon production, were contructed as being primarily personal, and Rachel's closing question, "do you think this will lead to peace?" arguably had more resonances in reference to their private relationships with David than to public policy, social relations, or the Middle-East peace talks. The conviction with which the Method-trained actors portrayed the personal crises of the characters and balanced the presentation, with equal conviction, of their different points of view, also served to resist resolution or the clear political positioning of the play itself. As the director, Ian Prinsloo said, employing a vocabulary fully congruent both with the major strains of director training in Canada, and with Method-style naturalism,

> I focus on the relationships between the characters on stage .... What is at stake for them personally? They are rich characters. They all have good reasons why they believe what they do. And each of them is right. (Lawless)

These approaches to acting and directing, together with the theatre's framing discourses of family and of genteel and balanced debate, its geographical, architectural, and audience composition, and its "house style," all worked, I suggest, to an extraordinary degree to contain potential political analysis or provocation within a generalized, polite, and ahistorical liberal pluralism. In fact, I suggest, the entire framing discourse and technology of theatrical practice at Tarragon militate against the production of *The Retreat* itself as being about "anything as ephemeral" —as site-specific and non-universal— as "political struggle." The political commitment of Wolf, Rachel's fight for equal consideration of Palestinian and Israeli settler claims to the West Bank, and even the moral issues surrounding David's betrayal of both his family and of Rachel —issues of *public* morality and responsibility that include gendered and economic power relations and raise such issues as harassment— are all and equally reduced, for their primary interpretative community at Tarragon, to the psychological struggles of sympathetic, naturalistically-realized characters to reconcile —or balance— their Stanislavskian "objectives" with the recognizable "realities" of living in the (implicitly unchanging and unchangeable) world. Change, in this discourse, can only come through individual psychological adjustment to supposed social inevitabilities; political commitment, almost inevitably, is either pathological, misguided or, as in the case of Wolf in the Tarragon production, funny; and tension, produced by dramatic conflict, exists in order to be resolved in formal cadences rather than to move audiences to action, or even to critical thought.

Most members of Tarragon's regular audience, then, will have left the theatre in February-March of 1996 with a healthy and balanced, liberal-minded and tolerant "understanding" that there are two sides to every issue, comfortable in the knowledge that the production had been balanced and fair-minded in its *explorations* of issues which, like the Arab-Israeli conflict, will remain forever unresolved. Above all, they will have left with a sense that they had witnessed "a beautiful [play] about a *man*, the, the *inner* life, his *struggle*." To have done otherwise would have required a significant investment on the part of an audience member intent on reading the play quite consciously from the other side of the tracks, and against the dominant discursive framework of Tarragon Theatre and the material circumstances within which *The Retreat* was produced, and produced its meanings.

*University of Guelph*

**WORKS CITED**

Belsey, Catherine. *Critical Practice*. London: Routledge, 1980.

Bennett, Susan. *Theatre Audiences: A Theory of Production and Reception*. London: Routledge, 1990.

Campau, DuBary. "Home for Irish, Canadian Drama." *Tele* 17 September 1971. Tarragon Theatre Archives, McLaughlin Library, University of Guelph.

Carlson, Marvin. *Places of Performance. The Semiotics of Theatre Architecture*. Ithaca: Cornell UP, 1989.

____. *Theatre Semiotics: Signs of Life*. Bloomington & Indianapolis: Indiana UP, 1990.

Case, Sue-Ellen & Janelle Reinelt, ed. *The Performance of Power: Theatrical Discourse and Politics*. Iowa City: U of Iowa Press, 1991.

Czarnecki, Mark. "The Regional Theatre System." Wagner 35-48.

Dollimore, Jonathan. "Shakespeare, Cultural Materialism and the New Historicism." Dollimore and Sinfield 2-17.

Dollimore, Jonathan and Alan Sinfield. "Foreword: Cultural Materialism." Dollimore & Sinfield, *Political Shakespeare* ix-x.

____. Ed. *Political Shakespeare: New Essay in Cultural Materialism*. Ithaca: Cornell UP, 1985.

Duchesne, Scott and Jennifer Fletcher. "Show, Don't Tell: Judith Thompson's *Sled* and The Tarragon Theatre's Public Workshop Program." Unpublished essay, University of Guelph, April 1996, presented in a revised version to the Association for Canadian Theatre Research, Brock University, Spring 1996.

Ehrenreich, Barabara and John Ehrenreich. "The Professional-Managerial Class." *Between Labour and Capital*. Ed. Pat Walker. Montreal: Black Rose Books, 1979. 5-45.

Flaherty, Kathleen. "Where's the Thrust? Putting Your Finger on the Conceptual Framework." *Theatrum* 14 (June/July/August 1989): 21-4.

Fletcher, Jennifer. "*The Retreat*: A Quest for Peace, Balance and Stability Within the Context of the Tarragon Theatre." Unpublished essay, University of Guelph, April 1996.

Gilbert, Mallory. Interview with Jennifer Fletcher, 8 March 1996.

Glassco, Bill. "Why Tarragon?" Tarragon Theatre Archives, McLaughlin Library, University of Guelph.

Hall, Stuart. "Encoding, Decoding." *The Cultural Studies Reader*. Ed. Simon During (London: Routledge, 1993). 90-103.

Harris, Marvin. *Cultural materialism: The Struggle for a Science of Culture*. New York: Vintage, 1980.

Jameson, Frederic. *Postmodernism, or, The Cultural Logic of Late Capitalism*. Durham: Duke UP, 1991.

Jauss, Hans Robert. *Toward an Aesthetic of Reception*. Trans. Timothy Bahti. Minneapolis: U of Minnesota Press, 1982.

Johnston, Denis. *Up the Mainstream: The Rise of Toronto's Alternative Theatres*. Toronto: U of Toronto Press, 1991.

Kareda, Urjo. "Director needs time to restore his creative energy." *Toronto Star* 15 March 1975. Tarragon Theatre Archives, McLaughlin Library, University of Guelph.

____. Introduction. David French. *Leaving Home*. Toronto: New Press, 1972. v-ix.

____. "Tarragon's Short History Buoyant with Successes." *Toronto Star* 15 March 1973. Tarragon Theatre Archives, McLaughlin Library, University of Guelph.

Kershaw, Baz. *The Politics of Performance: Radical Theatre as Cultural Interven-*

*tion*. London: Routledge, 1992.

Knowles, Richard Paul."Reading Material: Transfers, Remounts, and the Production of Meaning in Contemporary Toronto Drama and Theatre." *Essays on Canadian Writing* 51-2 (Winter-Spring 1993-4): 258-295.

____. "Shakespeare, 1993, and the Discourses of the Stratford Festival, Ontario." *Shakespeare Quarterly* 45 (Summer 1994): 211-225.

____. "Shakespeare, Voice, and Ideology: Interrogating the Natural Voice." *Shakespeare, Theory, and Performance*. Ed. James C. Bulman. London: Routledge, 1996. 92-112.

Lawless, Jill. "Failed Messiah Visits Writers in The Retreat." *Now* 22 February 1996.

Nellhaus, Tobin. "Performance, Hegemony, and Communication Practices: Toward a Cultural Materialist Analysis." *Theatre Annual: A Journal of Performance Studies* 49 (1996): 3-14.

Nunn, Robert. "Tarragon Theatre." *The Oxford Companion to Canadian Theatre*. Ed. Eugene Benson and L. W. Conolly. Toronto: Oxford UP, 1989. 517-18.

Salter, Denis. "Body Poliltics: English-Canadian Acting at NTS." *Canadian Theatre Review* 71 (Summer 1992): 4-14.

Sherman, Jason. *The Retreat*. Toronto: Playwrights Canada, 1996.

Sinfield, Alan. "Give an Account of Shakespeare and Education, Showing Why They Are Effective and What You Have Appreciated About Them. Support Your Comments with Precise References." Dollimore and Sinfield Political Shakespeare, 134-157.

Tarragon Theatre. "Coming on Strong: Tarragon Facts and Figures." Tarragon Theatre files.

____. *The Glass Menagerie*. Program. 1997.

____. *The Retreat*. Program. 1996.

____. "Tarragon Subscriber Households/Tarragon single ticket buyers by address" 01/30/95. Tarragon Theatre files.

____. "Tarragon Theatre Financial Statements." (30 June 1995). Tarragon Theatre files.

____. "Tarragon Theatre 96 97." Season brochure.

Taylor, Kate. "Popular Play Needs Balancing Act." *The Globe and Mail* 26 March 1997: C5.

Wagner, Anton, ed. *Contemporary Canadian Theatre: New World Visions*. Toronto: Simon & Pierre, 1985.

Wagner, Vit. "Gilbert Makes a Litte Tarragon go a Long Way." *Toronto Star* 9 April 1995: C5.

Williams, Tennessee. *The Glass Menagerie*. New York: New Directions, 1966.

# THE PLAY AND THE PRESENTMENT: TEXTS AND PERFORMANCES IN ENGLAND BEFORE 1642

John H. Astington

We will never be able to know very much about performances in early modern English theatres. Contemporary observers do not provide us with the kinds of information we are most hungry for — at their most expansive, like naive reviewers, they tell us what goes on in the fiction, or draw rather trite morals, suitable for use in the home, as Chekhov said. Although they appear to have been keenly interested in the skills of performance, following famous stars, comparing one actor with another, and even engaging in amateur competitions, like Hal and Falstaff, sixteenth- and seventeenth-century people who wrote about their playgoing did not make the particular and detailed remarks about style and effect which today we find so telling in accounts of Garrick or of Kean. The Oxford academic who in 1610 recorded the moving effect of the dead Desdemona's face still staring at the audience from the bed is exceptional in his specificity, and in recording an emotion created by performance.[1] No contemporary actors wrote memoirs about their lives and working methods, and although there are documents from the professional theatre amongst the treasure-trove Philip Henslowe and Edward Alleyn left to Dulwich College we can't be entirely confident about how some of them were used. Were the so-called plots, for example, call boards to assist overstretched actors, playing many plays in repertory from day to day, some among them taking two or three parts in given plays? Or were the plots, as has fairly recently been claimed, plans by the Elizabethan equivalent of the stage manager or the casting director to work out how play texts with a cast of twenty-odd speaking parts could be managed by a troupe of a fixed size: ten to twelve actors?[2]

The chief surviving example of an actor's part —the scroll containing all the lines of one character, prefaced by his cue lines, such as are distributed by Peter Quince in the second scene of *A Midsummer Night's Dream*— is also at Dulwich. The lines in it are for the lead role in a

---

[1] See Gamini Salgado, *Eyewitnesses of Shakespeare* (New York, 1975), p. 30.

[2] See David Bradley, *From Text to Performance in the Elizabethan Theatre* (Cambridge, 1992).

dramatic version of Ariosto's epic *Orlando Furioso*, a play usually ascribed to Robert Greene, and the part belonged to Alleyn, who probably first played the character of Orlando. In 1923 the textual scholar Walter Wilson Greg usefully published it, in modern transcription, in parallel with the text of the play as it was printed in 1594, so that matching passages from part and entire play may be compared on facing pages.[3] The two texts differ: Alleyn's scroll has more lines than the part of Orlando in the complete printed play. Verbal details, in generally similar verse lines, vary: for example the line in the manuscript which reads "those fluent springes of your lamenting *eyes*" in print becomes "Those fluent springs of your lamenting *teares*" (my italics).[4] Either works, as metre or as sense, and neither could strongly be preferred over the other on purely aesthetic grounds.

Yet Alleyn must have spoken only one of the two lines on the stage of the Rose in the early 1590s. Editors with a literary purpose will want to know precisely what Greene wrote; their end is to represent the writer's product, usually the most complete or artistically finished work of an *author*. The history of the editing of Shakespeare, from the early eighteenth century onwards, has largely been driven by such a philosophy, and editors have most usually treated the theatrical history of a text as a source of contamination or corruption of a pure authorial original, in Shakespeare's case ignoring his possible contribution to such a process as a performer in an acting company. If, however, we are looking for the performance text of *Orlando Furioso* —what the actors played and the audiences heard, as distinct from what the dramatist may have written— we might be led to distrust the 1594 quarto for other reasons. Surely the manuscript written out for the actor is likely to give us something nearer to the play in the playhouse? Perhaps so, but if what goes on in *A Midsummer Night's Dream* is any guide at all, parts were distributed and learnt before rehearsal began; during rehearsal, everyone knows, all kinds of pragmatic decisions are taken. Moreover, actors' scripts are one thing and their lines as spoken another. I have myself been reminded by stage managers quite late in rehearsal that what I was saying at certain points in performance was not what was printed in the script, and with the most scrupulous good will such reimaginings are by then very hard to dislodge. Variants on given lines must have happened frequently in Elizabethan playhouses, and it's easy enough to imagine that even if Alleyn originally spoke "lamenting eyes" he could on other occasions have said "lamenting

3 *Two Elizabethan Stage Abridgements: The Battle of Alcazar & Orlando Furioso* (Oxford, 1923 [dated 1922]).

4 *Ibid.*, pp. 150-51: Part, l. 86/Quarto, l. 713.

tears". Both monosyllables serve the sense, and it doesn't much signify —here— if one switches one word for another.

Sometimes the distinction between what was written and what was spoken was of crucial importance, as it was during the scandal of *A Game at Chess* in 1624. The script for that satirical play had been passed, rather remarkably, by the official censor, the Master of the Revels, Sir Henry Herbert. That mistake —if mistake it was— having been made, the subsequent commission of enquiry was eager to know if what was heard and seen at the Globe corresponded to the licensed text. The actors "produced a Booke being an Orriginall and perfect Copie of the play (as they affirmed)" and in reply to the question "whether there were noe other parts or passages represented on the Stage then those expressly contayned in the Booke, they confidently protested that they added or varied from the same, nothing at all".[5] Professional pride as well as submissive tact appears to accompany their claim. However true it might be, we might think that another professional skill of actors with blank verse and Elizabethan rhetorical vocabulary and syntax in their bones is likely to have been the ability to improvise a line or two if memory really stalled. The conventional nature of Greene's line allows one to play little variations on its basic shape ("Those flowing springs of your still-droppèd tears," and so on and so on).

Such changes, we should note, are unlikely to happen where the dramatic language is immediately connected to action, in its widest sense — that is, where the language is truly dramatic, as it is not in my sample line.[6] The general point is that minor verbal shifts by actors remain only part of the *performance* —uttered and heard— and do not alter the written *script* unless fortuitous changes or cuts are formally recorded as emendations. One recurrent suspicion of textual editors has been not only that the actors, like Hamlet's clown, spoke more, or less, than was set down for them, but that they then set down the altered text for themselves. Which returns us to Greg. His view of the text of the 1594 quarto of *Orlando* is not that it is unconnected with the theatre —quite the opposite— but that the manuscript part represents a portion of Greene's original script (and he can only assert rather than prove that this is so) which has been hacked about in various ways to produce the different text of 1594. He sums up his hypothesis in these terms: "This version differed considerably from that originally composed, most noticeably through extensive omissions and compressions, and less

5 Quoted in Richard Dutton, *Mastering the Revels* (London, 1991), p. 244.

6 On action and its relationship to speech, see Michael J. Sidnell, "Performing Writing," *Modern Drama*, 39 (1996), 547-57: 550.

extensive additions and expansions, and further through persistent corruption."[7]

That final word, heavy with moral and mortal overtones, signals disapproval that such a thing should be. The version "originally composed", we should notice, is not an extant document, but a third entirely speculative construction arising from the difference between one whole and one partial "version" of the play. "Versions", I suggest, is what today we would wish to call them, without the addition of judgmental adjectives — both are connected with the theatre, and show signs of use. They are chance survivals from a now vanished larger body of documents connected with the play in composition, production, and possible revision. These may have included papers in Greene's autograph, scenes by collaborators and revisors, copies of the whole play by scribes, one of which may have been marked up with cues and prompts for use in the theatre, and, of course, the parts of all the other actors. To tell a story as confidently as Greg does with only two pieces of the original paper trail seems rash, to put it mildly. No jury would convict on this evidence, one hopes, although with juries being what they are these days...

Many kinds of evidence demonstrate to us that texts for and in the theatre before 1642 did not remain in one ideal state. Greg was not ignorant of the functions and uses of theatrical writings, but his rhetorical framework is addressed to the defence of the unitary model of literary editing. He is in search of the whole, sound, pure, virginal, uncorrupted text. If such a view of theatrical texts seems a rather broad target for mockery these days, then all to the good. The editors still require embarrassing, because so much modern presentation of early theatrical texts, predominantly in the heavy industrial sector of Shakespeare editions, even at the very end of the twentieth century, has persisted in promulgating attitudes and speculative theories invented seventy-five or eighty years ago.

I say invented because many of the reasons Greg brings forward for the different state of the 1594 *Orlando* text have not been validated by subsequent scholarship. We have nothing approaching rational proof for the assertion, for example, that other states of a text were created by actors or others reassembling them from memory or shorthand notes: the theories of so-called "piracy", by which illicit editions were stolen from their playhouse owners, or of "memorial reconstruction", my favourite tissue of implausibilities, by which a lost text was recreated by actors dictating it to a scribe. The other bogeyman contaminating the purity of the true original text was that wretched creature the provin-

[7] *Op. cit.*, p. 351.

cial player. It used to be taken as an axiom that playing the provinces was a dreadful fate any halfway respectable actor would wish to avoid; the low characters in such troupes would sell their playtexts for sixpence, or less. Such an attitude may have been formed by the hierarchy of the late-Victorian and early twentieth-century profession. Who would play rep in Newcastle and live in digs when he or she might get a part in the West End?

While it is certainly true that the hundred years before 1642 saw the establishment of the metropolis as the major theatrical centre of England, it is not true that players in the sixteenth century or the first half of the seventeenth saw playing in the provinces as a second-best career, nor that all of them naturally aspired to London playing. The famous Queen's Men, founded in 1583, certainly played in London on occasion, and appeared frequently at court in the festival seasons, but we have far more records of them on provincial tours — at Norwich, Leicester, York, Bristol, Dover, and points between. There is no sign that they regarded touring from town to town as unprofitable, artistically or financially. A company with their status would have had no difficulty in acquiring a permanent location to play in London, had they wished to do so.

A frequent explanation for shorter variant texts, as Greg takes the 1594 *Orlando* to be, is that they were cut down to suit touring troupes, which generally, in the old theory, were taken to be smaller than the London companies, and which —although this is rarely acknowledged in these terms— were playing in any case to provincial hicks who wouldn't much mind what they got. Neither of these assumptions withstands much scrutiny. Where we find the licences of travelling players cited, particularly in the seventeenth century, they name large groups, usually including the principal actors of the troupe. There would be no reason for the actors to make extra work for themselves in adapting their repertoire when they had all the resources to play it in its current state of production. Moreover, provincial touring not infrequently took actors to the county seat of their noble patron, and to those of his friends and associates, sophisticated and travelled people who would not have expected to see some secondhand fare, or Royal Nonesuch. So Pembroke's Men, a company active in the early 1590s with which Shakespeare appears to have been associated at the start of his career, are known to have visited their patron the Earl of Pembroke, Lord President of Wales and member of the Privy Council, at Ludlow Castle in Shropshire, a place famous in literary history for the later performance there of Milton's *Comus*, but perhaps also distinguished as one of the places where Shakespeare's plays were first seen.[8]

The central issue, evidently, in considering texts is that of their adaptation for theatrical purposes; they are as likely to have been adapted within the London playhouses as elsewhere. Texts have always been so adapted, and always will be. Hamlet complains about improvised additions to theatrical texts, but he is not averse to doing a little script-doctoring himself. To take a hierarchical line, that the fullest authorial version is the "best" text, or that the putative "London" version is superior to the putative "provincial" version, is one approach: it does not have universal validity. Given the demands of the modern educational industry unitary edited texts obviously are required and will continue to be produced. The sixteen-year-old high-school student reading *Hamlet* will use a modern paperback —Signet, Bantam, Penguin, Folger, and so on— and will watch, say, the Kenneth Branagh and Mel Gibson movies (and here the enterprising teacher has the opportunity to introduce the issue of what a text is). The considerable seventeenth-century textual problems of *Hamlet* should not be something placed in such a student's way — far better to become interested in *a* version of the play, even if it's a version invented by editorial tradition, and a baggy monster never seen in that form in the playhouses of Shakespeare's time.

A senior colleague of mine at another university, whom I met recently at a conference, told me, in answer to my query about what he'd been doing lately, that he'd just finished editing *King Lear*. It was to be a conflated text, returning to the tradition of Kenneth Muir and older editors, after the more recent Oxford and Cambridge editions of separate texts of the 1608 *History* and the 1623 *Tragedy*; it was to be, he said, a text for *readers*. And fair enough. *King Lear* has had some distinguished readers; interestingly John Keats read it in the Folio version, not in an editorial conflation: "the fierce dispute/ Betwixt damnation and impassion'd clay" did not include the mad trial scene. What has frequently been wrong with editorial arguments in support of unitary texts, however, is that they claim to be restoring or re-establishing damaged wholes rather than creating a modern object. Moreover, the damage inflicted on the supposed whole has not uncommonly explicitly or implicitly been laid to the charge of the actors, the enemies of the integral text.

---

[8] See J. A. B. Somerset, "The Lords President, Their Activities and Companies: Evidence from Shropshire," *The Elizabethan Theatre X*, ed. C. E. McGee (Port Credit, 1988), pp. 93-111.

The whole text is not entirely a modern idea. What we now take to be the second edition of Shakespeare's *Hamlet* was published in 1604-05 with the claim that it was "Newly imprinted and enlarged to almost as much/ againe as it was, according to the true and perfect/ Coppie."[9] What it does *not* claim, significantly, is that it represented the text as performed, as does the text published in 1603, which says that it is "THE/ Tragicall Historie of/ HAMLET/ *Prince of Denmarke/* By William Shake-speare./As it hath been diuerse times acted by his Highnesse ser-/ uants in the Cittie of London: as also in the two V-/ niuersities of Cambridge and Oxford, and else-where". The old explanation that it is a pirated or surreptitious book fails to account for why one publisher oversaw both editions; one alternative explanation is that the acting text sold out as a literary product and that, seeing a commercial opportunity, Nicholas Ling acquired access to the fuller literary original —the true and perfect Coppie. A third explanation —and one much explored in the last fifteen to twenty years— is that *Hamlet* was a text in process of theatrical and literary development, driven by its great success in the theatre. The "true and perfect Coppie" would follow rather than precede the Q1 text in such a process, and that the process continued appears to be indicated by the different text of the third, later, Folio version of the play,

I don't want to entangle myself or you too much in the intricacies of the textual history, or mystery, of *Hamlet*, but to persist for a moment.[10] We have to recognise that the first edition of Shakespeare's play does not at some points make textual sense where the second one does —it seems indeed to be "corrupt"— garbled or mixed-up, and therefore somewhat suspect. On the other hand one can make too much of its supposed inferiorities; the phrasing in many instances is simply different from that of Q2: less poetically dense, plainer and more direct, but with the compensating virtues of such a style. Chiefly, it is an eminently playable text, with, arguably, a good deal more drive and dynamism than the four-hour version. How many of us have been truly

---

9 The "perfect Copie" of the play in the context of the enquiry into *A Game at Chess* in 1624 meant the text which had been approved by the Master of the Revels and which the actors claimed to have been using as an unaltered prompt copy (see above). But the phrase does not always necessarily mean this, since it is evidently used as a rhetorical claim on authority: see the title-page of *The Duchess of Amalfi,* cited below.

10 A sceptical view of older assumptions about the texts of *Hamlet* is taken by Paul Werstine in "The Textual Mystery of *Hamlet*," *Shakespeare Quarterly*, 39 (1988), 1-26. He continues his attack on such assumptions in "Narratives About Printed Shakespeare Texts: 'Foul Papers' and 'Bad' Quartos," *Shakespeare Quarterly*, 41 (1990), 65-86.

satisfied by modern performances of the full conflated text, which tend to succeed more often in part than as a whole, to lose rhythm and connectedness, to break apart in act four, to be marked by isolated successes in performance —a good Gertrude, a good Polonius, and so on— rather than by a convincing ensemble?

The shorter text of 1603 has proved itself to work when it has been given serious attention by modern actors. One observer of the 1985 production at the Orange Tree theatre in Richmond, Surrey, wrote "I have *never* seen Q2/F1 produced so skillfully, move so deftly, mount so surely in suspense. The thing was superb. The infelicities of diction *never* got in the way of the unfolding of the plot, the disclosure of character, the dignity or pathos of the action."[11] Nicholas Shrimpton, writing in *Shakespeare Survey*, frankly declared that "First Quarto is a lesser text than its alternatives". "But", he went on, "this production gave clarity, energy, and tension to the ideas which it does contain and offered the most entirely satisfactory piece of tragic acting of the year" — a year which included Ian McKellen as Coriolanus at the National Theatre and Ben Kingsley as Othello at the RSC.[12] Reviewers tend to speak of the short *Hamlet* as if it is a textual embarassment which can be saved by strong acting, but perhaps its very structure —compact, plain, and direct— delivers a good deal of the power which audiences are surprised to encounter when they see and hear it performed. What sense does it make to speak of such a theatrical vehicle as "corrupt", or to deny that it could possibly be the version of Shakespeare's play as performed at least up to 1604? As a version of a play called *Hamlet*, we should also note, it was merely one of a number played between 1594 or earlier and at least 1637 in the period before the civil wars.[13]

Shorter texts may indicate that a longer authorial original has been cut for performance, but may simply indicate a different authorial structure. As far as the actors were concerned a play may have had some ideal length — they would have had their eye on running time to fit within an afternoon's entertainment. But in fact play texts vary in length from around fifteen hundred lines to almost four thousand lines, and we cannot simply assume that all the long plays are uncut autho-

---

[11]Quoted in T. Clayton, ed., *The Hamlet First Published* (Newark, DE, 1992), p. 59.

[12]"Shakespeare Performances in London and Stratford-upon-Avon 1984-5," *Shakespeare Survey 39* (1987), 191-206: 197. A performance of the Q1 text by the Medieval Players, outdoors at Corpus Christi College, Cambridge in July 1992, and cast with only seven actors, is reviewed by Peter Holland in *Shakespeare Survey 46* (1994), 159-62.

[13]See E. K. Chambers, *William Shakespeare. A Study of Facts and Problems.* 2 vols. (Oxford, 1930); vol. 1, pp. 408-25.

rial versions and all the short ones theatrical texts. *The Tempest,* much admired by modern readers of the Shakespeare canon and frequently played in the modern theatre, is a short play —one of Shakespeare's shortest— but is not suspected of being incomplete. *The Tempest* is late, written, some think, for the newly available intimate theatrical conditions at the Blackfriars playhouse, but Shakespeare wrote plays of considerably differing lengths throughout his career. Somewhere near the start of it he wrote his shortest text, *The Comedy of Errors,* as well as one of his longest, *Richard III.* The short *Macbeth* contrasts with the long version of *Hamlet,* with *King Lear* and *Othello.* Some commentators have suspected *Macbeth,* which survives only in the single text of the Folio, of having been cut for the theatre; if so, whoever cut it did a masterful job, since the play as it stands has the most compelling rhythm and tension of all the tragedies, and it is difficult to imagine what might be missing of a hypothetically fuller Shakespearean version. In general terms, short texts need not be equated with cut texts.

When we take a large view of the theatrical culture of Shakespeare and his contemporaries variant texts appear everywhere. The notion of a unitary, authoritative, authorial text does not appear to have greatly concerned Thomas Middleton, whose play *A Game at Chess,* acted only once in 1624 in a nine-day run that was famously stopped by the protests of the Spanish ambassador, survives in various manuscript as well as two printed versions. One of the manuscripts is entirely in Middleton's handwriting; it differs from others which are also partly written by him. How different these various versions of the play are from the book which the actors showed to the commission of enquiry after the show had been stopped and which they claimed to be an exact record of what they acted we cannot know. Authors frequently wished to present revised or expanded texts in print, and they suggest in doing so that although the acting companies may have owned the true and perfect copy they did not necessarily perform all of it. The title-page to *The Duchess of Malfi* in 1623 claims that the publication contains "The perfect and exact Coppy, with diuerse/ *things Printed, that the length of the Play would/* not beare in the Presentment." In prefacing the collected plays of Beaumont and Fletcher in 1647 the publisher Humphrey Moseley also distinguished between "full" texts and acting texts: "When these *Comedies* and *Tragedies* were presented on the Stage, the *Actours* omitted some *Scenes* and Passages (with the *Authour's* consent) as occasion led them; and when private friends desir'd a Copy, they then (and justly too) transcribed what they *Acted.* But now you have both All that was *Acted,* and all that was not; even the perfect full Originalls without the least mutilation".

Rather than presenting the entire text, other publishers cleaned up what they clearly regarded as contaminated theatrical material for the refined sensibilities of readers. Richard Jones, prefacing his edition of what he calls the "two Tragicall Discourses" of *Tamburlaine* in 1590, says that he has "(purposelie) omitted and left out some fond & friuolous Iestures, digressing (and in my poore opinion) farre vnmeete for the matter, which I thought, might seeme more tedious vnto the wise, than any way els to be regarded, though (happly) they haue bene of some vaine-conceited fondlings greatly gaped at: what time they were shewed vpon the stage in their graced deformities". Jones, like Hamlet, is at pains to save the judicious from the unskilful, but he makes no mention of who might have been responsible for writing the "Iestures" he has excised — and they were surely written in order for them to have been omitted and left out. Marlowe, still alive in 1590, might have had some interest in Jones's editing, and he *may*, of course, have approved of it, although no edition of *Tamburlaine* mentions an author or assigns one to the play. The tone of the preface is that the dignified style of the text —the only text we can now read— has been trivialised by theatrical vulgarity, but we also know that one of the weaknesses of *Tamburlaine* as it stands is its sustained monotone in the high heroic vein, a mighty line that stretches to the crack of doom, with very little sign of the ironic grotesquerie, black farce, and sardonic humour which mark *Doctor Faustus*, *The Jew of Malta*, and *Edward II*. An authorial design which may have calculated its effect on the mixed style of Elizabethan popular theatre, mingling sonorous rhetoric with broad comedy, could in this case have been destroyed by an early editor looking for an integral and noble effect, for solemn decorum.

Texts of all kinds, then —published and unpublished— are records of various purposes and functions, some theatrical, some not, all surviving from some historical moment in a textual flux. Plays changed as they moved from author, or authors —and many plays were produced by collaborative teams of writers, like modern filmscripts— to playhouse scribes, to actors, through revisions, additions, copies, and printed versions. Some printed quartos found their way back into the playhouses to be used as promptbooks in later revivals, and to be marked up with manuscript cues, prompts, and cuts. So long as theatrical texts were used, they changed, and such texts as have survived by chance mark points on a curve of change. The final, definitive text is the dead text.

In one sense all sixteenth- and seventeenth-century texts are dead: we no longer use their codes, and neither speak nor receive their theatrical languages. How very hard it is for modern students to entertain the idea that boy Juliets or Cleopatras could have been anything but an awkward compromise, or for some modern theorists to imagine that they could have been regarded by male playgoers without pederastic desire. But the life and force of old texts as dramatic fictions has meant that they have been adapted to changing theatrical languages; some of them —many of the plays of Shakespeare principally— virtually continuously from their first performances until now. As modern versions, then, we have both the contemporary edited text, with modernised spelling and typeface, regularised act and scene division, explanatory stage directions, annotations, glosses, possibly presenting variant early versions in a conflation, and also the production text, probably based on some edited text, but changing somewhat from occasion to occasion. The working theatre selects from the supposedly stable text —the Penguin, or the Signet, the modern version of the true and perfect copy— a working text for production, usually cutting some of the original, possibly repositioning or amalgamating scenes, excising theatrically inconvenient minor characters, even, if you are John Barton, *adding* some lines of blank verse in modern pastiche.

Such constant theatrical reworking has provided us with an immense number of texts of certain plays. Our comparative examination of production texts —a regular pursuit of theatre historians— might be read backwards in the case of early plays. That is, where conformities and disconformities repeatedly appear we may be able to learn something of the probable early theatrical adaptations of a text, for all that the working assumptions in the modern theatre are in many ways very different. If continued theatrical change *is* revelatory, it is applied to only a very restricted number of texts. How useful it would be for scholars or simply admirers of Marlowe to have more professional productions of *Doctor Faustus* to compare, for example. Assuming, as I do, that *Faustus* is still an exciting play which can be made to work in a variety of styles and physical settings in the modern theatre, the director must face the question of text. The unitary text, once more, is a modern invention, and as one compares editions one finds different kinds of conflation of the two variant early texts. Published in 1604 and 1616, both appeared well after Edward Alleyn began acting in the play at the Rose playhouse, and after the playhouse text began to be adapted by later writers. *Faustus*, like *Hamlet*, was an immediate hit in the theatre and had a prolonged career. The shorter earlier text and the later one, longer by five hundred lines, are both viable versions of the play, theatrical adaptations of the shape that Marlowe originally gave it, whatever that may have been. Greg, who famously edited a parallel edition of the two texts in 1950, once again used his theoretical machinery to discredit one text and to validate the other: a whole generation of editions followed his example.

Today, less troubled by the idea of variability in theatrical texts, we need to consider the narrative and structural shape of both versions of *Faustus* as readers —an experience which the Oxford edition of Marlowe published in 1995 fairly allows us— but also to experience both in the theatre. The Royal Shakespeare Company, who opened their new Swan playhouse in 1986 with a production of Ben Jonson's *Every Man in his Humour*, a play which survives in two distinct authorial texts, might consider the experiment of rotating performances of variant versions of plays. This would, I hope, prove to be as interesting to actors as it would to audiences, especially when, as I assume to be true of the *Faustus* texts, they are both versions made in and for the theatre, with a different logic of performance in each case.

If this is altogether too archaeological an exercise for the modern theatre, which is not and should not be a scholarly instrument, then our own thinking about early modern theatrical texts should cast off the inappropriate vestiges of outdated theoretical models. Early plays are pieces designed to work in a theatre, and therefore subject to change and adaptation. Authors, or poets, as some of them preferred to call themselves, were certainly important figures within theatrical culture, but their texts were submitted to a working process of theatrical production which created more texts. In the case of surviving printed plays we might guess at what kind of manuscript text lies behind them —which of the many texts produced by theatrical activity made its way to the compositor's table— but often we can do no more than guess. The guesses, moreover, in the past have assumed regular and habitual ways of proceeding in a world that, like theatre at all times and in all places, while not being anarchic was frequently irregular, idiosyn-cratic, and particular. What was done on one occasion in preparing a manuscript play fresh from the author for production in the playhouse, it seems, was not an infallible model for what was done on another occasion, or by another company at a second playhouse. We have various kinds of surviving documents, for example, that can generally be described as early prompt copies: they contain a complete text of the play, and a variety of theatrical cues, giving warnings for entries by actors and for stage effects of one kind and another. But they do not all mark the same kinds of thing, they are not internally consistent, and they do not give us the kind of detailed information we would expect from a modern promptbook. That term, therefore, can be used about them only with caution.[14] We only partly understand the working methods they were

[14]On the problems of early promptbooks see William B. Long, "'A bed / for woodstock': A Warning for the Unwary," *Medieval and Renaissance Drama in England*, 2 (1985), 91-118; "*John a Kent and John a Cumber*, An Elizabethan

made to support, and to read them through later paradigms is to impose a sense on them that they do not and did not have.

Other kinds of regularisation and patterning have been imposed on what is more likely to be a more random and unpredictable history of texts by the theories of textual scholars, and particularly by the powerful and influential generation of Greg and his colleagues. Paul Werstine has recently demonstrated how entirely hypothetical are the categories of manuscript text of which such scholars spoke — the author's original draft, "foul papers", and so on, "of which there are no examples among extant dramatic manuscripts".[15] Empirical observation, Werstine argues, fails to support the idealised notion of an authorial manuscript text as a distinct category which might provide copy for the printers. Print, in any event, represents one point in a play's production history. If the play failed, the printed play may tell us most of its textual history; if it was successful then it is likely to have given rise to more texts, and when we are lucky suviving variant versions tell some of that story.

Attempts to break out of the old categories of explanation of variants sometimes betray themselves as being merely recycled versions of old prejudices. A recent example is the consideration by David Farley-Hills of the 1597 quarto of *Romeo and Juliet,* a text which used to be characterised as one of the so-called "bad" quartos, another term invented at the start of this century.[16] Its version of the play is different in a number of respects from that published in 1599, which is invariably taken as the copy for modern editions; the 1597 play has considerable theatrical interest, however, not least in its fuller stage directions. Attacking the old notion that the text was a "memorial reconstruction," Farley-Hills calls it a "redaction" of the 1599 version, and which he therefore assumes to have existed before the 1597 text was produced. Caught in old paradigms, he assumes that the text behind the 1597 edition was "a provincial acting text" (why "provincial"? we may ask) and in a revealing attempt to distance it from Shakespeare himself he characterises many of the differences as "clumsy" and therefore far beneath our famous and accomplished author: "Such clumsiness would argue strongly against Shakespeare as the redactor."[17] In his determination to find clumsiness, however, in one instance he revealingly mis-

---

Playbook and its Implications," *Shakespeare and DramaticTradition,* ed., W. R. Elton and W. B. Long (Newark, DE, 1989), pp. 126-43.

[15]Werstine, "Narratives," 75.

[16]David Farley-Hills, "The 'Bad' Quarto *of Romeo and Juliet," Shakespeare Survey 49* (1996), 27-44.

[17]*Ibid.,* 41, 31.

reads the theatrical sense of the text. The shorter 1597 version of the scene between Friar Lawrence and Juliet in which he gives her the sleeping potion, 4.1 in a modern edition, concludes with a short speech from Juliet, printed in the Q1 text like this: "Frier I goe, be sure thou send for my deare *Romeo.*"

Commending the general efficiency of what he takes to be cutting down of a longer original, Farley-Hills excepts "the calamitous last line." "Juliet's response, we can be sure, was entirely the redactor's work, and we can be equally sure (again) that Shakespeare was not the redactor."[18] I don't find myself able to say that I'm "sure" of a great deal when I consider the puzzles of early texts, but it seems to me that Juliet's speech is not one line, but two (strictly a fragmentary line of two poetic feet followed by a regular pentameter line), that it is a couplet, and as it was said in the theatre a perfectly conventional and recognisable signal of the ending of a unit of the action. Issues of authorship entirely aside, it is a competent and efficient theatrical "sign-off". Here is an instance of the not uncommon phenomenon of the printer setting verse as continuous text in order to make a little space, or simply misreading the spacing in the manuscript in front of him. Were we editing this text for modern readers, however, we would do something like this:

JULIET Friar, I go;
Be sure thou send for my dear Romeo.

Set in this fashion the text begins to reveal action: determined movement towards the stage door on the first three words, a pause and turn at the semi-colon, and a final phrase which has solemnity as well as urgency. It is hardly memorable poetry, but it has a theatrical purpose, and would play well. One could assemble a list, if one were so minded, of final couplets from the ends of scenes from Shakespeare plays which are as conventional and as "clumsy" as this one. The real test should be whether a scene looks and sounds as if it were written for performance on the contemporary stage, and 4.1 of the 1597 *Romeo and Juliet* clearly passes that test.

Since I have been cocking snooks at editors throughout this paper I should close by recording that an editorial introduction which has just appeared (in April 1997, when this paper was delivered orally, it was only a couple of weeks from publication) marks a refreshing change, and gives us a model of thinking about early dramatic texts we can recommend to our students. This is Stephen Greenblatt's introduction to the

---

[18] *Ibid.*, 31.

new *Norton Shakespeare*, a collected edition likely to be widely adopted across North American university campuses as a teaching text. The title of his chapter on the publication history of Shakespeare is significantly titled "The Dream of the Master Text". While to my mind he remains a little too respectful of certain ghosts from the editorial-theoretical cellarage he eloquently places the emphasis on the relationship between text and theatre exactly where it should be. Speaking, as everyone is drawn to do, of the theatrical additions made by Hamlet himself to the play he has acted before Claudius, he says "It seems likely that Shakespeare would have routinely accepted the possibility of such alterations. Moreover he would of necessity have routinely accepted the possibility, and in certain cases the virtual inevitability, of cuts in order to stage his plays in the two to two and one-half hours that was the normal performing time." Shakespeare the transcendent genius is placed back in the rehearsal hall. On text, Greenblatt goes on: "Neither the Folio nor the quarto texts of Shakespeare's plays bear the seal of final authorial intention, the mark of decisive closure that has served, at least ideally, as the guarantee of textual authenticity. We want to believe, as we read the text 'This is the play as Shakespeare himself wanted it read' but there is no licence for such a reassuring sentiment. To be 'not of an age, but for all time' means in Shakespeare's case not that the plays have achieved a static perfection but that they are creatively, inexhaustibly unfinished."[19] Variant texts of a play, by Shakespeare or other writers, give us the chance to explore something of the creative processes of early modern English theatres. As readers of the theatre rather than, especially and particularly, of authors, we should rejoice in our good luck in such cases, since they provide us, it seems, with two or more ways in which a text has been developed for production and performance. We should read them thoroughly, carefully, and comparatively, avoiding prejudicial hypotheses as much as we can through conscious effort. Early theatre texts still have a good deal to tell us, and deserve some new questions.

*University of Toronto*

---

[19] *The Norton Shakespeare* (New York, 1997), p. 67.

# SCENARIO AND PERFORMANCE IN COMMEDIA DELL'ARTE

Domenico Pietropaolo

When it is directly experienced and regarded only in the context of the cognitive mechanism that the encounter sets in motion, performance includes for the apprehending mind of the spectator the idea of something to which the performance process has been applied, something other than the performance itself, of whose material being as an aesthetic object it is the ultimate source. This otherness, on which the mind of the spectator seeks to rest, cannot be experienced in the theatre other than through the mediation of the performing process, though it is regarded as being both immanently present in the performance and prior to it in logic and time. In the most conventional form of theatre, for which the staging process is the aesthetic transformation of a literary into a performance text, this immanent otherness is the dramatic script, complete with fully developed characters, dialogue, and stage directions.[1]

This conception of double textuality, however we may conceive the relationship by which the two texts are linked, is very problematic when applied to commedia dell'arte. For while it is true that a commedia performance text also sends the mind to an immanent something, regarded as the present grounding of its material action and yet experienced as preceding it, that immanent something is not a play text but a scenario, in so far as the story is concerned, and a stage tradition, in so far as its characters are concerned. The scenario is at best the outline of a number of possible play texts, containing as it does patterns of action and interaction designed to guide the development of the performance process, protecting it from slipping into disorder, but not at all meant to determine the particulars of its articulation. And the stock characters, endowed with a rich existence in the theatrical tradition of the community to which the audience is presumed to belong, are at best lifeless inchoate forms awaiting fulfilment as living dramatic characters, so that they may discharge the responsibility of galvanising each other

1 This idea of "otherness" is derived from Marvin Carlson, *Performance* (London and New York: Routledge, 1996), p. 7 (concept of the "other" in all types of performance).

into the creative stage dynamism for which this type of theatre practice is famous. My purpose in this paper is to examine the chief parameters involved in the articulation of the story and the fulfilment of the characters in performance from the perspective of the phenomenology of perception, focusing in particular on the commedia story that has achieved the greatest distinction in our century, which is The Servant of Two Masters as staged by Giorgio Strehler, and on the one character who quintessentially represents the world of commedia for scholars and practitioners alike, that is to say Harlequin.

The most basic distinctive features of stock characters are familiar to the audience before the performance begins, as may also well be the story that the performance is about to tell, but the repertory of gestural and verbal actions through which the characters come to life and by means of which the story is told may be guessed at by individual spectators only to the degree that they are acquainted with the performance techniques of the actors in question. The scenario is a written structure that exercise rigid control over the narrative progress of the performance, but it is quite powerless before the vocal and gestural vocabulary through which the actors choose to transform lifeless stock figures, coming to them from a world outside the story, into the dramatic agents of the particular story being told. As a result, commedia dell'arte must be at once performative, in the sense that it gives material existence to a previously conceived plan of action and brings to renewed theatrical life for an audience characters already present in the collective imagination as memory, myth or iconography, and formative, in so far as, working creatively without a script, it actually synthesises on stage much of the material with which to bring that plan to material fruition as an aesthetic object and by means of which to give fullness of existence to the characters that sustain it.

If with respect to conventional literary theatre we can say that, for the spectator, prior to the performance the play existed only as dramatic text, that is to say as a silent one-dimensional play awaiting aesthetic fulfilment in performance, in the case of commedia dell'arte we are compelled to admit that, before the performance, the play does not exist at all, though both the logic of its plot and the mould of its characters certainly do. The consciousness of double textuality that informs audience perception of conventional theatre is here destabilised, since in the case of commedia the thing to which the mind is sent in the cognitive process has only a germinal kind of reality; therefore, the way in which a commedia performance is experienced must be quite different. This is by no means immediately clear, since, if the quality of performance is the same as that of conventional drama, the audience should have no way of determining that the actors are not working with a complete and detailed script. It would seem therefore that, in perception, commedia and scripted theatre should set in motion the same cognitive mechanism, giving rise in both cases to the intentionality of a full script sustaining the phenomenal reality of the performance. But that is not the case, since commedia audiences know before perception takes place that the performance they are about to see is the result of a different type of acting.

The point is made best by the actor Evaristo Gherardi, the Harlequin of the Com(die Italienne in late seventeenth-century Paris, who argued that, whereas all actors act from memory and imagination, since even actors who rigidly adhere to the instructions of a written text, which gives them both the dialogue and the characters in a linguistically finished state, must respond creatively to the vocal and physical gestures of other actors on stage, commedia actors act necessarily ìmore from imagination than from memory,î since they must construct the dialogue and attune to it the stock features of the characters who speak it or who react to it.[2]

Equipped with awareness of this principle, commedia audiences experience the textual otherness of performance as an entity both immanent and imaginary, an entity that has no existence outside the figurative consciousness of individual spectators, where, at every moment of the performance, it is posited as a script that dissolves immediately into nothingness. It is this continuous back and forth motion of consciousness from the performance text to an intentionality that is experienced as both real and imaginary that constitutes the unique aesthetic pleasure afforded by the art of commedia.

It is a consideration well worth making at this point, that in much of the literature concerning commedia the contribution of memory to performance is not regarded as especially significant. There is still such widespread confusion in popular accounts of commedia improvisation, and so general a conviction that the phenomenon can be easily understood in terms of post-Stanislavskian acting theories, as to justify any heavy underscoring Gherardi's statement.[3] Acting mostly from imagination does not mean creating speech from nothing, having become sufficiently acquainted with the inner life of a character to be able to do so; it means, rather, composing theatrical text, that is to say forming chains of composite units of acted speech from a largely shared

---

[2] Quoted in Pierre Louis Duchartre, *The Italian Comedy*, tr. R.T. Weaver (New York: Dover, 1966), p. 31.

[3] On commedia improvisation see my essay, "Improvisation as a Stochastic composition Process," in *The Science of Buffoonery: Theory and History of the Commedia delliArte*, ed. D. Pietropaolo (Ottawa: Dovehouse, 1988), pp. 167-175.

repertory of verbal and gestural signs, acquired through long practice and committed to memory. The purely imaginative part of performance concerns the selection of appropriate sign and the syntax of composition, both of which must be conducted with the insight and strategy required to provoke an appropriate audience response and to allow a logical development of the scene.

These observations on improvised discourse are borne out by contemporary witnesses and practitioners of commedia, from Pier Maria Cecchini, to Evaristo Gherardi, Andrea Perrucci and Luigi Riccoboni, though it is clear that the acting evidence on which they are based is for the most part inferential, since detailed performance analyses are actually quite rare. However, when we turn to character fulfilment, the evidence is direct, since in many cases it is possible to determine without difficulty the chief gestural signs available to the actors themselves, and hence the distinctive features of the characters they improvised. Among the witnesses and practitioners of commedia in this regard, Goldoni occupies a place of prominence, despite the fact the he is the playwright who, almost single-handedly, caused the demise of commedia. And the most significant contribution that he has made to our understanding of the actor's contribution to performance is without doubt The Servant of Two Masters, to which we shall now turn our attention.

As he explains in his address to the reader of the published text, Goldoni originally wrote this play as a commedia scenario for the company of Antonio Sacchi, while he was working as a lawyer in Pisa. The scenario consisted of a general outline of the plot and character relations, with a few completely scripted scenes for the serious roles, that is to say the lovers, in accordance with a generally accepted formula for the composition of scenarios in the second and third quarters of the eighteenth century. The plot was conceived by Goldoni along the lines of the compositional forms derived from the Aristotelian tradition: it had, he says, a complication, a change of fortune, and a catastrophe. The action sustained by this plot is a traditional love story, in which the lovers meet up with difficulties but manage to overcome them and finally get married. The dialogue and stage actions of the comic roles, that is to say Truffaldino, Brighella, Pantalone, the Dottore, and Smeraldina, were to be improvised by the highly skilled actors of Sacchi's company, with Sacchi himself in the role of Truffaldino, a variant of Harlequin that he had made famous, and that had made him famous, throughout Europe.

The most significant aspect of this scenario is that the plot does not revolve around the character of Truffaldino, whose involvement in it is in fact so minor as to induce Goldoni himself to observe that, were it not for the brief episode in which Truffaldino manages to get temporarily out of trouble by saying to each of his two masters that the other is dead, "the play could be staged without him."[4] His comic intrusion into the plot and his continued magnetism as the intended focus of the attention of the audience were left entirely to the performer. Antonio Sacchi improvised the role in Milan in 1747, and Goldoni was so impressed with his success that he resolved to reproduce the performance text as much as possible in written form, integrating his own scripted scenes and the ones improvised by the company into a single play text, which he published so that other actors, less imaginative and less skilled than Sacchi's troupe, might have some guidance for their own improvisations.

What this means is that the otherness to which the audience is sent back in its experience of the performance is not the plot outline in the scenario, since the play turns out to be dominated by Truffaldino rather than the lovers, but an elaborate imaginary script hung on that outline as if on a trellis. It is the knowledge that a script of such sophistication is actually constructed in the very act in which it is performed that causes the spectator to stand in awe of the actor's virtuosic power. The ability to awaken a sense of wonder in the audience by displaying the skill of performers improvising on stage is surely the most significant thing that commedia derived from the baroque aesthetics of the period in which it flourished. The imaginary script contains plot-related, structural and representational material, and plot-independent virtuosic improvisation, which supplies what is missing and colours what is given, transforming mere structure into aesthetic body and magnetising the attention of the audience onto it.

Sacchi was for Goldoni the ideal comic actor, so much so that he did not hesitate to say that, in the research that he had to carry out in order to come up with good comic roles for his scripted plays, he could do no better than to study the nuances of Sacchi's performances.[5] But he realised that other actors, with different skills and a different creative imagination, might measure up to the character of Truffaldino in a totally different way. He therefore regarded his scripted play as consisting of two intertwined, but ultimately separable parts: a prescriptive part, containing the plot and the dialogue of all the characters except Truffaldino, and a descriptive one consisting only of Truf-

---

4 "La commedia si potrebbe fare senza di lui," Carlo Goldoni, "L'autore a chi legge," in *Il servitore di due padroni*, in *Arlecchino servitore di due padroni*, con una nota di Giorgio Strehler (Milano: Rizzoli, 1996), p. 97.

5 "E volendo io provvedermi per le parti buffe delle mie commedie, non saprei meglio farlo, che studiando sopra di lui," in "L'autore a chi legge," p. 97.

faldinoís contribution to the text, as modelled on Antonio Sacchi's portrayal of the character. The descriptive part may be understood along the lines of the Parisian scenarios of Dominique Biancolelli, which describe in detail the stage behaviour of Harlequin while saying very little of the remaining characters in the play.[6]

The actor performing the role of Truffaldino, Goldoni believed, should not feel obliged to perform it as scripted in the published text, but should rather feel free to improvise it, provided, of course, that he has the ability to do so. The scripted version, describing as it does only Sacchi's interpretation of the character, is offered only as a guide to a performance type of proven success and admired by the author, but not as the verbal substance of a prescribed performance. "For this reason," Goldoni says, "I have taken the trouble to write it out in full, not in order to force the actors who will play the role of Truffaldino to speak the words that I have written, if they can come up with better ones, but in order to make my intention clear, and to direct them to the end along a straight path."[7]

Besides authorising textual cuts and rewrites of the most radical kind, this description of The Servant of Two Masters enables us to see firsthand how performative and formative elements were correlated in theatre practice and shows that acting, in the observable here and now of the present, is an indispensable means of research for the scholar intent on understanding the nature of commedia. For the givenness of a commedia character to consciousness is dominated entirely by the skill and creativity of the actor, who must act out his role principally from imagination. To be sure, historical documents provide us with a considerable quantity of information concerning the social attributes of stock characters, including class provenance, ideology, relations with others, and linguistic competence. But these ideas do not go very far in explaining the specifics of gestural and vocal text, since both of them depend very much on the physical and psychological attributes of the actor.

In other words, we know what Harlequin is like as a stock character, but if we wish to know something about how that stock character materialises on stage and becomes available for a real aesthetic experience, not as an abstraction but in the fullness of his being as an immanently present theatrical character, we must observe and interrogate

---

6 For a clear overview of Dominique Biancolelli's scenarios, see Cesare Molinari, *La commedia dell'arte* (Milano: Mondadori, 1985), pp. 221-222.

7 "Mi sono per questa ragione indotto a scriverla tutta, non già per obbligare quelli che sosterranno il carattere di Truffaldino a dire per l'appunto le parole mie, quando di meglio ne sappian dire, ma per dichiarare la mia intenzione, e per una strada assai dritta condurli al fine," in "L'autore a chi legge," pp. 98-99.

the actor, from whom the character is ultimately inseparable. As a stock character, Harlequin is an abstract model that is related to the real Harlequins perceived on stage the way the unreal human body in an anatomy textbook is related to the real bodies of living people, no two of which are exactly alike though they have much in common and may be regarded as different variations of the same form.

Each actor has inside knowledge of his own Harlequin, because he creates him anew in performance, and the substance that he uses in his creation is in part external, deriving from the stock attributes that the character has in the received tradition, and in part internal, or derived from his own physical and imaginative potential as an actor. The stock attributes are present in all Harlequins, but the rest is as unique to each of them as is the psycho-physical constitution of the actors that portray them in performance. In our quest to understand, both theoretically and historically, the nature of commedia theatre, we quickly reach a point where conventional scholarly sources are of little help, unless they are the result of a direct observation of the actors who perform it.

If we want to know what Harlequin was really like for and in a given age we must focus on the Visentinis, the Biancolellis, the Sacchis, the Gherardis, the Morettis and the Soleris, that is to say on the most distinguished Harlequin actors of each period of the history of commedia. In many respects our research is bound to be somewhat limited with respect to the past, which will always prove to be insufficiently documented, but it is likely to be very rich with respect to the present, when we can study living Harlequins with some precision, for, in addition to observing the actors directly, we can interrogate them for interior insight into their psycho-physical performance behaviour, confident that in doing so we are not thereby slipping into an inauthentic mode of scholarship. Now, the most distinguished Harlequin of our day is without doubt Ferruccio Soleri, who has played Harlequin for over thirty years in Giorgio Strehler's production of Goldoni's *The Servant of Two Masters,* for hundreds of audiences throughout the world. After being introduced to the character by Giacomo Colli, Soleri studied Marcello Moretti's representation of Harlequin under the direction of Strehler, and, in 1963, inherited the role and quickly made it his own.

Now, Soleri does not find it difficult to describe his character from the inside: in addition to considering him nevrotically hungry and childishly unpredictable, which are attributes of the stock character familiar to us from tradition, Soleri says that Harlequin is very much like a cat and would like to live in a space that is about a metre above ground level.[8] Harlequin's love of altitude is a reference to the constant high jumping with which he expresses his emotions, an attribute of the fictional character that is entirely dependent on the small physique of the real actor, which allows him to have a gravity-defying psychology, unavailable to the Harlequins of heavier and taller actors.[9] His feline movements, smooth, calculated and elegant even when they are most abrupt, are visually accentuated by his mask, which was especially designed for him by Amleto Sartori to suggest the idea of a cat, with its puffy cheeks and large, elongated and sinuous eye holes, rising at the outer edges from the lower eyelashes to well above the actor's eye brows, which are partly visible through them.

This last detail is especially significant and may in fact be regarded as the material fulcrum of Harlequin's physical and psychological dynamism in performance. Soleri's mask allows him to see just as well as he could without it. But seventeenth-century masks of Harlequin typically had very small round eye holes, no larger than the irises of the actors wearing them, and, naturally, could not fit snugly over the eyes, so that the openings, in addition to being very small, were at some distance from the pupils. Unlike Soleri, an actor wearing a mask of this type, such as Tommaso Visentini, who had himself painted holding a mask with eye holes actually smaller than the size of his irises, had an extremely small field of view and no lateral vision whatsoever: he could see only what was directly in front of him and more or less at eye level. As a consequence of this tunnel vision, he had constantly to make abrupt movements with his head, quickly turning toward all the different sources of noise and speech on stage, and bending his head to see were he was stepping when he moved from one place to the other. The acrobatics resulting from these combined movements would resemble those of a puppet rather than those of a cat, with the consequence that in the figurative consciousness of the audience his Harlequin could not be a composite of human and animal, but a hybrid of human and mechanical.

When a cat-like Harlequin crosses the stage, the audience is aware of only two vectors in his movement: one vertical, representing his body alignment, and the other horizontal, representing his linear direction forward. But when a puppet-like Harlequin performs the same action, the audience is conscious of a third line as well, a line that extends invisibly from his eyes to his intended point of visual contact. This invisible vector, which the phenomenology of dance would call the "focus"

---

[8] Loredana Stucchi e Mario Verdone, *Le maschere italiane* (Roma: Newton Compton Editori, 1984), p. 34.

[9] Soleri is 1.67 m high and weighs 60 kg. *Ibid.*, p. 34.

of the character's motion,[10] necessarily changes orientation with dizzying speed, giving a profoundly different impression of the internal geometry of the performance space, of the character's most natural form of movement in it, and of the psychology that informs his actions. As a consequence, the performance space is no longer experienced as a box-like container in which the characters move freely about their business, but as a configuration of lines irradiating from the moving characters, a space shaped, in other words, by the movement itself, so that the space of performance becomes itself a space performed.

The mask and the physical attributes of the actor determine what inner and outer life is available to the character and condition our experience of the space of his existence on stage, which becomes itself an inseparable part of the performance text. My purpose in comparing the two Harlequins was to show that the material conditions of performance are so much a part of the performance itself that the very construction of the text is unimaginable without them and that the characters are ultimately inseparable from the actors that play them. Outside of this commedia exists as iconography, as carnival costume, as story and as myth, but has no reality as theatre. What, then, is the final inference? It is that the study of commedia, whether in the context of history or in that of theory, must be conducted, as it were, starting, when this is possible, with a directly experienced performance, and describing what actually happens on stage as a unique moment in the life of commedia; and, when this is not possible, with a virtual performance envisioned on the basis of real performance conditions, and describing what can an cannot happen on stage as the upper and lower limits of a uniqueness no longer available to us. And this procedure should be followed in recognition, not only of the principle that performance is a necessary step in academic research in both the history and theory of commedia, but also of the fact that what is prior to performance is not yet commedia.

*University of Toronto*

---

[10] Maxine Sheets, *The Phenomenology of Dance* (Madison: University of Wisconsin Press, 1966), p. 122.

# *HISTOIRE ET RECUEIL DES LAZZIS*, A CASE OF EARLY PERFORMANCE ANALYSIS

David Trott

In his most recent book, *L'Analyse des spectacles*,[1] Patrice Pavis lays down a useful set of ground rules for the analysis of theatre performances. Emanating from the empirical object that a live performance offers to the combined senses and critical gaze of an "eye witness", the reception of this representational event involves a complex and still problematic series of operations which I shall invoke in the pages that follow. Furthermore, while Pavis aims his reflection at contemporary, intercultural spectacle as distinct from the historical reconstruction of earlier, Western performance practices, I shall argue that we can include past interpretations of live theatrical events, particularly where the existence of a focussed spectatorial gaze can be established. A rare example of such a focussed witnessing act is to be found in the early 18th-century French text, *Histoire et Recueil des Lazzis*.[2]

The description of theatrical performance has long tended to be overshadowed by the analysis of the play texts that were considered by many to generate them. The issue of which, a live performance or a written script, takes precedence over the other continues to bother theatre scholars and critics of all persuasions. Proponents of the primacy of text over staging frequently seek to anchor their judgements of a given live representation in an author's written dialogue or stage directions; for them, such and such a performance either "betrays" the author's text, or "does justice" to it. Although she acknowledges that some of her views over the years have evolved, theatre semiotician Anne Ubersfeld continues in re-editions of her 1978 *Lire le théâtre* to evoke the "matrices de représentativité" which call out for, or authorize, the performance options selected by directors, actors and other theatre

---

1 Patrice Pavis, *L'Analyse des spectacles*, Paris: Nathan, 1996.

2 *Histoire et Recueil des Lazzis*, édition critique par Judith Curtis et David Trott, *Studies on Voltaire and the Eighteenth Century*, Oxford: Voltaire Foundation, 1996, vol. 338.

"practitioners".[3] This accounts for the fact that, in 18th-century France at least, plot summary dominated many play reviews in journals and that the text-based, narrative attributes of unity and logical transition between segments, outshone more performance-based attributes such as virtuoso renderings of a specific scene by a great actor, or the effect on a particular audience group of a change in costuming practices.

A growing body of evidence is being gathered to suggest the extent to which playtexts (whether manuscript or edited, contemporary or from earlier periods) are shaped and determined by the exigencies of performance — for example, texts created for the talents of a particular actor or company; plays re-written in response to audience pressures at the time of opening;[4] or cuts of various proportions inflicted in the name of directorial vision or commercial acumen on long-standing editions of known authors' plays.[5] As a result, the text-performance relationship would appear to be somewhat looser. The two entities exist far more independently of each other, and, according to Pavis, the ways in which they are received can be quite distinct:

> Texte et représentation ne sont plus conçus dans un rapport causal, mais comme deux ensembles relativement indépendants qui ne se rencontrent pas toujours et nécessairement pour le plaisir de l'illustration, de la redondance ou du commentaire. (p. 23)

Where such "causal links" *are* taken for granted, theatre historians interested in early performance reconstitution can rely on a variety of sources of information to help them overcome the stumbling block of the irreversible inaccessibility of the event. These are the historiographic "documents" which Stephen Johnson outlines in his article in the present volume.[6] Some play reviews do of course include references to the performance as opposed to the text. Theatrical company archives

---

3 "Notre présupposé de départ est qu'il existe à l'intérieur du texte de théâtre des matrices textuelles de «représentativité»; qu'un texte de théâtre peut être analysé selon des procédures qui sont (relativement) spécifiques et mettent en lumière les noyaux de théâtralité dans le texte." *Lire le théâtre*, Paris: Éditions sociales, 1982, p. 20.

4 David Trott, "Production et réception du théâtre de Marivaux: le cas de *La Double Inconstance* et du *Jeu de l'amour et du hasard*", *L'École des lettres*, No. 8 - 1er février 1997, pp. 5-18.

5 See John Astington, "The Play and the Presentment: Texts and Performances in England before 1642", in the present volume.

6 See the article by Stephen Johnson, "Text and Translation in the Historical Reconstruction of Popular Dance: The Witness to Juba in 1848", in the present volume.

(where available) often specify details of set construction and stage accessories. There is a rich iconographic store of images displaying facial expression, costume and gesture. Musical scores and choreographic notations are available. Directorial notebooks can be found. Police reports record illicit performances. Private correspondences relate, in passing, individual theatrical events. Biographies and autobiographies feature insights into the art of many theatrical personalities. Authorities —church or state— contribute views ranging from the administrative to the philosophical about the place of theatre performances in the society of their time.

As was also pointed out, however extensive and rich these various accountings may be, they tend massively to be between one to several degrees removed from the actual, "live" theatrical event which they purport to record. The attestation of a fine performance in the section of the *Mercure de France* devoted to "spectacles", generally stands out as a fleeting digression in an otherwise text-based review stressing plot summary.[7] Evidence of the purchase of a Harlequin costume by the Comédie-Française in 1725 does not fully equal an eye-witness description of the performance by the actor who wore it.[8] Minute observations of legal infractions during a stage performance[9] are not driven by the same attention to detail that should, according to Pavis, motivate the focussed and knowledgable "spectateur/analyste".

---

7 For exemple, the May 1722 issue of the *Mercure* devotes seven paragraphs to Marivaux's *Surprise de l'amour*. Six of these deal with plot summary. The somewhat shorter final paragraph sums up the contribution of the four main actors thus: Silvia's performance "ne laisse rien à souhaiter"; Flaminia "a joué avec autant de feu"; Lélio acted "en perfection"; Arlequin performed predictably, "à la satisfaction de tout le public". One of only two fleeting references to some noteworthy stage business is cut short with a curt "nous n'en dirons rien pour ne pas entrer dans un trop grand détail." (quoted in Marivaux, *Théâtre complet*, éd. F. Deloffre, Paris: Classiques Garnier, 1968, tome premier, pp. 184-5).

8 In the entries for October 22 and November 21, 1725, the Comédie-Française *Registre* itemizes the following expenditures for the staging of *L'Impromptu de la folie*: "donné à Mr. Le Grand, père, pour un habit d'Arlequin... 100 livres" and "payé à Mr. Le Grand, père, pour le reste de labit d'Arlequin... 67 livres 14 sols 6 deniers". Behind such detailed financial record-keeping, we have a glimpse of a rare performative phenomenon: the presence of a *commedia dell'arte* masked character in the very "temple" of "French" theatre, the Comédie-Française.

9 Jules Bonnassies (*Les Spectacles forains ete la Comédie-Française*, Paris: E. Dentu, 1875) has included many police reports of fairground performances suspected of infringing the Comédie-Française monopoly on spoken, live, dramatic performances in the early 1700's.

* * *

*Histoire et Recueil des Lazzis* is a hitherto unpublished collection of frivolous, low-brow plays performed exclusively by, and for, eight individuals during the winter of 1731-32. Intended to enliven a series of sumptuous dinners, these individual entertainments, or "lazzis" as they were labelled, were gathered and bound into a single manuscript volume by one of the eight celebrants, in violation of their sworn commitment to maintain a wall of secrecy around the strictly private gatherings. More, however, than a simple anthology of silly private theatricals preserved for the personal satisfaction of a disloyal and indiscreet editor, the *Histoire et Recueil* also includes a set of notations about their performance and reception by the group. These notations account for over a fifth of the 44,000 word manuscript. Herein lies their theoretical interest for a conference devoted to the performance text. The *Lazzis* volume consistently highlights the *mise en scène* of the plays it contains.

In accordance with his contemporary focus on the analysis of performances, it is understandable that Patrice Pavis should favour recent stage spectacles. They are obviously more within our reach than enactments dating back several centuries. Furthermore, in a context of rapid globalization, these productions incorporate elements from non-Western cultures, not the least of which is a favouring of non-representational performance codes. For Pavis, then, the necessary ingredients for performance analysis are, in schematic form: 1) a concentration on live performance, or stage spectacle;[10] 2) recognition of the intentionality of a "mise en scène" or converging set of performance codes;[11] 3) an informed "eye witness", or spectator/analyst of the actual event.[12] Obviously, non-contemporary spectacles and long-dead spectators do not fit well into such an approach. Nonetheless, a closer reading of the *Histoire et Recueil* reveals that, within its own historical framework, it meets many of the requirements laid down by Pavis for performance analysis

---

[10]"L'analyse du spectacle part de l'objet empirique réalisé et ne cherche pas à remonter à ce qui a pu l'engendrer" (Pavis, p. 23).

[11]"L'analyse du spectacle... passe nécessairement par la reconnaissance de sa mise en scène" (p. 10).

[12]"Comme [Eugenio] Barba, on «pense à ces rares spectateurs capables de suivre ou d'accompagner l'acteur dans la danse de la pensée-en-action». Selon nous, ces spectateurs ne devraient pas être si rares, ils devraient plutôt être la règle générale: des amateurs de théâtre capables d'éprouver et d'expliciter les sensations et les mouvements de leur corps, de percevoir la pensée-en-action, le corps des *performers* et de la performance comme une *auto-bio-graphie,* au sens propre...." (p. 25)

as he technically defines it. The manuscript is devoted exclusively to the recording of actual performances; the staging of these resulted from a concerted, generative thrust; Anne-Claude-Philippe de Tubières, comte de Caylus, the anonymous recorder of the events, was in very direct contact with them.

While the title of the manuscript ("Recueil") implies an anthology of texts, it is not on the level of their "textual" or literary qualities that the *Lazzis* are primarily of interest. Indeed, as individual written works, they are frivolous, formulaic and crude. In addition, only half of the "lazzis" in the volume survive in the form of a fully written script; the remainder appear as summaries or scenarios, clearly less important than the scenic activity they served both to mould and to record.

Performance is rendered in the manuscript by the term "exécution" and its verbal derivatives.[13] Computer scanning[14] reveals that fully half the 22 occurrences throughout the entire text are clustered in Lazzis 2 and 4. The latter, involving a fairground number in which two members of the Lazzis circle imitate a famous dog and its trainer, followed by a change of costume to parody a well-known chorus from the third act of Fontenelle and Colasse's *Thétis et Pélée,* is an unscripted series of performative feats culminating with a spectacular display of fireworks in the royal kitchen of the Tuileries palace. The former gives rise to an instance of virtuoso acting by one of the two actors just mentioned who turns a three-character melodrama into a brilliant one-man show. The theatrical numbers thus "executed" are evaluated in terms of their practical difficulty and audience impact; the commentary highlights their degree of performative challenge[15] and subtlety of interpretation,[16] in addition to the pleasurable effect[17] they achieve on the enthusiastic intimate audience. It is the unfolding of performative events, and not at all their textual underpinnings, which are commented upon in the manuscript.

While, as we have been told, much of the experiencing of traditional Western performances has been primarily visual, *L'Analyse des*

---

[13]"exécuter", "exécuta", "exécutèrent", "exécuterai", etc.

[14]with the text retrieval software TACT

[15]"la pièce... qu'il exécuta lui seul..." (ms. 92); "les acheteurs les exécutent s'ils peuvent"(ms. 200); "bien difficile à exécuter"(ms. 103); "exécutés avec ... adresse"(ms. 128); "d'impossible exécution"(ms. 246). As the edition of *Histoire et Recueil des Lazzis* has included pagination from the original manuscript, all subsequent references to the text will use the "ms." number.

[16]"l'exécution la plus fine"(ms. 1); "l'exécution fine de Satyre"(ms. 128).

[17]"exécuté d'une façon vive"(ms. 299); "...plaisants dans l'exécution"(ms. 93); "l'agrément infini qu'une admirable exécution a pu y ajouter"(ms. 314).

*spectacles* widens the range of sensory stimuli offered to the modern spectator to include sound and mouvement. Pavis evokes "...un élargissement du paradigme favori de la représentation, la visualité, aux paradigmes de l'audition, du rythme et de la kinesthésie" (p. 291). The *Lazzis* volume focuses on a richness of concrete scenic elements similar to those given in Part II of Pavis' study.[18] Accordingly, the physical presence of actors is driven home, the actors' voices are characterized in terms of elocution ("prononciation", "façons de parler des acteurs de province" [ms. 73]), tone ("ampoulé"[ms. 380]) and even onomatopoeic barking ("hou, hou" [ms. 129]), musical interludes abound throughout the volume, the very fabric of costumes and accessories is specified ("laine", "peau de mouton", "ivoire", "toile", "bois", "taffetas"). Tactile and gustatory senses are teased ("souper magnifiques", "fruit" [ms. 127], "grillades et soupes à l'oignon" [ms. 134]).

Performance analysis is posited on the recognition of an intent to create a *mise en scène.* In the first third of the 18th century, the multiple competences associated with the directorial function had yet to coalesce into a single totalizing vision, although Anna Migliarisi writes convincingly in her recent thesis[19] that certain large scale productions such as Ingegneri's *Oedipus* at Vicenza and early baroque opeartic productions required such tight coordination. Small scale and intimate productions such as the "Lazzis" did not make the same demands. *Mise en scène* did not have to flow from one individual. Even in the context of our own day, Pavis allows for a certain looseness of the function by breaking it up into shared sets of artistic decisions made during the production process, but not necessarily taken by a single all-embracing "subject":

> ...c'est un sujet partiel et partial, démultiplié et à responsabilité limitée, qui se ramifie dans toutes les instances amenées, au cours de la production de la mise en scène, à prendre des décisions artistiques et techniques... (p. 4)

The "Lazzis" manuscript offers an example of such a multi-faceted "subject". The conception and overall framework of the pre- or post-dinner entertainments came from the fertile and probably amorous imagination of Comédie-Française actress, Jeanne-Françoise Quinault (1699-

[18] *L'Analyse des spectacles* breaks down the performance into the familiar set of constituent, concrete elements (Actor, Voice, Music, Rythm, Space, Time, Action, + Other material components--costume, makeup, accessories, lighting, smell/touch/taste).

[19] Anna Migliarisi, "Theories of Directing in Late Renaissance and Early Baroque Italy", Ph.D. thesis, University of Toronto, 1996.

1783). Her object: to win the favours of Jean-Frédéric Phélypeaux, comte de Maurepas (1701-1781), an influential minister of Louis XV. She pressed into service two fellow actors, cousin Marguerite Balicourt (d. 1746) and sister-in-law Catherine-Marie-Jeanne Dupré, Mlle Quinault-Dufresne (1705?-1767), two noted amateur thespians, le comte de Livry and le comte de Caylus —the latter being our anonymous analyst—, and two professional writers, Charles-Alexandre Salley (1700-1761) and Alexis Piron (1689-1773). The spectacular series of productions that followed lasted six months, was tightly knit and highly choreographed. However, each member of the circle became individually responsible for an evening's entertainment; each one tried to outdo the others; all of them had to remain strictly within the confines of the secret group where they sought the writing, acting and staging skills of their fellow "Lazzistes". The blend of creative concertation, intense spectator pleasure, and shared complicity on both sides of the "stage lights" was total. Description of the "Lazzis" by Caylus flowed from his initmate involvement with them at every stage, and from his deep awareness of their playful, creative thrust.

Part III of *L'Analyse des spectacles* describes the conditions of reception. While it outlines psychological, psychoanalytical, and sociocritical approaches, it is the anthropological/intercultural perspective that is presented as superceding and subsuming the others:

> Elle est... une méthode plurielle, en perpétuelle élaboration, qui fédère diverses approches et ne se réduit pas à un seul regard. (p. 249)

With appropriate compensation for the gap separating the 18th century from our own, the comte de Caylus, observant editor of *Histoire et Recueil*, fulfils some of the requirements of a forerunner to the modern anthropologist. An artist, engraver (whose several hundred prints form an important part of the collection in the Cabinet des Estampes of the Bibliothèque nationale) and the author of a learned study of the ancient cultures of Egypt, Greece and Rome,[20] Caylus describes the private performances in which he participated with particular acuity.[21]

[20] *Recueil d'antiquités égyptiennes, étrusques, grecques, romaines & gauloises*, Paris: 1767.

[21] "C'est grâce non seulement à son œil d'archéologue amateur, mais aussi à l'intérêt tout particulier qu'il porta au théâtre des Lazzistes en tant que phénomène social, que le regard de Caylus peut se qualifier d'«anthropologique avant la lettre»." Pour une anthropologie des théâtres de société au dix-huitième siècle", *Histoire et Recueil des Lazzis*, ed. Judith Curtis & David Trott, *Studies on Voltaire and the Eighteenth Century*, Oxford: Voltaire Foundation, 1996, vol. 338, p. 13.

While all eight members of the "Lazzis" circle appear in the manuscript under fictitious names (Mlle Quinault was called "Tonton", Maurepas, "L'Ingrat"), Caylus's presence is marked by two pseudonyms, "Luchon" AND "L'Historien", which indicate his double functions as involved participant and detatched, critical observer.

By virtue of his ambivalent involvement in the entertainments, Caylus assumed what Pavis calls the "interior anthropological perspective":

> L'observateur-participant s'immerge dans le spectacle, dans ce qui le précède comme dans ce qui le suit. Il participe à la vie du groupe théâtral et culturel, assiste et s'associe aux entraînements et aux répétitions, prend part aux choix esthétiques, se fond dans le groupe au risque de disparaître en tant qu'observateur et de devenir «un des leurs» (p. 251).

Serving as a go-between who facilitated bi-monthly dinner parties ("soupers") allowing Mlle Quinault to entertain Maurepas, Caylus wrote scripts and acted in most of the spectacles which he was simultaneously viewing with some critical detatchment. His evocation of spectator response was thus rooted in an intimate and shared appreciation of the audience's involvement not only with what they were seeing but with what they were perceiving and feeling as well. A computerized collocation of terms which gravitate around the word "spectateur" in the manuscript includes pleasure ("agréablement"), focus and concentration ("curieux", "attention", "écoutés"), and sudden, unexpected effect ("étonné", "étonnement", "surprise").[22]

For the group of "Lazzistes", the pleasure of a "Lazzi" springs from the recognition of a gap. Scenic images (or to borrow Nancy Copeland's suggestion, instances of "mimicry"[23]) are recorded by Caylus the spectator who immediately —in the form of explanatory notes—provides analytical insight into their fuller impact on the observers. On two occasions in the manuscript, Mlle Quinault cross-dresses, and assumes the identity of Maurepas; in Lazzi 6, *L'Audience*, she mimics him in a par-

---

[22]"étonnement pour les spectateurs" (ms. 128); "un bon Lazzi, suivant la nouvelle définition, est une plaisanterie dont la nouveauté faisant naître la surprise d'un spectateur étonné et curieux, interrompt agréablement la longueur difficile à remplir d'un souper...." (ms. 195); "Les spectateurs [complices] jettèrent alors leur mouchoirs" (ms. 351); "Les premiers vers du monologue... prononcés avec toute la variété de tons, et le détail qu'exige une exposition en sentiment, furent écoutés par les spectateurs avec cette attention qui s'efforce de trouver un sens juste à ce que l'on dit...." (ms. 382).

[23]See Nancy Copeland, "Mimicry and Hegemony: Feminist Performance Theory and Aphra Benn", in the present volume.

odic ministerial audience where a string of petitioners requests favours which Maurepas himself dutifully inscribes at the recording secretary's table to which he is relegated by way of visual irony throughout the performance. In Lazzi 1, the "[Carnaval Masked] Ball", Caylus describes from Maurepas' perspective the sudden visual encounter with his apparent double; Mlle Quinault appears with his face mask and wearing his own dressing gown and cap:

> ...pendant que ces plaisanteries occupoient l'Ingrat, qui de son côté ne s'oublioit pas, il apperçut tout d'un coup un masque dont le visage ressembloit au sien propre. Ce masque étoit vêtu de sa robe de chambre et de son bonnet de nuit. Cette surprise consacrée de droit au Lazzi, produisit des effets amusans, Tonton étoit le Masque en question.[24]

It is not enough to be physically present at —or even in— the staging of a play. To be what Pavis calls a "spectator/analyst", recognition by the observer of the artistic thrust of the event is required: "L'analyse du spectacle... passe nécessairement par la reconnaissance de sa mise en scène" (p. 10). Likewise, a degree of awareness of the per-

---

[24]La saisie quasi viscérale du décalage (conscient de soi -- se voyant autre) correspond à un instant de 'surprise' qui ouvre la voie aux 'effets amusants' produits par la réflexion. Plus cette réflexion est 'fine', plus les effets prennent de l'ampleur. La vue par Maurepas de son double fait place rapidement à l'apparition d'"une Espéce de Magicien" portant un chapeau 'tel que celuy du Mouphti du Bourgeois Gentilhomme' qui se transforme en une 'table chargée de fruits et d'entremets' au-dessous de laquelle sort Satire 'vêtu en Comus'. 'Quelque tems aprés l'on vit entrer un Ours paré des ailes et du carquois de l'Amour', ce qui donne lieu à une longue note explicative pour nous mettre au fait que ce déguisement se réfère à un vrai ours offert par 'le Comte de S[axe] à Mlle D[angeville], laquelle, étant actrice, 'venait alors de jouer une pièce nouvelle avec un habit semblable a celuy cy'.

Nous avons là les éléments constitutifs du concept de 'théâtralité' que pratiquaient les Lazzistes. Bien que le fond qui l'illustre ait été d'une frivilité indéniable, le plaisir qu'il crée est comparable à celui d'une oeuvre théâtrale plus complexe et sérieuse. La fin du Lazzi-faux Bal offre un premier exemple en microcosme, de 'cet enchainement de plaisirs' recherché par les huit Lazzistes. La configuration comporte une succession aussi rapide que possible de trois étapes: premier coup d'oeil + surprise immédiate + saisie de nouveaux sens. La connaissance/perception proposée par la première étape se volatilise aussitôt, mais non sans laisser ses traces physiques, viscérales (c'est l'étape de l'effet immédiat), pour faire place à une autre connaissance, différente et plus profonde, qui complète le circuit de la 'finesse'. Plus on découvre de sens cachés sous l'illusion, plus la théâtralité est fine. (David Trott, *Studies on Voltaire and the Eighteenth Century* 310, 1994, pp. 127-8) formative act is required on the part of the actor being observed: "...il faut aussi que l'observé ait conscience de jouer un rôle pour son observateur..." (p. 55). While this constitutes the essence of the contract between performers and spectators in *any* performative enactement, individual types of performance vary in terms of the stress they place on detachment or identification (ie. a "more willing" or a "less willing" suspension of disbelief). Diderot's theories of stage realism, for instance, aimed at the lulling of spectatorial critical awareness in order to enhance the emotional impact on his audiences' sensibility. Although there is now a tendency to associate instances of auto-reflexivity and complicitous self-awareness with performative traditions that diverge from Western, mainstream stage realism (ie. with contemporary and/or non-Western practices), we must also not forget the rich stream of Western, historical, self-conscious theatre[25] that naturalism sought to downplay or eradicate. Some "théâtre de société" or private theatricals was a part of "another" tradition which mainstream naturalism succeeded over the course of the 18th century in marginalizing.

To read performance, Pavis envisages going beyond what he calls, in a recent article on acting, "semiological analysis... in a mimetic situation of communication".[26] The direction to which he points is that of "vector theory" which he describes as the underlying principles of "... a kind of energy-based [communication] system that is divested of any mimesis or references to signs."[27] While he demonstrates the application of semiology and vector theory to two different performances —the gestures of Louis de Funès in a scene from Molière's *Avare* and the final sequence of the "choreographic theatre" piece *Ulricke Meinhof* by Johann Kresnik — it is worth noting that the distinctions on which he

---

[25] In *Histoire des Lazzis*, the phenomenon of auto-reflexivity is expressed in the manuscript by the 18th-century term "finesse". Having commented on the "grande finesse de jeu" (ms. 72) of the first Lazzi, Caylus immediately follows up with a reference to "la critique fine... de plusieurs défauts des pièces les plus connues" (ms. 72) which the tightly-knit audience viewing it could be expected to appreciate. He later adds: "Le goût fin, la délicatesse caractérisent les Lazzis..." (ms. 426).

[26] "Acting: Explication of gesture or vectorization of desire?" *Assaph C*, No. 8, 1992, p. 88.

[27] We must resist "...le modèle sémantique du signe et des niveaux de sens [qui est] peu adapté à la mise en scène contemporaine" (p. 26). Instead, the description of a performance must focus on the "vectorisation du désir--autant le désir du corps même de la représentation que celui du spectateur" (p. 26).

relies between text-based acting and "energy-based stage work"(103)[28] can be applied to the performances evoked in the *Lazzis* manuscript. By virtue of its self-propelled performative energy, the 1732 volume was as much the vectorization of the individual and collective desires of its combined spectator-cast as it was a parodic hommage to the great classical texts of Molière and Racine.

To what extent are the *Lazzis* mimetic? And to what extent are they self-sufficient/self-justifying acts of performativity? In other words, to what extent do they spring from what Pavis calls, "une énergétique coupée de toute mimesis et de toute référence ou signe" (p. 65)?. One is initially struck by the fact that they are rooted in the daily events of the Parisian winter of 1731-32. These events are political, religious, social and theatrical. As such, they must be placed in the category of realistic theatre the referents of which are the current events of their day.

Not all the activities observed by Caylus in the *Lazzis* manuscript fulfil the requirements of representational theatre, however. A good example of this is to be found in the seventh Lazzi which links the familiar elements of a fairground medecine show to create an entertainment culminating in what approximates near delirium. Following the pattern of the conventional opening compliment, one-act farce and final sales pitch, the seventh Lazzi may be considered mimetic primarily on the grounds of its imitation of the then quite familiar three-part performance the centrepiece of which was its "parade".

Performative exhuberance emanates from a succession of framed moments of alternating narration and dialogue, discourse and gesture, acting and singing, sensory theatre and spectacular gastronomy. Although richly larded with topical allusions to royal physicians, a Marivaux play opening, *Gulliver's Travels* and Czar Peter I, it is difficult to enclose this extended entertainment in a mimetic category. At best, its referent is the slick, transparent rhetoric of the fairground huckster whose speech fades into a night-long bout of song, revelry and feasting. It is perhaps better described as an orgy of the senses. But, however "orgiastic" the seventh Lazzi appeared, it had been choreographed with exquisite care, and recorded with rigour by Caylus whose manuscript notations of parentheses, italics and interjections provide textual evidence of a distinctly non-classical vectorisation of fluctuating intensities.[29]

---

[28]or "dream work", a term which enables Pavis to invoke Freudian concepts of of dream analysis to grasp the non-rational forces at play in such performances.

[29]The shifting levels of discourse in the 7th Lazzi make it difficult at times to distinguish between the narrating voice of editor Caylus and the authorial voice

* * *

*Histoire et Recueil des Lazzis* raises a number of important issues, none of which can be resolved in a short study such as this. These include:

1) a growing awareness of the marginal forms of spectacle which mainstream realism pushed aside or assimilated; among them, popular entertainment, fairground spectacle, some private theatre ("théâtres de société"), and the collective and "improvised" productions of *Commedia dell'Arte*; furthermore, to feed this process, the need to unearth further traces of such forms;
2) a recognition that the analytical criteria applied to spectacle must not only differ from those used for written texts (which are all too frequently the only surviving link between us and past performances of them) —this is self-evident—; but also a recognition that different kinds of performance demand a tailoring of critical methods to account for their specificity; in the case of *Histoire des Lazzis*, this has meant enriching conventional readings of its mimetic and referential nature by considering analytical tools such as vector theory to account for the waves of seemingly gratuitous, meaningless sensory pleasures derived from the experiencing of its pure performativity;
3) a realization that the title of the manuscript offers a useful illustration of the tensions which prevailed between the narrativity, even literariness, implicit in the term "Histoire" and the seemingly "meaningless", self-contained entertainment pieces suggested by the term "Lazzis"; the curious entertainments of 1731-32 occurred only three years after Luigi Riccoboni had defined "Lazzi" as "ces inutilités qui ne consistent que dans le jeu" and which "interrompent... la matière que l'on traite, et à laquelle on est pourtant toujours obligé de revenir"[30]; while Riccoboni was already clearly engaged in the shift toward "bookish" theatre that would ultimately harness the spontaneous performativity of early *Commedia*, the simultaneous wave of private theatrical activity which swept 18th-century France stands out as a secret expression of defiance against the repressive encroachment of mainstream realism.

Contemporary scholarship and theory share a need to distance their contribution from those of their predecessors and to affirm their originality in relation to what went before. Admittedly, there is al-

---

of playwright Salley. The resulting mix reflects a tension between description and prescription, distance and engagement.

[30] *Histoire du théâtre italien*, 1729.

ways a need to develop new critical tools in the face of ever-changing performance practices. Indeed, Pavis was moved to de-intellectualize current semiotic preoccupations with the ties that bind sign to meaning, in favour of "une expérience de sensorialité" (p. 286), to enable the beholder of non-representational performance to plunge into "des sensations de présence, d'équilibre qui essaient de neutraliser tout côté intellectualiste de l'expérience théâtrale" (p. 286). Just as *L'Analyse des spectacles* recognized that different *mises en scène* require different theories to account for them, I would like to conclude with a call to apply the maxim to past performances in the Western tradition as well. The entertainments which *Histoire et Recueil des Lazzis* finally make public do not measure up to the standards of mainstream, European, text-rooted theatre. They lack the edifying qualities of good writing and serious, meaningful intent. As said earlier, they are essentially frivolous when viewed from this perspective. Frivolity is a judgment based on textual classification by literary genre. The quality of performance cannot be judged by the "high" or "low" ranking of a text. It must be independent of a literary hierarchy. A challenging and rich performance is thus possible in the case of a script deemed to be "unworthy" of serious consideration. Thanks to the sharp eye and detailed notations of the comte de Caylus, it is clear that performance analysis does not have to restrict itself to the productions of our own lifetime.

*University of Toronto in Mississauga*

# CENSORING THE TEXT: A SIMPLE SKETCH ON A COMPLEX SUBJECT

Richard Plant

Like many things I do, the idea of talking about theatre censorship seemed a good idea at the time, a moment in the past when I said to Domenico Pietropaolo, our genial host and symposium organizer, that I would have something to speak about on the topic during this gathering. I am now regretting my boldness. My research progress has not been as quick as hoped.

Over the years I have had an on-going, but unsystematic interest in censorship, which has shown up mostly in topics on my course outlines. Two years ago this interest led me to agree to supervise an independent study conducted by Diane Morales, a student at the time in our drama department at Queen's University. Although the substance of my paper is quite distant from what Diane and I explored, her work has provided significant background for my overall views — and I wish to express my indebtedness to her. Similarly, I need to thank Rebecca Conolly, whose seminar presentation last year in my course at the Graduate Drama Centre has kept me thinking about censorship. Discussions this year with Michele Ballagh, whose research has been informed by her law studies and her theatre involvement, have also helped me.

The theme of this symposium seemed to line up with what I have been thinking. Given today's polarized climate, I find it hard not to be aware of censorship since it appears so frequently in any of several forms. This has led me to be intrigued by the way in which censorship treats the dramatic or performance text as well as how one theorizes the texts of censorship. I have also been interested in theorizing aspects of the relationship between theatre historiography and censorship. But trying to pull my ideas together for this paper has convinced me that my research has progressed barely to a point where I can speak in an informative manner about the subject. So, call it foolhardy or courageous, this is a tentative presentation showing the results of my preliminary research into a large, difficult topic. I present these several ideas with the hope that after my talk you will be willing to discuss the subject and from that will come further guidance for me.[1] I cannot safely say that you will be more enlightened by my thoughts than when you arrived here.

Since my original plan was to argue that there is no reason for censorship in the theatre, I have found the writing of this paper a surprise in some respects. I had believed that I am fundamentally at odds with censorship. I had believed that there is no overwhelming reason to curtail people's expression or reception; that the matters which censorship is claimed to deal with can be handled by existing legislation covering crimes and misdemeanors. Plato's oft-cited views, as expressed in *The Republic* and elsewhere, are ones I have long read in the context of ironic abstract discourse: fictions are dangerous and should be censored, now let's consider the fiction of a republic and the training of young rulers. I have since learned that I should be paying more attention to the complexity of Plato's dialogic irony which allows apparently opposing positions to co-exist. My ideological stance on censorship has proven to be far too limited.

My attention was caught a long time ago by commentary such as Ramon Hathorn's when he characterized the seventeenth-century "l'affaire *Tartuffe*" as "Canada's first theatrical conflict between church and state" (Hathorn, *Oxford* p 81). While his view is true in some senses, I understand censorship as a complex action which cannot be represented accurately in a statement of one-dimensional conflict. Even in instances where such a bi-polar set of interests appears to exist, closer reading of the circumstances reveals the presence of additional forces which have shaped the censorship actions.

I'll briefly try to sketch what I mean by citing five eclectic examples, starting with an elaboration of my previous comment about l'affaire *Tartuffe*. In 1694 the Count Frontenac decided that a performance of *Tartuffe* would be a worthwhile enterprise in Quebec. Perhaps the presence of Lieutenant Jacques de Mareuil, who could play the lead role, offered an opportunity Frontenac found hard to resist. But I wonder why such a venture would appeal to Frontenac? Certainly the production can be seen to be in keeping with the practice of holding vice-regal entertainments which he had carried on between his return from France in 1689 and this occasion. Again, I wonder why he undertook these activities? Might the reasons reveal anything about the censorship which ensued, or vice versa?

---

[1] I did receive encouraging suggestions including particularly helpful ones from Veronika Ambros and Ric Knowles which I have incorporated into this slightly revised text. As well, Leonard Doucette provided valuable refinements in my characterization of l'affaire *Tartuffe*.

Frontenac's "opposition," Msgr Saint-Vallier, Bishop of Quebec, would have had a professional and spiritual interest in seeing that the souls of his parishioners were protected from the perceived dangers of Moliere's controversial play — possibly protected against the perils of theatre more generally, if the Bishop's Jansenist beliefs held sway. Ostensibly to that end Saint-Vallier accused de Mareuil of blasphemy and excommunicated him; from his pulpit, he forbade such performances and challenged Frontenac to stop the production.

As Ramon Hathorn and others have argued, this appears to be a battle between the state and the church in which a high official of the church has invoked powers of censorship against a representative of the state. But what does that mean? Let's look at some further details.

Frontenac is recorded to have been an oppositional individual. He had been recalled to France in 1682 after quarrels with the clergy over his support of selling liquor to Native people. He had also quarrelled with the Intendant over their conflicting interests in the fur trade, and with various other officials over his extending his powers into civil areas and even imprisoning or exiling opposition. Frontenac had even gone against royal orders in setting up fur trading posts: ironically in light of the common historical view, fur trading was seen by the Crown in these years as a force which weakened the type of settlement desired. When the Count returned to Canada in 1689, he may have been less so, but he was still quarrelsome, and not above using his position and power to fulfill his own interests. By the time of *Tartuffe*, Frontenac was in need of money.

For his part, the Bishop was a notorious and disliked personality. He was a forceful and extremely pious man (Tartuffe-pious?), who saw himself as battling against evils in colonial society. Cornelius Jaenen describes him this way:

> In short time, however, he fell out with Governor Frontenac ..., with the military, cathedral chapter, Recollets, Jesuits, and almost the entire diocese. In return, his adversaries denounced his writings, *Catechism* (1702) and *Ritual* (1703), as heretical, and little effort was made to gain his release when he was captured and imprisoned in England. (*Canadian Encyclopedia* v 3, p 1924)

A further level of conflict might have been occasioned by Saint-Vallier's Jansenism less than ten years before it was outlawed by the Roman Catholic church.

Certainly as Ramon Hathorn indicates, Saint-Vallier was exercising a religious authority in what could be seen to be a more secular sphere — that is, one in which the authority of the state was seeking power. Moreover, he had a Jansenist's distrust of the theatre, although this may have been a relationship as complicated as that of many other clergy and Jansenists (such as Jean Racine) for he later attended a "réception" which he had asked to have composed in his honour.[2]

The Lieutenant, for his part, had an unsavoury past; not only was he an amateur actor, but he had previously been charged with blasphemy and clearly was no friend of the Bishop or the controls of the church. After this event he was sent back to France where his further activities earned him imprisonment.

As I expect you know, the *Tartuffe* matter was recorded to have been resolved when Frontenac did not stage the play and received a payment of a thousand "piastres d'indemnité" from the Bishop. What exactly was going on? Why was censorship invoked? A battle between church piety and state secularity? Who was representing what part of the church or what part of the state? These people seem to have a number of oxen which might be gored or gorged in the instance. In short, I have strong reservations about our being able to claim that censorship in this case was an exercise of church restraint to protect the parishioners from the dangerous effects of the play *Tartuffe*, which had been rewritten and performed in Paris approximately 30 years previously. It was much more than a battle between "the church" and "the state".

One of the aspects I find most interesting about the complexity of purpose in this act of censorship is that the Bishop's commands are noted by Canadian and Quebec theatre historians as prohibiting performances of *Tartuffe* for the next 200 years. As well, Robertson Davies seized on the event to write *Hope Deferred*, a short play in which a young Huron woman, an actress trained in France by the great Michel Baron, is caught in the battle between Frontenac and Saint-Vallier. Frontenac argues for staging *Tartuffe* and against "the tyranny of organized virtue" (Wagner p 175); Saint-Vallier offers reasons for not doing so. This allegorical piece is meant to reveal the manner in which artistry has been repressed or perverted over Canadian history. In other words, the characterization of the *Tartuffe* conflict in those terms has suited the construction of a particular line of interpretation in cultural history, which situates theatre as an embattled force of potential enlightenment in a world of philistinism and a vessel of truth amid religious and other hypocrisies. But this historiographical consideration will have to wait until there is more time.

A different circumstance prevails in the case of actions taken by legitimate theatre operators, artists and owners against variety theatres at the turn of the century in England. Variety theatre or music hall en-

---

[2] See L. E. Doucette's *Theatre in French-Canada: Laying the Foundations 1606-1867* pp 30-31

tertainment existed at the end of the 19th and the early part of the 20th century caught between the 1751 "police act" and the burden of the Licensing Act of 1843, which had been in part an attempt to deal with the residual definitional problems left from the supposedly temporary 1751 legislation. That is, stage performances not specifically included in the 1843 Licencing Act, which covered "... every Tragedy, Comedy, Farce, Burletta, Interlude, Melodrama, Pantomime, or other Entertainment of the Stage or any part thereof" (Schiede, p 124), fell into "variety" and were governed by the act of 1751. Its sense is captured in its title, the "Disorderly Houses Act," as well as in the preamble to Clause 36:

> Whereas the multitude of places and entertainments for the lower sort of people is another great cause of thefts and robberies, as they are tempted to spend the small substance in riotous pleasures, and in consequence are put on unlawful methods of supplying their wants and renewing their pleasures; in order, therefore, to prevent the said temptation to thefts and robberies, and to correct, as far as may be, the habit of idleness which is become too general over the whole kingdom, and is productive of much mischief and inconvenience... [the act goes on to establish licensing controls for "any House, Room, or Place opened for public dancing or music"]. (Schiede, p 123)

Subsequently, a "common informer" could accuse places of being disorderly houses "thereby subjecting them to the threat of fines or even closure" (Schiede, p 123), which is exactly what happened.

Variety's early 19th-century history as a notoriously bawdy entertainment helped form an impression that censorship on morally protective grounds was necessary. But by the late 19th century, many music halls had become "respectable," partly by including dramatic sketches in their programmes, a practice which developed widely by the 1870s. Many of these dramatic sketches, inserted as part of "well-regulated variety programme[s]," were of high aesthetic and production qualities, "seldom containing morally objectionable material." As the variety houses gradually drew a larger middle class audience, they came into greater competition with the legitimate houses. This situation continued until 1912 when an official accommodation was reached between the groups in a way which ironically contributed to the lessening of music hall as a commercially viable entertainment form.

As Frank Scheide reveals, over the years between 1890 and 1912 the legit theatres, often represented by their umbrella organization, the Theatrical Managers Association, initiated a series of litigations against the variety theatres, often represented in court by the London

Entertainments Protection Association. The legit claims were summarized in a 1904 statement, as follows:

> The music halls are permitted to have smoking and drinking in the auditorium, and standing in the corridors; their performances are not subjected to censorship ; they are, moreover, permitted in many instances to have what are called "promenades," and in other ways, they enjoy those free and easy attributes which have become associated with the music hall. The privilege of presenting stage plays, hitherto enjoyed by the theatre, is now claimed as a right by music halls, without their being subjected to the stringent regulations which control the theatre. (Sheide, p 125)

So much for a level playing field, I suppose. The variety owners viewed this in a different light:

> Music halls and sketches have grown into popularity because of the luxurious accommodation and the excellent entertainment that can be found therein, withal of a wholesome, instructive, and moral character. The theatrical managers are jealous; it is merely trade jealousy, nothing more [which prompts these law suits]. (Sheide, p 125)

As I said, though, the legits, with charges, testimony and "expert" reports from figures of the stature of Henry Irving, Harley Granville Barker and Beerbohm Tree were succcessful in securing a 1912 agreement governing the length of sketches (40 minutes or less) and the number of performers, as well as the number of sketches in any variety programme. Through this and continued lawsuits, they eventually gained greater control of the playing field. My view, which I find supported by Frank Schiede's work, is that one of the forces we see in the variety litigations is the use of censorship under the Lord Chamberlain's office to provide an advantage for the legitimate theatres in their competition for audiences. The law suits were on the grounds of smoking, morality, cleanliness — charges which would bring the particular music hall into the category of "disorderly houses"; there was even a charge against a ventriloquist and his dummy whom Barker tried to prosecute for presenting a duologue. But clearly, in addition to moral health, the litigation purposes included a greater share of attendance and box office. In terms of theatre historiography, it now suits my purposes to read the variety situation in this way.

I would like to turn very briefly to a couple of small personal examples. Recently I attended a student production of *Extremities* directed by a young woman in our department at Queen's. You may remember *Extremities* as a movie starring Farah Fawcett. Actually, I don't, but I can report that in this case the opening scene presented a young man who walked into a young woman's apartment and after increasingly suspenseful moments sexually assaulted her. As the frightening scene closed, she gained control by spraying him with wasp killer so that when the lights came up on the second scene, we found him secured in the fireplace. Then her roommates came home and eventually discovered that she may have tortured him and that he was inceasingly suffering from an allergic reaction to the spray. In addition, the intruder was able to create discord among the women by seeding their relationship with innuendoes about boyfriends and other personal details he picked up while watching them over the past months. Alas, since we saw only the first two scenes on this occasion, I do not know what happens after that. I can say that the question of what the rest of the play was like was much repeated by others who had been in the audience that night, and that my research has made it clear that I am not the only one to remain ignorant.

I am intrigued by the disappearance of my own and several of my colleagues' intellectual curiosity on this occasion. I wonder if it has anything to do with the palpably uncomfortable feeling I had (as did others) during that first scene as I watched at close hand a young man assaulting a young woman in convincingly realistic fashion? I remember that I said to someone after the show: "we don't really need that, do we?" What exactly did I mean? Was I relieved that the third act didn't get produced and I could leave? There was general agreement among us that the second act was poorly staged and acted, and that the play itself offered overly simplistic, sensationalized impressions. Was I simply letting myself off the hook in being able to dismiss the show at that point on aesthetic grounds? Most of all, what about my recurring confirmation during the first scene that I was watching students whom I knew in a presentation which was not "really" happening? My earlier position on theatre censorship was that it is inappropriate partly on the grounds of the fictionality of the art form. In theatrical presentations as such, there is no "clear and present danger," as would be required in Canadian law, although as history shows, theatre can become the site of "clear and present danger." Was I performing an act of self-censorship on my own serious consideration of the play?

Another personal instance, if you will allow a further brief indulgence. Many people have heard me speak in disparaging terms of musicals, particularly megamusicals. I was heard to decry their "outrageous expense" and call them "intellectual pap" in a recent class. This is the same person who used to appear in musicals and hugely enjoyed singing the roles. As well, I have been to see *Cats, Phantom, Showboat, Damn Yankees* and much more "intellectual pap". (Did I enjoy them? Do I have to say?) But I tend not to go to them. Am I exercising self-censorship control on the grounds of some pseudo-intellectual, high art principles or on the basis of my southwestern Ontario frugality or leftish principles of activist art?

One final example to make a further but quite different point. Most often censorship actions operate on the basis of someone laying a complaint which an enforcement agency, most often a police force, is called upon to investigate — if the incident is deemed worthy of investigation. These investigating officers must be trained in recognizing offences. Among the most interesting documents I have seen so far is a paper which was prepared a few years ago from the Office of the Crown Attorney of Ontario to serve "only as a general outline of the law of obscenity to provide police officers engaged in the investigation of obscenity offences with some legal background as a basis for their investigations." (De Julio, p 9) What has struck me about this document is the looseness of censorship law and the degree to which determination is left up to individual interpretation. For instance, while explaining to officers the manner in which court decisions are made, the paper outlines that:

> In determining whether the Crown has proven undue exploitation of sex as a dominant characteristic of the video tape, a jury should make this determination of all of the evidence having regard to the purpose of the producer, the artistic merit of the work, and the community standard of tolerance. (De Julio, p 6)

As laudable as the advice may be, I hardly need draw attention to the problems to be found in discerning purpose or artistic merit, nor to those in the following description:

> The test of undue exploitation of sex is to be determined according to contemporary community standards in Canada.... The community standards are not those of an individual community, such as a university community, but are those of all segments of the community. (De Julio, p 6)

Also in this paper, we learn from the R.V. Penthouse International Ltd case that, "notwithstanding ... that a dominant characteristic of the magazine was the exploitation of sex," the presence of "serious articles" can rescue a magazine from obscenity charges because each page is to be taken "more or less in isolation from the others." On the other hand, according to this judgement a novel requires that the offending parts be viewed in relation to the "entire work, and in the context of its theme." (De Julio, p 12) What does this say about a theatrical performance: would a revue be handled differently from *A Doll's House*? Actually, there might be assistance for officers who have to decide whether to lay charges or for courts dispensing justice in arts cases: "when judging novels the opinions of literary men are most helpful...." However, do I note a skeptical tone or just some humour in this paper's attitude to "experts": "Typically, an expert will be sworn in a particular field, e.g. literature, and, at some point in his testimony, will begin blithely expressing his views on obscenity, public good and community standards....In this regard, the police officers in charge of the case can assist the Crown by conducting a brief investigation into the witness' professional background and qualifications..."? (De Julio, p 22) My overall point here is quite simple, and one all of us are aware of, yet it bears mentioning: recognizing censorable material, determining whether to lay charges and even the decision making of the courts are enormously fraught with problems and personal interpretations which render censorship open to great variance and abuse. The level of training for that officer called upon to investigate the theatrical performance is just one troubling variable. As Alan Borovoy points out:

> In the early 1960s one trial judge, three appeal court judges, and four judges of the Supreme Court of Canada found that *Lady Chatterly's Lover* was obscene under the above definition ["undue exploitation of sex"]. However, five judges of the Supreme Court carried the day in a declaration that the book was not obscene. Despite the acquittal, the judicial head count was eight to five in favour of a conviction. During the same period the book *Fanny Hill* was found to be obscene by a trial judge and two appeal court judges, and not obscene by three other appeal court judges. Here the judicial head count wound up in a three-all tie.
>
> If the most eminent legal experts in the community disagree so sharply about what constitutes an "undue exploitation of sex", how is the lay citizen [or investigating officer] supposed to make such judgements? (*When Freedoms Collide,* p 55)

I have deliberately chosen this range of five examples to allow us to examine some of the boundaries and implications of what might be called censorship of the theatre: an action which prohibits or attempts to prohibit people's access to all of or part of a theatrical experience or dramatic text. Under existing law, censorship can be enacted on grounds of blasphemous, racist, or seditious acts or utterances, obscenity, pornography and morals offences, these last determined by "undue exploitation of sex" (*Martin's Annual*, p 239) judged on the basis of "community standards" (*Martin's Annual*, p 238) — by which is meant in some judgements (e.g. Goldberg and Reitman) a "national" standard and not that of an "elite". Where "true" censorship ends and either self-censorship or the "chill" effect begins is an important distinction since some people argue that true censorship exists only in the public domain where prohibition or punishment actually occurs. In that light, the first two censorship cases, l'affaire *Tartuffe* and the variety litigation, which occur in public, may appear to be markedly different from the second pair, putatively examples of "self-censorship," which occur in the private recesses of the mind. But the results are much the same: controlling of expression and reception in the theatre. They invoke either the explicit authority of public institutions or individual, personal values which have inherent in them "naturalized" codes of behaviour or values authorized by some institutional system, such as an academic, political or religious body. My abstinance (an interesting word in this context) from those megamusicals can be seen as an act of self-censorship, a type of Augusto Boal's "cops in the head" control, because like other censorship it constitutes "prior restraint," an action invoked to prevent what might happen: my implicit support of the evils of rampant commercialism, overwhelming capitalism, and "low-brow" sensationalist, popular entertainment. My reputation as an academic would be shot, eh? The debate in the area of "prior restraint," much more an American doctrine than a Canadian one, leans in the direction that control on the grounds of what might happen is both inappropriate as well as ineffective. One "right" is pitted against another: the right of people to be protected from a "clear and present danger" versus the right to freedom of expression and the right to receive that expression. Democracy, it is argued, is based on people's right and need to hear the truth. In 1914, *The Shewing up of Blanco Posnet* was cancelled at the urging of the censor of the Toronto police department, before it could be staged, on the basis of reports that it contained "blasphemy, profanity and language of the lowest type." (Hathorn, p 82) An argument can be presented that the public was denied the right to learn truth, in so far as Shaw's play presents truth. Alan Borovoy, the renowned civil liberties lawyer, would argue, I expect, that the dangers inherent in such a prohibition far outweigh the dangers in people's seeing *Blanco Posnet*. Borovoy would also argue that freedom of speech operates most effectively in a state of "constructive tension", to use his own term.[3] Censorship is a means of cutting off "constructive tension" — as I can be seen to be doing when I shut off *Extremities* or when I avoid megamusicals?

Incidents such as this have led me to question the nature of censorship, its efficacy and the reasons it has been and continues to be employed. A skeptical, some would say cynical, nature may be foremost in my considering that censorship is primarily an instrument which allows an individual or group advantage over another individual or

---

[3] See Alan Borovoy, *When Freedoms Collide*, pp 18-67

group. There appear to be ulterior motives in virtually all censorship actions I have examined, and there are virtually no instances of censorship in which single conflicts exist. The attacks by the Reverend Ken Campbell on Margaret Lawrence's novels and other "iniquitous" works gain for him fame in some quarters, notoriety in others, and through that a degree of power over a group of people which he would not have otherwise. He may claim he is protecting Canadian souls — and maybe he is — but that is not all he is doing. Censorship is argued in a way which involves choices by the prosecution and by the defence as to what grounds and motives form the strongest case — and the vagueness and variance in censorship determinations combined with the multiplicity of purpose, ulterior or otherwise, leave me unable to argue that censorship, in any of its forms, is a worthwhile action. However, I have much work to do yet and much to learn.

*Queen's University*
*Graduate Centre for Study of Drama, University of Toronto*

**WORKS CITED**

Borovoy, Alan. *When Freedoms Collide: The Case for Our Civil Liberties.*. (Toronto: Lester & Orpen Dennys, 1988)

*The Canadian Encyclopedia.* Vol 3, 2nd Ed. (Edmonton: Hurtig Publishers, 1988)

Doucette, L.E. *Theatre in French Canada: Laying the Foundations 1606-1867.* (Toronto/Buffalo/London: University of Toronto Press, 1984)

De Julio, Peter, "with the assistance of Mr. Donald Bellehumeur and Mr. Peter Griffiths." *Obscenity Prosecutions: A Crown Attorney's Perspective.* (Judicial District of York: Crown Attorney's Office, nd)

Hathorn, Ramon. "Censorship." *The Oxford Companion to Canadian Theatre.* Eugene Benson and L. W. Conolly, eds., (Toronto/Oxford/New York: Oxford University Press, 1989)

*Martin's Annual Criminal Code 1996.* (Aurora: Canadian Law Book Inc, 1995)

Sheide, Frank. "Legitimate Theatre v. The Music Hall: The Legal Repression of Dramatic Expression on London's Variety Stage, 1899-1912." *Free Speech Yearbook.* Vol 28, pp 120-131

Wagner, Anton, ed. *Canada's Lost Plays: Volume Three: The Developing Mosaic.* (Toronto: CTR Publications, 1980)